# Colorado Hut to Hut

## VOLUME 1: Northern and Central Regions

TEXT AND PHOTOGRAPHY BY Brian Litz

westcliffepublishers.com

**INTERNATIONAL STANDARD BOOK NUMBERS:**
**ISBN-10:** 1-56579-384-6; **ISBN-13:** 978-1-56579-384-2



**EDITOR:**
Bevin Wallace
**DESIGN AND PRODUCTION:**
Rebecca Finkel, F + P Graphic Design, Inc.; Boulder, CO
**PRODUCTION MANAGER:**
Craig Keyzer

**PUBLISHED BY:**
Westcliffe Publishers, Inc.
P.O. Box 1261
Englewood, Colorado 80150
**westcliffepublishers.com**

Printed in Hong Kong by World Print, Ltd.

*For more information about other fine books and calendars from Westcliffe Publishers, please contact your local bookstore, call us at 1-800-523-3692, or visit us on the Web at* ***westcliffepublishers.com.***

**LIBRARY OF CONGRESS CATALOGING-IN-PUBLICATION DATA:**
Litz, Brian, 1961–
Colorado hut to hut / text and photography by Brian Litz.
p. cm.
Includes bibliographical references and index.
Contents: v.1. Northern and central regions — v.2. Southern region.
ISBN: 1-56579-384-6 (vol. 1) — ISBN: 1-56579-385-4 (vol. 2)
1. Cross-country skiing — Colorado — Guidebooks. 2. All terrain cycling — Colorado — Guidebooks. 3. Tourist camps, hostels, etc. — Colorado — Guidebooks. 4. Colorado — Guidebooks. I. Title

GV854.5.C6 L575 2000
796.93′2′09788 — DC21 00-040428

**PLEASE NOTE:**
Risk is always a factor in backcountry and high-mountain travel. Many of the activities described in this book can be dangerous, especially when weather is adverse or unpredictable, and when unforeseen events or conditions create a hazardous situation. The author has done his best to provide the reader with accurate information about backcountry travel, as well as to point out some of its potential hazards. It is the responsibility of the users of this guide to learn the necessary skills for safe backcountry travel, and to exercise caution in potentially hazardous areas, especially on snowfields and avalanche-prone terrain. The author and publisher disclaim any liability for injury or other damage caused by backcountry traveling or performing any other activity described in this book.

**COVER PHOTO:**
*Skiers set out from Fowler/Hilliard Hut to hang some powder shots.*

# Acknowledgments

Through five printings and three editions of *Colorado Hut to Hut*, many, many super people have contributed ideas, information, time, words of encouragement, words of wisdom ("He who skis last skis tracks!"), technical expertise—even their precious bodies (as skiing companions and as models)—not only to help bring this project to fruition but also to keep it going. Without their help, this book would have been truly impossible—and it wouldn't have been nearly as much fun to do. Whether your help was by phone, in my office, or on the trail, it has been deeply appreciated! I would like to thank (in no particular order) the following people, who have added their special something to this book:

Bill Litz, Mary Kay Litz, Jon Alegranti, Bevin Wallace, Steve Grinstead, Clint Buckner, Kurt Lankford, Greg Doubek, Craig Gaskil, Jeff Cobb, Ken Morr, Pat Fortino, Beth Smith, Kirk Watson, Gordon Banks, David Hiser, Doug Johnson, Bruce Ward, Bernice Notenboom, Dan Schaefer, Lisa Paesani, Melissa Bronson, Judy Hampton, David "Cully" Culbreth, Rick and Kiki Sayre, Jordan "Du Telemark" Campbell, Bob Moore, Philippe Dunoyer, Paul Parker, Jeff Parker, Nancy Coulter-Parker, Mike Miracle, Rick Leonidas, Chris Quinn, Pete Stouffer, Doug Seyb, Mike O'Brien, David and Betsy Harrower, Ace Kvale, David Eye, John Scahill, Liz Klinga, Mark Collen, Joe Chervenak, Roland Pitts, Sally Moser, Dianne Howie, Suzanne Venino, and Amy Duenkel, Bruce Hayden, Dave Boardman, Steve Sterner, and the Geriatric Tele Society. Special thanks go to Lou Dawson for unwittingly helping me start down the path of guidebook writing.

The following members of organizations have been indispensable: John Fielder, Linda Doyle, Craig Keyzer, Carol Pando, Jenna Samelson, and Carolyn Acheson (Westcliffe Publishers); Rebecca Finkel (F + P Graphic Design, Inc.); Kim Reed (Reed Photo Imaging); Yvonne "Bootsie" Brodzinski and Linda Thompson (Never Summer Nordic); Steve Prim (Guinn Mountain Hut); Andy Miller (High Lonesome Hut); Bob Allison (Squaw Mountain Fire Lookout, Arapaho National Forest, Clear Creek Ranger District); Craig Steele (Outward Bound School); Ralph Thomas (Hidden Treasure Yurt);

Cindy and Curt Carpenter, David Schweppe, Peter Looram, Mary Sanders, Debbie Krohn, May Eynon, and Jenifer Blomquist (10th Mountain Division); Leigh Girvin and Dr. John Warner (Summit Huts Association); Scott Messina, Hawk Greenway, and Craig Ward (Alfred A. Braun Memorial Hut System); Jed Frame (Elkton Cabins); Tabor Allison (Gothic Cabin); Jean and Mary Pavillard (Cement Creek Yurt); "Stormy" Coleman (Lost Wonder Hut); Doug MacLennan (Southwest Nordic System); Mary Ann DeBoer (Cumbres Nordic Adventures); Mark Mueller and Sandra Kobrock (Wolf Creek Backcountry); Ken Kutac and Curtis Larson (San Juan Snowtreks); Mark Richter and Robert Sullivan (Phoenix Ridge Yurts); Jerry Gray and Colin Gray (Hinsdale Haute Route); Christopher George (Saint Paul Lodge); Mike Turrin, Joe Ryan, Josh Weinstein, and Mark Kelley (San Juan Hut System); and Dale Atkins, Knox Williams, and Scott Toepfer (Colorado Avalanche Information Center).

In this edition of *Colorado Hut to Hut,* we have teamed up with several sponsors. Not only do these people and companies produce some of the best products to take into the backcountry, but they are also friends. Thanks go to Tom Fritz, John Cooley, and Neil Munro (Marmot); Steve Hardesty (Cima/Tua Ski); Bruce Edgerly and Bruce McGowen (Backcountry Access); Mike Hattrup (K2 Skis); Mark Peterson (Ortovox USA); John Sweitzer and Gary Richter (Garmont USA); and Casey Sheahan and Ann Obenchain (Kelty Backpacks); Maile Buker, Jordy Margid, and Craig Hatton (Black Diamond Equipment Ltd.); and Mike Harrelson, Hal Thomson, and Vickie Achee (Patagonia).

Finally, I would like to thank the gang at Neptune Mountaineering, who kept my screws glued, edges sharp, and bindings (and attitude) adjusted—Gary Neptune, Chris Clark, Roland Fortin, Luke Gosselin, Scott Sutton, Mike Smith, Ryan Phinney, and Pete Mason.

*This book is dedicated to my mother, Jean Marie Litz.*

—BRIAN LITZ

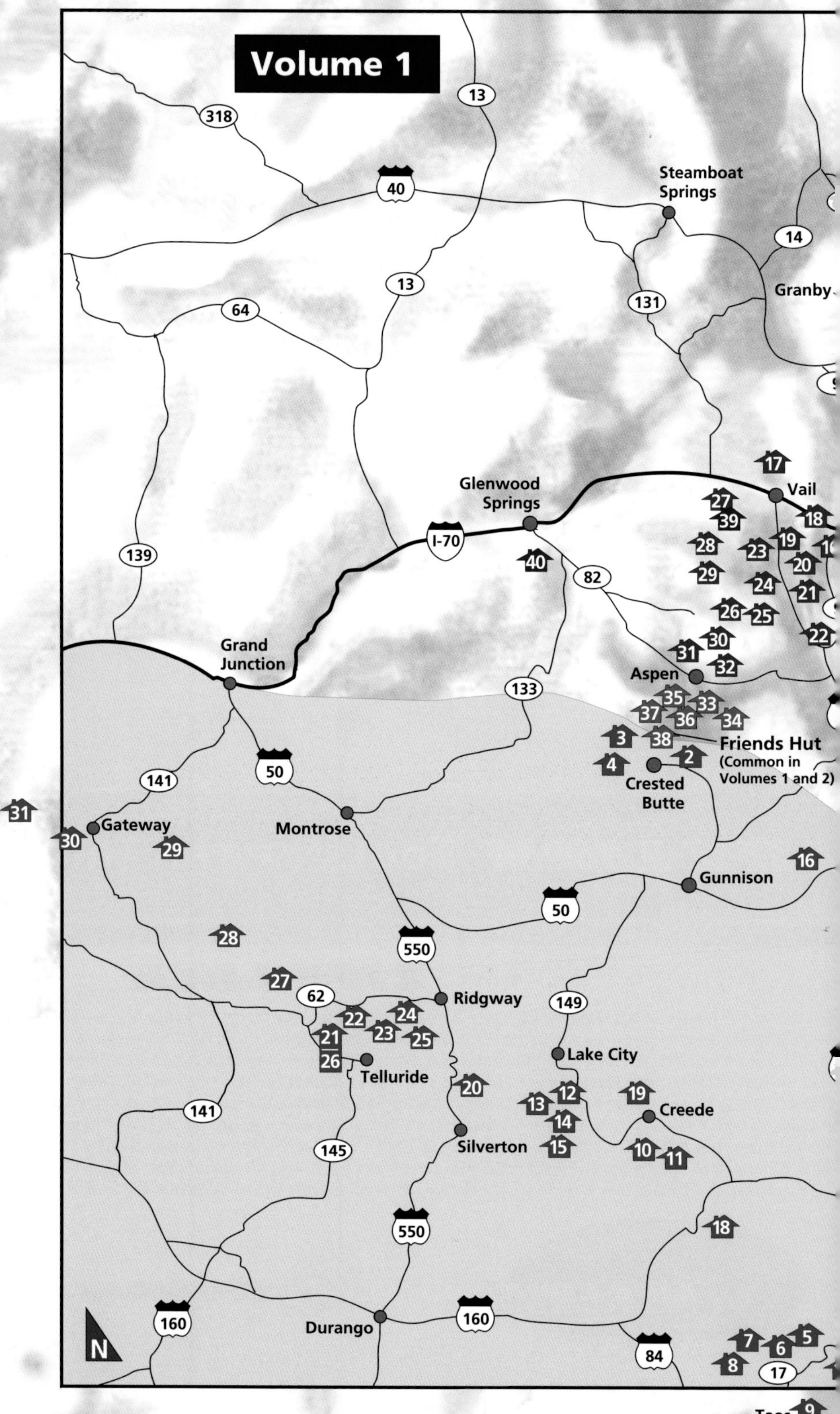

Volume 1
318
13
40
Steamboat Springs
14
Granby
64
131
139
Glenwood Springs
I-70
Vail
17
27
39
18
28
23
19
20
40
82
29
24
21
26
25
22
30
31
Grand Junction
32
Aspen
133
35
33
37
36
34
3
38
Friends Hut
(Common in Volumes 1 and 2)
50
2
4
Crested Butte
141
31
Gateway
Montrose
30
29
16
Gunnison
50
28
550
27
62
Ridgway
149
22
24
21
23
25
26
Lake City
Telluride
20
19
13
12
Creede
141
14
145
Silverton
15
10
11
18
550
160
160
Durango
7
5
6
N
84
8
17
Taos
9

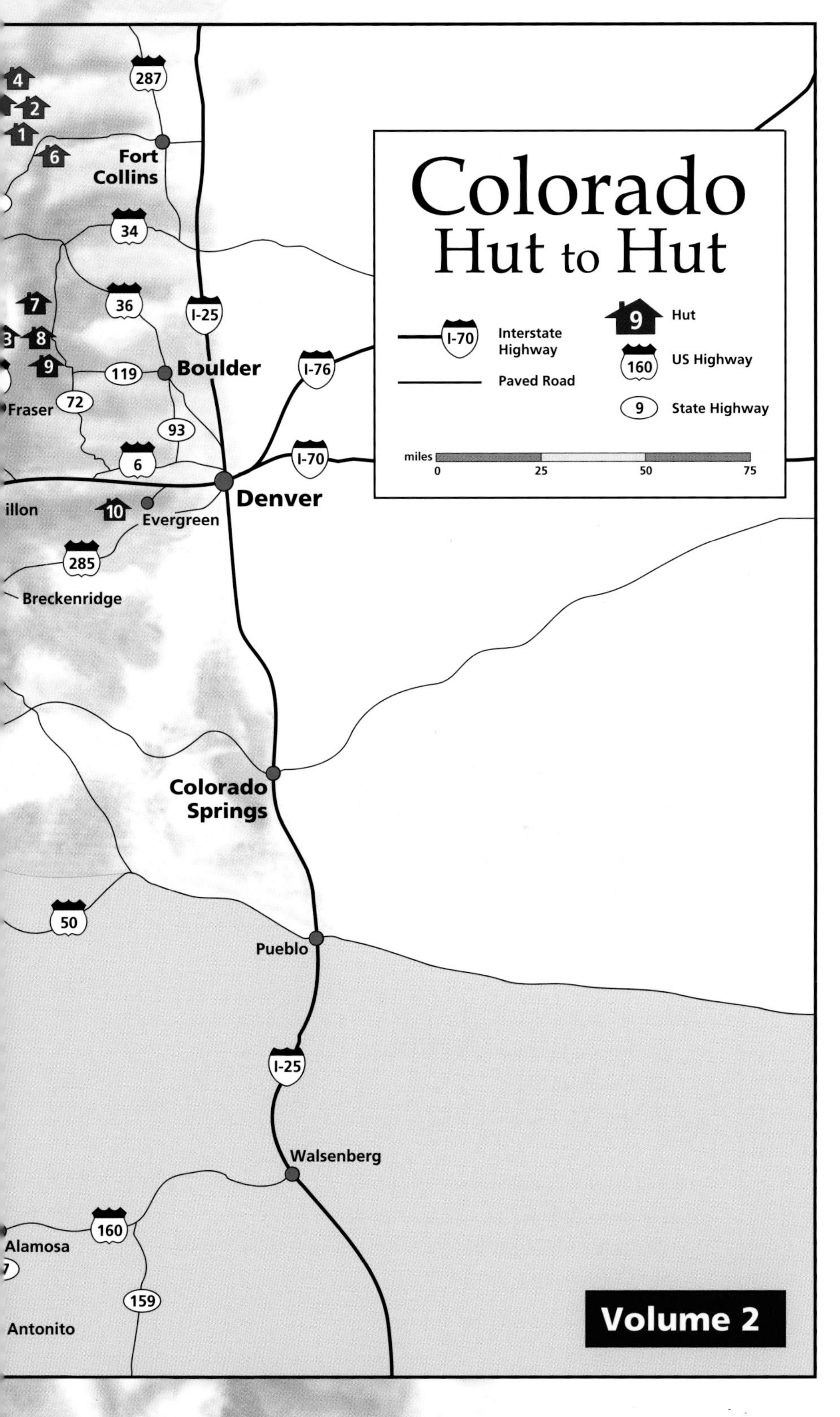

Colorado
Hut to Hut
Interstate Highway
Paved Road
Hut
US Highway
State Highway
miles
0
25
50
75
Volume 2
Fort Collins
Boulder
Denver
Fraser
Evergreen
Breckenridge
Colorado Springs
Pueblo
Walsenberg
Alamosa
Antonito
287
34
36
I-25
I-76
I-70
119
72
93
6
285
50
160
159

# Table of Contents

Foreword, John Fielder .......... 11
Preface, Brian Litz .......... 12
Introduction .......... 13
How to Use This Guide .......... 16
On the Trail .......... 21

**Northern Huts** .......... 35
*Never Summer Nordic Yurts and Nokhu Cabin* .......... 36
1 Grass Creek Yurt .......... 39
2 Montgomery Pass Yurts .......... 44
3 Ruby Jewel Yurt .......... 50
4 North Fork Canadian Yurt .......... 53
5 Dancing Moose Yurt .......... 56
6 Nokhu Cabin .......... 58

*Colorado Mountain Club and Northern Independent Huts* .......... 62
7 Brainard Lake Cabin .......... 65
8 Guinn Mountain Hut .......... 70
9 Tennessee Mountain Cabin .......... 75
10 Squaw Mountain Fire Lookout .......... 77
11 First Creek Cabin .......... 81
12 Second Creek Cabin (Gwen Andrews Hut) .......... 84
13 High Lonesome Hut .......... 87

**Central Huts** .......... 94
*Summit Huts Association* .......... 96
14 Section House and Ken's Cabin .......... 99
15 Francie's Cabin .......... 106
16 Janet's Cabin .......... 111

*10th Mountain Division Hut Association* .......... 120
17 Eiseman Hut .......... 126
18 Shrine Mountain Inn (Jay's, Chuck's, and Walter's Cabins) .......... 133
19 Fowler/Hilliard Hut .......... 141
20 Jackal Hut .......... 154

*10th Mountain Division Hut Association (continued)*
- **21** Vance's Cabin ........ 160
- **22** Sangree M. Froelicher Hut ........ 164
- **23** 10th Mountain Division Hut ........ 170
- **24** Uncle Bud's Hut ........ 176
- **25** Skinner Hut ........ 182
- **26** Betty Bear Hut ........ 188
- **27** Polar Star Inn and Carl's Cabin ........ 194
- **28** Peter Estin Hut ........ 204
- **29** Harry Gates Hut ........ 214
- **30** Margy's Hut ........ 222
- **31** McNamara Hut ........ 230
- **32** Benedict Huts: Fritz's and Fabi's Cabins ........ 233

*Alfred A. Braun Memorial Hut System* ........ 242
- **33** Barnard Hut ........ 245
- **34** Goodwin-Greene Hut ........ 254
- **35** Markley Hut ........ 256
- **36** Lindley Hut ........ 258
- **37** Tagert and Green-Wilson Huts ........ 262
- **38** Friends Hut ........ 272

*Central Independent Huts* ........ 278
- **39** Hidden Treasure Yurt ........ 280
- **40** Sunlight Backcountry Cabin ........ 285

**Appendix A:** Reservations and Information ........ 289
**Appendix B:** Road and Weather Conditions ........ 290
**Appendix C:** County Sheriffs and National Forests ........ 290
**Appendix D:** Guide Services ........ 291
**Appendix E:** Avalanche Training and Information ........ 291
**Appendix F:** Recommended Equipment Checklist ........ 292
**Appendix G:** Bibliography and Recommended Reading List ........ 295
**Appendix H:** Map Sources ........ 299
**Appendix I:** GPS Coordinates ........ 300
**Appendix J:** Difficulty Ratings for Tours ........ 300
**Appendix K:** Hut Rental Rates ........ 303
**Index** ........ 306

# Foreword

Many years ago I decided to take up backcountry skiing. I wasn't happy with the winter scenic photography I was producing from the roadside, and cross-country skiing by day did not reveal the remote early morning and late evening images I wanted.

To capture more secluded photographs of nature in winter, I had skied out of bounds from downhill ski areas for years, but I knew that eventually I'd be put in jail for violating Colorado law, which prohibits such activity.

I didn't want to make the investment in time to learn how to telemark ski (a nifty step up from cross-country skiing technique that employs much sturdier skis, boots, and bindings), but carrying 30 pounds of medium-format camera gear precluded anything less stable.

Then someone told me about alpine touring, or randonnée, equipment—skis, boots, and bindings that look much like downhill equipment but would allow me to release my heels to ski up and across mountains in the Nordic fashion, then lock down the heels to descend with the same parallel turns I used at downhill ski areas.

It was then that I also learned about the extensive and quickly expanding world of backcountry huts. The huts and randonnée skiing opened the door to the wintry backcountry world for a night—even a week—without the rigors and inconvenience of living in a snow cave.

Under the expert guidance of Brian Litz, I rapidly became comfortable with life in the winter outback, especially when I could retreat to a warm, cozy cabin after a long day on the snow trail. In fact, without these huts, I would not have been able to produce most of the Colorado winter images in my files.

Much of my best photography is accomplished when sunlight is saturated with color, at both ends of the day. And though all of the huts are in remarkably scenic locations, I often like to ski up to the high ridges around the huts to take pictures. This requires an hour or more of uphill skiing, which is slow work in fresh snow and usually means I must leave or return to the hut in the dark. If it weren't for the hut as a base of operations, I would not have the energy or desire to make good photographs—for it is usually well below zero at night at 12,000 feet!

The Colorado hut systems are a rare treasure, for me to make my living and for others as a way to enjoy what I've found to be the most tranquil of all seasons—a time when hardly a creature stirs and one can quietly contemplate the value of our natural environment.

I hope Brian's guidance and outstanding photographs will inspire you to discover for yourself the beauty of Colorado's backcountry.

—John Fielder
*Englewood, Colorado*

*Skiers carefully avoid an overhanging cornice as they ascend Pearl Peak en route to Jackal Hut from Fowler/Hilliard Hut via the High Traverse.*

# Preface

Some people are content to simply ride a chairlift up a mountain and ski down groomed slopes at the edge of the backcountry. Others are not: These lovers of the natural world retreat into the rugged backcountry for a few days or a few weeks to escape the bounds of everyday life. I am one of those people.

I remember my first winter-camping trip in 1976. My friend Brock Richardson and I watched as my father's car slowly pulled away from the Glacier Gorge parking lot in Rocky Mountain National Park. Two 14-year-old boys, we already considered ourselves hardened mountaineers with many seasons of "peak bagging" and downhill skiing under our belts. However, the backcountry in the winter was a new world to us, and we were determined to explore it. We received a blustery salutation from the ever-present wind as we hiked into the snow-covered mountains.

Our first night passed relatively uneventfully as we pitched our tent on the snow and burrowed into roomy down sleeping bags. The second night we slept in an abandoned snow cave, sequestered from the incessant winds and snug in our cozy home. At dawn, the feeling of well-being quickly dissipated when we awoke to find our doorway drifted over. During the night a blizzard had sealed us into a darkened world of ice and snow. We tunneled toward freedom and headed for home wearing frozen parkas and frozen smiles. I have never forgotten that early expedition, and I have never lost my love of the alpine world.

Today, adventurers can take advantage of an incredible range of resources to facilitate their travels to the high country. In addition to its alpine peaks, expansive grasslands, sandstone mesas, and swiftly flowing rivers, Colorado boasts the largest and most diverse selection of backcountry cabins, huts, and yurts in the lower 48 states. This eclectic collection of shelters provides any individual willing to strap on skis, lace up hiking boots, or mount a bike the opportunity to enjoy the incomparable beauty of this mountain paradise. The Colorado huts are waiting for you...hurry!

—Brian Litz

*Above: Stars streak the sky high above the North Fork Canadian Yurt in the Medicine Bow Mountains west of Fort Collins.*

# Introduction

Welcome to *Colorado Hut to Hut: Volume I, Northern and Central Regions.* There is much new in this third edition (and fifth printing) of this guidebook. In the introduction to the previous editions, I mentioned how popular hut-to-hut travel was becoming—illustrating with raw statistics the exaggerated growth curve that had defined the sport for 10 to 15 years. If anything, at the dawn of the new millennium this trend is accelerating. In fact, demand for 10th Mountain Division huts has become so vigorous that in 1999 the hut system instituted a lottery system to apportion its space.

Naturally, the hut supply tries to keep pace with hut demand, and since the last edition of this book, printed in 1995, Colorado's high country has sprouted roughly 20 new huts—a near 40 percent increase in five years. So, one of the first things you will notice is the presence of many new faces. All 20 of Colorado's new huts are covered, including six entirely new hut systems as well as additions to existing hut systems.

Concerns about the growing number of hut entries in the book along with the associated growth in the number of pages led to another major change: the metamorphosis of *Colorado Hut to Hut* from one book into a two-volume set. Volume I covers the huts detailed in the Northern and Central chapters of the old tome, while Volume II covers the Southern huts.

The line of demarcation runs east-west across the crest of the Elk Range and over to the southern end of the Sawatch Range near Monarch Pass. Although this splits the very centrally located Elk Mountains in two, it reflects the added

*Alan Keefe enjoys a cool combo—fresh powder and gravity.*

distance and time required for most hut users (based on the Front Range) to reach Monarch Pass and the Gunnison River Valley. It is also an attempt to balance the editorial coverage in each book. This division means that Alfred Braun Memorial Huts, which reside on the northern side of the Elk Range, will be found in Volume I while the Crested Butte area huts and the Lost Wonder Hut are found in Volume II.

Volume I covers huts in the northern and central areas. In the north, these include the five huts of the Never Summer Nordic Yurts and the Nokhu Cabin. Central huts include those of the Summit Huts Association, the 10th Mountain Division Hut Association, the Alfred A. Braun Memorial Hut System, and two independent huts (Hidden Treasure Yurt and Sunlight Backcountry Cabin). Volume II covers the Crested Butte area huts, the Bull of the Woods Yurt in Taos, New Mexico, and the entire San Juan Mountains, including the Cumbres Pass area in the South San Juans on the New Mexico border. The last section is a guide to the San Juan Huts mountain biking route going from Telluride to Moab, Utah.

New huts covered in this edition include the **Montgomery Pass Yurts** and the rebuilt Lake Agnes Cabin (now called the Nokhu Cabin) in the Never Summer Nordic Yurts; the **High Lonesome Hut** north of Winter Park; the **Squaw Mountain Fire Lookout** near Evergreen; the **Section House** and **Ken's Cabin** in Summit County; the **Hidden Treasure Yurt** near Edwards; and the **Eiseman Hut,** the **Sangree M. Froelicher Hut, Walter's Cabin,** and the **Benedict Huts,** which are additions to the 10th Mountain Division system. Even more new huts are in the planning stages (though most are several years away from opening their doors).

Taking on this book project certainly has proven to be a double-edged sword. When I first hatched the idea back around 1990, I did not envision the never-ending construction of huts that has forced me to continually update the guide. I figured that I would need to revisit it every five to eight years or so. This obviously was not to be, as every year sees a new hut welcoming weary, chilled skiers in the winter and rain-soaked, lightning-harassed mountain bikers and hikers in the summer.

Why is hut-to-hut travel becoming more and more popular? One reason, I believe, is that many alpine skiers have become bored with an increasingly packaged, groomed, and manufactured "product" at downhill ski areas. Also, many more people are moving to the Rocky Mountain region. Another factor is that outdoor-recreation gear has greatly improved in recent years; today's equipment is lighter and performs extremely well, allowing outdoor enthusiasts of all abilities to enjoy the backcountry. And finally, hut-to-hut travel is just plain fun! The backcountry beckons a wide variety of people with panoramic vistas, colorful sunsets, the challenge of unknown terrain, the thrill of virgin snow, and, finally, the chance to relax in a cozy cabin overlooking the heart of the Colorado Rockies.

Which all means lots of work for me. But, hey, it also keeps me out in the backcountry...doing field work! I still love this sport as much as I did the first time I strapped on a pair of old wooden Trysl-Knut skis and headed to the Markley and Tagert Huts with my Colorado Mountain Club Denver Junior Group buddies for our winter outing in January 1977. Here's to Colorado remaining the hut capital of the United States!

*John Oates chops cotton in the Elk Mountain backcountry near Aspen.*

# How To Use This Guide

Writing a guidebook presents the author with a quandary: provide directions as detailed as "go 100 feet and turn left at the 15th aspen tree" or provide only the basic data? Some guidebooks give so much information and conversation that the user becomes frustrated merely trying to assemble the relevant facts; other guidebooks are so tersely fact oriented that they leave the user cold and uninspired.

My vision for *Colorado Hut to Hut* was to create a field guide as well as a backcountry "wish book." It is intended to provide information and advice for aspiring hut-to-hut travelers and to inspire the seasoned ski mountaineer looking for new and unknown challenges. The beginner can read through the "On the Trail" section of this introduction and follow the detailed trail descriptions, while the expert might simply scan the trail summaries to get a quick overall feel for a tour or an untried hut system.

In addition to routes and hut-system information, *Colorado Hut to Hut* includes sections on equipment recommendations and hut etiquette, as well as avalanche information and help with some of the more common problems encountered on hut-to-hut expeditions. It also contains several appendixes with important phone numbers, including emergency and hut-reservation numbers. The Bibliography and Recommended Reading List (Appendix G) contains suggestions for further reading on a range of topics important to hut-to-hut skiers and bikers.

This book is certainly not the only source of information that should accompany adventurers into the wilderness, nor is it a substitute for experience. Every person heading into the backcountry needs to be proactive in obtaining the experience and knowledge necessary to ensure a safe, enjoyable adventure in the Colorado Rockies. Skiers, hikers, and bikers are strongly encouraged to carry a selection of maps, including United States Geological Survey's 7.5-minute topographic maps (topos), Trails Illustrated maps, and maps produced by the various hut systems. Books such as *The ABCs of Avalanche Safety, Snow Sense,* and *The Backcountry Medical Guide* are also invaluable resources for mountain expeditions. These books fit easily into a pack and cover important topics too complex to be detailed fully in this guidebook.

**To get the most out of this book,** please take the time to read the following brief summary of its overall organization.

*Colorado Hut to Hut: Volume I, Northern and Central Regions* and *Volume II, Southern Region* contain regional headings, each of which begins with a brief overview of the hut systems located in those areas, including a bit of local history, the type of skiing found nearby, and general descriptions of hut amenities.

Individual hut systems, huts, and tours are then described in detail, once again highlighting each hut's history and special features. Each tour description has two parts: The first is a capsule summary of the most important tour information, including level of difficulty, estimated travel time, mileage, elevation gain and loss, and pertinent map sources; the second portion is a detailed narrative of the route. A route is described in detail only once. That is, if a tour that runs from Uncle Bud's Hut to Skinner Hut is described under the Uncle Bud's Hut section, it will not be described again in reverse under the Skinner Hut entry.

Hut tours are separated into two categories: trails that travel from a trailhead to a hut, and tours that travel between huts—"hut to hut." As a general rule, the hut systems and trails that link huts within a system are described from north to south and/or from east to west. Many hut entries also include recommended day tours.

Annotated USGS 7.5-minute topo maps show routes to and surrounding each hut. These maps are for general reference only; you should purchase your own topo maps for route-finding.

*Craig Gaskill gets up close and personal with the Colorado snowpack.*

## Difficulty

Each tour is assigned a rating of overall difficulty. These ratings are subjective, but they do follow generally accepted criteria.

**Novice routes** present few difficulties, require less complex navigation, and feature minimal elevation gain. A novice rating does not mean a route is suitable for people who have never cross-country skied; a novice-level skier ideally should have completed at least 5 to 10 backcountry day trips and have a basic mastery of double poling and snowplowing. Because novice skiers are generally still gaining wilderness savvy in areas such as navigation and avalanche awareness, it is recommended that these skiers participate in guided trips or in group outings accompanied by more experienced skiers.

**Intermediate routes** are the most common type of tour in this book and most closely define the term "classic tour." Intermediate-level skiers usually have been skiing for at least several seasons and have participated in five or more hut trips. Their wilderness experience and fitness levels are solid, and they are able to ski to and from huts with ease. They also enjoy off-trail skiing, although they may not have completely mastered the telemark turn. Carrying heavy overnight backpacks is not new to these skiers.

**Advanced skiers** have generally been backcountry and hut skiing for many seasons, have skied and traveled in a wide variety of weather conditions, and can telemark down steep, timbered slopes and through diverse types of snow. They are very fit and have a full understanding of avalanches and rescue procedures. Most importantly, advanced skiers will never tell you where the best powder is!

**Advanced/Expert designations** indicate tours that go beyond the standard definition of "advanced"—tours that demand high fitness levels and mountain skills plus an extraordinary level of commitment. An example might be a tour with a passage over a pass or ridge that must be crossed to reach a hut. Once over the pass or ridge, you have to be committed to reaching the hut, as the distance and exertion required to retrace your steps may be simply too much. In addition, the high-altitude nature of this terrain might leave skiers particularly vulnerable to approaching storms—making a bail-out problematic, if not outright impossible. Other tours considered "expert" might require rock scrambling or extreme exposure to the elements, or the tour may be unusually long and physically taxing.

Most day-trip peak ascents are at least advanced in difficulty. Under good conditions, most peaks can be climbed quickly and safely, but it is amazing how quickly a storm can move in and within minutes drop the temperature and visibility to zero.

Advanced and expert tours are serious undertakings. In fact, any tour in this book can become advanced under certain conditions.

## Icons

Icons indicating cross-country skiing, snowshoeing, bicycling, and/or hiking accompany each tour description. Hut routes with all four icons are open year-round for skiing, snowshoeing, biking, and hiking. Some huts are open only in winter (due to permit restrictions), so only winter icons will be shown. Because bicycles are prohibited in Wilderness Areas, routes that pass through them are closed to mountain bikers; therefore no bicycle icon will be shown.

## Time

The travel times listed are general guesstimates of how long the average group of skiers will take to complete a route. They include time for a lunch break and several shorter breaks. While stronger parties can easily make quick work of most trails, slower groups—those new to backcountry skiing or those breaking trail in powder snow—might consider using a figure of one mile per hour plus one hour per 1,000 feet of elevation gain in estimating tour lengths.

## Distance

The distance listed in each section is one-way mileage as measured from trailhead to hut or from hut to hut. (Mileage to a trailhead, as detailed in the text portion of the tour, may be slightly off due to variances in car odometers.)

## Elevations

Three elevations are given in the capsule information for each tour. The first elevation is for the point where the trail begins, whether it is a trailhead or a hut. The second elevation is for the destination hut. The final pair of elevations represents the gain (+) and loss (–) accumulated over the length of a trail. (These figures should be reversed if you are traveling in the opposite direction.) In trail descriptions, an elevation that corresponds to a USGS 7.5-minute topo map reference is referred to as an "Elevation Point."

*Major avalanche runs such as these above the trail to the Tagert and Green-Wilson Huts pose a threat to winter travelers.*

## Avalanche

In this guidebook I use the avalanche-hazard rating system created by Richard and Betsy Armstrong, which I have used in previous skiing guides. This system is extremely useful because it gives an overall feel for the terrain. This is important because daily or seasonal avalanche hazards may change but terrain does not.

Avalanche warnings in the summaries at the beginning of each trail discussion pertain only to that specific trail, not to other hut-to-hut trails in the area or to any day tours in the area. For example, a trail to a hut or in between huts might be extremely safe and carry with it a "minimal danger" avalanche rating while the recommended day tours included with a specific hut origin might have much more dangerous ratings. A rating of "minimal danger" in a tour description has no relationship to the severity of the avalanche terrain and hazards above and around the huts.

Snow conditions can change rapidly; the decision to ski or not ski a potential avalanche route is entirely yours. Remember that many people are caught in small slides that occur in unlikely or unobvious avalanche terrain, such as in a creek drainage or in the middle of a forest. To be safe, always assume that you will be traveling in avalanche conditions.

The four categories of avalanche terrain used in this guidebook are:

**1. Minimal danger.** This route is safe under all conditions. However, it is still recommended that you remain alert and play it safe; an avalanche, while unlikely, is never totally impossible.

**2. Some avalanche terrain encountered; easily avoided.** This route is still safe in all conditions when skiers remain on standard trails. There is some dangerous terrain in the general vicinity, but it should be easy to spot and avoid.

**3. Route crosses avalanche runout zones; can be dangerous during high-hazard periods.** This trail's normal route lies below a known avalanche path. Skiers will not likely serve as a trigger, although they could be caught in a spontaneous slide.

**4. Route crosses avalanche slopes; prone to skier-triggered avalanches during high-hazard periods.** This route travels directly across a known hazard, and skiers can easily set off a slide given the right combination of conditions.

*Note:* If the Colorado Avalanche Information Center says the avalanche hazard is high, avoid trails with ratings of three or four as listed above. (See Appendix E for avalanche information phone numbers and Appendix G for recommended reading.)

## Maps

*Colorado Hut to Hut* lists relevant USGS 7.5-minute topographic maps, National Forest maps, Trails Illustrated maps, special maps for each tour, and references for maps included in this book.

USGS topo maps are the mainstays of mountaineers and skiers, providing the greatest detail of elevations, contours, and natural features. National Forest maps are large-scale maps that are almost useless for navigation; however, they do provide road and trailhead information, as well as an overview of the area. Trails Illustrated maps are very useful for backcountry travelers—especially mountain bikers—because they cover the equivalent of eight USGS topo maps. These maps are up-to-date and virtually indestructible. Trails Illustrated maps are listed only if they are available for the area. Specialty maps include any maps produced by a hut association, such as the 10th Mountain Division Hut Association. These maps are revised often and are very popular.

Schematic maps included in this book are referenced by page number after each tour heading. These maps are for basic orientation only; use the maps recommended in the capsule information for route navigation. Also, keep in mind that a map's degree of usefulness is directly related to its date of publication. Old maps will not have the most current information on roads, trails, etc. Remember to check the publication date of any map.

*Note:* A 1:160,000-scale "topo atlas" published by DeLorme Mapping is available for Colorado. This is one of the single most useful sources of information for anyone traveling the back roads of the state and is highly recommended. See Appendix H for map sources.

# On the Trail

## Before You Go

As someone (perhaps a backcountry skier) once said: "Education teaches us the rules. Experience teaches the exceptions." The mountains can be a very dangerous and unpredictable place for the unknowing and ill prepared—as well as for the highly skilled and seasoned backcountry traveler. Skiers, snowshoers, hikers, and mountain bikers must understand that even the "easiest" trail can be very challenging, that weather patterns can and do change quickly and dramatically, and that equipment fails. Those headed to even the most readily accessible huts must accept responsibility for their own and their companions' safety and well-being. A self-sufficient mindset is a must.

For individuals who are interested in learning more about hut-to-hut travel, courses are offered by major outdoor-equipment retailers, guide services, universities, and recreational clubs, as well as many city and county recreation departments. These classes range from "layering clothes for cold weather" and "basic mountain bike repair and maintenance" to weekend avalanche seminars. These evening and weekend sessions can be excellent sources of basic and more advanced backcountry information.

Successful and safe expeditions do not just happen—they are the result of organization and planning. Use the following outline to aid in organizing your hut-to-hut adventure:

**1. Use *Colorado Hut to Hut*** to choose trips that match your group's interests and skill level. Talk to the hut systems' personnel to help plan a trip that is appropriate for your group's experience and fitness level, and to help you decide whether your group needs a guide. (See Appendix A for hut-system addresses, phone numbers, and websites.)

**2. Call the hut system to reserve the hut(s) and dates you want.** Remember that weekends, holidays, and nights with full moons are usually reserved first. Be prepared to pay for the trip in full when you make your reservation.

**3. Designate a leader for your group.** The leader should be responsible for disseminating information and seeing that all risk waivers (if required) are returned to the proper hut system.

**4. Purchase any necessary trail and road maps.**

**5. Plan meals and snacks.** Purchase food and repackage to reduce bulk.

**6. Inspect equipment** (zippers, pack straps, etc.) and take it for a dry run. Purchase flashlight and avalanche transceiver batteries, ski waxes, skin glue, etc. Restock first-aid and repair kits. Make sure that all binding screws are tight and that binding cables (if any) are in good repair. Organize group gear. Rent any gear necessary. Test avalanche transceivers.

**7. Practice packing your pack.** Make sure essential and often-used items (sunglasses, goggles, sunscreen, maps, headlamps, compass, snacks, knives) are in a handy location.

**8. Plan car shuttles.** (Call the hut system if you need assistance in planning car shuttles; its staff may be able to recommend shuttle services.)

**9. Before you leave for the trailhead,** be sure to call the Colorado Avalanche Information Center (CAIC), the U.S. Weather Service, and the Colorado Department of Transportation (see Appendixes B and E) to check avalanche, weather, and road conditions.

**10. Provide a responsible party back home with your trip itinerary,** expected time of return, where you plan to park, and hut-system phone numbers.

**11. Establish an emergency plan and assess the group's first-aid knowledge.**

**12. Finally, DO NOT forget hut lock combinations and/or keys.** Play it safe and have several individuals carry these. Keep a flashlight handy in case you arrive at the hut after dark.

## Gear

Today, a staggering amount of durable, high-performance equipment is available for conveyance through the backcountry. Though the vast majority of hut visitors arrive in winter, and on skis, more people are traveling by snowshoe and in the summer.

*Though modern free-heel gear is a far cry from simpler, less stout Nordic gear of yore, it still can break.*

There is little to say about what kind of equipment to use in the summer. Bikers use standard mountain bikes, though the cyclo-cross type of bike has become more popular. Appropriate footwear for hikers ranges from heavy-duty "approach" shoes and boots to heavy-duty backpacking boots. Some summer visitors drive high-clearance or four-wheel-drive vehicles to the huts and use them as base camps for day hiking and biking trips. Many huts and hut systems are not open in the summer, so please check with each system for specifics.

Winter is the time when things are hopping in the huts, and there is much debate regarding the best equipment for winter travel. Snowshoes are steady and reliable, easy to master, require minimal skills to operate (especially when pointed downhill), are not temperature-temperamental (like waxes and skins), can easily be rented, and are a great choice for non-skiers who would like to sample the hut experience without the anxiety that can accompany the beginning ski experience. Even though snowshoeing is a fulfilling outdoor pursuit, I believe it ranks well below skiing on the fun scale. Think about it—you walk up a hill, then you walk back down the hill. With skis, you walk up the hill (aided by skins or waxes), then slide down the hill on a gravity-propelled free-fall.

The fact of the matter is that most of the huts in Colorado were conceived of as ski huts—plain and simple. All in all, skis are the ideal mode of transportation for those willing to master their use. You can walk on them, kick and glide on them, herringbone on them, carry them on your pack, and, most importantly, be transported straight to nirvana on them when under the influence of gravity in powder snow.

For the most part, any type of non-track (Nordic center) ski can be used in Colorado's hut systems. I have acquaintances who occasionally "skate," or kick-and-glide, their way to the huts. This usually is done only under optimal conditions. Though most of the huts and trail systems were designed for and built when most people were skiing on heavy-duty, metal-edged touring skis and when moderate-duty, free-heel telemark gear reigned supreme, today an equal number of skiers are using alpine resort-grade free-heel gear. And more and more people—though the numbers are still relatively small—are using alpine touring or ski-mountaineering equipment. It all works, and the final choice really depends on the skiers' intentions, abilities, and the type of gear they own.

Virtually every novice- to intermediate-level trail on a road can be tackled using metal-edge touring gear. Even beginners can scoot to and from huts and snowplow down roads on this gear. This category includes waxable and waxless skis with partial to full metal edges with a shovel of roughly 50 to 70 millimeters in width. If you intend to travel above treeline, off-trail (cross-country), with heavier packs, or want to make some turns on day trips, then a wider, sturdier, more aggressive heavy-duty backcountry touring or moderate-duty telemark setup would be preferable—along with a heavier all-leather or lighter-weight plastic boot.

For many modern skiers who rip at the lift-accessed resorts using telemark and parallel turns, want to spend a lot of time skiing off peaks and ridges and through steep trees, and do multiday tours with heavy packs, the choice is the latest generation of high-end performance free-heel gear. These skis are derived from alpine ski technology. They are not meant to be waxed with "touring" waxes. Rather, they are used most often with climbing skins for forward and upward mobility. In addition, they have a single-camber construction that is optimized for turning on the steeps in a variety of snow conditions—from the deepest powder to the most problematic, wind-compacted sastrugi above treeline. For the most part, skiers using this type of "heavy metal" will most likely sport the latest generations of burly plastic boots or race-grade leather telemark boots.

Alpine touring gear hails primarily from the central European alpine countries (free-heel telemark gear originated in Scandinavia), and has been available for decades in North America. Alpine touring gear's proponents—usually introduced to it in the Alps by mountaineers who climb peaks while wearing leather or plastic mountaineering boots—are growing. This increase in popularity is for good reasons, including the fact that as "tele" gear has become higher-performance and heavier, Alpine touring gear has become increasingly light and comfortable. The bindings, which can pivot at the toe for touring and lock down like a standard resort alpine binding for downhill skiing, also incorporate sophisticated release features that appeal to skiers concerned about leg injuries from falls.

The lock-down feature also allows skiers to ski exactly as they would on standard resort equipment. This feature is beneficial for competent resort skiers who would like to experience the backcountry and do not want to learn an entirely new turn. Alpine touring gear allows downhill skiers to directly transfer their skills into backcountry skiing.

In summary, don't obsess about gear. In fact, if you make many sojourns to the huts, you can and will see every type and combination of gear imaginable. If you are new to the sport, go to a good shop and talk to experienced salespeople. Talk to friends. Keep an open mind and don't get led astray by philosophical zealots. You can find many good books and how-to videos that go over the basics (see Appendix G). Most gear is rentable. Experiment before you buy. Bottom line? It is more important to go out there and have fun while cranking face plants than to worry about what kind of gear you are using.

A note about equipment care: Modern equipment is so well-made and sophisticated that many people have become complacent concerning the proper maintenance and routine inspection of their gear. Take the time to check your equipment thoroughly. Look for loose screws and loose cables on bindings, worn laces on boots, bent poles, broken zippers, loose brakes on bikes, etc. Make sure that you have all of your gear (see checklist in Appendix F). Carry a repair kit and know how to use it. The time to learn how to repair gear is before you leave home—not while huddled under a spruce tree in the middle of a blizzard at midnight.

## General Trail Considerations

When traveling in the backcountry, be sure that your group arrives at the trailhead early; traveling hut to hut requires an equally early start. Try to build extra time into your schedule just in case problems arise.

The three rules of backcountry travel are: Stay together, stay together, and—of course—stay together. Think what could happen if someone in the back of the group breaks a binding or needs a blister kit while the leader speeds away in a Zen-like trance. Any member of your group could end up lost—or dead—if he or she makes a wrong turn in a winter whiteout. Consider using a buddy system to ensure that each member of your group is accounted for.

Each group should carry emergency equipment consisting of rudimentary camping gear, such as a stove, a pot, and a tarp, in case emergency shelter is necessary. Also, each person should carry high-energy snack food and quick trailside meals (such as soups), as well as a first-aid kit, flashlight, and avalanche gear. Be sure to test your transceivers as a group each and every day and discuss emergency procedures before your group heads into the backcountry.

*Steve Sterner, Bill Litz, and Bruce Hayden depart the Fowler/Hilliard Hut.*

Finally, each member of the group should carry maps and a compass. Many skiers and mountain bikers have become too dependent on guidebooks; map reading, navigation, and compass use are crucial skills that all backcountry travelers should acquire and practice. It is essential to keep maps and compasses handy and refer to them often, especially when confronted with a trail intersection, confusing route, and/or foul weather. Get in the habit of matching real-world landmarks to features on the map and watching out for trail markers—both the obvious and the not so obvious.

Backcountry trail markers exist in a variety of forms: blue diamonds for Nordic ski trails, orange diamonds for snowmobile routes, old tree blazes, and others. On the trails covered in this book, you may encounter any or all of these markers—or none.

## GPS Coordinates

If there ever was anything that is part art and part science, it is land navigation. Though the subject is too large to cover in detail here—and there are many fine books dedicated solely to this pursuit—I find it necessary to touch on the subject, especially with regard to Global Positioning System (GPS) units and coordinates. GPS coordinates are beginning to appear in many guidebooks. This is because more people are requesting them, not necessarily because people absolutely need to have them to navigate in Colorado under normal conditions. I have been uneasy about including them and, in fact, as we went to press, I chose to leave them out entirely in this edition.

One reason is the coordinates that were available at press time, provided by the hut operators, came with caveats such as "remember that these are only as good as the person who took them," or "so-and-so did these coordinates a long time ago and we think they are *reasonably* accurate," and "we have two sets of numbers that differ, and we are going to do them again in the future."

This lack of confidence in the current data—much of which are many years old—is a function of several factors, including the evolution of both the sophistication of commercially available GPS units over time and advancements in the general science of equipment usage in the field. In addition, the competence of the GPS operator affects the accuracy of the readings, as does the ability of the GPS unit to lock onto a maximum number of satellites—the latter being affected by local topography and forest cover. Historically, GPS units have been less effective in giving elevational readings, as opposed to latitude and longitude.

Perhaps most important, up until a few months before this book went to press, the U.S. military had purposefully hindered the accuracy of civilian units for reasons of national defense. The U.S. government's decision now allows GPS units to achieve highly accurate readings. So during the next few years, prepare for a steady stream of accurate, dependable coordinates to be available through a variety of sources, including each hut system.

And finally, bear in mind the sales hype that accompanies the arrival of GPS units that are sold today. Believe all of it, and it could lead you to swear that by carrying one (or an altimeter or a compass, for that matter), you will be immune to getting lost. What if the batteries die? Or you could come to the conclusion that GPS units' divining-rod abilities allow you to shut off your brain while you are led directly to your chosen destination. They don't and won't.

GPS units only tell you where you are—and roughly at that—not where to go. Nor will they tell you whether an avalanche path, a cliff band, or unskiable trees are in your way. Ultimately, you have to select the route.

## Navigation Tips and Tools

The bottom line is that GPS units are useful for navigating in Colorado's mountains, but no more so than a map, a compass, or an altimeter. You can travel through the high country safely and efficiently by following these guidelines:

1. **Give yourself time to develop a feel for the land,** rates of travel, and the orientation of the mountains.

2. **Learn to pay attention to landmarks.**

3. **Master the use of basic navigation tools such a compass and USGS topo maps**—7.5-minute quads still being the best tools available for navigation—and the ability to match them to the terrain around you.

4. **Skillfully employ your brain** (first and foremost).

In addition to good maps, everyone should have a quality compass. This, like the topo map, is an essential tool for travel. Buy a good compass that is capable of shooting real bearings, and learn how to use it. State-of-the-art compasses cost around $40 to $60 and will last forever. (Don't get hoodwinked into buying a techy, battery-operated one—the fewer the batteries, the better.) Keep your map and compass handy and break them out at every stop.

More and more people are now carrying altimeters, which are on the next tier of essential tools for navigation in the mountains. Units such as the Suunto Vector provide a steady stream of information for the user from their sophisticated altimeter/barometer, log functions, watch functions, and built-in digital compass. The compasses in these devices are actually quite nice, though still not a substitute for a quality hand-held compass. Used properly, altimeters can provide helpful information on changing weather conditions, elevation, and rate of travel; however, the key to using them is to understand what their limitations are.

## Hypothermia, Frostbite, and the Sun

Hypothermia and frostbite are the two most common cold-weather injuries afflicting skiers and winter mountaineers. Both are preventable—and reversible—if caught in their earliest stages.

**Hypothermia** is a general cooling of the body's core temperature. It takes only a minor change in this core temperature to produce noticeable effects such as feeling chilled or cold, impairment of muscle coordination (especially of the hands), apathy, confusion, and shivering. Try to stay dry and warm, drink warm fluids, snack regularly, and check each other during the course of the day.

**Frostbite** is a localized freezing of soft tissue due to exposure to temperatures at or below freezing. Keep all body parts protected from the wind and cold and keep them dry! Watch for skin that turns whitish and loses sensation (frost nip and mild frostbite).

You can avoid both frostbite and hypothermia by staying dry, warm, and rested and by limiting your skin's exposure to the cold air and bitter winds. Carry and wear a variety of clothes, layering them so you can quickly regulate your body's temperature and humidity by shedding or adding garments, especially a wind-protection layer.

**Your skin and eyes need "clothing," too.** Pack plenty of sunblock and lip protection, at least SPF 20 to 30. Consider bringing moisturizing lotion or aloe to soothe skin. Purchase high-quality sunglasses that screen out the most dangerous ultraviolet radiation, and carry an extra pair in the first-aid kit. On mountain bike trips, bring light-colored clothes, such as thin tights and long-sleeved T-shirts, that you can wear during the day to shield your skin from the sun.

## Altitude

*Snowmelt is the source of water for most Colorado huts.*

Colorado's huts are roughly between 8,500 and 12,000 feet in elevation. Unless you have been routinely exercising at higher elevations, you will probably feel the effects of altitude. Because there is less oxygen at these high elevations, your body will consequently be forced to work harder during physical exertion. It is not unlikely that you will experience the effects of altitude sickness, with symptoms such as shortness of breath, dizziness, headaches, lack of appetite, and nausea.

Slow acclimatization is the best way to minimize and eventually eliminate the effects of altitude. It takes about three weeks of continual exposure to a given altitude to become fully acclimatized. Fortunately, the human body adapts quickly, and you can easily lessen the effects of altitude by building a little time into your trip and starting out slowly. If you are visiting the mountains from a lower elevation, say, 6,000 feet or below, plan a day or two at the beginning of your trip to stay at a mountain town before hitting the trailhead. Additionally, choose an itinerary that allows your group to gain elevation gradually; hut-system personnel can help you plan an appropriate trip. Also, stay several nights at one hut so you can further acclimatize. Remember that a hut trip is not a race—take your time and enjoy it.

Be sure to consult a physician if you have any questions concerning your health and your ability to function at high altitude.

## Nutrition and Hydration

Dehydration is one of the single biggest factors contributing to Acute Mountain Sickness (AMS) and High-Altitude Pulmonary Edema (HAPE), as well as leading to headaches, nausea, restless sleep, and a feeling of malaise. Colorado's dry climate and high elevations cause human bodies to work harder. It is almost impossible to drink too much water. Plan on at least three to four quarts per person per day.

Rather than waiting and watching for signs of dehydration, prevent it! Make sure you drink plenty of fluids each morning when you get up, at meals, and throughout the day. Drink tea or water after a hard day of skiing, biking, or hiking. Begin dinner with a light soup and keep a bottle of water next to your bed. Consider carrying two water bottles or one water bottle and a thermos. Fill one container with plain water and a second with soup, cider, or a fruit-flavored electrolyte-replacement beverage.

Because hut skiing allows you to travel with less camping gear, there is no excuse for not bringing enough food. Cook good, nutritious meals with plenty of carbohydrates and protein. Soups are excellent for times when your appetite is suppressed. Have healthy snacks handy on the trail and snack routinely. Taking a steady supply of fuel and liquid into the body throughout the day will work wonders at warding off exhaustion.

## Weather

Colorado weather is predictable in that it is unpredictable. The weather is generally sunny and clear. Winter storms sometimes descend out of Canada, sending temperatures far below zero for extended periods, but these storms usually moderate rapidly. In winter, the midday temperatures in the high country normally remain in the +15 to +30 degree (F) range, with nighttime temperatures dropping to zero to –10 degrees. When storms move in, they seldom stay for more than a few days.

Early-season skiing (late November through early January) can range from excellent to nonexistent. During this time of year, it is often possible to travel hut to hut on packed trails, though day skiing is often limited because of shallow snow cover that leaves rocks and logs exposed. Late in the season, as snowstorms become more frequent and the snow has a higher moisture content, conditions start improving. Good off-trail skiing usually begins in January, when the snowpack starts to settle and skiers are able to float well above any obstacles beneath it, like rocks and tree stumps. The more southern huts tend to get a deeper snowpack earlier and often have great skiing as early as December.

As spring approaches, the days become longer and warmer, although winter-like storms are still very real threats in the high country. This is when storms with heavier, moisture-laden snow move through the mountains and the deepest snowpack accumulates. Many skiers—both Nordic and downhill—feel February to April is the best time to ski, especially at higher elevations.

In the summer, the high country belongs to hikers and mountain bikers. Colorado summers are beautiful, with warm to hot days and cool nights. Probably the greatest dangers to people using huts during the summer are dehydration and lightning. Summer thunderstorms build with extreme rapidity and can easily strand groups on exposed mountain peaks, high passes, or in the middle of treeless parks. These storms, which usually hit in the afternoon, often move off as quickly as they arrive. Watch the skies, including the sky behind you.

Storms should not be treated lightly. If you are caught in a storm during summer or in winter (yes, there are occasional lightning storms even in winter and spring), immediately leave high points such as ridges, passes, or peaks. Move away from lone objects such as boulders, trees, or bicycles. Sit on the ground, not in caves or gullies (because of ground currents), and wait until the storm passes.

Many Coloradans feel that autumn is the finest season in the Rockies. The weather is stable, with crisp daytime temperatures and chilly nights. Normal temperatures range from the 60s and 70s during the day to the high 30s and 40s at night. This is probably the best time of year for mountain biking and hiking. Fall can also see turbulent weather as rainstorms move across the mountains, dusting the highest peaks with snow. Keep an eye out for rainbows.

## Avalanches

Perhaps the most spectacular, most widespread, and least understood threat to the winter backcountry traveler is an avalanche. By its most basic definition, an avalanche is a large mass of snow that moves downhill under the force of gravity. Avalanche activity is a very complex process that belies its apparent simplicity.

More and more people are dying in avalanches because more and more people are skiing, snowshoeing, snowboarding, and snowmobiling. People new to backcountry skiing should consider a guided trip their first time out. The purpose of this discussion is to give you a rudimentary understanding of just what an avalanche is, how to avoid one, and what to do if you must cross an avalanche slope.

The best way to prepare yourself to travel safely in the Rockies is to first read *Snow Sense* and *The ABCs of Avalanche Safety.* Carry these with you. For further information, read *The Avalanche Handbook* and *Avalanche Safety for Climbers and Skiers.* Enroll in an avalanche course and spend some time really digging into the snowpack. Or check out some of the videos that have hit the market in recent years, including *Winning the Avalanche Game.* (See Appendix G for information on how to obtain these titles.)

Avalanches come in two basic varieties. The first is the loose-snow or point-release avalanche. Point-release avalanches usually begin at a specific point and flow downhill in a structureless mass, forming an inverted V. The second kind is the slab avalanche, which begins when a large, cohesive slab or sheet of snow starts sliding all at once, leaving a well-defined fracture line. Slab avalanches are the more dangerous of the two types of slides because they involve huge amounts of hard, often wind-packed snow. Slab avalanches kill the most people and cause the most property destruction.

A slab avalanche is initiated when something serves as a trigger to upset the snowpack, which may have very little internal strength. Likely triggers are the wind, weather, temperature, and, of course, people. Think of the snowpack as a cake; a cake may be made up of a single, stable layer or it may have several layers. Now think of what will happen when that cake is tilted at an angle. Often these layers are held together in a delicate equilibrium and may stay in this precarious state for days or weeks. Then, along comes a potent snowstorm, a warm spell, a wild animal, or a skier to disrupt that delicate balance.

Backcountry travelers should consider three factors when assessing a slope's potential for sliding: terrain, weather, and snowpack. When thinking about the terrain, remember that most avalanches occur on north- and east-facing slopes with angles between 25 and 55 degrees. The vast majority of avalanches occur on slopes with angles between 30 and 45 degrees. Avoid snow cornices that overhang ridges away from the prevailing winds. Keep in mind, however, that wet-snow avalanches can occur on slopes of even 10 degrees, especially on south-facing slopes during spring. Remember to check the ground cover; the more rocks and trees there are to anchor the snow, the better.

Weather factors include rapid changes in conditions such as wind, air temperature, and snowfall. Any of these factors can create a change in the structure and equilibrium of the snowpack, causing a slide. Most avalanches occur immediately after a storm as the new snow slides off the old surface. Be especially watchful during periods when there are constant winds over 15 miles per hour. Also watch for storms that dump more than one inch per hour or have a total accumulation of six inches or more. An increase in the air temperature can also strongly affect the internal integrity of the snowpack.

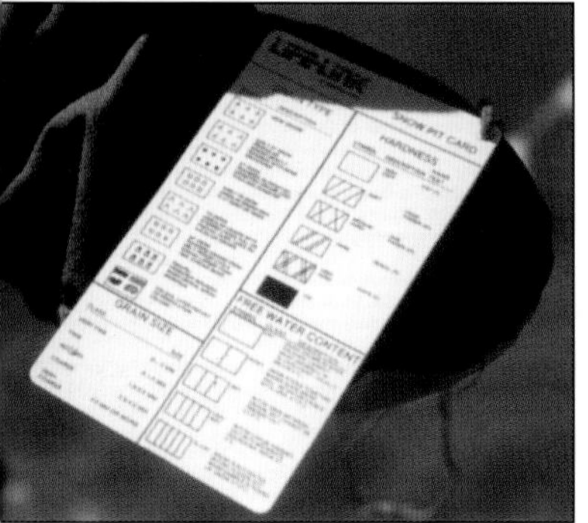

*Snow crystal cards are indispensable for interpreting the dynamics of the snowpack.*

The third factor, snowpack, is a little more difficult to observe, as it requires digging into the snow and having some training in assessing just what you're looking at when you do. A Life-Link snow crystal card is extremely useful for assessing snow type.

Once in the backcountry, the most important thing that skiers can do to avoid tragedy is to make simple, informed observations. These include:

**1.** taking note of any slides or movements of snow

**2.** noticing any old slide paths

**3.** paying close attention to any settling of the snowpack (particularly after you ski across it)

**4.** listening for the "whumpfing" sounds that occur when air is being forced out from under the snowpack

**5.** looking for any cracks in the snow

Try to avoid avalanche slopes by staying in the forest or skiing along the crest of a ridge. If you must cross a known or suspected avalanche slope, first remove all ski leashes and pole straps and loosen or undo pack straps and waist belts. Cross the slope one skier at a time and observe the others in your group as they cross.

Every member of your group should wear a transceiver; make sure that your transceiver is turned on and set to transmit on the same frequency as everyone else's in your group. The new standard worldwide frequency is 457 kHz. The old 2.275 kHz transceivers that have been the standard in the United States are now being phased out. In recent years, several fully digital and analog-with-digital-function transceivers have hit the market. This means the units are getting easier to use. However, technology is still not a substitute for practice, practice, practice. No matter which model you own, you should know it intimately.

In addition to transceivers, backcountry skiers must carry a shovel and either ski poles that convert to an avalanche probe pole or a dedicated probe. Recently, more people have begun carrying lightweight dedicated probes because of their superior ability to penetrate hard snow, their simplicity, and their length, which allows them to probe more deeply into the snowpack. Obviously, you want reliable, durable gear that is still light enough not to be left at home.

If you do get caught in a slide, attempt to "swim" in the snow, shedding any gear. When you sense that the slide is coming to a stop, place your hands in front of your face to create an air pocket. Remain calm and wait for rescuers to reach you. Individuals not caught in the slide should begin rescue operations immediately.

Before you leave on a hut trip, be sure to call the Colorado Avalanche Information Center to get the most recent snow conditions and avalanche activity reports (see Appendix E).

*Ahh, yes...hut life!*

## What You'll Find at the Hut

You've struggled all day breaking trail through two feet of fresh snow, arriving at the hut's front door late in the afternoon—spent but happy to be "home." Inside, you'll find the huts well-furnished for comfortable living. The huts do not have exactly the same assortment of stoves, lighting systems, beds, or kitchenware, but here is what you can generally expect to find.

First, all of the huts have some type of woodstove for heat. In huts with only one stove, it is used not only for heat but also to melt snow for water (accomplished with large pots), to dry wet clothes, and for limited cooking. The primary source of water for the huts is snowmelt, though a few have well water. To avoid contamination of the water, dogs are banned from the huts. Most huts also are stocked with firewood.

Larger huts, such as those in the 10th Mountain Division system and the Summit Huts Association, usually have a second wood-burning stove dedicated to cooking tasks. This second stove most often is a large, classic, old-time stove featuring an oven and warming bays underneath a flat cooking surface. Although few people cook with wood today, you would be surprised at the incredible meals and baked goods that can be produced on these stoves.

In addition to a wood-burning stove, nearly every hut is equipped with some type of propane cookstove. Fueled by large exterior tanks, these simple-to-operate workhorse stoves pull duty for most of the hut cooking and for heating drinking water. Because of the high cost of propane, using propane stoves to melt snow for water is discouraged unless there is an emergency. Though firing up a woodstove is slower when you first arrive at the hut, producing water on a woodstove is the most efficient method. Finally, a few huts have older suburban-home-style propane stoves with integrated propane ovens.

Hut kitchens are fully stocked with the pots, pans, skillets, cups, glasses, knives, forks, and spoons that most people require. Huts typically end up with a basic assortment of spices, cooking oils, and a few staples—which can be helpful in emergency situations. Except in a few instances, however, the huts are not stocked with food. Leaving excess food is also strongly discouraged, as it can attract the local rodent population. You pack it in, you pack it out—eaten or uneaten.

The standard hut has a lighting system powered either by the large propane tanks used for cooking or by a contemporary photovoltaic lighting system. In addition, you should carry headlamps and candles. Headlamps are handy for late-night forays to the outhouse, for reading in bed, and for use on the trail.

Each hut visitor must bring a sleeping bag. Don't worry about a foam pad, as all huts have some type of foam pads for comfortable sleeping. Some huts have pillows and some do not. If you can't sleep without a pillow and can't stand the thought of using a pillow that someone else has used, bring a small camp pillow of your own. Sleeping bag stuff-sacks are useful as makeshift pillows when stuffed with extra sweaters.

For evenings and while relaxing at the huts, bring an extra pair of pants, shorts, dry socks, hut booties or slippers, and a T-shirt. Most hut visitors just walk around in their fleece tights, which cuts down on the weight in your pack. An extra set of lightweight clothes for lounging does add a bit of weight but more than makes up for it when your ski clothes are damp and smelly and you want to get out of them.

*This view is out of the Fowler/Hilliard Hut across the headwaters of Resolution Creek.*

## Hut Etiquette

Hut life can be joyous, or it can be hellish. Huts are often large enough to hold up to 20 people, and more than one group may be booked at the same time. The quality of the hut experience depends on the groups sharing a hut treating each other with respect and courtesy. If sharing a hut with strangers does not appeal to you, be sure to reserve the hut exclusively for your own group. Here are a few rules to keep in mind—whether you are sharing a hut with another party or have it to yourselves. These courtesies extend to groups that may be arriving after your group departs.

#### When you arrive:

1. Leave skis and poles outside.
2. Clean snow from boots and clothes outside.
3. Read any hut instructions and post reservation confirmation lists.
4. Build a fire, shoveling out old ashes if necessary, and begin to melt water. Chop lots of wood.
5. Turn on electricity and propane.
6. Be tidy. Do not drop clothing and equipment all over the communal living area.
7. Be polite and quiet, especially in the evening.
8. Wash dishes promptly and thoroughly.
9. Leave your dog at home with a multiday steak bone. "Just say no to yellow snow."

#### Before you leave:

1. Make sure fires are out.
2. Shut and lock all windows and doors.
3. Turn off propane (if required) and photovoltaic electric system.
4. Shut outhouse doors.
5. Pour out water to prevent freezing.
6. Sweep floor.
7. Pack out trash and extra food.
8. Chop some wood and kindling for the next group.

## Cellular Phones

Believe it or not, cell phones have become an issue in the backcountry. They can be a very effective way to summon help in the event of an emergency. The problems arise in the hut. Many people find them to be an unnecessary intrusion of technology into the serenity of a wilderness adventure. Use them judiciously and thoughtfully.

# Northern Huts

Northern Colorado offers a wealth of diverse skiing within relatively short distances of major population areas and mountain resorts. From the Never Summer Nordic Yurts in the Medicine Bow Mountains to the Guinn Mountain Hut just south of the Indian Peaks Wilderness, Nordic skiers of all skill levels will enjoy fine trail skiing and excellent telemark terrain amid the beauty of northern Colorado's rugged, glaciated peaks.

The backcountry shelters covered in this section have relatively short approach routes, and most require only modest skiing ability. In addition to serving as overnight destinations, they make ideal base camps for extended day trips and backcountry powder skiing.

True hut-to-hut skiing, mountain biking, and hiking are available in northern Colorado only at the Never Summer Nordic Yurts. Privately owned and operated, these tentlike structures are modern descendants of the movable animal-skin tents used by Mongolian nomads. Today's yurts typically are made of coated or laminated canvas and nylon. What makes these yurts so special is their cozy, "cabiny" feel, complete with wood-burning stoves. All of the Never Summer Nordic Yurts can be reached with ski tours of 2 miles or less, and connecting them into a multiday trip is also easy. With this edition we add two new yurts to the system. The Montgomery Pass Yurts sit side by side and open up an entirely new drainage to overnight recreation.

The Colorado State Forest has closed one northern hut, the Lake Agnes Cabin, because of its deteriorating condition, but a new structure called the Nokhu Cabin was built just north of the old Lake Agnes Cabin site in the fall of 1999. The brief 1.5-mile approach to the cabin makes it one of the shortest advanced-skill tours covered in this guide.

Well to the south of the Never Summer Nordic Yurts, hidden away in Colorado's Front Range, are the cabins owned and operated by the Colorado Mountain Club (CMC), the state's largest outdoor recreation club. The Brainard Lake Cabin and Guinn Mountain Hut have been favorite haunts of Front Range skiers for decades. The CMC huts are located near areas of archetypal Nordic skiing and classic backcountry trails. They are popular destinations for introductory overnight trips and jumping-off points for longer cross-country excursions, such as skiing over Rollins Pass. The First Creek Cabin and Second Creek Cabin (a.k.a. Gwen Andrews Hut) are closed indefinitely while the U.S. Forest Service conducts site evaluations.

This section also includes several independently operated huts, including the Tennessee Mountain Cabin, which lies within the Eldora Nordic Center west of Boulder and Nederland. This hut is easy to reach, and there are a number of routes to the cabin via the Nordic area's groomed trails.

New additions to the northern section in this edition include the High Lonesome Hut in Grand County north of Winter Park and the unusual Squaw Mountain Fire Lookout atop Squaw Mountain west of Evergreen and Bergen Park. Throughout other western states, many defunct fire lookouts have been converted to public use as overnight huts. The Squaw Mountain Fire Lookout is an excellent addition to our state's recreation shelters and is unlike anything else in Colorado.

*Carrie Thompson at Jewel Lake below the southwest face of Clark Peak.*

## Never Summer Nordic Yurts and Nokhu Cabin

The Never Summer Nordic Yurts are located within the Colorado State Forest, which is operated as a State Park. Situated on the eastern edge of North Park, the yurts are hemmed in by the valley's flat expanse on the west and the ridgelike ramparts of the Medicine Bow Mountains and the Rawah Wilderness Area to the east. Remote and beautiful, this environment is ideal for moderate ski touring, mountain biking, and hiking.

Recently, this hut system has come of age with the addition of the Montgomery Pass Yurts and replacement of the Lake Agnes Cabin with the Nokhu Cabin, built and operated by Never Summer Nordic. The Montgomery Pass Yurts, in particular, provide access to great new terrain and several trails that climb far onto the high ridges and peaks near Montgomery Pass. The routes are ideal for mountain bikers as well as for skiers.

In addition, a new intermediate trail has been laid out directly from the Montgomery Pass Yurts north to the Ruby Jewel Yurt. Consequently, more capable skiers can tour cross-country via a less obvious, higher-altitude path rather than dropping all the way back down on the easy-to-follow roads. The Montgomery Pass Yurts also are being used by those skiing to and from trailheads on the eastern (Fort Collins) side of Cameron Pass near the Zimmerman Lake Trailhead.

*Lisa Paesani kicks back on the deck of the North Fork Canadian Yurt.*

All of the yurts are reached by routes that follow obvious trails and roads. Old logging roads provide easy access to the yurts. Although this area has been logged over the years, the terrain around the yurt feels pristine and deserted. Whether you are a beginner or a more experienced skier or biker, you can easily spend several days exploring the areas around these remote shelters. Telemarkers will find many acres of skiable terrain to satisfy their appetites for challenging backcountry skiing.

During the winter of 1999–2000, the Lake Agnes Cabin was closed by the state because of deteriorating conditions, and Never Summer Nordic built the Nokhu Cabin to replace it. The Nokhu Cabin sits to the north—back down the trail—from the site of the Lake Agnes Cabin. Unlike the other huts in the system, the Nokhu Cabin is a small wooden cabin, not a yurt.

North Park is home to a herd of moose. These animals, once indigenous to the area but later eradicated through hunting, were reintroduced here in 1978. The incredible creatures roam free and are an added attraction to the other abundant wildlife species in the Medicine Bow Mountains.

Because the Never Summer Nordic Yurts are in the Colorado State Forest, a valid day/overnight State Parks Pass is required. Passes are available from a self-service dispenser near the entrance during the winter and also at the entrance booth during the summer. The daily fee is about $4.

The yurts are circular white-canvas tents atop wooden substructures. Each yurt sleeps four to six people on bunks and mattresses, except the new Dancing Moose Yurt, which sleeps 8 to 12. With the woodstove stoked, occupants stay warm even on the coldest winter night. However, yurts, unless extremely well-insulated, will not hold their heat as well as a hut will—especially if the fire is allowed to go out. Consequently, I recommend bringing a warmer sleeping bag when going to yurts.

**RESERVATION NOTE:** Tours to the yurts and the Nokhu Cabin are normally self-guided, but guided trips can be arranged through the Never Summer Nordic Yurt system. A single group can book the hut exclusively on a nightly basis. Rates vary according to the season and night of the week. Friday, Saturday, and Sunday nights are more expensive, as is Christmas week. Make reservations in advance. Last-minute reservations are accepted based on space available; availability can be checked by visiting the website listed in Appendix A. Make reservations through Never Summer Nordic Yurts (see Appendix A).

**DIRECTIONS TO TRAILHEADS:** Take CO 14 to the entrance of the Colorado State Forest, 19 miles east of the town of Walden or roughly 2 miles west of Gould. (From the Fort Collins area, the entrance is approximately 72 miles west of the intersection of CO 14 and US 287.) The turnoff into the State Forest is marked by a large KOA campground sign.

The road from the park entrance to the trailheads for the Never Summer Nordic Yurts is narrow, winding, traveled by heavy vehicles, and often snow-covered. Drive carefully! For specific trailhead parking directions, refer to individual hut listings.

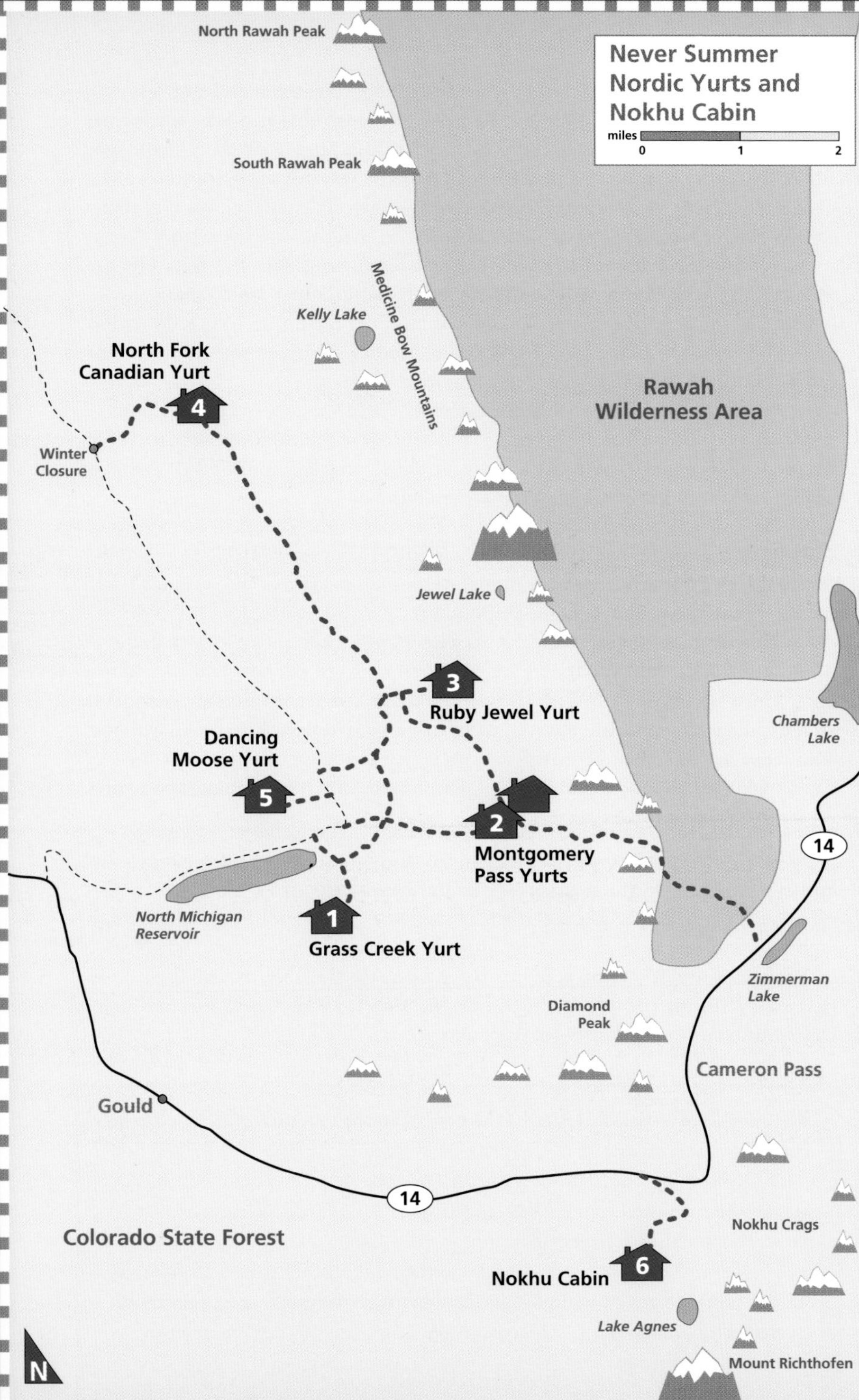

Never Summer Nordic Yurts and Nokhu Cabin
miles
0
1
2
North Rawah Peak
South Rawah Peak
Medicine Bow Mountains
Kelly Lake
Rawah Wilderness Area
North Fork Canadian Yurt
4
Winter Closure
Jewel Lake
3
Ruby Jewel Yurt
Chambers Lake
Dancing Moose Yurt
5
2
Montgomery Pass Yurts
14
to Walden
North Michigan Reservoir
1
Grass Creek Yurt
Zimmerman Lake
Diamond Peak
Cameron Pass
Gould
14
Colorado State Forest
Nokhu Crags
6
Nokhu Cabin
Lake Agnes
Mount Richthofen
N

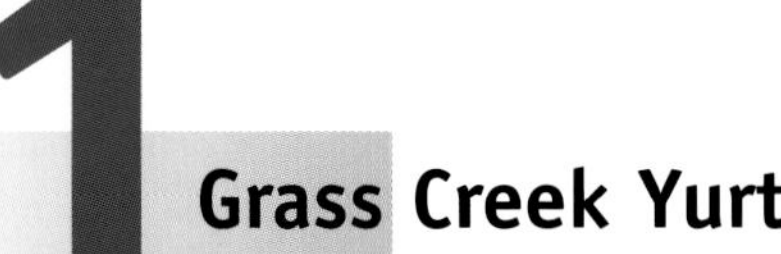

# 1 Grass Creek Yurt

| | |
|---|---|
| **HUT ELEVATION** | 9,040' |
| **DATE BUILT** | 1986 |
| **SEASONS** | Year-round (except possible closure in early spring due to conditions) |
| **CAPACITY** | 7 |
| **HUT LAYOUT** | 16-foot yurt with 2 bunks (1 double and 3 single beds) plus 2 mattresses for the floor |
| **HUT ESSENTIALS** | Woodstove for heat, propane cookstoves, all kitchenware, outhouse |

The Grass Creek Yurt is the southernmost of the yurts in this system and is located less than 1 mile from the trailhead—an example of just how readily accessible backcountry shelters can be. Once at the shelter, skiers can continue up Grass Creek via the road for a day tour or climb Gould Mountain for intermediate to advanced off-trail telemarking.

Grass Creek Yurt is the perfect introduction to overnight winter camping for individuals and families. Make reservations through Never Summer Nordic Yurts (see Appendix A).

**RECOMMENDED DAY TRIPS:**

**Return to the road on the north side of Grass Creek.** Turn south and tour along the road through this gentle valley, heading upstream parallel to Grass Creek. You will find nice, moderate trail skiing here. Total distance is roughly 1.5 miles, one way.

**Gould Mountain** has acres of hidden telemark glades and slopes and is laced with oodles of old logging roads well suited for skiers and bikers alike. For an intermediate run, ascend to Elevation Point 9,700' (south of the yurt) and ski down Lary's Run. This run drops east/northeast from the small saddle immediately south of Elevation Point 9,700' and takes you back down to the road.

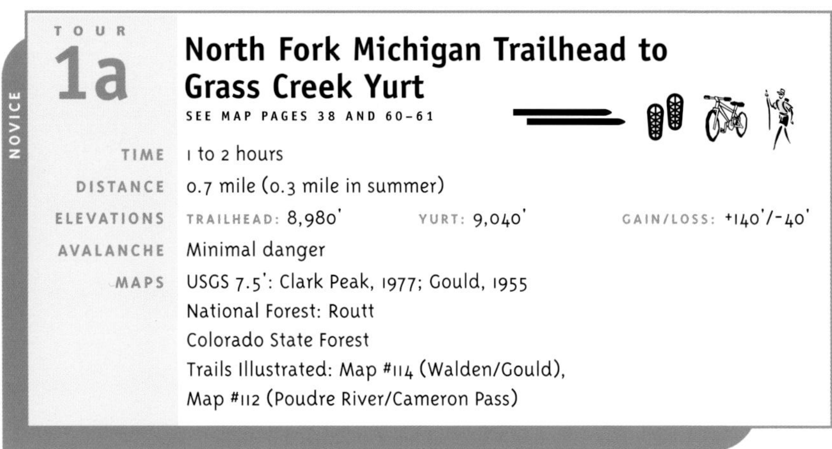

NOVICE

TOUR

# 1a North Fork Michigan Trailhead to Grass Creek Yurt

SEE MAP PAGES 38 AND 60–61

| | |
|---|---|
| TIME | 1 to 2 hours |
| DISTANCE | 0.7 mile (0.3 mile in summer) |
| ELEVATIONS | TRAILHEAD: 8,980′ YURT: 9,040′ GAIN/LOSS: +140′/-40′ |
| AVALANCHE | Minimal danger |
| MAPS | USGS 7.5′: Clark Peak, 1977; Gould, 1955<br>National Forest: Routt<br>Colorado State Forest<br>Trails Illustrated: Map #114 (Walden/Gould), Map #112 (Poudre River/Cameron Pass) |

**TOUR OVERVIEW:** This main route to the hut is one of the least complicated and arduous trails to a hut in Colorado. It is an ideal route for hut newbies and for families with younger skiers.

**DIRECTIONS TO TRAILHEAD:** Proceed through the entrance for the Colorado State Forest (for directions to entrance, see page 37) and follow the road to North Michigan Reservoir. Drive to the far end of the reservoir near the 3.0-mile road marker (3.3-mile odometer reading). On the left is a small parking area that is plowed in winter. Just beyond this area is a wood X-fence and a cattle guard.

**THE ROUTE:** After parking, cross the road (carefully!), drop off the roadbed, and head toward the lake via a small road through the sagebrush down to a summer parking/picnic area. Normally a hut-system sign here marks the egress point from the roads. Now follow the trail across the North Fork of the Michigan River.

Once you've crossed the river, head south/southeast away from the road, toward the Grass Creek drainage (be sure to remain inside the fenced-in area). Ski through a break in the fence on the far side of the river and continue up into Grass Creek, remaining on its left (east) side, gaining roughly 80 to 100 feet in elevation. Intercept the Grass Creek Road near the creek, cross the road and the creek, and continue south/southwest away from the creek, following the eastern edge of the forest and gaining very little altitude. Grass Creek Yurt is located near the edge of the trees, 0.3 mile from the creek.

**SUMMER NOTE:** During the summer you can drive almost directly to the yurt via a different summer route. To reach the yurt in summer, take a right turn that heads off to the east. This turnoff is also for the North Michigan Campground and is roughly 1 mile from the turnoff at CO 14. After leaving the main road, follow this road along the south side of the reservoir and follow markers to the parking area for the yurt.

NOVICE/INTERMEDIATE

TOUR **1b**

## Grass Creek Yurt to Montgomery Pass Yurts

SEE MAP PAGES 38 AND 60–61

TIME 3 to 5 hours

DISTANCE 3.7 miles

ELEVATIONS GC YURT: 9,040' MP YURTS: 9,620' GAIN/LOSS: +820'/-200'

AVALANCHE Minimal danger

MAPS USGS 7.5': Clark Peak, 1977; Gould, 1955
National Forest: Routt
Colorado State Forest
Trails Illustrated: Map #114 (Walden/Gould), Map #112 (Poudre River/Cameron Pass)

**TOUR OVERVIEW:** This tour splices the bulk of the standard trailhead tours to both of these yurts together with a unique section of trail that traverses between the two drainages that are the homes to these shelters. This route also shares some common ground with the Grass Creek to Ruby Jewel Tour. This route is pleasant and well-marked, and except for the traverse section between these two drainages, it follows large, obvious roads.

*Carrie Thompson, Dan Schaefer, and Lisa Paesani enjoy the amenities of the Ruby Jewel Yurt.*

**THE ROUTE:** From the Grass Creek Yurt, retrace your approach steps north, back across the creek, until you near the lake. Several hundred feet south of the creek, a signed turnoff leads you onto a trail that heads east on a traverse that reaches the road that is the route to the Montgomery Pass Yurts. The traverse passes a gate near the creek and then makes a short climb up to the road near the 0.8-mile point on the approach tour for the Montgomery Pass Yurts. This intersection is also the point where the trail that heads to the Ruby Jewel Yurt leads north away from this same spot.

From this point, follow the standard description for the approach trail (Tour 2A) to the Montgomery Pass Yurts.

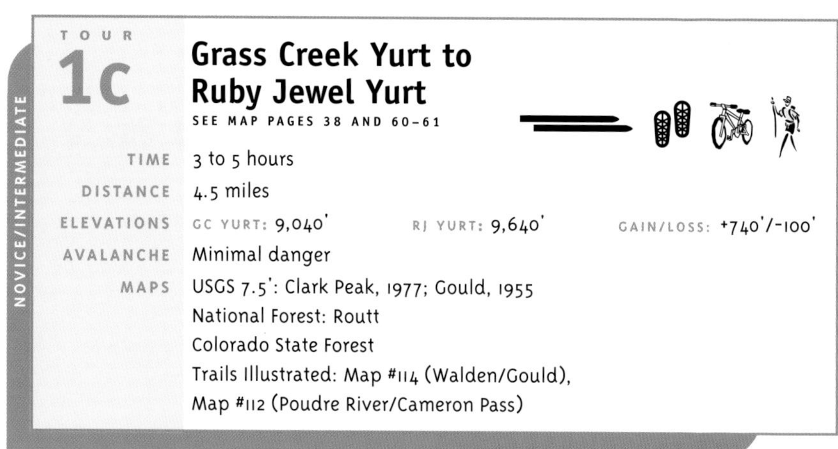

TOUR 1c

NOVICE/INTERMEDIATE

## Grass Creek Yurt to Ruby Jewel Yurt

SEE MAP PAGES 38 AND 60–61

| | |
|---|---|
| TIME | 3 to 5 hours |
| DISTANCE | 4.5 miles |
| ELEVATIONS | GC YURT: 9,040' RJ YURT: 9,640' GAIN/LOSS: +740'/-100' |
| AVALANCHE | Minimal danger |
| MAPS | USGS 7.5': Clark Peak, 1977; Gould, 1955<br>National Forest: Routt<br>Colorado State Forest<br>Trails Illustrated: Map #114 (Walden/Gould), Map #112 (Poudre River/Cameron Pass) |

**TOUR OVERVIEW:** This tour traverses the foothills of the higher forested slopes, crossing in and out of several creek drainages en route. After reaching the standard approach trail to the Ruby Jewel Yurt, the route climbs more steadily.

**THE ROUTE:** To travel from the Grass Creek Yurt to the Ruby Jewel Yurt, leave the Grass Creek Yurt and retrace your tracks to the point immediately southeast of the North Fork of the Michigan River. Instead of returning to the parking area, turn east and traverse the slope south of the Michigan River through the forest, following a single-track trail marked by blue ski diamonds.

After just over 0.5 mile, you will reach a trail that drops to the north across the North Fork of the Michigan River. As you near the river and the Montgomery Pass Road, you will merge onto a gated road that climbs up from the creek to the Pass Road. Cross the prominent Montgomery Pass Road and continue in a northerly direction, ascending slightly over a rise onto a second road.

Turn skier's left (west) and follow this second road until you cross a small creek, then leave the road on a diagonal off to the right (north). Continue north through open country and tour through a small basin up onto the feature marked as Point 9,180'. Once on top of this feature, drop off the northern aspect and follow the route as it skirts the edge of the forest. This entails looping slightly downhill to the west before resuming the climb toward the Ruby Jewel Road. As you approach the road to Ruby Jewel Yurt, you will find a spur logging road that merges into the final stretch of the route. Follow the signs to the Ruby Jewel Yurt.

**SUMMER NOTE:** The summer mountain bike route returns to the North Michigan Reservoir Trailhead, heads north along the road, then follows the Ruby Jewel Trail to the yurt. Total length is 5.8 miles, with an elevation loss of 140 feet and roughly 500 feet of gain.

*The cozy Ruby Jewel Yurt glows in a winter's night.*

# 2 Montgomery Pass Yurts

| | |
|---|---|
| **HUT ELEVATION** | 9,620' |
| **DATE BUILT** | 1998 |
| **SEASONS** | Year-round<br>(except possible closure in early spring due to conditions) |
| **CAPACITY** | 7 in each yurt (2 yurts total) |
| **HUT LAYOUT** | Two 16-foot yurts, each with 2 bunks (1 double and 3 single beds) plus 2 mattresses for the floor |
| **HUT ESSENTIALS** | Woodstove for heat, propane cookstoves, all kitchenware, outhouse, propane lights |

The spectacular Montgomery Pass Yurts are the latest offspring of this northern Colorado hut system. Well-positioned on the crest of a forested ridge, they occupy the most commanding spot in the system. Surrounding these yurts—practically off the front porch—is ample terrain for making turns. These twin yurts open up many new possibilities for skiing, and hut interconnecting in this system is a welcome addition.

Like the rest of the system, mountain biking is excellent in the area surrounding these yurts. Long, old logging trails lead up from behind the hut toward the high peaks to the east, offering many opportunities for shorter day excursions. In addition, the roads throughout the North Fork of Michigan River Valley are ideal for bike and ski touring.

The two yurts sit a stone's throw away from each other and can be reserved in tandem for large groups. The huts are a fine destination on their own, as well as for extended hut-to-hut tours in the system.

**RECOMMENDED DAY TRIPS:**

**There is much to do in this area winter and summer.** Skiers and bikers can continue along the road beyond the yurts and explore many miles upslope toward the high peaks and ridges to the east. Though south-facing, the basin to the south of the yurts (which you climbed through) has many acres of perfectly angled terrain for skiing. In addition, the slopes just to the north of the yurts are eminently skiable. As mentioned, some of the best biking in the area can be found upstream in the Upper Michigan Creek Valley.

A tour for the really adventurous person leaves the yurts and continues uphill via the approach logging road all the way to tree line and the high ridge to the east—near the radio towers. Pass a gate and continue up onto the ridge-crest. Once on the ridge, drop south along the ridge-crest to Montgomery Pass. From there, drop down west and back to the turnoff to the logging road that leads you up to the yurts on the final approach climb.

NOVICE/INTERMEDIATE

TOUR
# 2a North Fork Michigan Trailhead to Montgomery Pass Yurts

SEE MAP PAGES 38 AND 60–61

| | |
|---|---|
| TIME | 2 to 4 hours |
| DISTANCE | 2.8 miles |
| ELEVATIONS | TRAILHEAD: 8,980' MP YURTS: 9,620' GAIN/LOSS: +680'/-40' |
| AVALANCHE | Minimal danger |
| MAPS | USGS 7.5': Clark Peak, 1977; Gould, 1955<br>National Forest: Routt<br>Colorado State Forest<br>Trails Illustrated: Map #114 (Walden/Gould), Map #112 (Poudre River/Cameron Pass) |

**TOUR OVERVIEW:** This trail follows well-marked and obvious logging roads throughout the journey. The first 2 miles climb gently through lowland meadows, wetlands, and woods, and the latter half climbs steadily, though manageably, up south-facing slopes through logging cuts in a side valley up to the yurts. Perhaps the greatest potential difficulties will be found by the secondary roads and intersections encountered on the tour. Keep an eye on the trail markers.

**DIRECTIONS TO TRAILHEAD:** Proceed through the entrance for the Colorado State Forest (for directions to entrance, see page 37) and follow the road to North Michigan Reservoir. Continue past the lake and follow the road to a well-marked intersection with the Montgomery Pass Road near the 3.6-mile mark. The Montgomery Pass Road is on the right (southeast) side of the main road, and is the trail to the yurt. It is not plowed in the winter. It also is marked as the trailhead for the yurts and as a route back to CO 14.

**THE ROUTE:** Leave the intersection and glide along the Montgomery Pass Road. From the trailhead, the route immediately switchbacks to the north down across the creek, then south, before striking up into the main drainage of the North Fork of Michigan Creek. Ascending gently through open country, the road intersects the trails that head south to the Grass Creek Yurt and north to the Ruby Jewel Yurt at roughly 0.5 mile.

Near the 1.0-mile mark you will arrive at another, more utilized intersection near a large wooden X-fence that is marked with several prominent signs. A large, secondary road cuts through the fence to the north and heads into the Bockman Lumber Camp. This is the road that heads back west and is used for a short stretch by the traverse routes to the Ruby Jewel Yurt.

*Bypass the turnoff* to the lumber camp and instead follow the primary road to the right (southeast) across the creek. The proper route is marked by blue diamonds; it is signed as Road #380 and as the route to Montgomery Pass and CO 14.

From here, the road heads almost due south on an ascending traverse through increasingly dense woods. Eventually you will come to another well-signed intersection at the 1.7-mile mark. A road indicated by blue diamonds forks off to the left (east/northeast) and climbs more noticeably. Take this left fork. Climb the road steadily until you bypass another old logging road by skiing left at a fork. This intersection was not marked when I made a visit. Note that there are fewer blue diamonds along this final section of trail. In general, though, the road ascends up through intermittent clear-cuts and remaining stands of evergreen trees.

As you get closer to the huts, the road alternatively climbs and traverses along the bottom edges of several clear-cuts before veering directly and more steeply up to the crest of the ridge. Near the top of the ridge, a signed turnoff leads to the left into the trees. The twin yurts sit amidst several logged areas on top of the ridge. The distance of this final climb from the Montgomery Pass Road is roughly 1.1 miles.

**SUMMER NOTE:** In the summer months—after mud season—you can drive directly to the yurt. This enables you to use the yurt as a base camp for lightweight day trips.

ADVANCED/EXPERT

TOUR

## 2b Zimmerman Lake/Montgomery Pass Trailhead to Montgomery Pass Yurts

SEE MAP PAGES 38 AND 60–61

| | |
|---|---|
| TIME | 4 to 7 hours |
| DISTANCE | 5 to 6.5 miles, depending on the route |
| ELEVATIONS | TRAILHEAD: 10,020' MP YURTS: 9,620' GAIN/LOSS: +980'/-1,380' |
| AVALANCHE | Some avalanche terrain encountered; easily avoided |
| MAPS | USGS 7.5': Clark Peak, 1977; Gould, 1955<br>National Forest: Routt<br>Colorado State Forest<br>Trails Illustrated: Map #114 (Walden/Gould), Map #112 (Poudre River/Cameron Pass) |

**TOUR OVERVIEW:** This is another trail suggestion for these new yurts. It is the most challenging route in the Never Summer Nordic Yurt system. Although the overall distance is not too great, the nature of the tour is alpine and exposed to the elements. The route necessitates a committing passage directly over the high, rugged ridge that separates the eastern slope of the Front Range and North Park to the west via Montgomery Pass. And, depending on the exact route chosen on the west side (there are two main choices), it also may be necessary to ascend along this ridge to the north in search of a sometimes difficult-to-locate logging road that descends to the yurts. Consequently, solid navigation and high-mountain travel skills are mandatory for this rewarding expert tour—especially under adverse weather conditions.

The ascent up the eastern aspect of the ridge from the pass is one of the most popular winter and summer trails in the Cameron Pass area. The trail usually is broken and follows an obvious, identifiable path.

**DIRECTIONS TO TRAILHEAD:** The trailhead for these routes lies 1.2 miles north of the summit of Cameron Pass, on the Fort Collins side. Park at the plowed parking area for Zimmerman Lake.

**THE ROUTE:** From the parking area, cross the road and begin skiing up the Montgomery Pass Trail. A new section of trail connects the Zimmerman Lake parking area to the old four-wheel-drive trail up to the pass. Though it is printed on the Trails Illustrated maps, this short stretch of trail does not appear on the USGS 7.5-minute topos. Rarely will the section of this tour up to Montgomery Pass require serious trail-breaking, as this is an extremely popular day tour. Near the pass, too, are many acres of great free-heel downhill skiing. Once on the main trail, follow it upward along a subtle forested ridge up to just below 11,000 feet, where the route veers slightly to the northwest to the pass.

Atop the pass, two main routes on the western side lead to the yurts. The simplest route navigation-wise drops directly off the western side following the Montgomery Pass Road. The upper slopes, just below the west side of the pass, are not skied often and may require a bit of route-finding until you pick up the road lower down. Once on the road, follow it downstream for 4.0 miles to the signed intersection with the logging road on the right (northeast) that leads 500 feet back up to the yurts.

The second and recommended route to the yurts is shorter and more direct, doesn't have excessive elevation loss on the west side, and is identical to the other route up to Montgomery Pass. In this case, however, you ascend northward from the pass along the ridge-crest, heading for the radio towers on the ridge. Once you reach roughly the 11,350' elevation level, and before the radio towers, you begin a gently descending traverse off the crest, heading northwest. Ultimately what you are aiming for is a trail/logging road marked by a gate. This gate can be hard to find in the winter. In general, the correct route off the ridge to the gates takes you on the aforementioned descending traverse past a rounded, ridgelike feature, and on the broad, moderate terrain flowing down from the summit of Elevation Point 11,622'.

Poke around and find the logging road proper. Follow it 2.0 miles downward to the yurts, but be careful not to get sucked onto the road that connects the Montgomery Pass Yurts to the Ruby Jewel Yurt. This fork is just uphill from the turnoff to the yurts.

NOVICE/INTERMEDIATE

TOUR

# 2c Montgomery Pass Yurts to Ruby Jewel Yurt (Valley Route)

SEE MAP PAGES 38 AND 60–61

| | |
|---|---|
| TIME | 3 to 5 hours |
| DISTANCE | 3.9 miles |
| ELEVATIONS | MP YURTS: 9,620' RJ YURT: 9,640' GAIN/LOSS: +740'/-700' |
| AVALANCHE | Minimal danger |
| MAPS | USGS 7.5': Clark Peak, 1977; Gould, 1955<br>National Forest: Routt<br>Colorado State Forest<br>Trails Illustrated: Map #114 (Walden/Gould), Map #112 (Poudre River/Cameron Pass) |

**TOUR OVERVIEW:** Like most interconnect routes in this system, the bulk of the trail is cobbled together from sections of other routes. This route has variety, including downhill schussing on trails, touring through rolling meadows, and a bit of climbing. It is generally well-marked.

**THE ROUTE:** Leave the yurt and head back toward the trailhead. Ski 2.0 miles all the way back to the Grass Creek/Ruby Jewel Trail intersection near the 0.8-mile mark. *Note:* The adventurous could drop off the ridge from the yurts heading northwest and ski down to the Bockman Lumber Camp, then take the main Montgomery Pass Road back down near the Bockman Camp intersection.

*The Montgomery Pass Yurts get a white-washing by a late spring snowstorm.*

Either way, once back at the intersection, follow the trail to the Ruby Jewel Yurt by exiting the Montgomery Pass Road and skiing north up over a small rise. Atop the rise, gain another road. Turn left on the road and follow it for several hundred feet until you cross a creek. Near the creek, the trail exits this road and ascends cross-country through a small basin and over a ridge near Elevation Point 9,180'. Once over the ridge, the trail descends slightly, then heads north and east, following the forest's edge on a short, moderate climb to the standard Ruby Jewel approach route. Continue along that path on a steady climb to the yurt. For more details on the final approach, refer to Tour 3a.

INTERMEDIATE

TOUR **2d**

## Montgomery Pass Yurts to Ruby Jewel Yurt (High Traverse Route)

SEE MAP PAGES 38 AND 60–61

| | |
|---|---|
| TIME | 3 to 5 hours |
| DISTANCE | 3.9 miles |
| ELEVATIONS | MP YURTS: 9,620' RJ YURT: 9,640' GAIN/LOSS: +250'/-200' |
| AVALANCHE | Minimal danger |
| MAPS | USGS 7.5': Clark Peak, 1977; Gould, 1955<br>National Forest: Routt<br>Colorado State Forest<br>Trails Illustrated: Map #114 (Walden/Gould), Map #112 (Poudre River/Cameron Pass) |

**TOUR OVERVIEW:** This direct route between these yurts is a recent addition and one that charts roadless, less traveled terrain. It is a shorter, more direct route that avoids the significant loss in elevation incurred by skiing back down the standard approach tour to the Grass Creek/Ruby Jewel route. But it does not follow obvious, well-defined summer logging roads. The route has less traffic and a generally deeper snowpack. Consequently, it actually can place greater demands on skiers.

**THE ROUTE:** From the Montgomery Pass Yurts, return to the approach road. Follow the road uphill until you reach the logging road that cuts off left (north). Turn onto this road and descend roughly 140 feet. The trail to the Ruby Jewel Yurt exits this road and winds merrily through the woods along the 9,600-foot contour level. Though the route is marked, an altimeter is useful along this traverse.

Eventually the trail crosses the dagger-shaped ridge immediately south of the Ruby Jewel Yurt and intercepts that yurt's standard approach route near the 9,590' mark printed on the maps. From there, follow that route uphill to the yurt, bypassing the turnoff to the North Fork Canadian Yurt en route.

Those seeking a bit more adventure or more turns can climb directly over the ridge behind the Ruby Jewel and ski down the slopes above the yurt.

# 3 Ruby Jewel Yurt

| | |
|---|---|
| **HUT ELEVATION** | 9,640' |
| **DATE BUILT** | 1986 |
| **SEASONS** | Year-round |
| **CAPACITY** | 7 |
| **HUT LAYOUT** | 16-foot yurt with 2 bunks (1 double and 3 single beds) plus 2 mattresses for the floor |
| **HUT ESSENTIALS** | Woodstove for heat, propane cookstoves, all kitchenware, outhouse, propane lights |

The Ruby Jewel Yurt is at the highest elevation of the Never Summer Nordic Yurts. It is also the most remote and offers the greatest variety of backcountry challenges. East of the yurt is Jewel Lake, a tiny alpine tarn cradled in a glacial cirque below the southwest face of Clark Peak. Skiing, biking, or hiking to the lake makes a very scenic intermediate-level day trip from the yurt.

Nearby telemark excursions include skiing to Jewel Lake, climbing the ridge south of the yurt to the 10,804-foot level, and skiing on and around Margi's Knoll, the ridge that juts to the southwest of Jewel Lake. (Margi's Knoll is suited for strong intermediate to advanced skiers.) Make reservations through the Never Summer Nordic Yurts (see Appendix A).

## RECOMMENDED DAY TRIPS:

**From the yurt, ski east** on an obvious roadbed through the forest to a small clearing where the trail begins to contour sharply to the southeast. This site, known as the Saw Dust Pile, marks the end of the novice skiing terrain.

At the south edge of the clearing, the trail splits into three separate roads. The first two forks on the right do not appear on the maps. The first road switchbacks up to Elevation Point 10,804'. The middle road goes into the valley on the north side of Elevation Point 10,804' (known locally as Lynx Gulch) and is an intermediate tour.

**Jewel Lake** (11,260'), at the top of the left fork, is the best day trip in the area. Climb the road to the summer vehicle closure. Ski up the valley along the path of least resistance, remaining close to the creek. As you leave the forest, be sure to stay near the creek, avoiding the avalanche slopes on the north side of the valley. The tour is 5 miles round-trip, with 1,620 feet of elevation gain.

NOVICE

TOUR 3a

## Jewel Lake Trailhead to Ruby Jewel Yurt

SEE MAP PAGES 38 AND 60–61

TIME 2 to 4 hours

DISTANCE 2 miles

ELEVATIONS TRAILHEAD: 9,146' YURT: 9,640' GAIN: +494'

AVALANCHE Minimal danger

MAPS USGS 7.5': Clark Peak, 1977; Gould, 1955
National Forest: Routt
Colorado State Forest
Trails Illustrated: Map #114 (Walden/Gould), Map #112 (Poudre River/Cameron Pass)

**DIRECTIONS TO TRAILHEAD:** Drive from the Colorado State Forest entrance (see directions, page 37) past North Michigan Reservoir to a small parking area on the right near the 5.2-mile mark. Plowed in winter, this parking area is on the east side of a small hairpin curve and is marked with a Jewel Lake/Ruby Jewel Yurt sign.

*Note:* Immediately north of the plowed parking pullout for the Ruby Jewel Yurt (0.1 mile) is a distinct logging road that forks off to the right (east) away from the main Colorado State Forest road. This leads a few hundred feet up through a logged area to another secondary fork. The righthand fork, though not the normal Ruby Jewel route, is flagged with a blue diamond and eventually merges with the regular route roughly a mile up the trail. To avoid confusion, it is better to simply return to the regular trailhead and proceed from there.

**THE ROUTE:** From the parking area, ski to the southeast and immediately intercept the snow-covered four-wheel-drive road that leads to the yurt. Begin gently climbing as you contour to the northeast. Once on the road, navigation is no problem; follow the road toward the high peaks. The steepest section is near a noticeable switchback in the road as you climb onto a forested ridge. This switchback is near Elevation Point 9,590'.

Be aware of three turnoffs: One heads south toward the Grass Creek Yurt, the second turns north and leads to the North Fork Canadian (NFC) Yurt, and another new turnoff to the right heads to the Montgomery Pass Yurts. The first turnoff is only 0.7 mile from the trailhead; the second is reached after ascending through the aforementioned switchback and is marked by a sign that reads Ruby Jewel Yurt/North Fork Canadian Yurt.

After skiing several hundred yards past the marked turnoff to the NFC Yurt, watch for a small sign on the south marking the turnoff to the Ruby Jewel Yurt, which is 75 feet from the trail in a small clearing.

Should you decide to tour the area, be aware that many secondary logging roads do not appear on the maps. Even though these logging roads make fine tours, pay attention to where you're going so you don't get lost.

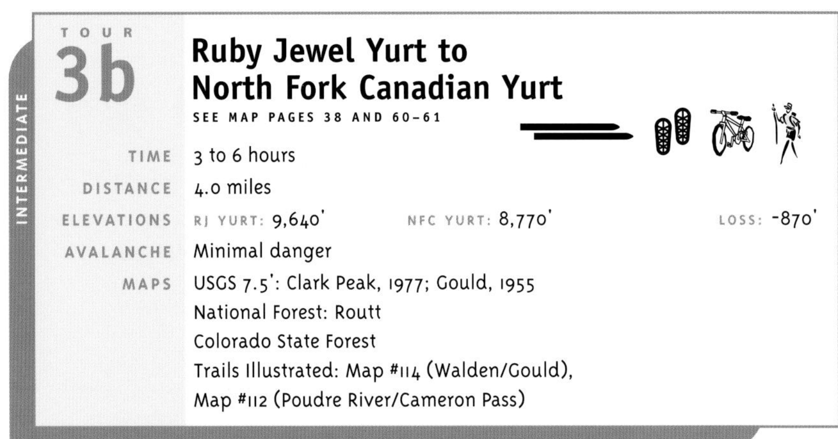


**TOUR OVERVIEW:** Skiing between the Ruby Jewel Yurt and the North Fork Canadian Yurt can be either a fast descent or a steady climb. The trail connecting the yurts drops consistently from 9,640 feet at the Ruby Jewel Yurt to the North Fork Canadian Yurt at 8,770 feet. The recommended direction of travel is from south to north, making for a fun run down through the forest on a wide, twisting trail. The trail is marked with blue diamonds and is easy to follow.

**THE ROUTE:** The south end of the trail begins 0.6 mile west of the Ruby Jewel Yurt at an obvious, marked fork in the trail and descends immediately. You will quickly reach a second fork in the trail (this is a new logging road not yet on the topo map). Here, follow the right fork down through a fast turn across the South Fork of the Canadian River. A very short climb takes you out of this drainage and the descent continues. Eventually, the trail breaks out into a meadow lined with evergreen and aspen trees. Cross the meadow, exiting west through thin stands of trees into a second meadow.

Next you will arrive at a marked turnoff. Here the ski trail leaves the well-traveled (shared by snowmobilers) route and heads north into stands of aspen. At Elevation Point 8,800' is another meadow, which you enter from the south. Ski through the center of the meadow, heading north. The North Fork of the Canadian River borders the north end of the meadow. Blue trail diamonds lead down to and across the river, through a short stretch of willows, and up across the open, south-facing bank to the yurt.

# 4 North Fork Canadian Yurt

| | |
|---|---|
| **HUT ELEVATION** | 8,770' |
| **DATE BUILT** | 1986 |
| **SEASONS** | Year-round (except possible closure in early spring due to conditions) |
| **CAPACITY** | 7 |
| **HUT LAYOUT** | 16-foot yurt with 2 bunks (1 double and 3 single beds) plus 2 mattresses for the floor |
| **HUT ESSENTIALS** | Woodstove for heat, propane cookstoves, all kitchenware, outhouse, propane lights |

The North Fork Canadian Yurt is on an open slope above the North Fork of the Canadian River—really more of a creek than a river. The south-facing yurt has great views of the peaks to the east. The skiing to and around the yurt is very gentle and well-suited for beginning backcountry skiers.

When the State Forest road is plowed to its end, the tour is less than a mile from the parking area. The road is normally plowed, but call the State Forest or the yurt system to confirm this. Add 5 miles to the mileage if the road is not plowed. Make reservations through the Never Summer Nordic Yurts (see Appendix A).

**RECOMMENDED DAY TRIPS:**

Fine backcountry touring may be found by exploring **Mossman Pole Patch Creek** and also by heading north and east from the yurt up to Elevation Point 9,200'. Follow the ditch north uphill to the Kelly Lake Trail as far as your group feels comfortable skiing.

TOUR 4a

NOVICE

## North Fork Canadian Trailhead to North Fork Canadian Yurt

SEE MAP PAGES 38 AND 60–61

| | |
|---|---|
| TIME | 1 to 2 hours |
| DISTANCE | 1.1 miles |
| ELEVATIONS | TRAILHEAD: 8,680' YURT: 8,770' GAIN/LOSS: +170'/-80' |
| AVALANCHE | Minimal danger |
| MAPS | USGS 7.5': Clark Peak, 1977; Gould, 1955<br>National Forest: Routt<br>Colorado State Forest<br>Trails Illustrated: Map #114 (Walden/Gould), Map #112 (Poudre River/Cameron Pass) |

**DIRECTIONS TO TRAILHEAD:** From the Colorado State Forest entrance (see directions, page 37), pass the reservoir, proceed to the end of the plowed road, and park. This parking area is approximately 8.9 miles away from CO 14 and is where the plowed road forms a turnaround loop.

**THE ROUTE:** Ski through a gate and follow a road east down and across to the north side of the North Fork of the Canadian River. This initial stretch of trail follows the road to Kelly Lake and Clear Lake. Once across the creek, the road climbs a short hill through a small S curve. On the east side, heading southeast across the open slopes roughly 80 feet above the creek, is the marked trail to the yurt. Follow the contour of the land southeast on a traverse above the creek for several hundred yards to the yurt. Watch for moose! They like to feed on willow bushes in the creek bed.

*Throckmorton Coupersthwaite trims the trees in the northern Colorado Rockies.*

# 5 Dancing Moose Yurt

| | |
|---|---|
| HUT ELEVATION | 9,120' |
| DATE BUILT | 1992 |
| SEASONS | Year-round |
| CAPACITY | 9 comfortably |
| HUT LAYOUT | 20-foot yurt with 3 bunks (double beds on bottoms, singles on top) |
| HUT ESSENTIALS | Woodstove for heat, propane cookstoves, all kitchenware, outhouse, propane lights |
| OTHER GOODIES | Wheelchair-accessible (primarily in summer) |

The Dancing Moose Yurt is the largest structure in the Never Summer Nordic Yurt system. It is not really a backcountry yurt but, rather, a large structure that works well as a base camp for day tours, as a place to spend the night before launching a trip to the other yurts, or as a destination for anyone wanting to experience hut/yurt life without undertaking a major expedition. It is very close to the road, and it takes only about 10 to 20 minutes to ski to it. With a capacity of 8 to 12 people, it is a great spot for families or large parties (as in people, not festivities). And finally, it is fully wheelchair-accessible during the summer and fall. Make reservations through Never Summer Nordic Yurts (see Appendix A).

*Kelly Stone and Barbie Schmidt break trail.*

NOVICE

TOUR **5a**

## Dancing Moose Trailhead to Dancing Moose Yurt

SEE MAP PAGES 38 AND 60–61

| | |
|---|---|
| TIME | ½ hour or less |
| DISTANCE | 0.25 mile |
| ELEVATIONS | TRAILHEAD: 9,080′ YURT: 9,120′ GAIN: +140′ |
| AVALANCHE | Minimal danger |
| MAPS | USGS 7.5′: Clark Peak, 1977; Gould, 1955<br>National Forest: Routt<br>Colorado State Forest<br>Trails Illustrated: Map #114 (Walden/Gould), Map #112 (Poudre River/Cameron Pass) |

**DIRECTIONS TO TRAILHEAD:** Drive from the Colorado State Forest entrance (for directions, see page 37) past North Michigan Reservoir and the Grass Creek Yurt Trailhead. Near the 4.6-mile mark there is a small, narrow plowed parking area on the right (northeast) side of the road. This area is on the north end of a large clearing. To the west, the clearing spans the creek.

**THE ROUTE:** The yurt is almost visible from the road and sits to the west, in a finger of the clearing that reaches up into the forest. The route itself is straight-forward and self-evident. Cross the road, then drop off the road, passing the hut sign. Follow a road down across the wetlands along the creek/valley bottom. Once over the creek, continue several hundred feet up to the yurt.

*Lenore Anderson in pursuit of powder.*

# 6 Nokhu Cabin

| | |
|---|---|
| **HUT ELEVATION** | 10,000' |
| **DATE BUILT** | 1999 |
| **SEASONS** | Year-round |
| **CAPACITY** | 6 |
| **HUT LAYOUT** | 2 bunks (single beds on top, doubles on bottom) |
| **HUT ESSENTIALS** | Woodstove for heat, propane cookstoves, all kitchenware, outhouse, propane lights |

The Colorado State Forest closed the Lake Agnes Cabin in late 1999 because of the cabin's deteriorating condition, and the new Nokhu Cabin has replaced it. Nokhu Cabin is located north of the Lake Agnes Cabin site, along the access road.

The mountains above the hut to the south lie along the northern border of Rocky Mountain National Park and include the northern extension of the Never Summer Mountains. Lake Agnes sits at the bottom of a rugged alpine cirque formed by these peaks. The skiing in this area is a closely guarded secret of Fort Collins skiers and others in the know. This is excellent skiing all winter long; challenging descents of the peaks and couloirs are a spring treat. If you are looking for something unusual and out of the way, check out this "Cache la Poudre." Contact Never Summer Nordic Yurts for current information (see Appendix A).

**RECOMMENDED DAY TRIPS:**

**You'll find several options for day trips in this area.** The glades north/northwest of the lake offer some nice terrain for winter telemark skiing. Skiers also can tour along the Michigan Ditch.

Surrounding the hut to the south is a magnificent cirque wall with many skiable lines. Unfortunately, most of these do not come into safe conditions until the springtime in addition to being steep and serious. This is really the playground of savvy, experienced skiers, and final route selection will be left to them. Some possibilities include ski descents off the north face of the unnamed peak immediately west of Lake Agnes, off Peak 12,493, down from the saddle west of Mount Richthofen, and even down the steeply tilted north face of Richthofen.

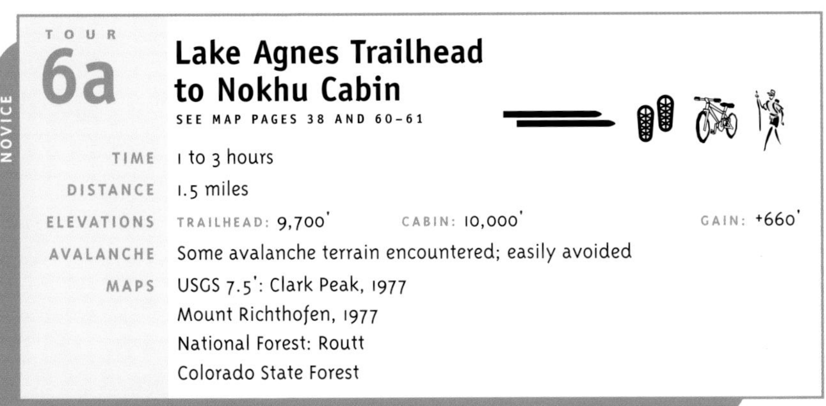

NOVICE

TOUR 6a

## Lake Agnes Trailhead to Nokhu Cabin

SEE MAP PAGES 38 AND 60–61

| | |
|---|---|
| TIME | 1 to 3 hours |
| DISTANCE | 1.5 miles |
| ELEVATIONS | TRAILHEAD: 9,700' CABIN: 10,000' GAIN: +660' |
| AVALANCHE | Some avalanche terrain encountered; easily avoided |
| MAPS | USGS 7.5': Clark Peak, 1977<br>Mount Richthofen, 1977<br>National Forest: Routt<br>Colorado State Forest |

**DIRECTIONS TO TRAILHEAD:** The trailhead for the cabin is 2.5 miles west of Cameron Pass. The parking area is on CO 14, approximately 20 miles east of Walden or 59 miles west of the intersection of CO 14 and US 287 (north of Fort Collins). On the south side of CO 14 is a small parking area. In winter the road is closed by a gate.

**THE ROUTE:** Ski past the gate and proceed down the access road 0.5 mile to the entrance to the State Forest. Turn right onto a summer four-wheel-drive trail marked for Lake Agnes.

Cross the creek and ascend through a hairpin curve. At a fork in the road, take the right (west) fork. Contour to the southwest and ascend into the Lake Agnes Creek drainage. Follow the road upward for approximately 1.5 miles to the cabin.

The area is in the Colorado State Forest, and a valid daily or annual State Park Pass is required on all vehicles. The passes may be purchased at a self-service station at the forest entrance or at the office near the turnoff to the Never Summer Nordic Yurts (for directions, see page 37).

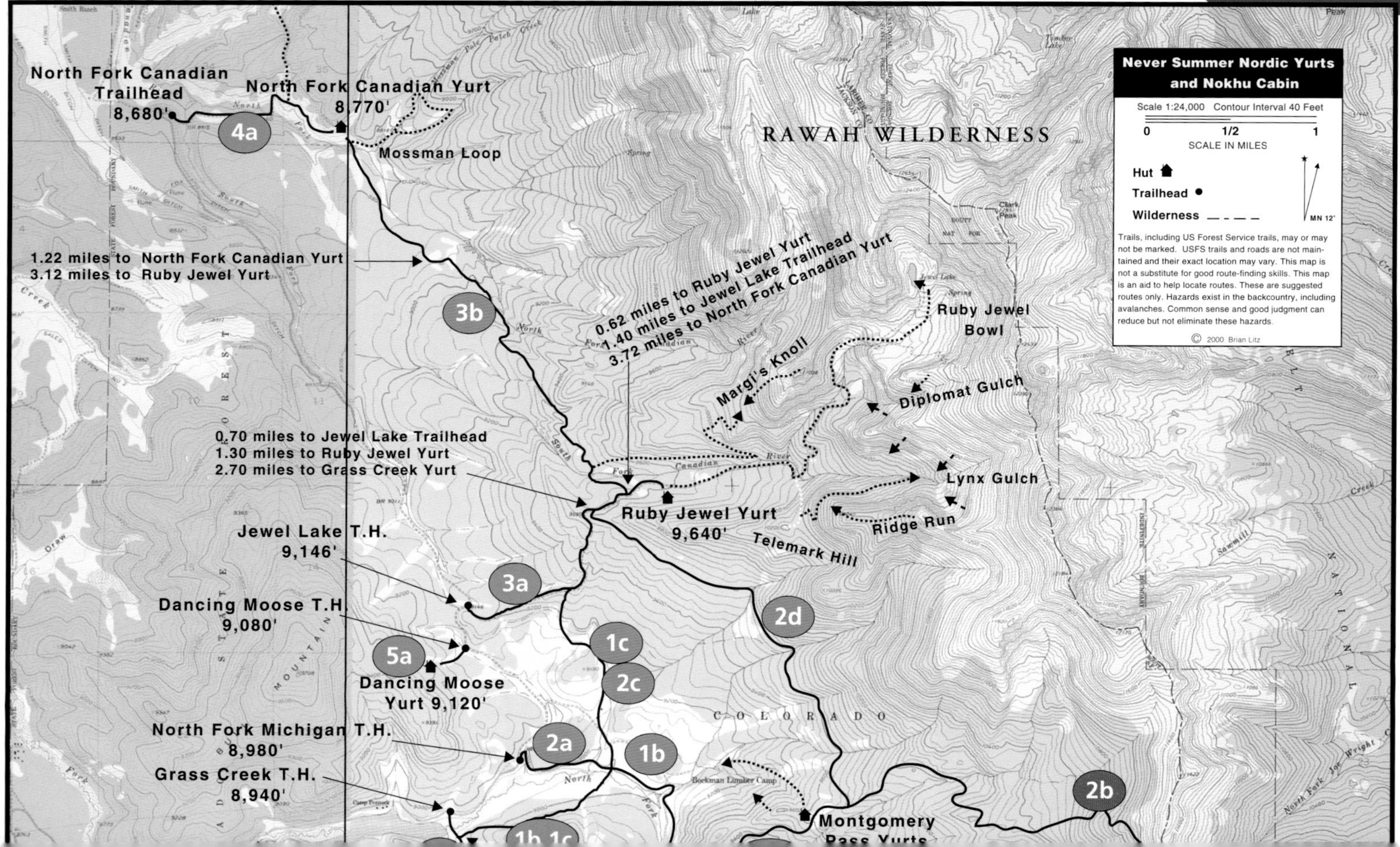

Never Summer Nordic Yurts and Nokhu Cabin
Scale 1:24,000 Contour Interval 40 Feet
0 1/2 1
SCALE IN MILES
Hut
Trailhead
Wilderness
MN 12°
Trails, including US Forest Service trails, may or may not be marked. USFS trails and roads are not maintained and their exact location may vary. This map is not a substitute for good route-finding skills. This map is an aid to help locate routes. These are suggested routes only. Hazards exist in the backcountry, including avalanches. Common sense and good judgment can reduce but not eliminate these hazards.
© 2000 Brian Litz
RAWAH WILDERNESS
North Fork Canadian Trailhead 8,680'
North Fork Canadian Yurt 8,770'
Mossman Loop
4a
1.22 miles to North Fork Canadian Yurt
3.12 miles to Ruby Jewel Yurt
3b
0.62 miles to Ruby Jewel Yurt
1.40 miles to Jewel Lake Trailhead
3.72 miles to North Fork Canadian Yurt
Ruby Jewel Bowl
Margi's Knoll
Diplomat Gulch
Lynx Gulch
Ridge Run
Telemark Hill
0.70 miles to Jewel Lake Trailhead
1.30 miles to Ruby Jewel Yurt
2.70 miles to Grass Creek Yurt
Ruby Jewel Yurt 9,640'
Jewel Lake T.H. 9,146'
3a
Dancing Moose T.H. 9,080'
5a
Dancing Moose Yurt 9,120'
1c
2c
2d
COLORADO
North Fork Michigan T.H. 8,980'
2a
1b
Grass Creek T.H. 8,940'
Montgomery Pass Yurts
2b
1b 1c

Never Summer Nordic Yurts & Nokhu Cabin
COLORADO STATE FOREST
Zimmerman Lake T.H.
10,020'
0.20 miles to North Michigan Trailhead
Lary's Run
Lake Agnes Trailhead
9,700'
Nokhu Cabin
10,000'
6a
GOULD
JACK CREEK RANCH
CLARK PEAK
MOUNT RICHTHOFEN
U.S.G.S. QUADS
Gould Mountain
Diamond Peaks
Cameron Pass
Seven Utes Mountain
Nokhu Crags
Lake Agnes
Static Peak
COLORADO STATE FOREST

# Colorado Mountain Club and Northern Independent Huts

For many decades, mountaineers and skiers have enjoyed several shelters operated by various chapters of the Colorado Mountain Club (CMC), as well as several privately owned cabins and lodges. These include a variety of huts within a one- to two-hour drive of the Denver metro area.

Perhaps the best-known Front Range hut is the storied Brainard Lake Cabin in the Indian Peaks Wilderness. The trailhead for this popular spot is just off CO 72, the Peak to Peak Highway, north of the town of Ward.

Two huts are perched high above the Eldora Nordic and downhill ski areas, west of the historic mining community of Nederland. The Guinn Mountain Hut and the Tennessee Mountain Cabin are favorite destinations for Boulder-area skiers and hikers and are open year-round. These two huts work well for shorter trips and as base camps for ski, mountain bike, and hiking trips. They share a common trailhead at the base of the Eldora Ski Area, near the Nordic Center office. The Guinn Mountain Hut is operated and maintained by the Boulder chapter of the Colorado Mountain Club; the Tennessee Mountain Cabin is operated by the Eldora Nordic Center.

Between Interstate 70 and the town of Winter Park, on US 40, is the infamous Berthoud Pass. This sinuous road climbs over the Continental Divide through some of the finest ski terrain in northern Colorado. Since the early part of the century, Berthoud Pass and its environs have provided many Colorado skiers with their first backcountry tree-skiing experiences and deep-powder face plants.

The two huts in the Berthoud Pass area, First Creek Cabin and Second Creek Cabin (Gwen Andrews Hut), are closed indefinitely while the U.S. Forest Service conducts site evaluations. Contact the Sulphur Ranger District of the Arapaho National Forest for current information (see Appendix C).

Additions to the huts of northern Colorado include two new and very different offerings. North of Fraser and Winter Park is the High Lonesome Hut. Though close to Granby, Grand Lake, and Winter Park, this hut is situated in a seldom visited patch of National Forest wedged in between the towns.

The second new hut is the closest hut to Denver. Though not possessing access to natural skiing terrain, the Squaw Mountain Fire Lookout—a 1940s-era Front Range fire lookout—may be the most spectacularly positioned hut in Colorado.

*Kurt Lankford nears the top of Charles Ridge on a late afternoon powder excursion near Peter Estin Hut, with Elk Mountains in the distance.*

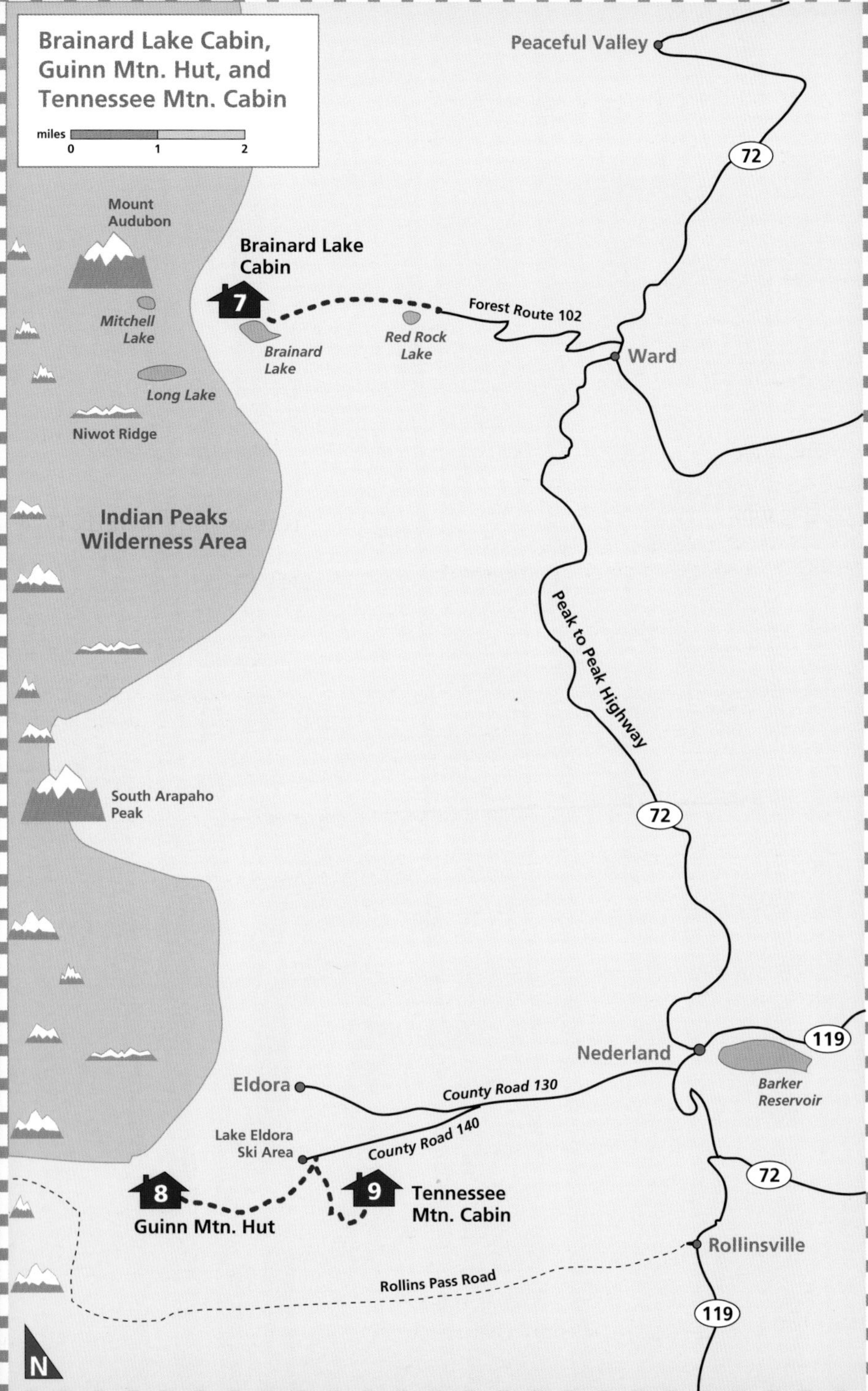

to Allenspark
Brainard Lake Cabin, Guinn Mtn. Hut, and Tennessee Mtn. Cabin
miles
0
1
2
Peaceful Valley
72
Mount Audubon
Brainard Lake Cabin
7
Mitchell Lake
Brainard Lake
Red Rock Lake
Forest Route 102
Ward
Long Lake
Niwot Ridge
Indian Peaks Wilderness Area
Peak to Peak Highway
South Arapaho Peak
72
Nederland
119
Barker Reservoir
Eldora
County Road 130
Lake Eldora Ski Area
County Road 140
8
Guinn Mtn. Hut
9
Tennessee Mtn. Cabin
72
Rollinsville
Rollins Pass Road
119
N
to Central City and US 6

# 7 Brainard Lake Cabin

| | |
|---|---|
| **HUT ELEVATION** | 10,400' |
| **DATE BUILT** | 1928 |
| **SEASONS** | Year-round |
| **CAPACITY** | Up to 20, though 8 to 10 is preferable |
| **HUT LAYOUT** | 2-story log cabin with a dorm-style sleeping loft equipped with foam sleeping pads upstairs; 1 semiprivate room upstairs |
| **HUT ESSENTIALS** | Wood-burning stove for heat and cooking, fireplace, foam sleeping pads, outhouse, running water in nearby creek (should be treated) |
| **OTHER GOODIES** | The cabin is open for day visitors throughout the winter for $1 per person; hot water, tea, coffee, cocoa, and a warm fire are provided; volunteer hut hosts |

Built in 1928, the historic Brainard Lake Cabin is well-hidden in the trees, surrounded by some of the most diverse Nordic touring terrain in the Denver-Boulder vicinity. Ironically, though the cabin sits among the summer parking areas for trailheads to some of the most popular trails, peaks, and wilderness in the state, many people drive by the hut and never see it, so well is it hidden. In the winter and spring, the Brainard Lake area is laced with superlative day skiing, whether you enjoy energetic treks along winding trails, climbing to alpine lakes, or ski mountaineering.

West of the cabin is the Indian Peaks Wilderness Area, which certainly ranks as one of the most spectacular Wilderness Areas near a major population center. The glacially carved valleys that lead from the cabin to the high peaks hold seemingly endless acres of incredible telemark skiing terrain. Peaks such as Mount Audubon are excellent goals for winter and spring mountaineering.

The cabin, which is open year-round, sleeps up to 20 people comfortably and has two levels. The rustic and cozy main floor is the cooking and socializing area, and the second level is for sleeping. Water can be obtained by melting snow or from the creek flowing across the road to the west. (Though you often will have to break through the ice, this is recommended.) Creek water should be boiled or treated before using.

The Brainard Lake Cabin is one of the best pure Nordic huts in the state. In fact, it is one of the original backcountry huts in the state, created with a true European-style community spirit. Weekends may be very crowded, though, as the cabin also serves as a warming hut for day skiers for a small fee. In addition, throughout the winter, the hut is hosted on an intermittent basis by volunteers. Two sleeping spaces are reserved for hut hosts.

The cabin is open to members and non-members of the Colorado Mountain Club. Non-members will pay more for staying overnight and must sign a liability waiver. Drop-ins are a big no-no! Skiers will find many maps in the cabin, marking day tours in the area. The CMC also produces a map of nearby Nordic trails. Candles and other types of open flame (other than the fireplace) are strictly prohibited because of fire danger. For CMC membership information and reservations, call the club at the number listed in Appendix A.

**RECOMMENDED DAY TRIPS:**

From Brainard Lake Cabin, you can ski to either **Mitchell or Blue Lake** (skiing to Mitchell Lake is for intermediate-level skiers; Blue Lake is for strong intermediate to advanced skiers). From the road near the cabin, continue north around a large curve to the west, up to a large meadow/parking area. On the west edge of this clearing, near two small wooden structures, is the trailhead to Mitchell and Blue Lakes.

Enter the forest and climb west into this spectacular valley. The trail goes up and across the main creek via a small bridge, then along the south side of the stream to Mitchell Lake. Beyond Mitchell Lake, the trail gets steeper and the terrain more alpine as the trees begin to thin out. Blue Lake is near tree line as the trail ascends along the north side of the creek. This trail is less traveled than the section below Mitchell Lake, and route-finding to Blue Lake is slightly more difficult.

The trail to **Long Lake** is for easy touring. From the cabin, head south and take the turnoff to the Long Lake Trailhead parking area, proceeding past the trail marker into the forest. Ski for roughly 0.25 mile until you reach the clearing that surrounds the lake.

The trail continues along the north edge of the lake. At the far northwest edge of the lake, you may return along the same path or tour around the south shore via the Jean Lunning Trail, which will bring you back to the outlet at the east edge and a rendezvous with the main Long Lake Trail.

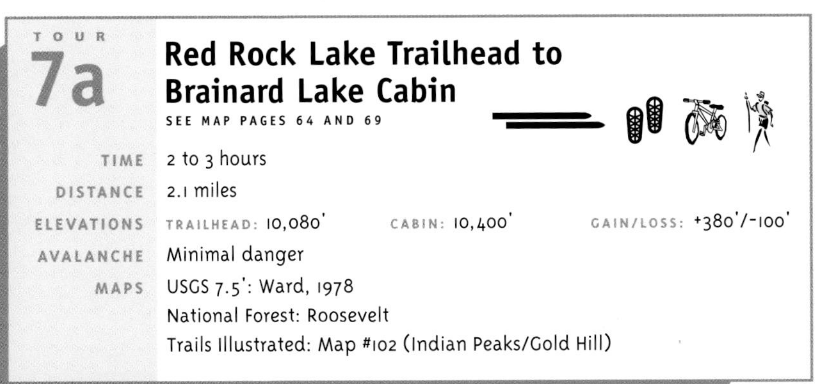


**TOUR OVERVIEW:** The gentle and straightforward Brainard Lake Road is the simplest approach to the cabin and one of the most scenic of the introductory-level tours in this book. Nearly anyone who can strap on a pair of skis should be able to manage this trail. The tour follows a wide road that is quite distinct and nearly free of elevation gain. Throughout the tour, skiers enjoy vistas of the central Indian Peaks. Stretches of this road often are blown clear of snow.

**DIRECTIONS TO TRAILHEAD:** Drive on CO 72 (the Peak to Peak Highway) to the turnoff to the Brainard Lake Recreation Area (Forest Road 102). The turn is immediately north of the town of Ward and just south of the Millsite Inn (great bluegrass music on Saturday nights!).

Occasionally, this turn is somewhat obscured by large snowbanks, so drive slowly and keep an eye open for signs. Once on the curvy road, drive west 2.6 miles to the winter public-road closure. There is ample parking here except on weekends, when day skiers are present.

**THE ROUTE:** Leave the west end of the parking area, ski past a metal barricade, and continue along the road as it contours northwest up and around a hill. Once past this incline, the trail gently rolls west and is easy to follow. The road eventually reaches the east end of the open meadowlands that surround the lake. Aim for the north side of the lake and cross the bridge and dam at the outlet stream. Contour around the north edge of the lake in the trees.

On the northwest corner of the lake (in the forest) is a turnoff to the Long Lake and Mitchell Lake Trailheads. Take this turn and follow this road as it bends sharply to the north. Pass a left turn to the Long Lake parking area and then pass a "Parking in designated areas only" sign. Finally, as you reach the southeast edge of a clearing, you'll arrive at a sign marking the trail to the cabin and the CMC Waldrop Trail. The Brainard Lake Cabin is directly east of the sign in the trees. Remember to follow the primary road and avoid any turnoffs to other ski trails, summer campsites, or secondary roads.

TOUR
# 7b North and South Trails to Brainard Lake Cabin

INTERMEDIATE

SEE MAP PAGES 64 AND 69

TIME 2 to 4 hours (each tour)

DISTANCE 2.6 miles (each tour)

ELEVATIONS TRAILHEAD: 10,080' CABIN: 10,400' GAIN/LOSS: +420' (NT), +110'/-360' (ST)

AVALANCHE Minimal danger

MAPS USGS 7.5': Ward, 1978
National Forest: Roosevelt
Trails Illustrated: Map #102 (Indian Peaks/Gold Hill)

**TOUR OVERVIEW:** Slightly more demanding routes to the cabin are found on the CMC North and South Trails. Guidelines on the proper direction of travel have changed: The North Trail (the Waldrop Trail) is now the recommended route to the cabin, and the South Trail is designated for return trips to the parking lot. Both of these trails are slightly more advanced than the Brainard Lake Road but are still quite manageable for most skiers.

**THE ROUTE:** To reach the North Trail, ski west from the Red Rock Lake parking area, past the barricade. As you begin to round the corner on the road's initial climb, you will reach a large trail sign marking the turnoff to the North Trail. Drop off the road and head north into the forest.

From here, the trail contours around to the west and then parallels the main road on the north. The trail, which lies below the road, heads west above South Saint Vrain Creek. Eventually it begins a gradual descent to the creek.

Cross the creek and climb northwest to an intersection with the South Saint Vrain Trail. Turn west/southwest, then ski down and around a steep curve that crosses South Saint Vrain Creek for a second time. This well-marked trail climbs steadily to the southwest through thick evergreen forests until it reaches a clearing near the Mitchell Lake Road and the Brainard Lake Cabin. The easiest way to find the cabin is to ski to the road and head south to the sign marking the turnoff to the cabin.

To return to the parking area, leave the cabin and return to the Mitchell Lake Road. Turn south, pass the turnoff to the Long Lake Trailhead, and continue to the main Brainard Lake Road. Ski along the road around the west edge of the lake. As the road begins to contour to the east around the south edge of the lake, turn off into the trees near a meadow that is thick with willows. Enter the forest, passing some old freestanding chimneys and the turnoff to the Little Raven Trail.

The well-marked and well-traveled South Trail follows the south edge of the lake in the forest. It is less strenuous and technical than the North Trail but slightly harder than the Brainard Lake Road. There is a short descent just before it reaches the parking area. This drop is steep; take off your skis and walk if necessary. Skiers ascending a trail have the right-of-way, so watch for skiers climbing up this hill—and for those who have crashed and are recovering their belongings alongside the trail!

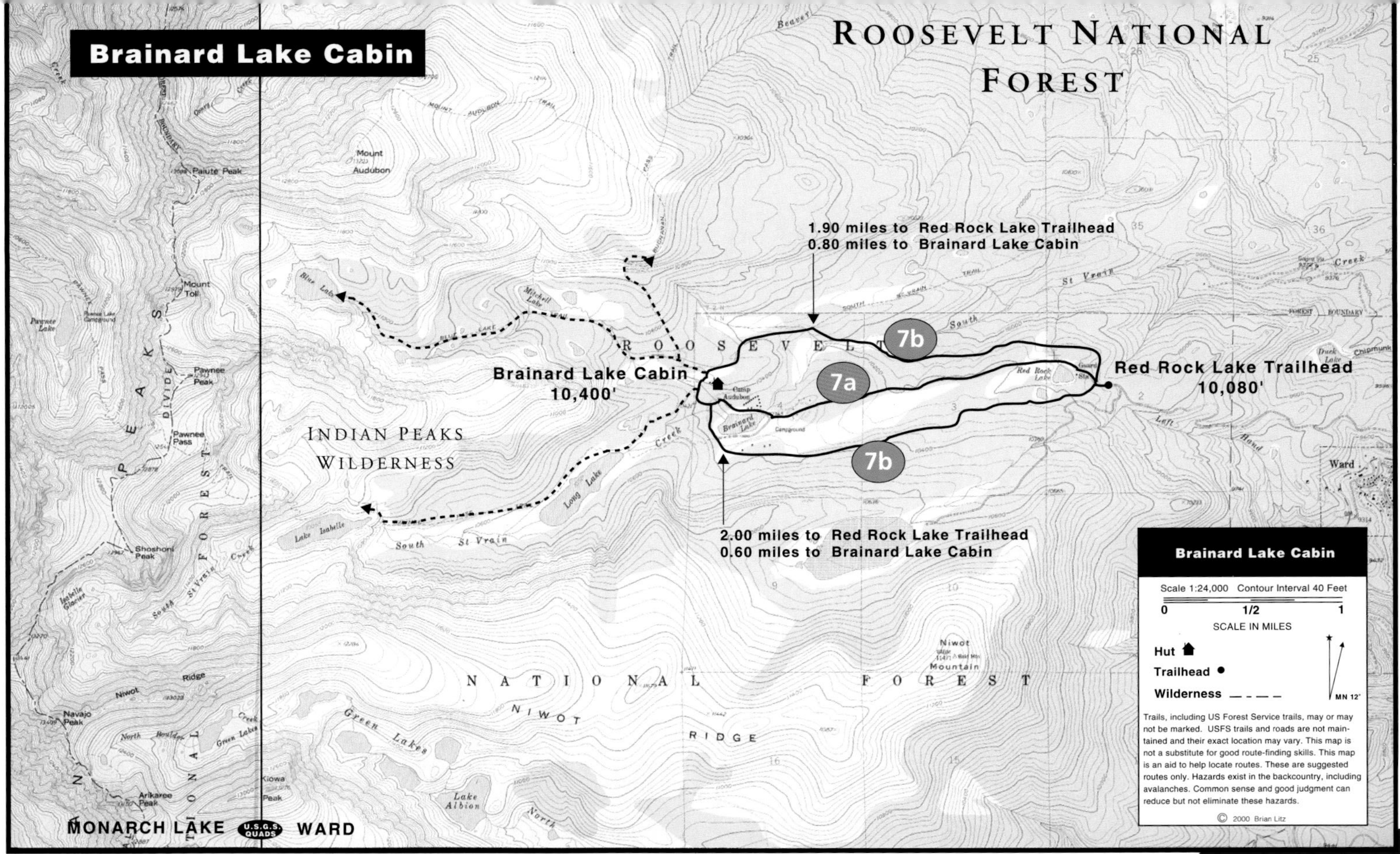

Brainard Lake Cabin
Roosevelt National Forest
1.90 miles to Red Rock Lake Trailhead
0.80 miles to Brainard Lake Cabin
Red Rock Lake Trailhead
10,080'
Brainard Lake Cabin
10,400'
7a
7b
7b
2.00 miles to Red Rock Lake Trailhead
0.60 miles to Brainard Lake Cabin
Indian Peaks Wilderness
Mount Audubon
Paiute Peak
Mount Toll
Pawnee Peak
Pawnee Pass
Shoshoni Peak
Navajo Peak
Arikaree Peak
Kiowa Peak
Niwot Mountain
Niwot Ridge
Blue Lake
Mitchell Lake
Long Lake
Lake Isabelle
Brainard Lake
Red Rock Lake
Green Lakes
Lake Albion
Ward
National Forest
Brainard Lake Cabin
Scale 1:24,000 Contour Interval 40 Feet
0 1/2 1
SCALE IN MILES
Hut
Trailhead
Wilderness
MN 12°
Trails, including US Forest Service trails, may or may not be marked. USFS trails and roads are not maintained and their exact location may vary. This map is not a substitute for good route-finding skills. This map is an aid to help locate routes. These are suggested routes only. Hazards exist in the backcountry, including avalanches. Common sense and good judgment can reduce but not eliminate these hazards.
© 2000 Brian Litz
MONARCH LAKE U.S.G.S. QUADS WARD

# 8 Guinn Mountain Hut

| | |
|---|---|
| **HUT ELEVATION** | 11,120' |
| **DATE BUILT** | 1972 |
| **SEASONS** | Year-round |
| **CAPACITY** | 7 |
| **HUT LAYOUT** | 12' x 14' wooden hut with sleeping benches |
| **HUT ESSENTIALS** | Wood-burning heat stove, foam sleeping pads, kitchenware; bring your own camping cookstove and fuel, and candles for light |

Guinn Mountain, elevation 11,200', sits just between the Eldora Ski Area and Rollins Pass. Perched just below and to the east of the summit is the diminutive Guinn Mountain Hut. It is the brainchild of Boulder residents Ingevar and Jofrid Sodal, who wanted to build a cabin similar to the cross-country huts found in their native Scandinavia. This hut is also known as the Arestua Hut; *arestua* means "shelter" in Norwegian.

Protected from Front Range winds and with a commanding view of the Great Plains, this hut is a favorite overnight refuge for skiers. The trail to the hut is steep and strenuous, but the sight of the twinkling lights on the plains far below makes the journey worth the effort. The skiing around Guinn Mountain is limited and often windblown. However, an ascent to the summit provides skiers with a panoramic view of the Front Range peaks. The Guinn Mountain Hut is also a good place to spend the night for groups planning to cross the Continental Divide to Winter Park via Rollins Pass.

A wood-burning stove, wood, and pots and pans are provided, but you will want to bring a small backpacking stove for meal preparation. Pressurized camp stoves are allowed in the cabin. Be careful! Also note that there is no source of water during the summer.

This hut is open year-round on a first-come, first-served basis. There is no fee, but a donation is appreciated. The cabin is maintained by volunteers, and all donations go directly to upkeep.

Access across the Eldora Ski Area is a courtesy of the resort. Do not park in the Eldora parking areas or your car may get locked in. Parking is available just in front of the gate near a sign for the Jenny Creek Trail.

**RECOMMENDED DAY TRIPS:**

**Day-tour possibilities are actually quite limited** around the hut on the large ridge upon which the hut sits. Skiers can tour east and west along the crest of the ridge.

ADVANCED

TOUR **8a**

## Eldora Nordic Center Trailhead to Guinn Mountain Hut

SEE MAP PAGES 64 AND 73

| | |
|---|---|
| TIME | 4 to 6 hours |
| DISTANCE | 4.5 miles |
| ELEVATIONS | TRAILHEAD: 9,360′ HUT: 11,120′ GAIN/LOSS: +1,991′/-180′ |
| AVALANCHE | Minimal danger |
| MAPS | USGS 7.5′: Nederland, 1972; East Portal, 1958<br>National Forest: Roosevelt<br>Trails Illustrated: Map #103 (Winter Park/Central City/Rollins Pass) |

**TOUR OVERVIEW:** The trail to the Guinn Mountain Hut through Jenny Creek has been a popular tour for decades. In its relatively short 4.5 miles, it packs in some strenuous climbing. Descending from the hut into the Jenny Creek drainage is equally challenging down the narrow, south-facing trail.

*Gail Keefe looks out from the Guinn Mountain Hut.*

**DIRECTIONS TO TRAILHEAD:** Drive on CO 119 southwest from the town of Nederland to the well-marked turnoff (north) to County Road 130 and the Eldora Ski Area. After 1.5 miles, take the left fork onto County Road 140, ascending the steep south wall of the valley. Parking is available just outside of the Eldora Ski Area entry gate. Don't park in the resort lots! Not only is this forbidden, but you may return to find your car locked in for the night! Look for signs for Jenny Creek and Guinn Mountain Trails. Once on the trail, which passes through the resort, look for CMC Cabin signs, too.

**THE ROUTE:** From the parking area just outside of the ski resort gate, follow the marked trail past the Nordic Center and parking lots and through the downhill area via a signed public right-of-way. Stay well east of the ski lift (watching for downhill skiers and Nordic area touring trails) and follow the signs into the forest just above the top of the ski lift. From here, the trail crosses a rolling, forested ridge before the wild and exciting descending traverse to Jenny Creek (avoid a left fork that leads to private property). Jenny Creek, on the south side of Guinn Mountain, is a fine tour in itself.

Ski west up Jenny Creek for 0.25 mile until you reach a trail intersection. Turn to the northwest and start climbing. From this point, the route climbs almost constantly to the Guinn Mountain Hut. After another 0.5 mile, turn west, then northwest at another trail marker. Continue over moderate terrain until you reach a cabin ruin at the top of a treeless meadow.

Follow the trail west past the ruin to the top of the small gully and re-enter the forest. From here the trail becomes sinuous and less steep. Watch for trail markers above the ruin; they are sometimes difficult to see. Near the top of the mountain, you will enter a meadow. Start searching the south edge of the clearing for the hut against a stand of evergreen trees.

The two greatest challenges of this tour are finding the trail into the woods just past the cabin ruin and locating the hut once you enter the small meadow. If you pay attention at these spots, you shouldn't have any trouble. During the summer, the trail past the ruin is a faint animal trail and may be hard to follow; some orienteering skills may be required.

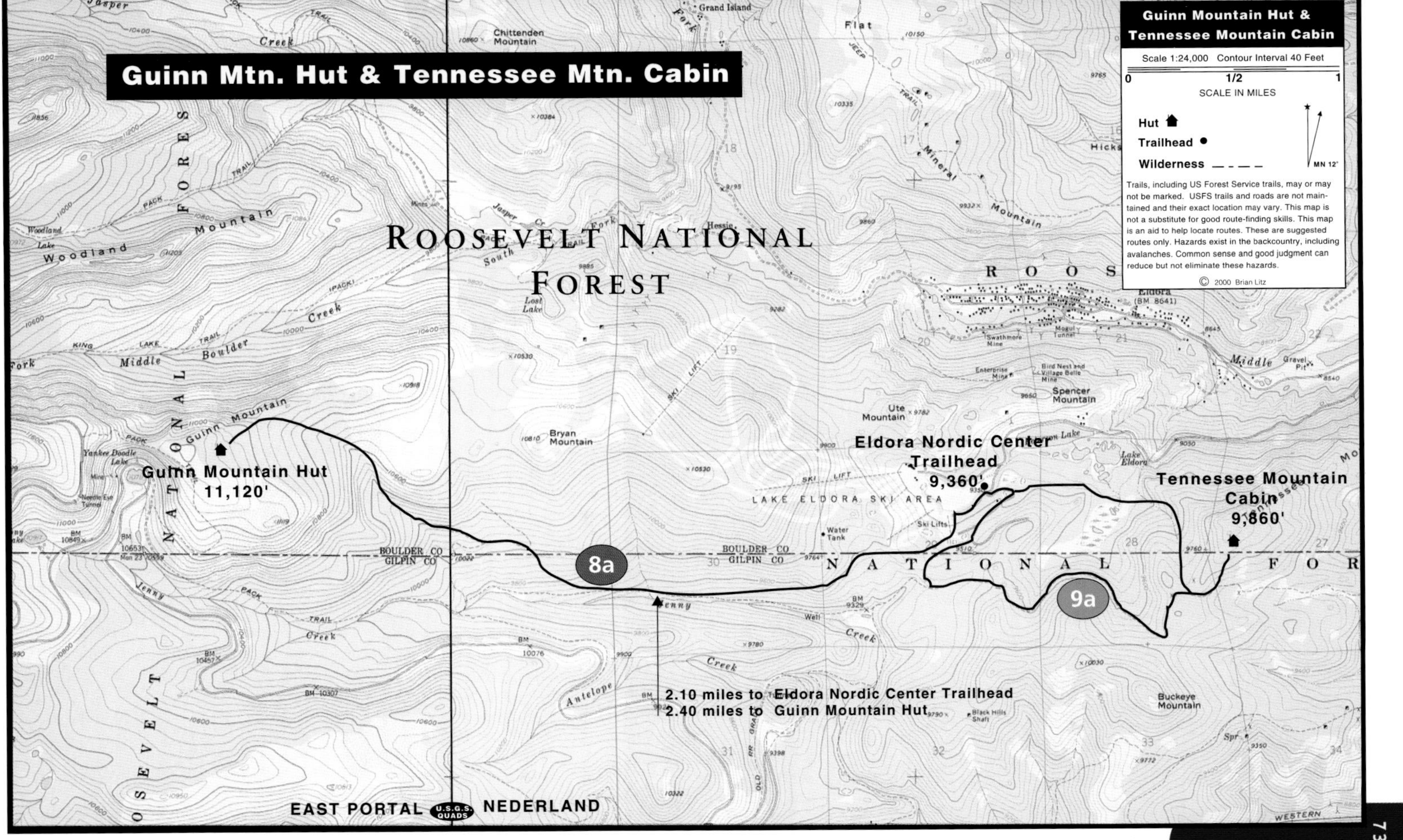
Guinn Mtn. Hut & Tennessee Mtn. Cabin
Guinn Mountain Hut & Tennessee Mountain Cabin
Scale 1:24,000 Contour Interval 40 Feet
0 1/2 1
SCALE IN MILES
Hut
Trailhead
Wilderness
MN 12°
Trails, including US Forest Service trails, may or may not be marked. USFS trails and roads are not maintained and their exact location may vary. This map is not a substitute for good route-finding skills. This map is an aid to help locate routes. These are suggested routes only. Hazards exist in the backcountry, including avalanches. Common sense and good judgment can reduce but not eliminate these hazards.
© 2000 Brian Litz
ROOSEVELT NATIONAL FOREST
Guinn Mountain Hut
11,120'
Eldora Nordic Center Trailhead
9,360'
Tennessee Mountain Cabin
9,860'
8a
9a
2.10 miles to Eldora Nordic Center Trailhead
2.40 miles to Guinn Mountain Hut
LAKE ELDORA SKI AREA
BOULDER CO
GILPIN CO
Chittenden Mountain
Bryan Mountain
Ute Mountain
Spencer Mountain
Buckeye Mountain
Guinn Mountain
Mineral Mountain
Woodland Mountain
Eldora
Lost Lake
Lake Eldora
Yankee Doodle Lake
Grand Island
Hessie
EAST PORTAL
U.S.G.S. QUADS
NEDERLAND

# 9 Tennessee Mountain Cabin

| | |
|---|---|
| **HUT ELEVATION** | 9,860' |
| **DATE BUILT** | 1970s |
| **SEASONS** | Same as Eldora Nordic Center; dependent on winter weather |
| **CAPACITY** | 10 (8 comfortably) |
| **HUT LAYOUT** | 1 room with a 4-person loft, plus 4 underneath and 2 benches with pads |
| **HUT ESSENTIALS** | Wood-burning stove for heat, sleeping pads, lanterns and candles, cookware, some utensils (recommended that you bring your own); bring your own stove for cooking |
| **OTHER GOODIES** | Quick access to many kilometers of groomed trails at the Eldora Nordic Center |

Tennessee Mountain Cabin is an independently owned hut located on the south flank of Tennessee Mountain near the Eldora Ski Area. You can reach this cozy shelter by following the groomed Nordic area trails; skiers may opt for lighter touring equipment.

Day tours from the hut are limited mainly to the Nordic area's trails, but the large capacity of the hut, its close proximity to the Denver-Boulder metro area, and straightforward approach make this hut a nice choice for large groups.

A valid Nordic area pass is required to use this cabin and the network of trails on the mountain. The passes are complimentary for cabin users and can be picked up at the Eldora Nordic Center. Reservations are made through the Eldora Nordic Center (see Appendix A).

**RECOMMENDED DAY TRIPS:**

The short tour to the top of **Tennessee Mountain** makes for a quick and scenic day trip that offers views of the Indian Peaks Wilderness.

*Winds moving transversely (right to left) across this ridge from the west formed the potential problematic drifts and pillows on the lee side.*

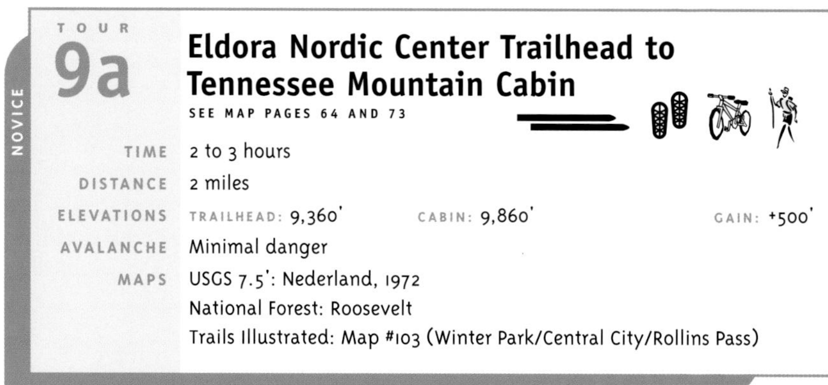

TOUR **9a** NOVICE

## Eldora Nordic Center Trailhead to Tennessee Mountain Cabin

SEE MAP PAGES 64 AND 73

TIME 2 to 3 hours

DISTANCE 2 miles

ELEVATIONS TRAILHEAD: 9,360' CABIN: 9,860' GAIN: +500'

AVALANCHE Minimal danger

MAPS USGS 7.5': Nederland, 1972
National Forest: Roosevelt
Trails Illustrated: Map #103 (Winter Park/Central City/Rollins Pass)

**TOUR OVERVIEW:** The normal routes to the cabin are somewhat strenuous. Because these are maintained trails, route-finding is not a problem and skiers rarely need to break trail.

**DIRECTIONS TO TRAILHEAD:** Drive on CO 119 southwest from the town of Nederland to the well-marked turnoff (north) of County Road 130 to the Eldora Ski Area. After 1.5 miles, veer left onto County Road 140, ascending the steep south wall of the valley. Park in the first parking lot to the left. The trail begins near the Nordic ski area office. Stop at the office to obtain trail passes and to pick up a trail map.

**THE ROUTE:** The most direct route starts at the office and heads east on a trail named Dixie. Next, follow the Mill Iron Trail to Buck Eye Basin Loop, then on to Rising Sun, which climbs directly to a saddle southwest of Tennessee Mountain. At an intersection with the Tennessee Mountain Trail, turn east, and follow the Tennessee Mountain Trail up to the cabin.

*Note:* In the summer, follow the trail marked 17th Avenue to either Twin Twisted or Phoebe B, then connect with Rising Sun (near Siding and Sawmill) and follow that route up onto the Tennessee Mountain Trail.

# 10 Squaw Mountain Fire Lookout

| | |
|---|---|
| HUT ELEVATION | 11,486' |
| DATE BUILT | 1940s |
| SEASONS | Year-round |
| CAPACITY | 4 |
| HUT LAYOUT | 2 rooms, 2 beds up and 2 down |
| HUT ESSENTIALS | Electric range, refrigerator, baseboard heat |
| OTHER GOODIES | Best view of the Front Range and the Great Plains |

The Civilian Conservation Corps constructed the Squaw Mountain Fire Lookout in the 1940s. For decades it served as the early warning detection system for wildfires along the Front Range from Longs Peak to Pikes Peak. Though mothballed in recent decades, the lookout now returns to active duty as a high-alpine retreat for hikers, bikers, and skiers.

The lookout crowns the radio-tower festooned summit of Squaw Mountain. Immediately west of Evergreen and Bergen Park, Squaw Mountain rises like an island above the foothills of the Front Range, providing one of the most scenic and spectacular vistas in all of Colorado, bar none. The first story of the two-story hut is built of native stone that blends seamlessly into the tumbledown talus that spills into the valleys below. The second story features giant, panoramic windows and a narrow balcony that circumnavigates the building. Directly to the west is the massif of Mount Evans and Mount Bierstadt, both Fourteeners.

Because of the steepness and ruggedness of the surrounding terrain, there is essentially no downhill turning terrain for skiers. Rather, this hut, with its short, straightforward approach route, works ideally as an overnight getaway, winter or summer.

*Kurt Lankford, Greg Doubek, and Craig Gaskill "go fishing" at the Estin Hut.*

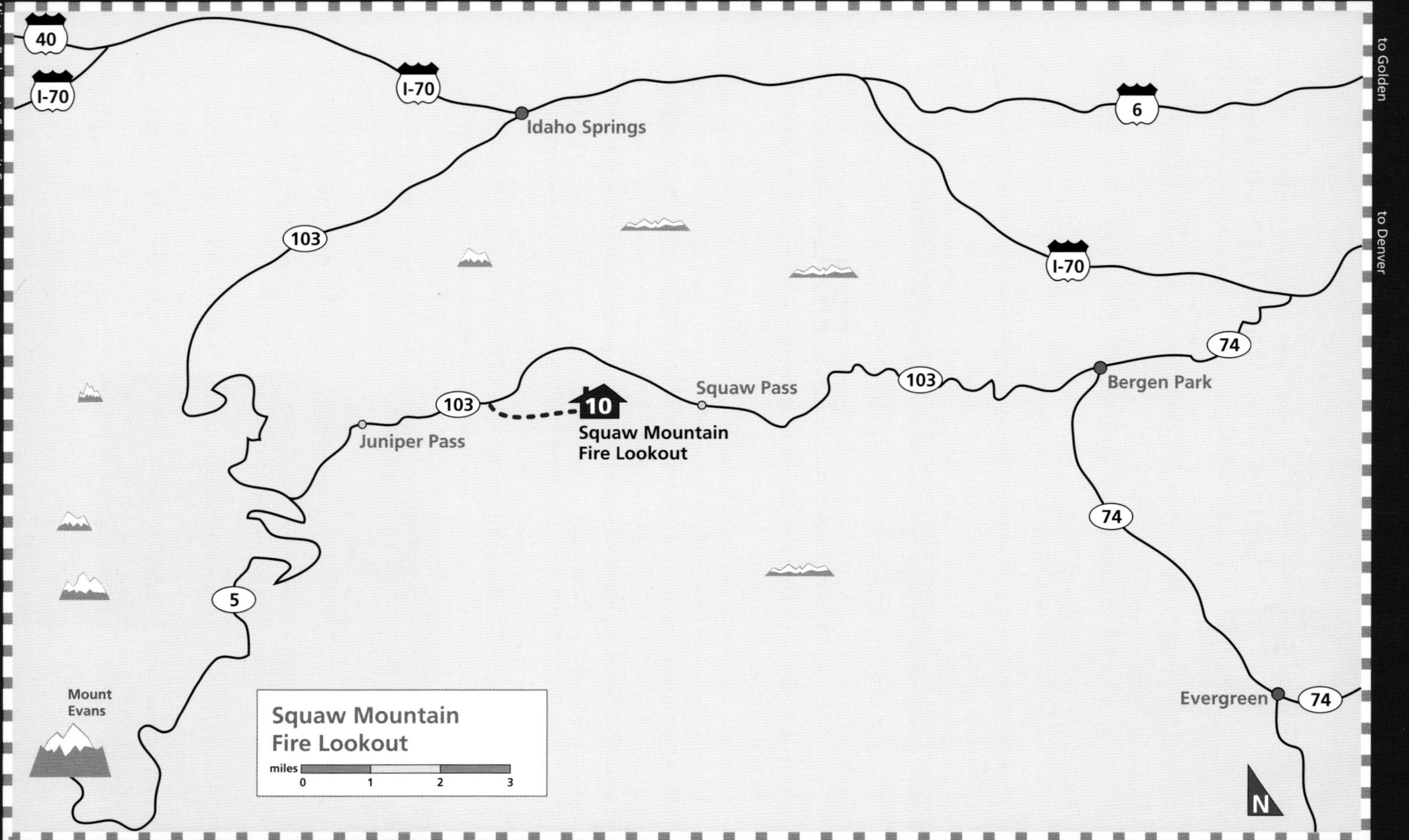

Squaw Mountain
Fire Lookout
miles
0
1
2
3
to Winter Park
to Summit County
to Golden
to Denver
40
I-70
I-70
I-70
6
Idaho Springs
103
103
103
Juniper Pass
10
Squaw Mountain
Fire Lookout
Squaw Pass
74
Bergen Park
74
Evergreen
74
5
Mount
Evans
N

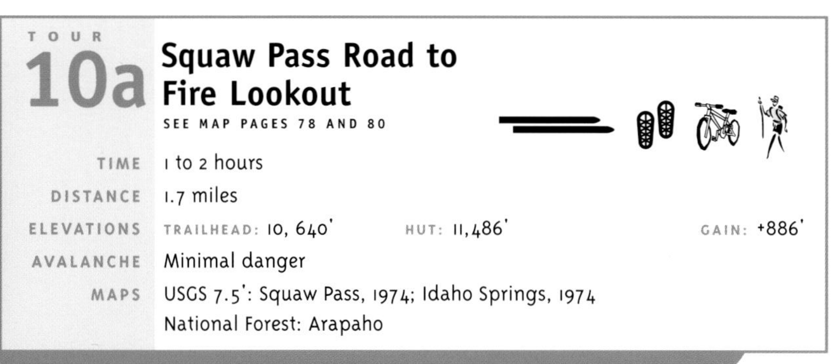

NOVICE

TOUR **10a**

## Squaw Pass Road to Fire Lookout

SEE MAP PAGES 78 AND 80

| | |
|---|---|
| TIME | 1 to 2 hours |
| DISTANCE | 1.7 miles |
| ELEVATIONS | TRAILHEAD: 10, 640' HUT: 11,486' GAIN: +886' |
| AVALANCHE | Minimal danger |
| MAPS | USGS 7.5': Squaw Pass, 1974; Idaho Springs, 1974<br>National Forest: Arapaho |

**TOUR OVERVIEW:** The trail to the lookout is straightforward and easy to follow. In addition, the road gains only 500-plus feet. But it is located in a high-altitude mountain environment and is exposed, especially in the upper section, to the elements.

Winter visitors park at the intersection with CO 103. Summer visitors can drive up the dirt approach road for 0.7 mile to a parking area before the switchback and a locked gate.

**DIRECTIONS TO TRAILHEAD:** The trailhead to the fire lookout trail begins along the sinuous Squaw Pass Road (CO 103) leading from the towns of Evergreen and Bergen Park to Idaho Springs, which sits along I-70. The trailhead is approximately 18.5 miles east of Idaho Springs (an odometer reading, though it sits near the 19-mile marker). If approaching from Bergen Park/Evergreen, at the intersection with CO 74, the trailhead is approximately 12.3 miles (odometer reading). To reach Bergen Park, take the El Rancho/Evergreen Parkway exit from I-70 (Exit 252) and head south along CO 74 to the intersection with the Squaw Pass/Echo Lake/Mount Evans Road (CO 103). There is a stoplight at this intersection. As you approach the trailhead, look for an unmarked, though obvious, dirt road forking off to the east.

*From the Squaw Mountain Fire Lookout, you can see Mount Evans in the distance.*

**THE ROUTE:** Summer or winter, head out along the easy-to-follow road to the east on a gently rising traverse across the northern slopes of Chief Mountain. The road traverses onto a saddle near the 0.7-mile mark. This is a summer parking area. Continue on, passing a short, sharp switchback and a large metal gate. Above the gate, the route takes on a more alpine flavor as the road climbs toward the rocky, windswept summit of Squaw Mountain. As you approach the summit, the rocky road switchbacks up to the peak. The lookout is obvious, sitting on the southern corner of the ridgelike summit crest.

# Squaw Mountain Fire Lookout

# 11 First Creek Cabin

*Note:* During the winter of 1999–2000, the First Creek Cabin was closed so the U.S. Forest Service could conduct a site evaluation to assess if the hut is in safe, habitable condition; if it merits formal designation as a historic place; and if it should be replaced by a new hut. The closure remains in effect for the 2000–2001 season and for the foreseeable future. Although we continue to include a tour to the hut in this guide, please respect the closure until a permanent solution is found. Contact the Sulphur Ranger District of the Arapaho National Forest for current information (see Appendix C).

First Creek Cabin was an excellent destination for short trips when skiers were interested in getting away without logistical complications. The trail to this log structure is short, steep, and often unbroken. And, although the cabin is less than 1 mile from US 40, it can be difficult to find. The valley where the cabin is located is small, and the west end of the valley is precipitous, with several avalanche slopes. Backcountry skiing is limited to short tours around and west of the cabin along several benches.

For more information, call either the Sulphur Ranger District of the Arapaho National Forest or the Grand Huts Association (see High Lonesome Hut, Appendix C).

*One of the most important daily chores—drying out the gear.*

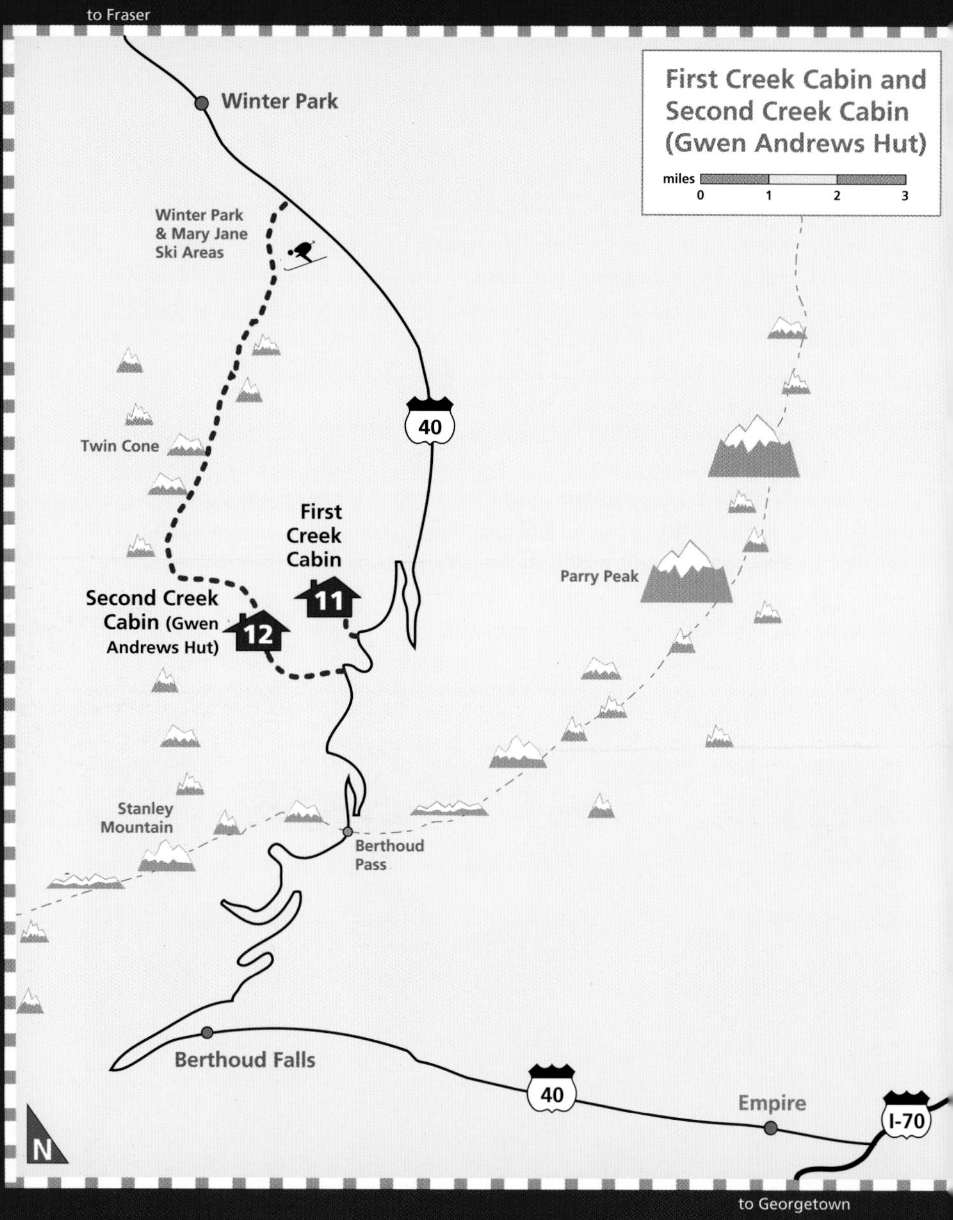

## First Creek Cabin and Second Creek Cabin (Gwen Andrews Hut)

miles 0 1 2 3

to Fraser

Winter Park

Winter Park & Mary Jane Ski Areas

Twin Cone

40

First Creek Cabin

11

Second Creek Cabin (Gwen Andrews Hut)

12

Parry Peak

Stanley Mountain

Berthoud Pass

Berthoud Falls

40

Empire

I-70

N

to Georgetown

NOVICE/INTERMEDIATE

TOUR

# 11a Berthoud Pass Road to First Creek Cabin

SEE MAP PAGES 82 AND 86

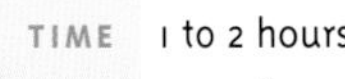

| | |
|---|---|
| TIME | 1 to 2 hours |
| DISTANCE | 0.7 mile |
| ELEVATIONS | TRAILHEAD: 10,442' CABIN: 10,920' GAIN: +478' |
| AVALANCHE | Route crosses avalanche slopes; prone to skier-triggered avalanches during high-hazard periods |
| MAPS | USGS 7.5': Berthoud Pass, 1957<br>National Forest: Arapaho<br>Trails Illustrated: Map #103 (Winter Park/Central City/Rollins Pass) |

**TOUR OVERVIEW:** This route covers very few miles, but you must pay attention to the map and the terrain.

**DIRECTIONS TO TRAILHEAD:** Take US 40 over Berthoud Pass, between the town of Empire (near I-70) and Winter Park. The parking area and the trailhead lie just over 4 miles down the Winter Park (north) side of the pass at the third obvious drainage. The first two drainages are Current Creek and Second Creek, which are also very popular touring areas. Park on the west side of the road in a plowed turnout.

**THE ROUTE:** The cabin is up the hillside, almost due north of the parking area. Leave the trailhead and ski into the trees along the creek. The trail climbs to the hut in a giant S by first heading west up the creek, curving up and around to the east, then back to the north, and finally west to the cabin.

*Mike Miracle takes the plunge.*

# 12 Second Creek Cabin (Gwen Andrews Hut)

*Note:* During the winter of 1999–2000, the Second Creek Cabin (Gwen Andrews Hut) was closed so the U.S. Forest Service could conduct a site evaluation to assess if the hut is in safe, habitable condition; if it merits formal designation as a historic place; or if it should be replaced by a new hut. Currently, it appears that the hut may be replaced with a modern hut built and operated by a not-for-profit permittee like other hut systems throughout the state. The closure remains in effect for the 2000–2001 season and for the foreseeable future. The Forest Service has tried to keep the structure locked, but vandals continue to break in and ransack the tiny A-frame—further expediting its deterioration. Although we continue to include a tour to the hut in this guide, please respect the closure until a permanent solution is found.

Formerly a Forest Service cabin, the quaint Second Creek Cabin is also known as the Gwen Andrews Hut. It has long been one of the most popular backcountry-skiing destinations in the state and with good reason: It is close to Denver; it is surrounded by many acres of small bowls and glades—excellent terrain for ski tourers and telemarkers of all abilities; and the snow is generally superb. The tour to this cabin is short and scenic.

For more information, call either the Sulphur Ranger District of the Arapaho National Forest (see Appendix C) or High Lonesome Hut (see Appendix A).

**RECOMMENDED DAY TRIPS:**

**For an intermediate-level tour from the cabin,** climb directly west up to the Nystrom Trail. Tree line is easily reached as you follow upper First Creek to the alpine ridge to the west. The bowls in this area offer superb intermediate telemark skiing. Due south across the basin from the hut is more terrain that fewer people visit for touring. Some of the terrain near the top of the ridge can avalanche during high-hazard periods, so keep an eye out. Stay well away from the obvious, east-facing, avalanche-prone face on the southwest edge of the drainage.

**Winter Park Ski Resort** is easily reached from the hut. Combining a night at the hut with a tour to the base of the ski area is a classic Colorado backcountry adventure. From the hut, climb west up through the creek drainage onto the high ridge to the west. From there, turn north and tour over the snow-covered tundra, aiming for the top of Parsenne Bowl atop Mary Jane Resort. Once at the resort, choose a descent route suited to your group's ability by following the trail maps. Return to your car at Second Creek with a shuttle car.

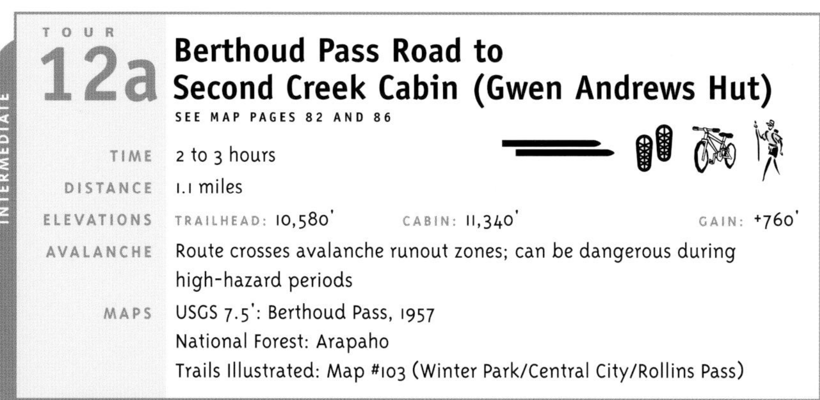

INTERMEDIATE

TOUR 12a

## Berthoud Pass Road to Second Creek Cabin (Gwen Andrews Hut)

SEE MAP PAGES 82 AND 86

| | |
|---|---|
| TIME | 2 to 3 hours |
| DISTANCE | 1.1 miles |
| ELEVATIONS | TRAILHEAD: 10,580' CABIN: 11,340' GAIN: +760' |
| AVALANCHE | Route crosses avalanche runout zones; can be dangerous during high-hazard periods |
| MAPS | USGS 7.5': Berthoud Pass, 1957<br>National Forest: Arapaho<br>Trails Illustrated: Map #103 (Winter Park/Central City/Rollins Pass) |

**TOUR OVERVIEW:** Second Creek is one of the most popular touring areas in Colorado. On weekends it can be difficult to find parking—as well as untracked snow! The route to the hut is usually broken, though telemark tracks and wandering trails can lead you astray. All in all, this is a pleasant, classic climb through a beautiful mountain cirque.

**DIRECTIONS TO TRAILHEAD:** Take US 40 over Berthoud Pass, between the towns of Empire (near I-70) and Winter Park. The parking area and the trailhead are just under 3 miles down the Winter Park (north) side of the pass, at the second obvious drainage. (You pass the first drainage, Current Creek, another popular touring area, while driving down the pass.) Park on the west side of the road in a large, plowed turnout.

**THE ROUTE:** The most popular and safest route through this short valley departs from the trailhead and ascends along the north side of the creek. The forest here is broken and navigation is fairly straightforward.

Ski west in and out of small clumps of trees for several hundred yards, departing from the main creek en route. Climb slightly to the northwest as the terrain opens up even more. The steepest section of the tour, a treeless slope, is reached near the halfway point. The easiest route up this steep slope climbs the north, or righthand, side. As the grade becomes gentler, ski around the south end of a small ridge with rocky outcrops. Some skiers climb directly to the cabin via a small ridge immediately to the north of the small outcrops. Most skiers, however, contour around the south edge of the ridge.

Enter the flat basin below the huge, avalanche-prone mountain to the west. The route contours to the north up the shallow gully several hundred feet north. The Second Creek Cabin is hidden in a stand of evergreen trees and can be difficult to see until you ski right up to it.

When skiing to the hut, stay away from the avalanche slopes off the eastern aspect of Elevation Point 12,092' and from the avalanche runout zones at the base of the slopes! This is a very dangerous area.

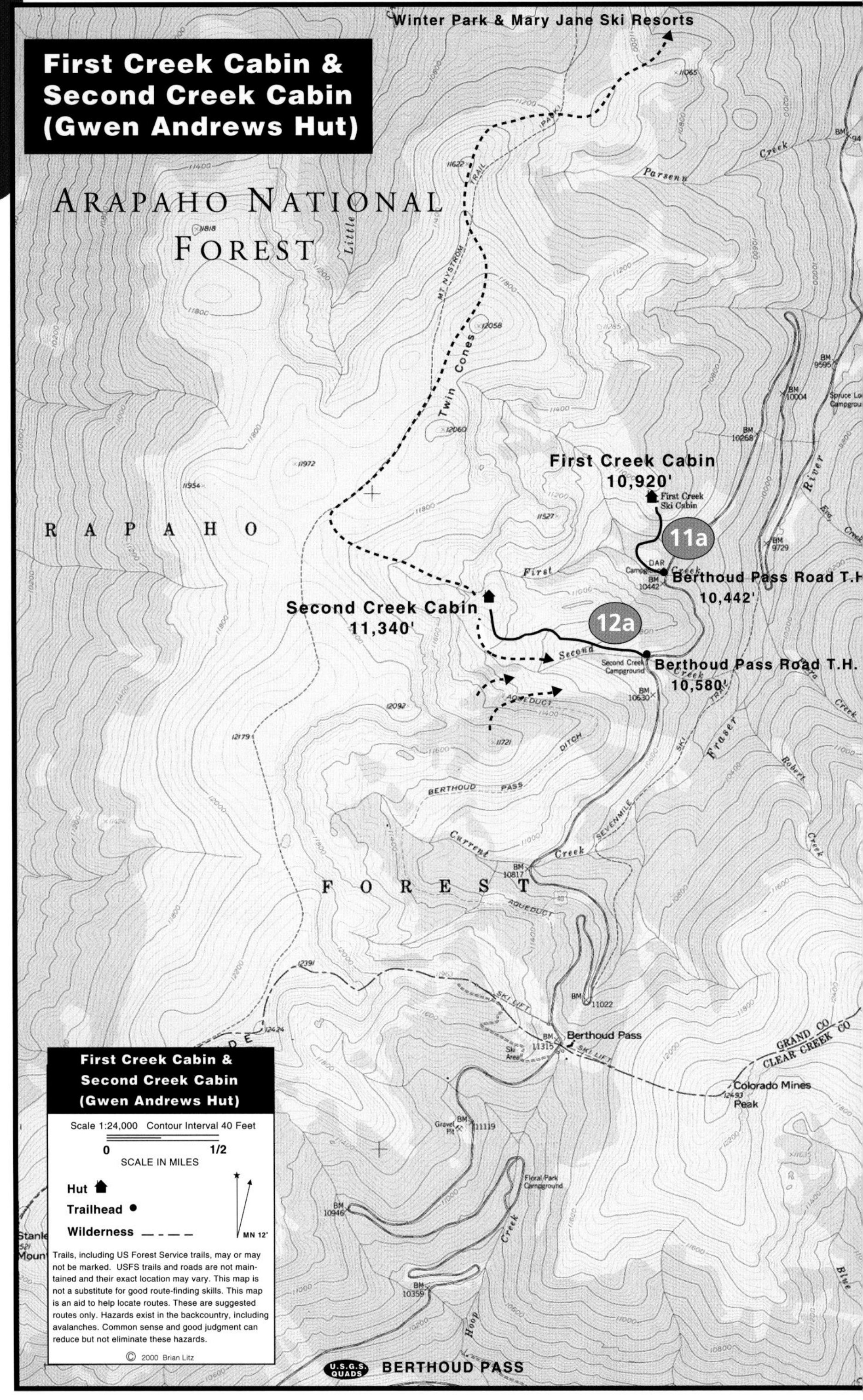

Winter Park & Mary Jane Ski Resorts
First Creek Cabin & Second Creek Cabin (Gwen Andrews Hut)
Arapaho National Forest
First Creek Cabin
10,920'
11a
Berthoud Pass Road T.H
10,442'
Second Creek Cabin
11,340'
12a
Berthoud Pass Road T.H.
10,580'
Berthoud Pass
Colorado Mines Peak
Grand Co
Clear Creek Co
First Creek Cabin &
Second Creek Cabin
(Gwen Andrews Hut)
Scale 1:24,000 Contour Interval 40 Feet
0
1/2
SCALE IN MILES
Hut
Trailhead
Wilderness
MN 12°
Trails, including US Forest Service trails, may or may not be marked. USFS trails and roads are not maintained and their exact location may vary. This map is not a substitute for good route-finding skills. This map is an aid to help locate routes. These are suggested routes only. Hazards exist in the backcountry, including avalanches. Common sense and good judgment can reduce but not eliminate these hazards.
© 2000 Brian Litz
U.S.G.S. QUADS
BERTHOUD PASS

# 13 High Lonesome Hut

| | |
|---|---|
| HUT ELEVATION | 9,140' |
| DATE BUILT | 1995 |
| SEASONS | Year-round |
| CAPACITY | 12 |
| HUT LAYOUT | 3-story hut with 2 bunks on main floor and a sleeping loft with a "slumber party" atmosphere on the top floor; plenty of beds and mattresses for sleeping |
| HUT ESSENTIALS | Photovoltaic lights, kitchenware, propane cookstove, Finnish wood-burning stove for heat, cooking, and baking located in the basement |
| OTHER GOODIES | Flush toilets and a shower, running water, barbecue grill |

The High Lonesome Hut lies in an area of National Forest that is a blank on the map for most backcountry skiers and mountain bikers. The area has working ranches, quiet hidden valleys, and lower-elevation peaks. Overlaid with a thick forest of lodgepole, spruce, and fir trees, this area is more reminiscent of Scandinavian ski touring through boreal forests.

During the winter, the local topography is perfect for cross-country skiing on traditional Nordic equipment using waxes (remember those?) as well as for snowshoes. Heavier gear is appropriate, too. But don't expect technical skiing down couloirs off treeless summits. Instead, plan on forest tours and glade skiing. Because the short approach tour follows a rolling road and is not excessively challenging, beginners, families, and younger, budding adventurers can enjoy this hut. In the warm summer months, the hut is even easier to reach for mountain bikers by the same route.

Though most visitors arrive from the south, via the aforementioned trailhead located south of Fraser, a longer, more demanding northern trail links the hut to the Arapaho Bay Road. This road travels along the southern edge of Shadow Mountain Reservoir to Monarch Lake. The turnoff to this road lies north of the town of Granby on the way to Grand Lake.

Once at the hut, there is plenty to do. Radiating out in all directions from the hut is a network of trails laid out by the hut's owner, Andy Miller. In addition, the forest on the property is undergoing selective logging, the by-product of which is the creation of excellent glades for skiers of all abilities on the hills and ridges surrounding the hut.

**RESERVATION NOTE:** On weekends during peak summer and winter seasons, the entire hut must be rented, with a two-night minimum (December 15 to April 15 in winter, July 4 to August 15 in summer). During non-peak times, more than one group may share the hut.

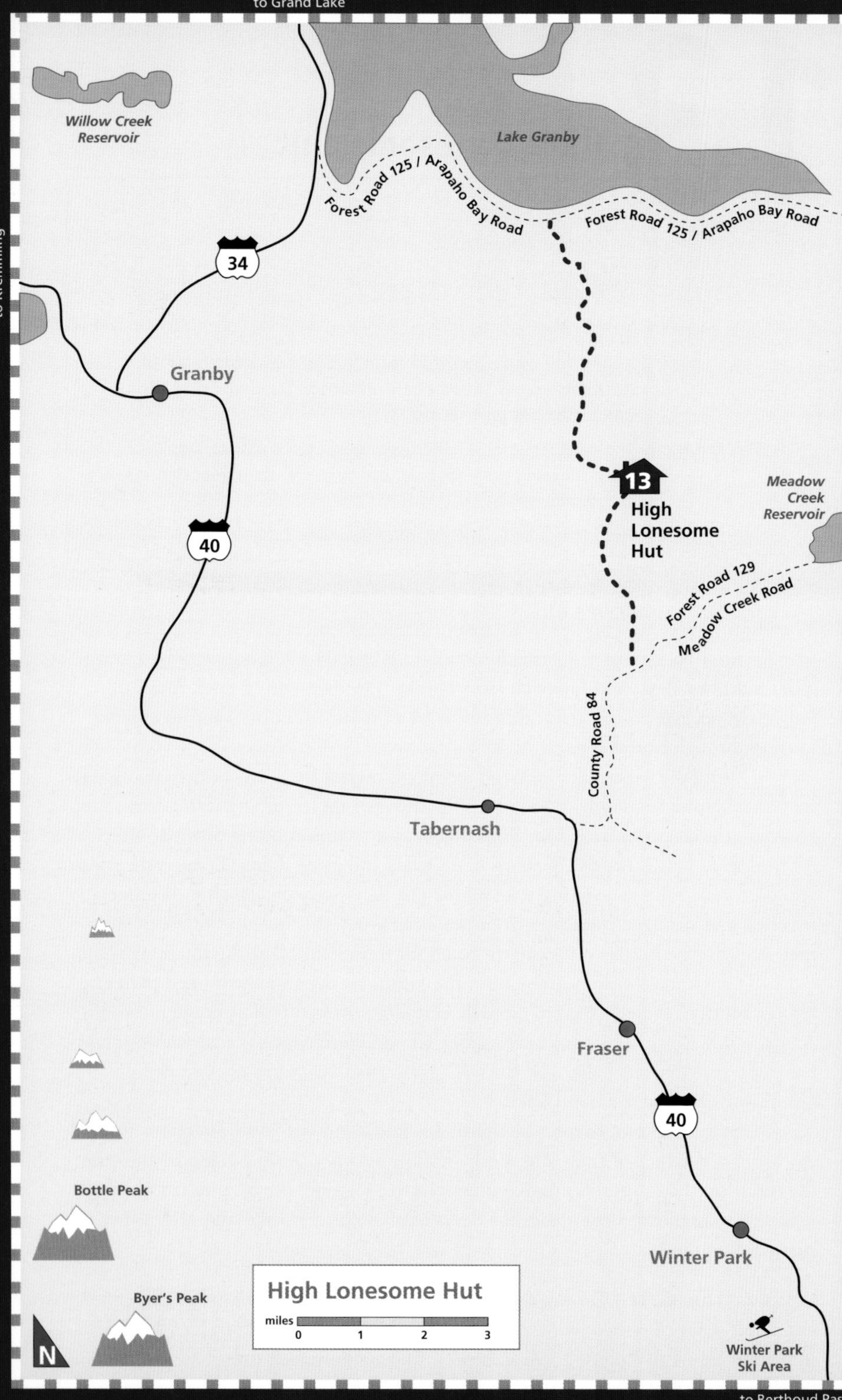
to Grand Lake
to Kremmling
Willow Creek Reservoir
Lake Granby
Forest Road 125 / Arapaho Bay Road
Forest Road 125 / Arapaho Bay Road
34
Granby
13
High Lonesome Hut
Meadow Creek Reservoir
40
Forest Road 129
Meadow Creek Road
County Road 84
Tabernash
Fraser
40
Bottle Peak
Winter Park
High Lonesome Hut
miles
0
1
2
3
Byer's Peak
N
Winter Park Ski Area
to Berthoud Pass and I-70

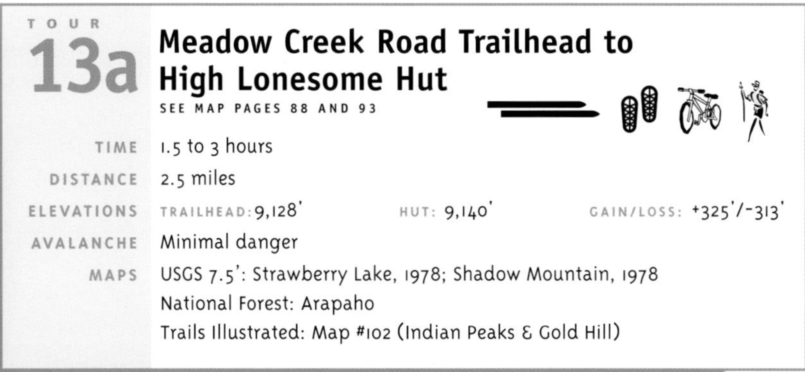

NOVICE

TOUR 13a

## Meadow Creek Road Trailhead to High Lonesome Hut

SEE MAP PAGES 88 AND 93

| | |
|---|---|
| TIME | 1.5 to 3 hours |
| DISTANCE | 2.5 miles |
| ELEVATIONS | TRAILHEAD: 9,128' HUT: 9,140' GAIN/LOSS: +325'/-313' |
| AVALANCHE | Minimal danger |
| MAPS | USGS 7.5': Strawberry Lake, 1978; Shadow Mountain, 1978<br>National Forest: Arapaho<br>Trails Illustrated: Map #102 (Indian Peaks & Gold Hill) |

**TOUR OVERVIEW:** This is the beeline to the hut, as it is the shortest route, is the least problematic, and is the closest trailhead to the Denver metro area. In the summer it is an easy walk or mountain bike trip. The same goes for winter visits unless there is much deep, unbroken snow. Generally, though, there is enough winter traffic to maintain a reasonably packed trail.

**DIRECTIONS TO TRAILHEAD:** The trailhead is closest to the tiny town of Tabernash, which lies to the north along US 40 from Winter Park and Fraser. From the northern edge of Fraser, drive north along the very straight section of highway through the wide-open valley bottom. As you approach Tabernash, the highway veers markedly to the west, making an almost 90-degree bend near where the road runs right along the Fraser River.

Just prior to this bend in the highway, a road forks off to the east and crosses the Fraser River. This is the start of County Road 83 and Forest Road 129. After crossing the river, the road forks. The right fork is CR 83, which eventually leads to the Devil's Thumb cross-country ski area.

Take the left fork onto FR 129 to Meadow Creek Reservoir. Continue past a small housing development on the right and follow the signs as the road crosses over Meadow Creek, then passes roads to the left and right. Now the road climbs more steeply, passes through two switchbacks, and arrives at a flat area at exactly 4.0 miles, where the road switchbacks to the south, then east on its way up to the reservoir. The trailhead is at this flat area. Park on the northwest side of the curve.

**THE ROUTE:** The trail to the hut lies behind the metal gate and is marked by signs. Beware of logging roads in the area that don't lead to the hut. Pass the gate and begin a gentle descent along the road. Continue down the road until you travel into a flat, open clearing at the bottom of the Meadow Creek drainage. This spot is 0.5 mile from the gate. The road, and route, fork here, and you must choose between two alternatives for the remainder of the journey. The main road takes the left fork and begins climbing along the right side of a drainage, heading to the northwest and then to the north.

At 2.1 miles, crossing over an indistinct pass at the head of the drainage, you will come to the property boundary marked with a "private property" sign. Bypass the sign and continue to another fork, with a horse corral in the middle, at 2.2 miles. Take the right fork and descend easily a few more hundred feet to the hut.

If you choose the right fork back at the 0.5-mile mark, you will travel around the eastern flank of Elevation Point 9,438'. By following the signs, you will arrive at the hut from the southeast, crossing a meadow/wetland just before reaching the building.

*Bob Moore and Cully Culbreth carry out a Rutschblock test on Mount Yeckel near Margy's Hut to check for snowpack stability.*

INTERMEDIATE/ADVANCED

TOUR **13b**

# High Lonesome Hut to Arapaho Bay/Doe Creek Trailhead

SEE MAP PAGES 88 AND 93

TIME 5 to 7 hours

DISTANCE 7.0 miles

ELEVATIONS HUT: 9,140' TRAILHEAD: 8,380' GAIN/LOSS: +660'/-1,420'

AVALANCHE Minimal danger

MAPS USGS 7.5': Strawberry Lake, 1978; Shadow Mountain, 1978
National Forest: Arapaho
Trails Illustrated: Map #102 (Indian Peaks & Gold Hill)

**TOUR OVERVIEW:** This is without question the most challenging route to the High Lonesome Hut. The distance is moderate, and if you must break trail, you should plan on a fairly long day. There is snowmobile traffic along much of the route, and the trail is flagged with orange snowmobile route diamonds that aid greatly in navigation. Still you need to pay attention to route selection, as there are few visible peaks or landmarks to use for navigation.

In addition, the route travels through and slices across several creek and river drainage systems, requiring a bit of thought. Also, on the northern end, the trail winds through lodgepole forest, which can add to navigation difficulties because of their uniform, evenly spaced trees.

In the summer, this is a pleasant hike or enjoyable mountain bike route. Note that officially this trail is known as the Doe Creek Trail, even though it only lasts a short time in the Doe Creek drainage.

**DIRECTIONS TO TRAILHEAD:** The trailhead at Doe Creek lies along the Arapaho Bay Road on the south side of Shadow Mountain Reservoir. The turnoff to this road is 4.6 miles north of Granby and is well-marked. This is also Forest Road 125, and it crosses the dams of the reservoir. Once on the Arapaho Bay Road, drive 4.6 miles along the southern edge of the reservoir to a small, plowed parking area on the right (south) side of the road. Snowmobilers use this for winter parking, too, so please use the parking space efficiently.

**THE ROUTE:** *This route will be described as an exit route from the hut* (remember to leave a shuttle car on the northern end), but it can easily be reversed as an ingress route. From the steps leading up to the front door of the hut, head north from the hut past the tree-fort and then veer to the northwest across a meadow into the woods.

Pick up the road and begin the gradual 1.2-mile descent to the confluence at 8,843' with the southeast fork of Strawberry Creek, which comes in from the east. A good landmark (especially in summer) is a small concrete and steel structure built into the streambed of Strawberry Creek immediately east of the spot where the road fords the creek.

From the meadow at the confluence, continue north downstream, following the creek to the next river confluence, which is with Little Strawberry Creek—the one that flows from the lake of the same name. Once you reach this spot in a lovely open clearing near the 2.0-mile mark, you will encounter one of the trickier sections of the route. Cross the creek and begin ascending a short distance upstream along Little Strawberry Creek.

Near the southeast corner of Elevation Point 8,882', a signed trail leads into the woods and traverses north along the base of Elevation Point 8,882', flirting with the edge of the trees and the meadow. Note that this intersection is marked with a wooden trail sign stuck into a pile of rocks. This sign can and does fall over, so beware.

The trail continues north just inside the trees on public land; the valley bottom is private ranch land. After roughly 0.5 mile, you will come to another tricky intersection near the ruin of a large cabin. At this point, the trail abruptly leaves the confines of the valley bottom and climbs northwest via a good trail on the hardest climb of the trip. Though the trail may be obscured by snow in the winter, it does follow a maintained trail that switchbacks to a saddle north of Elevation Point 9,492' and is well-marked with orange snowmobile markers.

*The High Lonesome Hut lives up to its name.*

Once on top of the "pass," the trail turns left and travels uphill slightly toward Elevation Point 9,492' along the crest before it veers back to the northwest on a descent into Doe Creek drainage. The route drops gently at first through the lodgepole pines, then it again changes course abruptly and turns sharply to the northeast, and plunges into the Doe Creek drainage.

Now the trail follows Doe Creek down to around the 8,800-foot level. Abandoning its namesake creek, the trail climbs moderately over another forested pass before descending moderately (with views to the Never Summer Mountains to the north) into a stunning wetland or snow-covered meadow—depending on what time of year you travel this route.

The trail enters this meadow from the southeast and tours diagonally across it to a well-marked exit on the north/northwest edge. From here, the route begins the final descent first along a trail, and finishes up on a logging road that appears on the USGS topos. You know you're getting close when the road switchbacks sharply from the northeast to the northwest.

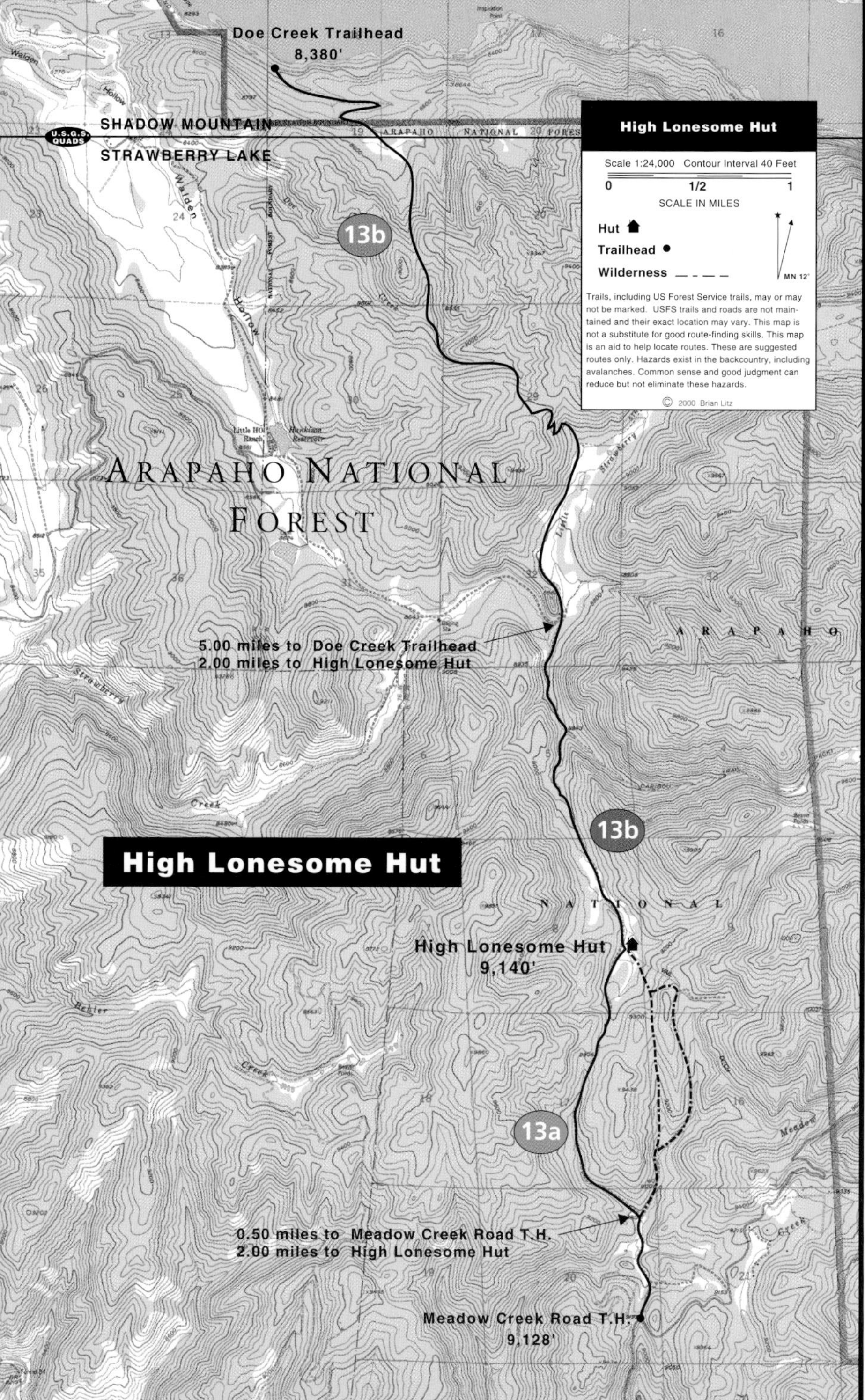

High Lonesome Hut
Scale 1:24,000 Contour Interval 40 Feet
0 1/2 1
SCALE IN MILES
Hut
Trailhead
Wilderness
MN 12°
Trails, including US Forest Service trails, may or may not be marked. USFS trails and roads are not maintained and their exact location may vary. This map is not a substitute for good route-finding skills. This map is an aid to help locate routes. These are suggested routes only. Hazards exist in the backcountry, including avalanches. Common sense and good judgment can reduce but not eliminate these hazards.
© 2000 Brian Litz
Doe Creek Trailhead
8,380'
SHADOW MOUNTAIN
STRAWBERRY LAKE
U.S.G.S. QUADS
13b
ARAPAHO NATIONAL FOREST
5.00 miles to Doe Creek Trailhead
2.00 miles to High Lonesome Hut
A R A P A H O
13b
High Lonesome Hut
N A T I O N A L
High Lonesome Hut
9,140'
13a
0.50 miles to Meadow Creek Road T.H.
2.00 miles to High Lonesome Hut
Meadow Creek Road T.H.
9,128'

# Central Huts

The central Colorado Rockies contain spectacular and diverse topography, including many of the state's highest and most famous peaks. The Mount of the Holy Cross, Mount Massive, Mount Elbert, Castle Peak, the Maroon Bells, and Pyramid Peak are just a few of the 14,000-foot mountains found here. Thick boreal spruce forests and aspen groves have overgrown glacially scoured valleys. Mirrorlike alpine lakes speckle the landscape. From the igneous and metamorphic rocks of the Gore and Sawatch Ranges to the violet-hued sedimentary cliffs of the Elk Mountains, the state's complex geologic past is vividly apparent to visitors.

The central mountains are a focus of Colorado hut-to-hut travel because they offer skiers, hikers, and mountain bikers the greatest variety of huts, trails, peaks, and backcountry glades in the state. Four hut systems are covered in this section, beginning with the Summit Huts Association. Conceived in the mid-1980s, the Summit Huts Association has benefited from careful planning and the dedicated commitment of staff and volunteers. When completed, this will undoubtedly be one of the finest hut-to-hut systems in the Rockies.

The inaugural Summit hut, Janet's Cabin, is one of the most majestic huts in the state. This thoughtfully crafted cabin has made an enduring statement on the future of hut-to-hut adventure in Colorado. A second hut, Francie's Cabin, became operational in January 1995. More recently, Summit Huts worked with the Forest Service to renovate several nearby building ruins atop Boreas Pass to create their newest sister huts, the Section House and Ken's Cabin.

Southwest of Vail Pass is perhaps the most famous hut system in existence. Named in honor of the soldiers of the 10th Mountain Division, the 10th Mountain Division Hut Association system is by far Colorado's largest and most sophisticated hut system. It provides access to a staggering selection of backcountry challenges. Skiers and mountain bikers could spend several years' worth of vacations exploring the trails and old roads that lace the mountains between Aspen, Vail, and Leadville, let alone all the hidden bowls and windblown peaks accessible from the huts. Most of the 10th Mountain Division huts share a similar architecture—rustic, roomy, and fully equipped for large numbers of skiers. The 10th Mountain group has several new huts, which are covered in this guide, including the Eiseman Hut, the Sangree M. Froelicher Hut, and the Benedict Huts (Fritz's and Fabi's Cabins).

Forming a linear partition between swank Aspen and rural Crested Butte, the towering peaks and avalanche-prone valleys of the Elk Mountain Range discourage winter travel; nevertheless, the Elk Mountains are home to the first true backcountry hut system in Colorado to be created specifically for skiers and snowshoers. The six huts of the Alfred A. Braun Memorial Hut System provide access to some of the best alpine skiing in Colorado and are favorites among experienced skiers.

On the Crested Butte side of the Elk Mountains, the Friends Hut is available to all skiers, especially those less experienced in off-trail skiing and winter wilderness travel. (The Friends Hut is also discussed in *Colorado Hut to Hut, Volume II: Southern Region,* along with the rest of the Crested Butte area huts; see Note, page 243.)

This section covers two independent huts. The historic Sunlight Backcountry Cabin is less than a mile west of the Sunlight Mountain Resort ski area near Glenwood Springs and is a great destination for novice skiers and anyone who wants to experience the backcountry without a major time commitment. And the Hidden Treasure Yurt makes its *Colorado Hut to Hut* debut. This yurt lies on the northwestern flanks of New York Mountain near the 10th Mountain's Polar Star Inn.

*Crossing the bridge in Castle Creek en route to the Tagert & Green-Wilson Huts.*

## Summit Huts Association

Historically, Summit County was the mountain homeland of the Ute Indians, the dominant tribe in the Colorado Rockies. During the warm summer months, small bands of Utes lived in the high valleys, hunting game and gathering plants such as the wild yampa root. Diverse wildlife provided an abundant source of meat for the Utes, though on occasion they ventured onto the plains to hunt buffalo.

The Ute way of life first began to change during the 1500s and 1600s, when Spanish explorers swept through North America in search of mythical cities

*Liz Klinga skis past the old rail-line water tank on the Boreas Pass Road near the Section House.*

of gold—and came into contact with Native Americans with increasing frequency. Not until the 1800s, however, did the Ute lifestyle change dramatically. With the discovery of gold and silver in the Colorado high country, a rush of humanity in search of wealth soon drove out the indigenous people.

Precious metals were first discovered in Summit County in the early 1800s. From that moment on, the area would never be the same. Tents and mining shacks appeared in the high valleys, as prospectors chipped away at mountains in eager pursuit of the mother lode. Along with the miners came assay offices, hardware stores, brothels, saloons, churches, and rail lines. The population swelled as mining towns sprang up in valleys and basins throughout the Colorado Rockies.

Summit County somehow survived the notorious boom-and-bust cycles inherently associated with mining and has remained one of Colorado's most profitable mountain areas. Today, Summit County's scenic beauty draws explorers seeking the natural treasures of the great outdoors.

The Summit Huts Association is based in Breckenridge, the southernmost town in Summit County. One of Colorado's busiest resort communities, Breckenridge offers year-round recreation ranging from Nordic and alpine skiing to mountain biking and fly-fishing, as well as sailing and kayaking on Dillon Reservoir.

With the growing popularity of hut-to-hut skiing and the success of the 10th Mountain Division Hut Association, skiers in Summit County decided that a hut system connecting the eastern and western parts of the county would be appropriate and popular. When the system is completed, backcountry skiers will be able to tour from the Keystone area to the Copper Mountain area near Vail Pass, spending each night in a warm, comfortable cabin. From Copper Mountain, skiers then will be able to connect with the 10th Mountain Division hut system and ski continuously hut to hut all the way to Aspen, across the heart of the Colorado Rockies.

The first hut in this system, Janet's Cabin, immediately became one of Colorado's most frequented Nordic lodges. Francie's Cabin, the closest hut to Breckenridge, is equally popular. The newest huts in the system and in this book, the Section House and Ken's Cabin, sit side by side at the top of Boreas Pass. Both of these historic buildings were built in the 1800s and were recently renovated.

At press time, Summit Huts was actively looking at several hut sites for future expansion, including an area near the head of Stafford Creek—between Janet's Cabin and the Shrine Mountain Inn/Vail Pass. Contact the Summit Huts Association for current information on the status of this and other future plans (see Appendix A).

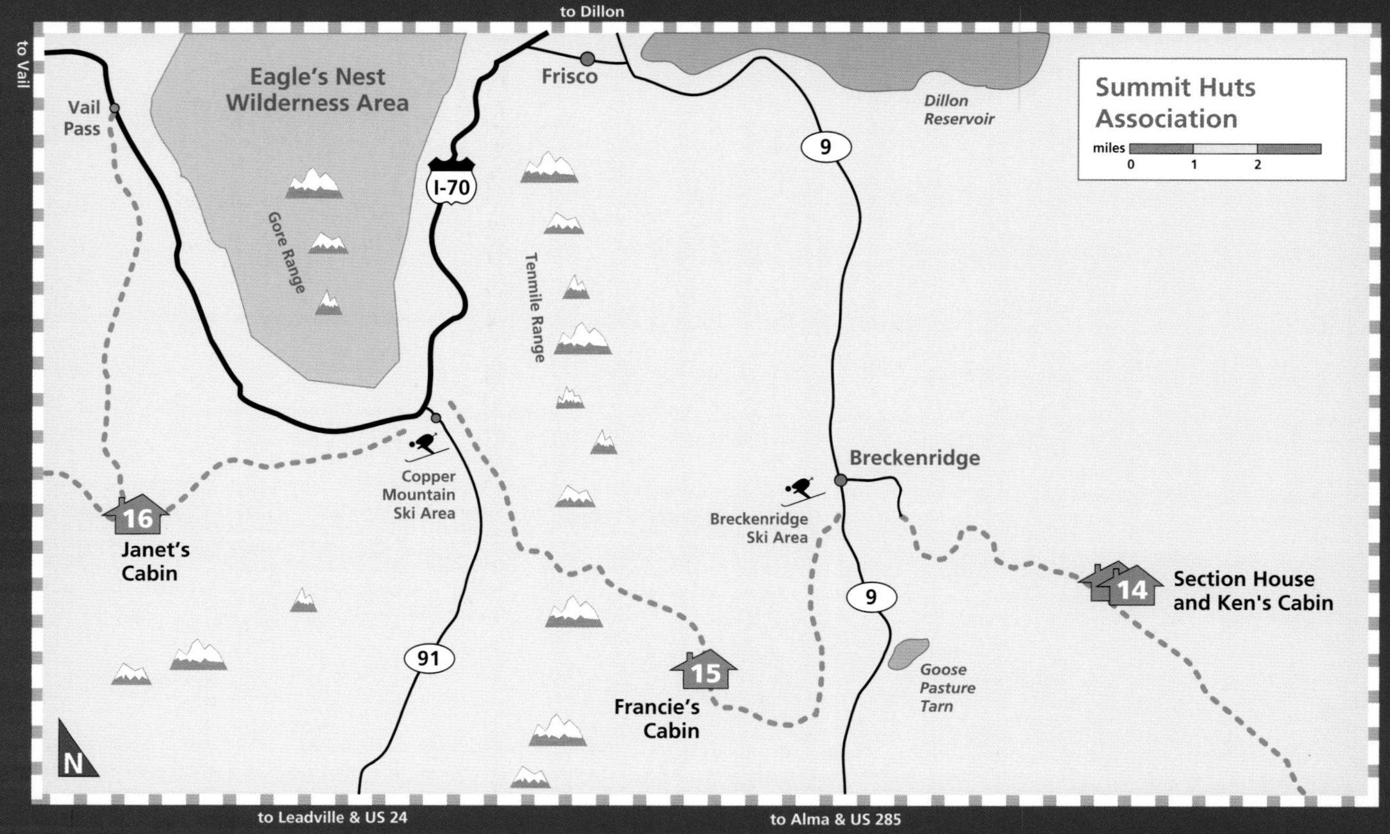

Summit Huts Association

miles 0 1 2

to Dillon

to Vail

Vail Pass

Eagle's Nest Wilderness Area

Gore Range

I-70

Frisco

Tenmile Range

9

Dillon Reservoir

Copper Mountain Ski Area

Breckenridge

Breckenridge Ski Area

16

Janet's Cabin

91

15

Francie's Cabin

14

Section House and Ken's Cabin

Goose Pasture Tarn

N

to Leadville & US 24

to Alma & US 285

# Section House and Ken's Cabin

| | |
|---|---|
| **SECTION HOUSE** | |
| **HUT ELEVATION** | 11,481' |
| **DATE BUILT** | 1882; refurbished 1996 |
| **SEASONS** | Thanksgiving through early May |
| **CAPACITY** | 12 |
| **HUT LAYOUT** | Upstairs, 1 bedroom with a single and a double bed, 1 bedroom with a double and 3 singles; main floor, 4 single bunks |
| **HUT ESSENTIALS** | Woodstove for heat, wood cookstove with oven, propane cookstove, all kitchenware, photovoltaic electric lights, outhouse |
| **OTHER GOODIES** | Period furnishings and lots of wind. Ghosts! |
| **KEN'S CABIN** | |
| **HUT ELEVATION** | 11,481' |
| **DATE BUILT** | 1860s; refurbished 1996 |
| **SEASONS** | Thanksgiving through early May |
| **CAPACITY** | 3 |
| **HUT LAYOUT** | 1 room with a double brass bed and a bench/single bed |
| **HUT ESSENTIALS** | Woodstove for heat, propane cookstove, sink, table with chairs, all kitchenware, photovoltaic electric lights |
| **OTHER GOODIES** | Period furnishings and even more wind. Smaller ghosts! |

The Section House and Ken's Cabin are at once the newest and the oldest huts in the Summit Huts system. These two Victorian-era structures sat as near ruins and are the only surviving members of a once thriving Boreas Pass rail stop at the crest of the Continental Divide between Summit County and Park County. It took a joint effort of the Summit Huts system and the Forest Service to bring these lovely, historic buildings back to life—not only as overnight huts but also as living museums. In addition to being a scenic and technically moderate (though long) tour, a trip here is a unique voyage back in time.

The multistory, many-roomed Section House was, literally, a "section" house, where a resident family lived while maintaining a section of rail line. Rail workers and occasional guests would take refuge from the hostile alpine climate in this bastion of warmth and hospitality. Both buildings are built out of massive logs that easily stand up to the rigors (wind) of the area. Today, an archive of fantastic photos and interpretive posters hangs on the walls of the Section House, telling the story of this tiny, bustling community on the summit of Boreas Pass during Colorado's mining era.

Ken's Cabin is a much smaller satellite hut a short walk away. It is a cozy, minimalist shelter ideal for a couple or a small (close-knit) group.

NOVICE/INTERMEDIATE

TOUR

# 14a Boreas Pass Trailhead (Breckenridge) to Section House and Ken's Cabin

SEE MAP PAGES 98 AND 104–105

| | |
|---|---|
| TIME | 3 to 6 hours |
| DISTANCE | 6.4 miles |
| ELEVATIONS | TRAILHEAD: 10,350′ HOUSE/CABIN: 11,481′ GAIN +1,130′ |
| AVALANCHE | Minimal danger |
| MAPS | Summit Huts Association Map: Boreas Pass<br>USGS 7.5′: Breckenridge, 1988; Boreas Pass, 1988<br>National Forest: Arapaho<br>Trails Illustrated: Map #109 (Breckenridge/Tennessee Pass) |

**TOUR OVERVIEW:** Long a popular day-ski tour, the old railroad grade from Breckenridge to Boreas Pass is the most popular route to the Section House and Ken's Cabin. Although relatively long, high, and exposed to the elements, the ascent remains at a novice technical level throughout and the route is easy to follow. The historic ambiance of this journey is highlighted by Bakers Tank—the old water tower once used to top off the trains as they made the climb to the pass, which you pass at the 3-mile mark.

Because of the popularity of this southerly exposed trail with ski tourers, Nordic racers, and snowshoers, ski conditions generally consist of packed trail. Under these conditions, the tour passes quickly; some local, lightly clad Nordic skate skiers often make it in under an hour. If a skier is breaking trail or fighting a winter storm, though, it can take considerably longer.

**DIRECTIONS TO TRAILHEAD:** The turnoff to the trailhead is at the south end of Breckenridge's frenetic Main Street, along CO 9. Look for the well-marked Boreas Pass road turnoff to the east. Take the road and follow it up through the houses and condos until you reach the end of the plowed road.

**THE ROUTE:** Gear up and continue along the road, immediately passing through a rock cut that provides passage to the south-facing road with its commanding view of the upper Blue River valley below and the Tenmile Range to the west. From here, the route ahead is an obvious, steady haul up to the hut and does not need a detailed description—just follow the main road. The upper reaches of the road lie above timberline and are the most exposed to the elements. Enjoy this fine high-country tour.

NOVICE/INTERMEDIATE

TOUR
# 14b Peabody Trailhead (South Park) to Section House and Ken's Cabin

SEE MAP PAGES 98 AND 104–105

| | |
|---|---|
| TIME | 4 to 6 hours |
| DISTANCE | 7.1 miles |
| ELEVATIONS | TRAILHEAD: 10,090' HOUSE/CABIN: 11,481' GAIN: +1,385' |
| AVALANCHE | Minimal danger |
| MAPS | Summit Huts Association Map: Boreas Pass<br>USGS 7.5': Boreas Pass, 1988; Como, 1994<br>National Forest: Pike<br>Trails Illustrated: Map #109 (Breckenridge/Tennessee Pass) |

**TOUR OVERVIEW:** This is the southern access route from Park County and sprawling South Park and is the southern half of the abandoned Boreas Pass railroad grade. Like its Breckenridge counterpart, this route faces south and can have marginal skiing conditions—especially down low. Don't be surprised if you have to hoof it on sections of this tour. For consistently better skiing, consider taking the forested Gold Dust Trail, which parallels this route to the west (Tour 14c).

**DIRECTIONS TO TRAILHEAD:** Drive on US 285 to the turnoff to Park County Road 50 and the tiny town of Como. Turn onto Park County 50 and proceed northwest through Como. After 3.8 miles you will reach the turnoff to the Boreas Pass Road. Note that this road can be muddy and may require a four-wheel-drive vehicle.

**THE ROUTE:** Park off the main road and begin the sinuous ascent. Like the tour from the Breckenridge side, this route follows an easy-to-follow roadbed for its entire length.

*Liz Klinga relaxes by the fire at the Section House.*

INTERMEDIATE

TOUR

# 14c Gold Dust Trailhead to Section House and Ken's Cabin

SEE MAP PAGES 98 AND 104–105

| | |
|---|---|
| TIME | 4 to 6 hours |
| DISTANCE | 4.9 miles |
| ELEVATIONS | TRAILHEAD: 10,330' HOUSE/CABIN: 11,481' GAIN/LOSS: +1,271'/-120' |
| AVALANCHE | Minimal danger |
| MAPS | Summit Huts Association Map: Boreas Pass<br>USGS 7.5': Boreas Pass, 1988; Como, 1994<br>National Forest: Pike<br>Trails Illustrated: Map #109 (Breckenridge/Tennessee Pass) |

**TOUR OVERVIEW:** The complete Gold Dust Trail leads all the way from near Como to an intersection with the Boreas Pass Road just to the southeast of Boreas Pass and the Section House. The upper section of the Gold Dust Trail is the shortest route to the Section House. It also provides the best consistent ski and snowshoe conditions and is the "wildest" route, as it doesn't follow a road.

**DIRECTIONS TO TRAILHEAD:** Drive on US 285 to the turnoff to Park County Road 50 and the tiny town of Como. Turn onto Park County 50 and proceed northwest through the town of Como. After 5.5 miles you will reach the Gold Dust Trailhead, which is not well-marked. Parking can be a little tight in this area, so you may need to exercise a little creativity to get your car off the main road.

*Liz Klinga and Leigh Girvin depart from the Section House below Mount Baldy near Boreas Pass.*

**THE ROUTE:** Perhaps the most difficult task relating to this trail is to find the start to the upper section that climbs up through North Tarryall Creek. From the trailhead, the tour climbs to the west/northwest, first up through an indistinct drainage and then up on a moderate traversing ascent through the woods well west of the creek.

Eventually, the trail crosses the creek, crosses a road, and then climbs more steeply up south-facing slopes up to the Boreas Pass Road. Once on the Boreas Pass Road, follow it to the northwest up to the huts and the pass.

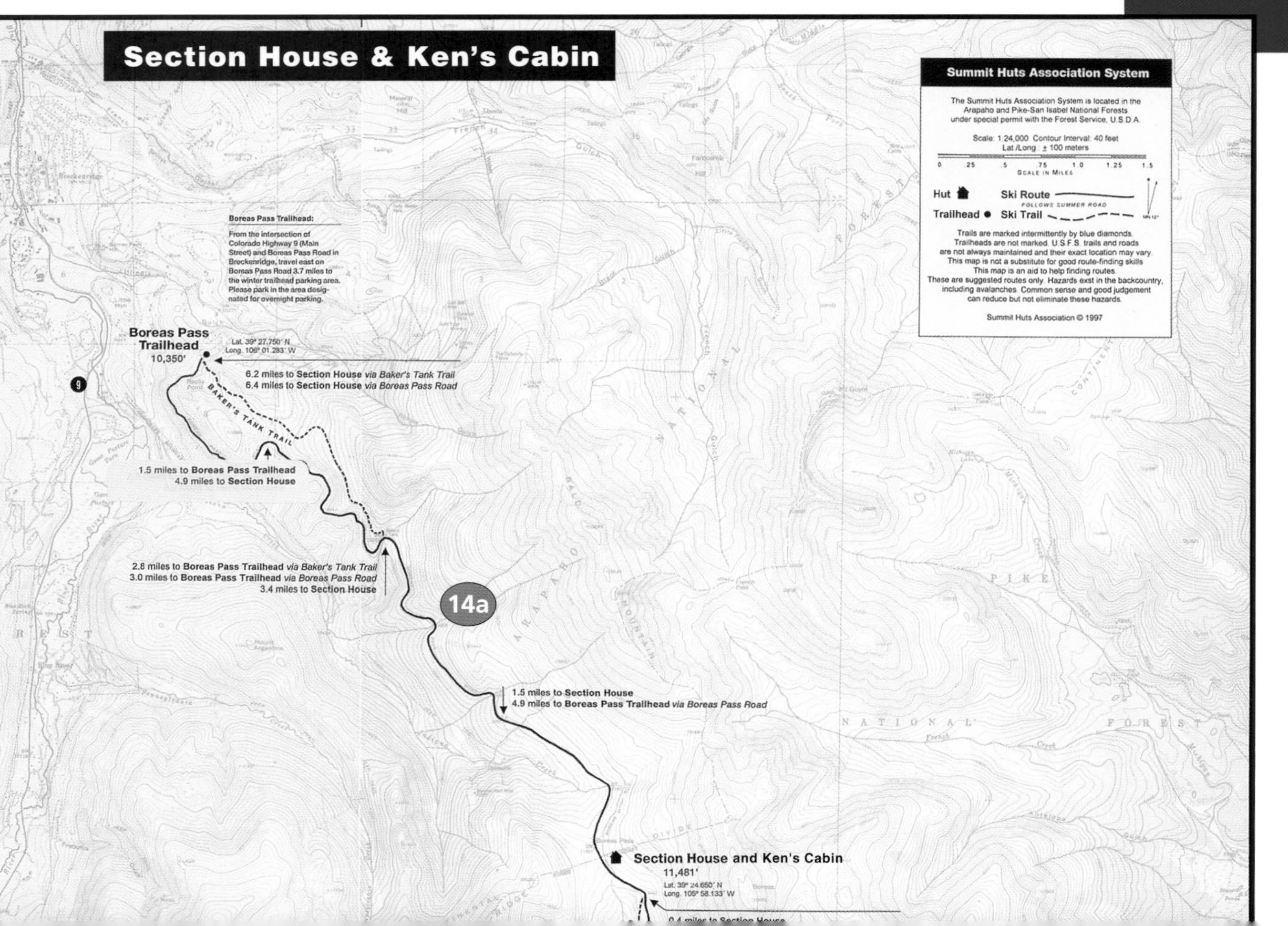
Section House & Ken's Cabin
Summit Huts Association System
The Summit Huts Association System is located in the Arapaho and Pike-San Isabel National Forests under special permit with the Forest Service, U.S.D.A.
Scale: 1:24,000 Contour Interval: 40 feet
Lat./Long.: ± 100 meters
0 .25 .5 .75 1.0 1.25 1.5
Scale in Miles
Hut
Ski Route
Follows summer road
Trailhead
Ski Trail
Trails are marked intermittently by blue diamonds. Trailheads are not marked. U.S.F.S. trails and roads are not always maintained and their exact location may vary. This map is not a substitute for good route-finding skills. This map is an aid to help finding routes. These are suggested routes only. Hazards exist in the backcountry, including avalanches. Common sense and good judgement can reduce but not eliminate these hazards.
Summit Huts Association © 1997
Boreas Pass Trailhead:
From the intersection of Colorado Highway 9 (Main Street) and Boreas Pass Road in Breckenridge, travel east on Boreas Pass Road 3.7 miles to the winter trailhead parking area. Please park in the area designated for overnight parking.
Boreas Pass Trailhead
10,350'
Lat. 39° 27.750' N
Long. 106° 01.283' W
6.2 miles to Section House via Baker's Tank Trail
6.4 miles to Section House via Boreas Pass Road
BAKER'S TANK TRAIL
1.5 miles to Boreas Pass Trailhead
4.9 miles to Section House
2.8 miles to Boreas Pass Trailhead via Baker's Tank Trail
3.0 miles to Boreas Pass Trailhead via Boreas Pass Road
3.4 miles to Section House
14a
1.5 miles to Section House
4.9 miles to Boreas Pass Trailhead via Boreas Pass Road
Section House and Ken's Cabin
11,481'
Lat. 39° 24.650' N
Long. 105° 58.133' W
ARAPAHO NATIONAL FOREST
PIKE NATIONAL FOREST
BALD MOUNTAIN
CONTINENTAL DIVIDE
9

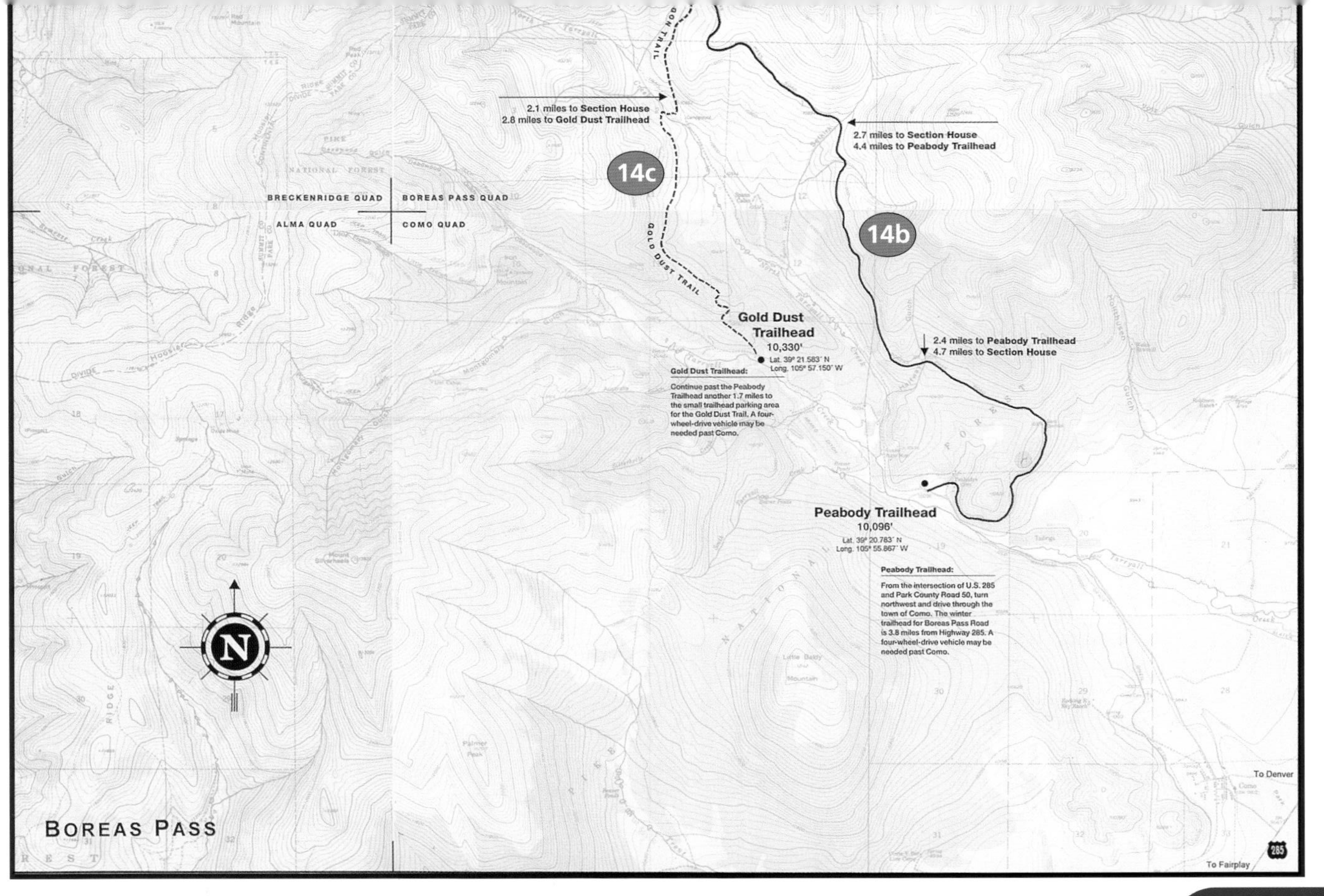

BOREAS PASS
2.1 miles to Section House
2.8 miles to Gold Dust Trailhead
2.7 miles to Section House
4.4 miles to Peabody Trailhead
14c
14b
BRECKENRIDGE QUAD
BOREAS PASS QUAD
ALMA QUAD
COMO QUAD
GOLD DUST TRAIL
Gold Dust Trailhead
10,330'
Lat. 39° 21.583' N
Long. 105° 57.150' W
Gold Dust Trailhead:
Continue past the Peabody Trailhead another 1.7 miles to the small trailhead parking area for the Gold Dust Trail. A four-wheel-drive vehicle may be needed past Como.
2.4 miles to Peabody Trailhead
4.7 miles to Section House
Peabody Trailhead
10,096'
Lat. 39° 20.783' N
Long. 105° 55.867' W
Peabody Trailhead:
From the intersection of U.S. 285 and Park County Road 50, turn northwest and drive through the town of Como. The winter trailhead for Boreas Pass Road is 3.8 miles from Highway 285. A four-wheel-drive vehicle may be needed past Como.
To Denver
To Fairplay
285
N

# Francie's Cabin

| | |
|---|---|
| **HUT ELEVATION** | 11,360' |
| **DATE BUILT** | 1995 |
| **SEASONS** | Thanksgiving through early May (winter); limited basis July through September (summer) |
| **CAPACITY** | 20 (winter), 14 (summer) |
| **HUT LAYOUT** | 2 bedrooms with 2 single beds each, 3 bedrooms with 4 single bunks, upstairs; 1 bunk bed, 2 single beds on main floor |
| **HUT ESSENTIALS** | Woodstove for heat, propane cookstove, all kitchenware, photovoltaic electric lights |
| **OTHER GOODIES** | Sauna, indoor composting toilets, large bay windows |

Francie's Cabin is a memorial to Frances Lockwood Bailey, a Breckenridge resident who died in a plane crash. This lovely and roomy log shelter sits at tree line in the Crystal Creek drainage. Precipitous alpine peaks and colorful sunrises lie just beyond the warmth of the cabin's crackling woodstove. During the winter the cabin is accessible via a classic, moderate cross-country trail, although the last mile does climb quite steeply.

Once at the cabin, skiers are within 100 yards of true alpine terrain and its accompanying hazards, that is, avalanches. Consequently, touring around the hut is somewhat limited and is recommended only for groups of experienced skiers who have the proper equipment and knowledge for traveling in avalanche country.

Francie's Cabin is open during the summer for bikers and hikers and is accessible to people with disabilities, although the approach road is rough and requires a high-clearance, four-wheel-drive vehicle. The route to Wheeler Flats Trailhead (Tour 15B) is also rough and is really appropriate only for summer hikers; it is not recommended for biking or skiing. Also note that the location of Francie's Cabin does not lend itself to true hut-to-hut travel. Make reservations through the 10th Mountain Division Hut Association (see Appendix A).

INTERMEDIATE

TOUR
# 15a Burro Trail Trailhead to Francie's Cabin

SEE MAP PAGES 98 AND 110

| | |
|---|---|
| TIME | 3 to 5 hours |
| DISTANCE | 4 miles |
| ELEVATIONS | TRAILHEAD: 9,730' CABIN: 11,360' GAIN: +1,680' |
| AVALANCHE | Minimal danger |
| MAPS | Summit Huts Association Map: Francie's Cabin<br>USGS 7.5': Breckenridge, 1988<br>National Forest: Arapaho<br>Trails Illustrated: Map #109 (Breckenridge/Tennessee Pass) |

**TOUR OVERVIEW:** The trailhead for the Burro Trail is at the base of Breckenridge Ski Area's Peak 9, on the south side of the Beaver Run Resort near the southwestern edge of town. Keep in mind that there is no official designated parking for Francie's Cabin, and because no overnight parking is allowed at the E lot (the closest parking area) in winter, parking instructions are different for winter and summer.

**DIRECTIONS TO TRAILHEAD:** To reach the drop-off spot for the trail (winter or summer), drive to the southern end of Main Street in Breckenridge and turn right at a stoplight onto Park Street. Head west and turn left onto Village Road, which leads directly to the Beaver Run Resort. Continue up the hill until you reach the ski area and a large parking lot to the south of the Beaver Run complex. Enter this lot and cross to the south side. You can park here in the summer. (*Note:* Please read parking information in your confirmation packet for the most current parking instructions—things can change!)

In the winter you must park in one of the lower town lots and ride a shuttle bus back up to the trailhead. Drop off your gear near the trailhead (following the directions above), leaving someone to watch over it, then drive back down Village Road to Park Street. Turn left onto Park Street and proceed north, past Ski Hill Road and the Miner's parking lot on the right, and park in the Tailings parking lot. Catch the Beaver Run shuttle bus back to the trailhead.

If downhill skiers are not yet parking at the Tailings and no shuttle buses are servicing this lot, walk south to the Miner's lot bus stop. If the Miner's lot is not open yet, walk south to the intersection of Park Street and Ski Hill Road. From the bus stop on Ski Hill Road, in front of the 1st Bank, take either the Breckenridge Town Trolley or the ski area bus back up to the Beaver Run Resort and the trailhead. This is all a test: If you can negotiate these parking procedures, skiing to the hut will be no problem! *Note:* Be sure to leave the parking permit that is part of your reservation packet in the window of your vehicle; make copies of the permit for all of the cars in your group.

**THE ROUTE:** When you are ready to hit the trail, leave the parking area and head south, past the maze for the Beaver Run quad chairlift, to the ski school area. Watch out for skiers coming downhill! Near the creek and the ski school yurt, a Forest Service sign marks the trailhead. Launch onto the trail, which is marked by blue diamonds, cross the creek, and begin skiing south along the eastern edge of the creek. The trail runs along this side of the creek for 0.7 mile. Be sure to avoid a left fork that goes uphill to a plowed road and huge homes. Instead, take the right fork and ski past a small yellow sign.

Continue on the trail, gradually ascending through the forest for 1.2 miles until the trail veers west. The trail climbs a small hill and intercepts an old jeep trail. Turn left (south) onto this trail, which is marked by a diamond with a small black arrow. Follow this obvious trail south on a very gradual ascending traverse for 2.4 miles until you reach another trail intersection. Three trails lead off from this intersection: A trail marked by blue diamonds leads southwest to Spruce Creek Road; downhill to the east is a steep trail; and uphill to the west is the continuation of the trail to the hut. It is unmarked and steep. (The route back to Breckenridge is marked by a Burro Trail sign.)

*An all-women "Babes in the Backcountry" course heads out into the classroom from Francie's Cabin.*

Shift into low gear (you may want skins for the rest of the climb) and begin the final 1-mile climb to the hut. The trail contours and climbs west into the Crystal Creek drainage, where it intercepts the aqueduct road on the south, marked by a "No Snowmobilers" sign. Continue on the trail past a "Motorized Restriction" sign, break through a final stand of trees, and enter a clearing near tree line. There are two posts with brown trail diamonds just beyond the edge of the trees. From this spot Francie's Cabin is a long stone's throw away. Turn to the north and climb up through the clearing, over a hill crest, and ski to the hut.

ADVANCED

TOUR **15b**

## Wheeler Flats Trailhead to Francie's Cabin

SEE MAP PAGES 98 AND 110

**TIME** 5 to 8 hours

**DISTANCE** 6.5 miles

**ELEVATIONS** TRAILHEAD: 9,730' HUT: 11,360' GAIN/LOSS: +1,300'/-200'

**AVALANCHE** Not recommended as a winter route

**MAPS** USGS 7.5': Copper Mountain, 1987; Vail Pass, 1987
National Forest: Arapaho
Trails Illustrated: Map #108 (Vail/Frisco/Dillon); Map #109 (Breckenridge/Tennessee Pass)

**TOUR OVERVIEW:** The Wheeler Flats Trail crosses the Tenmile Range through a pass between Peak 8 and Peak 9. It is recommended as a summer-use-only route, because of the high avalanche hazard at the pass. At 12,390 feet, far above Breckenridge and Copper Mountain, this passage can be very taxing. Get an early start; this trail is exposed to the vagaries of mountain weather.

**DIRECTIONS TO TRAILHEAD:** This tour begins near the intersection of I-70 and CO 91 at Copper Mountain (immediately south of I-70). Turn east off CO 91 onto the frontage road. Then veer north, proceeding 0.4 mile to an obvious parking area.

**THE ROUTE:** Leave the parking area, pass the Forest Service sign, and begin the Wheeler Flats Trail by crossing Tenmile Creek via a footbridge. After the bridge, turn east and follow the trail south along a gas-line road until you begin climbing the Wheeler Flats Trail/Colorado Trail. (Be sure not to follow the Colorado Trail northeast to Frisco.)

This is an easy route following a well-traveled summer trail. Be sure to continue on a southeast course over the Tenmile Range. From the top of the pass, the trail descends the eastern side steeply and continues southeast across the slopes of Peak 9 and Peak 10. Once in the Crystal Creek drainage, the trail intercepts the Crystal Trail, then the Crystal Creek four-wheel-drive road. Follow this road to Francie's Cabin.

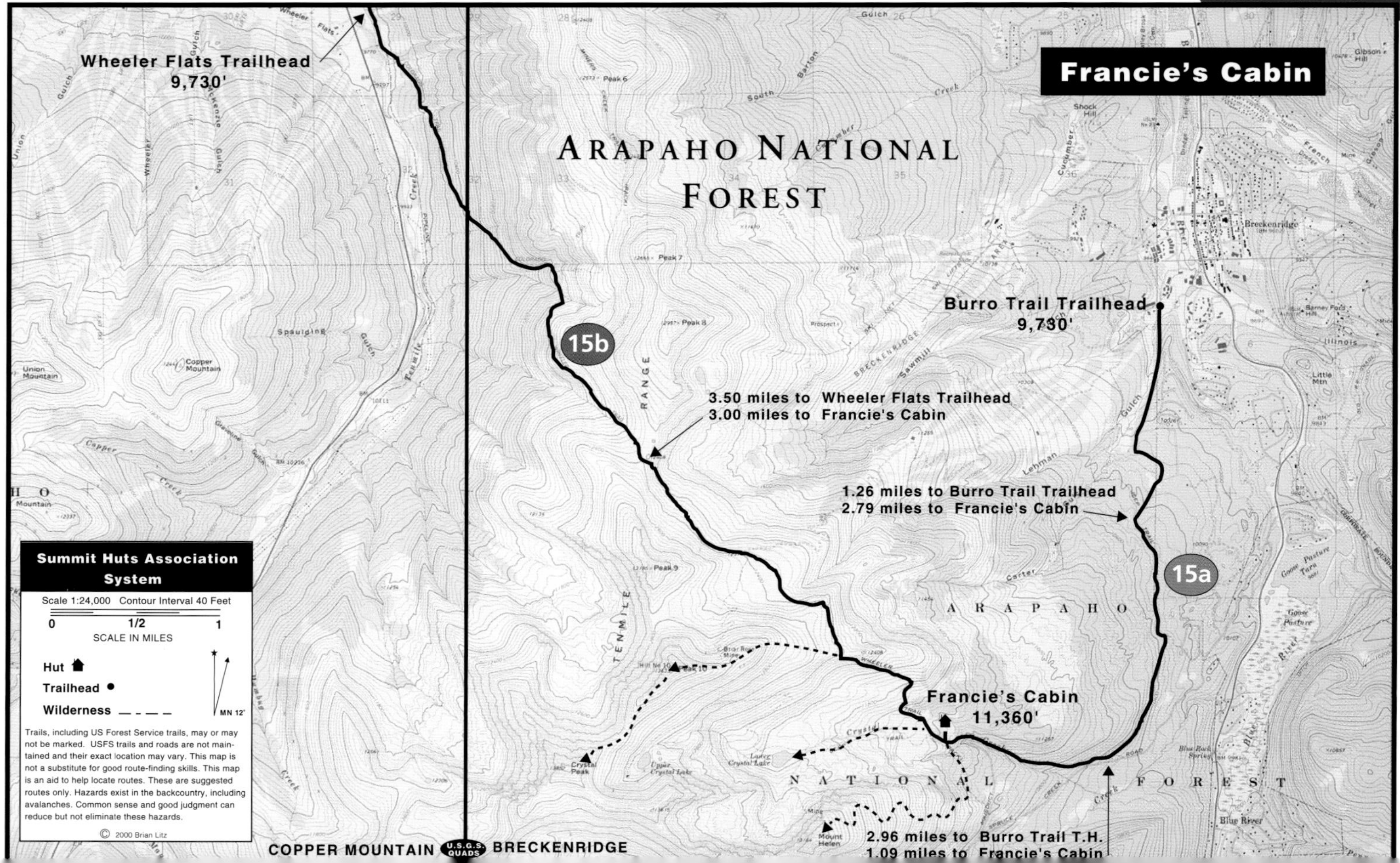

# Francie's Cabin

Wheeler Flats Trailhead
9,730'

ARAPAHO NATIONAL FOREST

Burro Trail Trailhead
9,730'

15b

3.50 miles to Wheeler Flats Trailhead
3.00 miles to Francie's Cabin

1.26 miles to Burro Trail Trailhead
2.79 miles to Francie's Cabin

15a

Francie's Cabin
11,360'

2.96 miles to Burro Trail T.H.
1.09 miles to Francie's Cabin

COPPER MOUNTAIN U.S.G.S. QUADS BRECKENRIDGE

**Summit Huts Association System**

Scale 1:24,000 Contour Interval 40 Feet

0 1/2 1
SCALE IN MILES

Hut
Trailhead
Wilderness

MN 12°

Trails, including US Forest Service trails, may or may not be marked. USFS trails and roads are not maintained and their exact location may vary. This map is not a substitute for good route-finding skills. This map is an aid to help locate routes. These are suggested routes only. Hazards exist in the backcountry, including avalanches. Common sense and good judgment can reduce but not eliminate these hazards.

# 16 Janet's Cabin

| | |
|---|---|
| **HUT ELEVATION** | 11,610' |
| **DATE BUILT** | 1990 |
| **SEASONS** | Thanksgiving through early May |
| **CAPACITY** | 20 |
| **HUT LAYOUT** | 2 bedrooms that sleep 6 each, and 2 bedrooms that sleep 4 each, all single beds |
| **HUT ESSENTIALS** | Woodstove for heat, propane cookstove, all kitchenware, photovoltaic electric lights |
| **OTHER GOODIES** | Sauna, indoor composting toilets |

Janet's Cabin is a memorial to Janet Boyd Tyler, a colorful fixture on the Colorado ski scene for many decades. The cabin is at the head of Guller Creek, adjacent to the Colorado Trail. This is one of the most popular backcountry huts in Colorado and may be crowded on weekends. Much of its popularity stems from the fact that the trailhead is a very short drive from the center of Summit County and not far from Vail and the Denver metro area.

The relatively short and uncomplicated tour to the hut also contributes to the popularity of Janet's Cabin; skiers of all abilities can ski to this hut. The hut's location allows intermediate and expert skiers access to the fine bowl skiing near Searle Pass and Sugarloaf Peak, an area used extensively for winter training by the U.S. Army's 10th Mountain Division ski troops during World War II.

This roomy structure is state-of-the-art and fully equipped to sleep 20 people. The main floor is huge and has couches and tables for several groups, as well as plenty of cooking space. Also located on the main floor are composting toilets, a ski/boot room, and a large south-facing deck. (The cabin cannot be accessed via the south deck, so skiers have to enter the cabin from the north entrance.) Upstairs are several large bedrooms. This luxurious hut even has a sauna; the Nancy Dayton Memorial Sauna was airlifted to the cabin in October 1991.

Janet's Cabin is not open for day use. Nor is it open in the summer, because of wildlife-habitat studies nearby. Make reservations through the 10th Mountain Division Hut Association (see Appendix A).

*The soft pastel colors of dawn paint the landscape above Janet's Cabin.*

Janet's Cabin

INTERMEDIATE

TOUR **16a**

## Union Creek Trailhead to Janet's Cabin

SEE MAP PAGES 98, 118–119, 124–125, AND 152–153

| | |
|---|---|
| TIME | 3 to 5 hours |
| DISTANCE | 4.6 miles |
| ELEVATIONS | TRAILHEAD: 9,820' CABIN: 11,610' GAIN/LOSS: +1,970'/-180' |
| AVALANCHE | Minimal danger |
| MAPS | 10th Mountain Division: Resolution Mountain<br>USGS 7.5': Copper Mountain, 1987<br>National Forest: Arapaho<br>Trails Illustrated: Map #108 (Vail/Frisco/Dillon); Map #109 (Breckenridge/Tennessee Pass) |

**TOUR OVERVIEW:** The Union Creek Trailhead is the most popular route to Janet's Cabin. It runs up the center of a long, almost treeless valley where navigation is easy and skiers will rarely need to break trail. But this route is a true backcountry trip to a high-altitude cabin, so don't let the high skier volume lull you into nonchalance. Be prepared, and get an early start.

The most confusing part of the trip is finding the parking area, getting to the shuttle buses, and finding your way out of the Copper Mountain ski area.

**DIRECTIONS TO TRAILHEAD:** Drive to the Copper Mountain Resort. Drive south on CO 91 past Copper's main entrance, then take the next right into Alpine Lot, formerly East Lot. As of press time, Copper Mountain was allowing Janet's Cabin guests to park in the northeast corner of Alpine Lot. This may change, so look for signs directing you to Janet's Cabin parking. Hop on a shuttle bus (buses run between 7 a.m. and 10 p.m.) and ride to the farthest stop west, Union Creek, which is at the Nordic center and shuttle-turnaround point. The route begins on the west side of the Nordic center building. *Note:* Please read parking information in your confirmation packet for the most current parking instructions—things can change!

**THE ROUTE:** Ascend the west edge of the ski area until you reach a public access trail that traverses into Guller Creek. This ascent can be accomplished by one of two methods: One option is to strap on your skins and climb a ski run named West Tenmile Trail (while dodging downhill skiers and keeping a sharp eye out for the trail entrance); the second and more popular choice is to present your hut-reservation slip (good for one complimentary ride) to either the ticket window or the lift operators and ride up Copper's K or L lift to the top. From the top of the lift, descend West Tenmile Trail for a few hundred feet to the access trail. The point of entry for the trail is marked with a blue diamond and a Forest

*Carrie Thompson and Dan Schaefer depart from Janet's Cabin.*

Service sign. Finding this trail is tricky because the entrance is in the forest on the west edge of the ski run, just below the top of the lifts; most skiers usually drop down too far.

Follow the Nordic trail into the woods on a steep drop, then along a traverse into the Guller Creek drainage. You will intersect the Colorado Trail/Guller Creek Trail at a point where the trail crosses Guller Creek. A sign reading "Vail Pass/Backcountry Uses in Winter," which used to mark the intersection, is now gone.

For the next 0.5 to 1 mile, the trail cruises up Guller Creek, first on the northwest side of the creek, then crossing to the southeast side midway through a large meadow. As you approach the head of the valley—marked by steep, forested slopes—begin a gradual ascent along the forest's edge. Continue along the southeast edge of the valley until you enter a distinct, treeless gully that climbs steeply south toward alpine peaks and bowls. Janet's Cabin, its roof visible to a sharp eye, is at the top of this gully on the right, hidden in a stand of trees.

*Dan Schaefer finds a late afternoon respite in Janet's Cabin.*

ADVANCED

TOUR

# 16b Vail Pass Trailhead to Janet's Cabin

SEE MAP PAGES 98, 118–119, 124–125, AND 152–153

| | |
|---|---|
| TIME | 4 to 7 hours |
| DISTANCE | 5.7 miles |
| ELEVATIONS | TRAILHEAD: 10,580' CABIN: 11,610' GAIN/LOSS: +1,300'/-200' |
| AVALANCHE | Route crosses avalanche runout zones; can be dangerous during high-hazard periods |
| MAPS | 10th Mountain Division: Resolution Mountain<br>USGS 7.5': Copper Mountain, 1987; Vail Pass, 1987<br>National Forest: Arapaho<br>Trails Illustrated: Map #108 (Vail/Frisco/Dillon); Map #109 (Breckenridge/Tennessee Pass) |

**TOUR OVERVIEW:** Decidedly more difficult than the standard Guller Creek Trail to Janet's Cabin, this less-traveled route is very enjoyable and scenic. The trail is a rolling, high-altitude traverse that gives skiers a taste of tree-line skiing as well as more challenging route-finding. Vail Pass also makes a nice trailhead for those wishing to ski to Janet's Cabin and exit via Guller Creek, which is part of the Janet's Cabin to Shrine Mountain Inn route (see Tour 16d).

**DIRECTIONS TO TRAILHEAD:** Drive on I-70 to the Vail Pass exit (Exit 190), 15 miles east of Vail or 5 miles west of Copper Mountain. From the exit, proceed west to the overnight parking area above the rest-stop building.

**THE ROUTE:** Begin the tour by walking down to the lowest part of the parking area. Ski south across West Tenmile Creek and begin a moderate traverse that contours south, then southwest down into Wilder Gulch. Cross Wilder Creek and begin the longest ascent of the tour by skiing southwest up the blunt northeast ridge at Elevation Point 12,207'. This ridge forms the southeast boundary of Wilder Gulch.

After gaining roughly 700 feet of elevation, the ridge begins to narrow noticeably near a shoulder. From here, the route leaves the ridge and begins to climb through the forest in generally the same direction below the steep southeast side of the ridge.

Make a dogleg around a subtle shoulder directly below Elevation Point 12,207'. The route then skirts the head of Stafford Creek. Cross over a low point (near tree line) on the westernmost part of the ridge that separates Guller Creek and Stafford Creek. Make the final gentle descent to Janet's Cabin. As you approach the cabin, continue to traverse directly toward the highest reaches of Guller Creek, just above tree line.

ADVANCED

TOUR

# 16c Janet's Cabin to Fowler/Hilliard Hut

SEE MAP PAGES 98, 118–119, 124–125, AND 152–153

| | |
|---|---|
| TIME | 4 to 6 hours |
| DISTANCE | 5.5 miles |
| ELEVATIONS | J CABIN: 11,610' F/H HUT: 11,500' GAIN/LOSS: +950'/-40' |
| AVALANCHE | Route crosses avalanche slopes; prone to skier-triggered avalanches during high-hazard periods |
| MAPS | 10th Mountain Division: Resolution Mountain<br>USGS 7.5': Copper Mountain, 1987; Vail Pass, 1987<br>National Forest: Arapaho<br>Trails Illustrated: Map #108 (Vail/Frisco/Dillon); Map #109 (Breckenridge/Tennessee Pass) |

**TOUR OVERVIEW:** Machine Gun Ridge runs north from Sugarloaf Peak. During World War II the 10th Mountain Division ski troops trained in this area. They fortified the ridge with a machine gun pit and sniper positions, and they often lived in makeshift shelters on the ridge. (For more information on the history of the 10th Mountain Division, see Appendix G, History).

Machine Gun Ridge is not an official 10th Mountain Division hut-to-hut trail, but it makes for a direct and spectacular route between Janet's Cabin and the Fowler/Hilliard Hut. Consider this route only when avalanche and weather conditions are stable. Strong beginner or intermediate skiers should be accompanied by skiers experienced in untracked, backcountry skiing.

**THE ROUTE:** From Janet's Cabin, follow the Vail Pass/Janet's Cabin route (see Tour 16b) west for a little over 0.5 mile. Then strike off due west, aiming for the 12,140-foot low spot north of Sugarloaf Peak. There are several dangerous slopes on the eastern aspect of this ridge, but there is a series of small benches that access the pass. To find them, ski directly toward the low spot, which forms a subtle, low-angle ramp up to the pass.

Once on the pass, follow the ridge north, over Elevation Point 12,293' and across a flat saddle, then begin climbing toward Elevation Point 12,370'. Contour west about 200 feet below the top of Elevation Point 12,370'. Begin a descending traverse to the road, switchbacking below the south side of Ptarmigan Pass. Once on the road, descend west until you can turn onto the main Resolution Creek Road (Forest Road 751). Begin climbing this road, contouring around the south face of Ptarmigan Hill. Follow the road for 2 miles to the forested pass east of the hut, where the road intersects with the Shrine Mountain Inn Trail from the north. From the wooded pass, follow a trail along the ridge to the southwest, past a gate and over a small knoll to the Fowler/Hilliard Hut.

ADVANCED

TOUR

# 16d Janet's Cabin to Shrine Mountain Inn

SEE MAP PAGES 98, 118–119, 124–125, AND 152–153

| | |
|---|---|
| TIME | 5 to 8 hours |
| DISTANCE | 8.4 miles |
| ELEVATIONS | J CABIN: 11,610' SM INN: 11,209' GAIN/LOSS: +829'/-1,320' |
| AVALANCHE | Route crosses avalanche runout zones; can be dangerous during high-hazard periods |
| MAPS | 10th Mountain Division: Resolution Mountain<br>USGS 7.5': Copper Mountain, 1987; Vail Pass, 1987<br>National Forest: Arapaho<br>Trails Illustrated: Map #108 (Vail/Frisco/Dillon); Map #109 (Breckenridge/Tennessee Pass) |

**TOUR OVERVIEW:** Skiing between these two huts makes for a long day; be sure to get an early start. The route combines Tour 16b (Vail Pass Trailhead to Janet's Cabin) and Tour 18a (Vail Pass Trailhead to Shrine Mountain Inn). Refer to those tours for complete descriptions.

*Gore Range as viewed from above Janet's Cabin.*

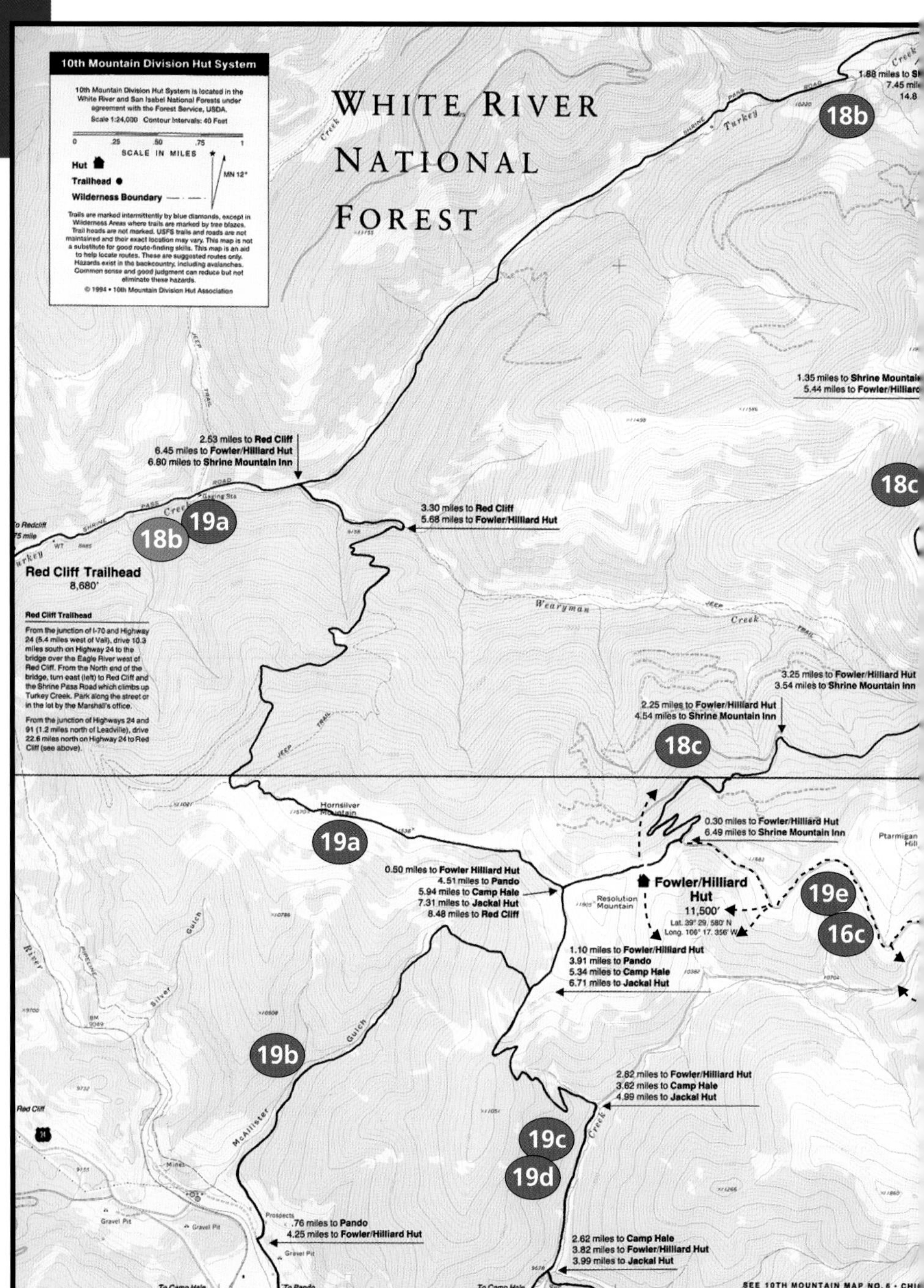
10th Mountain Division Hut System
10th Mountain Division Hut System is located in the White River and San Isabel National Forests under agreement with the Forest Service, USDA.
Scale 1:24,000 Contour Intervals: 40 Feet
0 .25 .50 .75 1
SCALE IN MILES
MN 12°
Hut
Trailhead
Wilderness Boundary
Trails are marked intermittently by blue diamonds, except in Wilderness Areas where trails are marked by tree blazes. Trail heads are not marked. USFS trails and roads are not maintained and their exact location may vary. This map is not a substitute for good route-finding skills. This map is an aid to help locate routes. These are suggested routes only. Hazards exist in the backcountry, including avalanches. Common sense and good judgment can reduce but not eliminate these hazards.
© 1994 • 10th Mountain Division Hut Association
WHITE RIVER NATIONAL FOREST
18b
1.88 miles to Sh
7.45 mile
14.8
18c
1.35 miles to Shrine Mountain
5.44 miles to Fowler/Hilliard
2.53 miles to Red Cliff
6.45 miles to Fowler/Hilliard Hut
6.80 miles to Shrine Mountain Inn
3.30 miles to Red Cliff
5.68 miles to Fowler/Hilliard Hut
19a
18b
To Redcliff
.75 mile
Red Cliff Trailhead
8,680'
Red Cliff Trailhead
From the junction of I-70 and Highway 24 (5.4 miles west of Vail), drive 10.3 miles south on Highway 24 to the bridge over the Eagle River west of Red Cliff. From the North end of the bridge, turn east (left) to Red Cliff and the Shrine Pass Road which climbs up Turkey Creek. Park along the street or in the lot by the Marshall's office.
From the junction of Highways 24 and 91 (1.2 miles north of Leadville), drive 22.6 miles north on Highway 24 to Red Cliff (see above).
Wearyman Creek
3.25 miles to Fowler/Hilliard Hut
3.54 miles to Shrine Mountain Inn
2.25 miles to Fowler/Hilliard Hut
4.54 miles to Shrine Mountain Inn
18c
Hornsilver Mountain
19a
0.30 miles to Fowler/Hilliard Hut
6.49 miles to Shrine Mountain Inn
Ptarmigan Hill
0.50 miles to Fowler Hilliard Hut
4.51 miles to Pando
5.94 miles to Camp Hale
7.31 miles to Jackal Hut
8.48 miles to Red Cliff
Resolution Mountain
Fowler/Hilliard Hut
11,500'
Lat. 39° 29.580' N
Long. 106° 17.356' W
19e
16c
1.10 miles to Fowler/Hilliard Hut
3.91 miles to Pando
5.34 miles to Camp Hale
6.71 miles to Jackal Hut
Silver Gulch
19b
McAllister Gulch
Red Cliff
2.82 miles to Fowler/Hilliard Hut
3.62 miles to Camp Hale
4.99 miles to Jackal Hut
19c
19d
Creek
.76 miles to Pando
4.25 miles to Fowler/Hilliard Hut
Gravel Pit
2.62 miles to Camp Hale
3.82 miles to Fowler/Hilliard Hut
3.99 miles to Jackal Hut
To Camp Hale
To Pando
To Camp Hale
SEE 10TH MOUNTAIN MAP NO. 8 • CHI

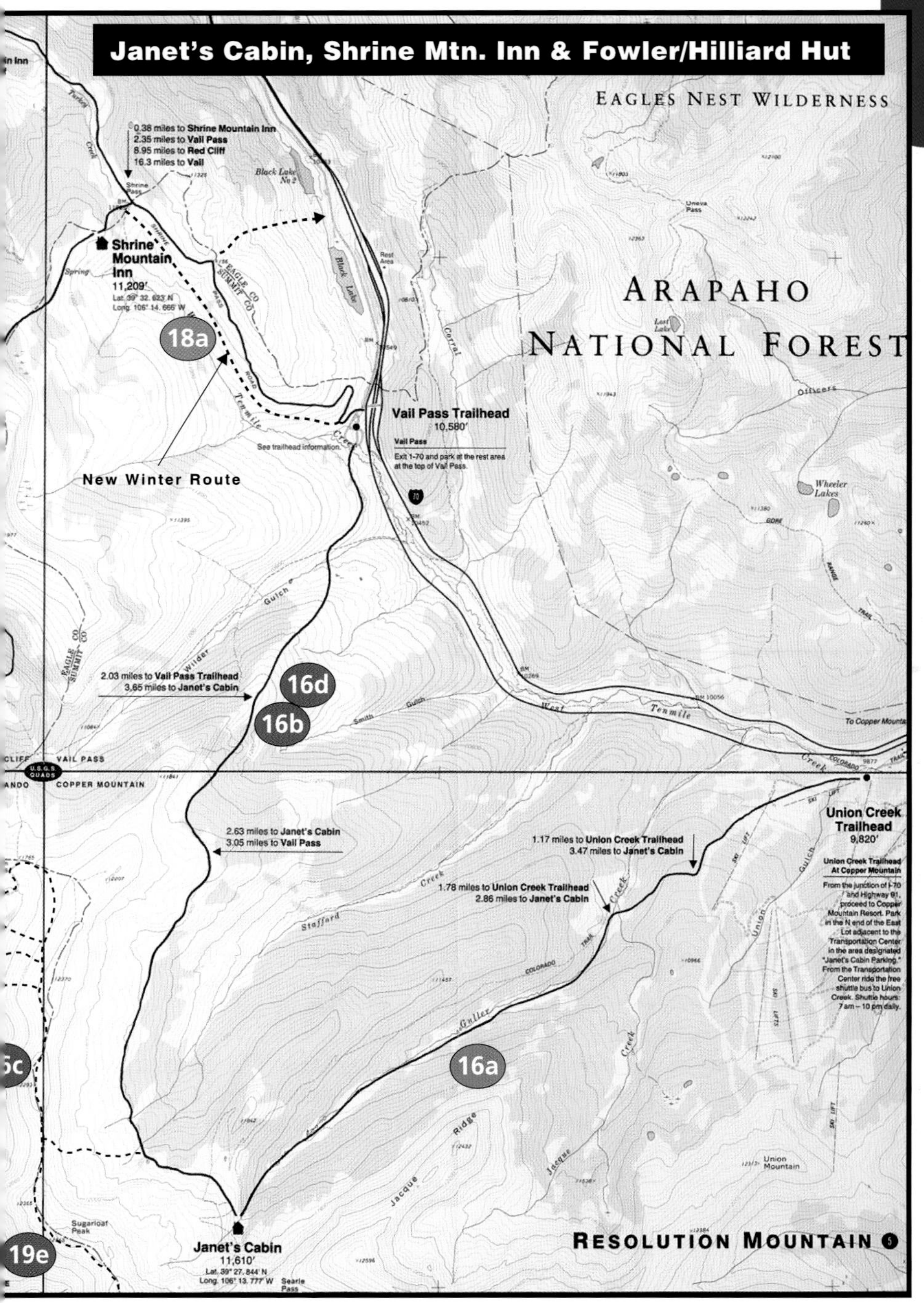
Janet's Cabin, Shrine Mtn. Inn & Fowler/Hilliard Hut
EAGLES NEST WILDERNESS
ARAPAHO NATIONAL FOREST
0.38 miles to Shrine Mountain Inn
2.35 miles to Vail Pass
8.95 miles to Red Cliff
16.3 miles to Vail
Shrine Mountain Inn
11,209'
Lat. 39° 32. 623' N
Long. 106° 14. 666' W
18a
New Winter Route
Vail Pass Trailhead
10,580'
Vail Pass
Exit 1-70 and park at the rest area at the top of Vail Pass.
See trailhead information.
Black Lake No 2
Black Lake
Tenmile Creek
Wheeler Lakes
2.03 miles to Vail Pass Trailhead
3.65 miles to Janet's Cabin
16d
16b
West Tenmile Creek
To Copper Mountain
VAIL PASS
COPPER MOUNTAIN
2.63 miles to Janet's Cabin
3.05 miles to Vail Pass
1.17 miles to Union Creek Trailhead
3.47 miles to Janet's Cabin
1.78 miles to Union Creek Trailhead
2.86 miles to Janet's Cabin
Union Creek Trailhead
9,820'
Union Creek Trailhead At Copper Mountain
From the junction of I-70 and Highway 91, proceed to Copper Mountain Resort. Park in the N end of the East Lot adjacent to the Transportation Center in the area designated "Janet's Cabin Parking." From the Transportation Center ride the free shuttle bus to Union Creek. Shuttle hours: 7 am – 10 pm daily.
16a
Stafford Creek
Guller
Jacque Ridge
Union Mountain
Sugarloaf Peak
Janet's Cabin
11,610'
Lat. 39° 27. 844' N
Long. 106° 13. 777' W
Searle Pass
19e
RESOLUTION MOUNTAIN

# 10th Mountain Division Hut Association

The 10th Mountain Division huts have become synonymous with the finest that backcountry hut skiing has to offer. Situated between the mountain communities of Aspen, Vail, and Leadville, the 10th Mountain Division hut-to-hut system is the most extensive backcountry hut system in the United States. In fact, the 10th Mountain Division huts are so well-known that it is nearly impossible to open an outdoor magazine and not find a reference to them.

The hut system is named in honor of the soldiers of the U.S. Army's 10th Mountain Division, an elite ski corps commissioned during World War II for duty in the European Alps. For three winters, from 1942 until 1945, some 14,000 soldiers were based at Camp Hale, the division's training center north of Leadville. Wearing 7-foot-long skis and 90-pound packs and camouflaged in winter whites, these "phantoms of the snow" roamed throughout the mountains on maneuvers in the Gore and Sawatch Ranges. On windswept ridges in temperatures far below zero, they engaged in military exercises and mock warfare as they trained for combat against the Nazis.

When the war ended, a number of men returned to the mountains they had come to know so well, and many of these veterans became the moving forces behind the Colorado ski industry. Today, little remains of Camp Hale, just the concrete foundations of old army barracks and facilities. But the memory and the spirit of the 10th Mountain Division soldiers live on. For those interested in more information on the history of the 10th Mountain Division, refer to *Ski the High Trail: World War II Ski Troopers in the High Colorado Rockies,* the memoirs of Private Harris Dusenbery (see Appendix G, History).

The first hut in this system was built in 1982. Today there are 20 huts (13 owned by the 10th Mountain Division Hut Association and 7 owned by private groups) and several hundred miles of trails providing a wide array of skiing, hiking, and mountain biking adventures for backcountry enthusiasts of every ability and temperament. The 10th Mountain Division Hut Association located the huts so that nearly all are accessible to intermediate-level skiers. Many hut routes are also within the abilities of novice skiers, while a few are reached only via strenuous or technically demanding trails. Avalanche hazards do exist, but most routes were planned to avoid the most threatening slopes.

The majority of the trails linking the 10th Mountain Division huts are classic cross-country tours through dense evergreen forests. The hut association envisioned a comprehensive series of trail markers (blue diamonds) along the most popular routes. However, it is impossible—and unnecessary—to staple markers to each and every tree. Indeed, the trails often pass through meadows and above tree line, as well as through federally designated Wilderness Areas, where it is illegal to mark trails permanently.

Each individual participating in a trip to 10th Mountain Division huts must be prepared for serious backcountry travel, must understand basic route-finding and map and compass reading, and must have at least a rudimentary knowledge of avalanche hazards and rescue protocol. Anticipating a warm shelter

*Doug Seyb skis on the High Traverse between the Fowler/Hilliard Hut and the Jackal Hut.*

at the end of the trail, too many wilderness skiers travel imprudently and ill prepared. Several well-qualified guide services offer a variety of trips throughout the year. If you are new to the backcountry, consider hiring a guide for a satisfying and safe wilderness experience.

Remember that this is a communal living experience and you will probably be sharing your hut with other skiers, hikers, or bikers. If your group is uncomfortable with this reality, consider getting a large group together to rent an entire hut or going to a different hut system with smaller huts.

The 10th Mountain Division huts are open during the winter and summer months but not during spring or late fall. The exception is McNamara Hut, which is closed during the summer.

*A word on trailhead parking:* Over the past few years, there has been increasing vandalism to cars parked at the trailheads, especially the South Camp Hale Trailhead, Crane Park, Turquoise Lake, and the summer Skinner Hut Trailhead on the south side of Turquoise Lake. The Turquoise Lake parking area has now been moved 2 miles back down the road to a location just east of the Arkansas River/Tennessee Creek and the Denver & Rio Grande Western Railroad tracks. This parking lot is more open, lighted, and on the sheriff's patrol route. Nevertheless, do not leave valuables in your car and, if possible, do not leave expensive cars at the lots mentioned above.

Skiers visiting the western 10th Mountain Division huts have used the Diamond J Ranch for years, as a parking/jumping-off point for trips in the Upper Fryingpan area. The guest cabins and rooms of the ranch are also commonly used as a layover spot when connecting Margy's Hut to the Betty Bear or Harry Gates Huts. This is because no convenient 10th Mountain hut is situated centrally between any of these three huts.

After a brief hiatus, the Diamond J is operating business-as-usual once again. It offers not only lodging but also homestyle meals and shuttle service for one-way trips. The Diamond J can be contacted at the number listed in Appendix A.

In addition, there is a bed-and-breakfast downriver, at Meredith, called the Double Diamond, which in recent years has been offering similar services. The Double Diamond may be contacted at the number listed in Appendix A.

**RESERVATION NOTE:** During the spring of 1999, a new reservation lottery system was instituted and seems to be working successfully. Interested parties now must submit a lottery form that allows them to request up to 10 trips. Forms are pulled at random on March 1 for the following season. Weekends, full moons, and holidays go first. After the lottery, any remaining nights are available on a first-come, first-served basis.

The 10th Mountain Division website (www.huts.org) has an exhaustive, frequently updated "hut availability" page, which indicates vacancies. Remember that huts closer to Summit County, Vail, and Denver are the most popular, and those closer to Aspen tend to have more spaces available later in the reservation season. The 10th Mountain Division website also provides a page for swapping and selling reservations. Also note that payment is due at the time reservations are made. For reservations, call the 10th Mountain Division Hut Association (see Appendix A).

KELTY

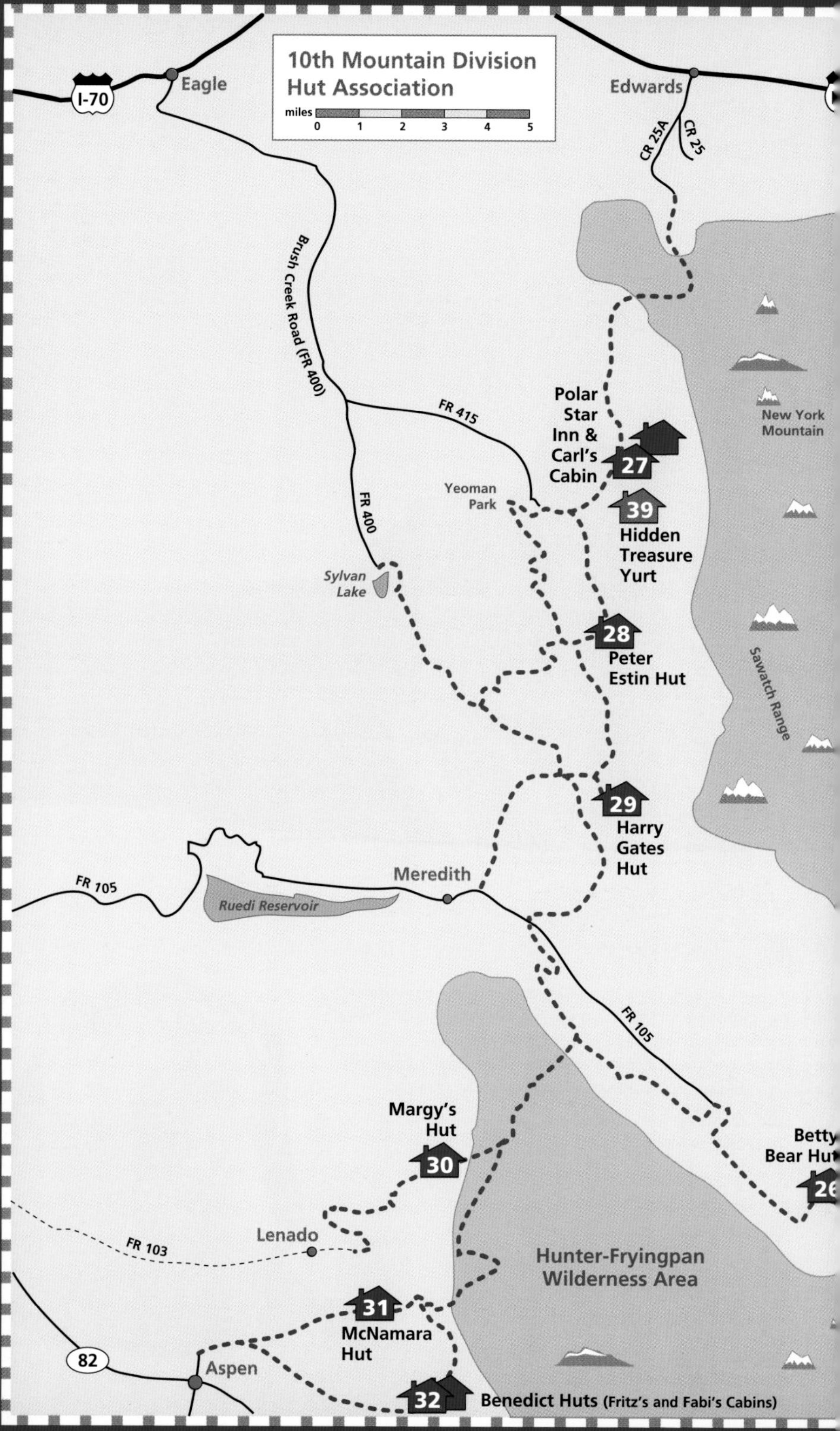

## 10th Mountain Division Hut Association

miles 0 1 2 3 4 5

to Glenwood Springs

I-70

Eagle

Edwards

CR 25A

CR 25

Brush Creek Road (FR 400)

FR 415

Polar Star Inn & Carl's Cabin

27

New York Mountain

Yeoman Park

FR 400

39

Hidden Treasure Yurt

Sylvan Lake

28

Peter Estin Hut

Sawatch Range

29

Harry Gates Hut

to Basalt & CO 82

FR 105

Ruedi Reservoir

Meredith

FR 105

Margy's Hut

30

Betty Bear Hut

26

to Woody Creek

FR 103

Lenado

Hunter-Fryingpan Wilderness Area

31

McNamara Hut

to Basalt

82

Aspen

32

Benedict Huts (Fritz's and Fabi's Cabins)

17 Eiseman Hut
Vail
Beaver Creek
er Creek
Area
Minturn
Vail Ski Area
Eagle's Nest
Wilderness Area
Gore Range
24
Vail
Pass
18
Shrine
Mtn. Inn
(Jay's, Chuck's,
and Walter's
Cabins)
Red Cliff
19
Fowler/
Hilliard Hut
16
Janet's
Cabin
Copper
Mtn. Ski
Area
to Dillon
to I-70
Holy Cross
Wilderness Area
ount of the
ly Cross
20
Jackal
Hut
FR 703
Vance's
Cabin
21
10th Mtn.
Div. Hut
23
estake
ervoir
Homestake
Peak
Ski Cooper
Tennessee
Pass
Climax Mine
24
Sangree M.
Froelicher Hut
22
91
24
Uncle
Bud's Hut
Skinner
Hut
25
Turquoise Lake
rman
FR 105
Leadville
Mount Massive
Wilderness Area
Mt. Massive
N
to Buena Vista

# 17 Eiseman Hut

| | |
|---|---|
| **HUT ELEVATION** | 11,180' |
| **DATE BUILT** | 1996 |
| **SEASONS** | Thanksgiving through April 30 (winter);<br>July 1 through September 30 (summer) |
| **CAPACITY** | 16 |
| **HUT LAYOUT** | 2 bedrooms with double beds, 12 single beds in communal sleeping area |
| **HUT ESSENTIALS** | Woodstove for heat, wood-burning cookstove with oven, propane cookstoves, all kitchenware, outhouse, photovoltaic electric lights |

*Jordan Campbell and Tyler Moore enjoy the superb ski terrain and expansive views of the Gore Range from the popular Eiseman Hut.*

The Eiseman Hut is notched into the crest of a towering ridge on the west side of the Gore Range. This stand-alone shelter, the only 10th Mountain Division hut north of Vail and I-70, has quickly become one of the most popular huts in the system—especially with stronger skiers and those who place a premium on cranking turns. In addition to the great local skiing, there are views of Mount of the Holy Cross, Vail ski area, and the high peaks of the Eagles Nest Wilderness. Put on your skis in front of the hut and dangle the tips over the inviting glades that drop for many hundreds of feet directly below the hut, and you'll quickly come to understand the allure of the Eiseman Hut.

Strong beginning skiers certainly can and do visit the hut, but this is not a beginner's hut. Experienced intermediates and experts will get the most out of a visit to the area. The Eiseman is a one-story ranch-style hut with large panoramic windows and an airy, open feel inside. It was built as a memorial to Dr. Ben Eiseman, a longtime supporter of the 10th Mountain Division system.

**RECOMMENDED DAY TRIPS:**

**All one has to do is stumble out the front door to find some of the best ski slopes near any 10th Mountain Division hut.** Let gravity pull you downward for hours of sweet turns, and use skins to lay tracks back up, following the old logging roads. For an adventurous little trip, climb east of the hut along the narrowing ridgetop. Pass an exposed section with drop-offs to the south by down-climbing along the northern edge of the ridge-crest—being mindful of potential avalanche conditions—to a small saddle. Either scramble straight up the ridge to Elevation Point 11,770' or descend north from the saddle (again being very careful about avalanche hazards) and traverse north across the west aspect of Elevation Point 11,770'; make a final climb up the more moderate north ridge to the same summit. The western flanks of this northern ridge harbor nice, steep glades. Additionally, there are several chutes and slopes that drop directly north off the ridge east of the hut that can be excellent, though steep. Extreme caution should be exercised in this area.

More adventurous peak baggers can continue east beyond Elevation Point 11,770' to the ridges and peaks along the western edge of the Wilderness Area. And finally, the less reckless can drop down the slopes north of the hut and explore the upper reaches of the south fork of Red Sandstone Creek.

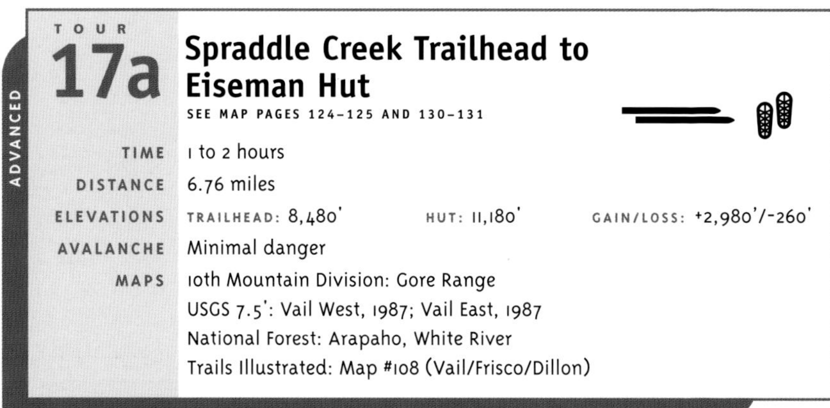

ADVANCED

TOUR **17a**

## Spraddle Creek Trailhead to Eiseman Hut

SEE MAP PAGES 124–125 AND 130–131

| | |
|---|---|
| TIME | 1 to 2 hours |
| DISTANCE | 6.76 miles |
| ELEVATIONS | TRAILHEAD: 8,480' HUT: 11,180' GAIN/LOSS: +2,980'/-260' |
| AVALANCHE | Minimal danger |
| MAPS | 10th Mountain Division: Gore Range<br>USGS 7.5': Vail West, 1987; Vail East, 1987<br>National Forest: Arapaho, White River<br>Trails Illustrated: Map #108 (Vail/Frisco/Dillon) |

**TOUR OVERVIEW:** The two routes to the Eiseman Hut are very different. The Red Sandstone route follows Forest Service and logging roads, and Spraddle Creek follows a trail steeply up through several creek drainages, forests, and clearings. The Spraddle Creek trail can surprise skiers with its nearly 3,000 feet of elevation gain. Although the trail climbs steadily throughout its length, the final blast out of the head of Middle Creek frequently pushes skiers to the limit after a long day. Get an early start.

Also, remember that this route has a sunny, southern exposure, so it can have sections of crusty, sun-baked snow. Consider heading down from the hut via the Red Sandstone route for less technical downhill skiing and better, colder snow on your return. A car shuttle is required if you ascend one of the routes and descend the other.

**DIRECTIONS TO TRAILHEAD:** Drive on I-70 to the main exit into central Vail (Exit 176). Once you are off I-70 and on the north side of the intersection, take the frontage road that heads east along the north side of the interstate. This road is marked with a sign for Spraddle Creek Road. There are two parking areas for the Spraddle Creek Trail. The first is a secondary Forest Service access parking area on the left side of Spraddle Creek Road down low at 0.1 mile. The second, main parking area is farther up the road and closer to the trailhead. Drive 0.75 mile to the gate at Spraddle Creek Estates. Turn right immediately before the gate and drive another 0.1 mile to the parking area. It may be necessary to leave some cars below and shuttle gear and people up to the trailhead.

**THE ROUTE:** Ski up the Spraddle Creek Road. At 1.81 miles the trail veers off the road to the north, switchbacks across the creek, and begins a traversing ascent back west/southwest until entering a clearing atop the crest of the ridge that forms the eastern slopes of Middle Creek. Keep an eye out for the trail, which may be obscured here. Round the crest of the ridge and begin the gentle traversing descent into the Middle Creek drainage.

From here the trail works its way steadily up the valley as it swings to the east. Initially, the trail is on the righthand (eastern) side of the creek, then it's on the left (west and north), and finally, for a short stretch as you near the upper end of the valley, it's back on the righthand side (south). You will begin to see the higher, treeless slopes of Bald Mountain and the Gore Range above. So far, so good.

The final climb to the hut is a deceptive stretch that is nearly 2 miles long and gains roughly 750 feet. Cross the creek and head north up onto the steeper slopes. A series of steep switchbacks deposits you just below the hut, on top of the ridge. Work your way up to the right (northeast) to the hut.

*Jordan Campbell, David Harrower, and John Meyer ascend a ridge east of the Eiseman Hut with the central Gore Range behind.*

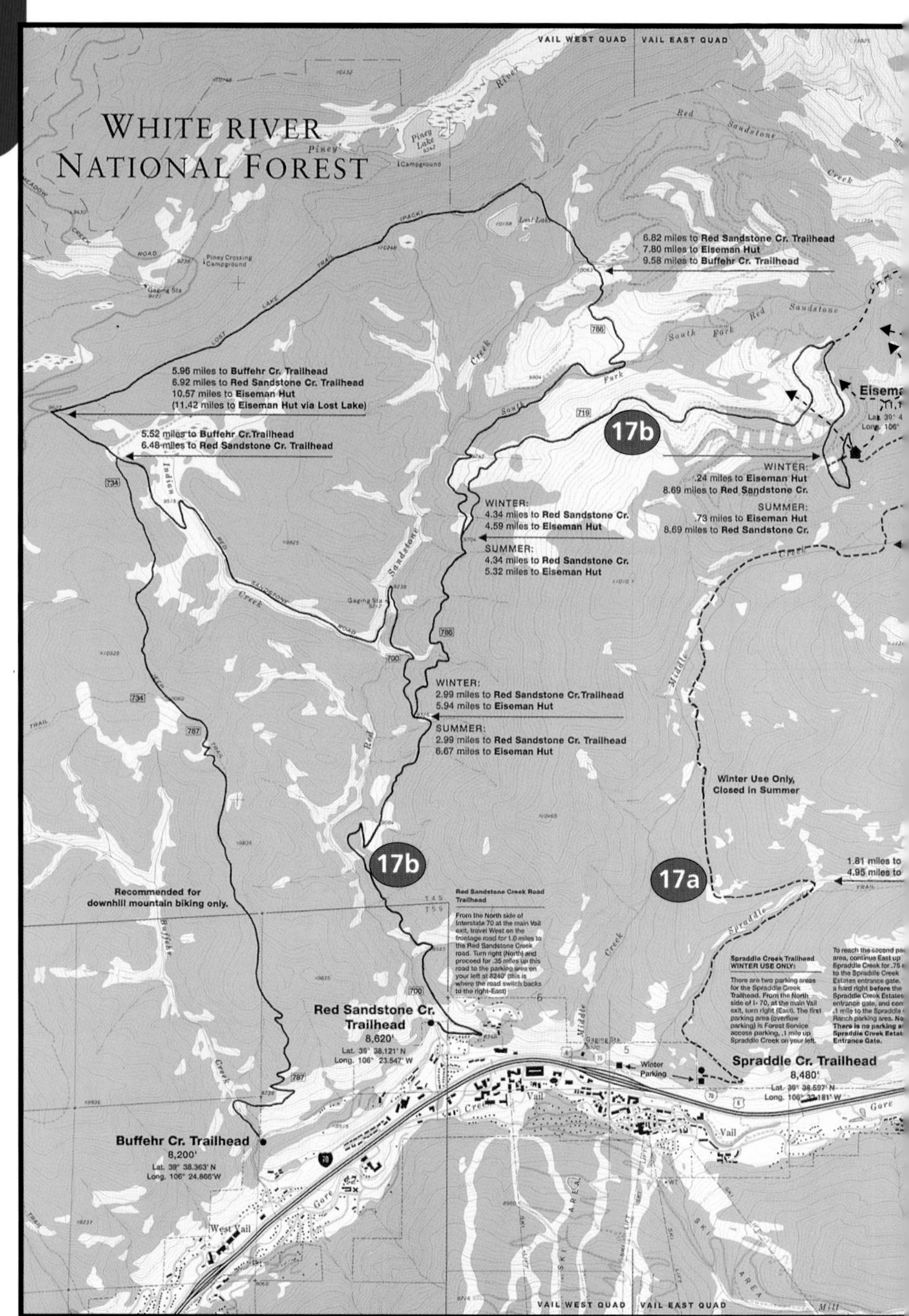

VAIL WEST QUAD
VAIL EAST QUAD
WHITE RIVER
NATIONAL FOREST
Piney Lake
Campground
Piney Crossing Campground
Gaging Sta.
Lost Lake
Red Sandstone Creek
South Fork Red Sandstone
6.82 miles to Red Sandstone Cr. Trailhead
7.80 miles to Eiseman Hut
9.58 miles to Buffehr Cr. Trailhead
5.96 miles to Buffehr Cr. Trailhead
6.92 miles to Red Sandstone Cr. Trailhead
10.57 miles to Eiseman Hut
(11.42 miles to Eiseman Hut via Lost Lake)
5.52 miles to Buffehr Cr.Trailhead
6.48 miles to Red Sandstone Cr. Trailhead
17b
WINTER:
.24 miles to Eiseman Hut
8.69 miles to Red Sandstone Cr.
SUMMER:
.73 miles to Eiseman Hut
8.69 miles to Red Sandstone Cr.
WINTER:
4.34 miles to Red Sandstone Cr.
4.59 miles to Eiseman Hut
SUMMER:
4.34 miles to Red Sandstone Cr.
5.32 miles to Eiseman Hut
WINTER:
2.99 miles to Red Sandstone Cr.Trailhead
5.94 miles to Eiseman Hut
SUMMER:
2.99 miles to Red Sandstone Cr. Trailhead
6.67 miles to Eiseman Hut
Winter Use Only,
Closed in Summer
17b
17a
1.81 miles to
4.95 miles to
Recommended for
downhill mountain biking only.
Red Sandstone Creek Road Trailhead
From the North side of Interstate 70 at the main Vail exit, travel West on the frontage road for 1.0 miles to the Red Sandstone Creek road. Turn right (North) and proceed for .35 miles up this road to the parking area on your left at 8240' (this is where the road switch backs to the right-East)
Spraddle Creek Trailhead WINTER USE ONLY:
There are two parking areas for the Spraddle Creek Trailhead. From the North side of I- 70, at the main Vail exit, turn right (East). The first parking area (overflow parking) is Forest Service access parking, .1 mile up Spraddle Creek on your left.
To reach the second pa
area, continue East up
Spraddle Creek for .75
to the Spraddle Creek
Estates entrance gate.
a hard right before the
Spraddle Creek Estates
entrance gate, and con
.1 mile to the Spraddle
Ranch parking area. No
There is no parking a
Spraddle Creek Estat
Entrance Gate.
Red Sandstone Cr.
Trailhead
8,620'
Lat. 39° 38.121' N
Long. 106° 23.547' W
Winter Parking
Spraddle Cr. Trailhead
8,480'
Lat. 39° 38.597' N
Buffehr Cr. Trailhead
8,200'
Lat. 39° 38.363' N
Long. 106° 24.866' W
Vail
West Vail
Gore Creek
Buffehr Creek
Middle Creek
SKI AREA

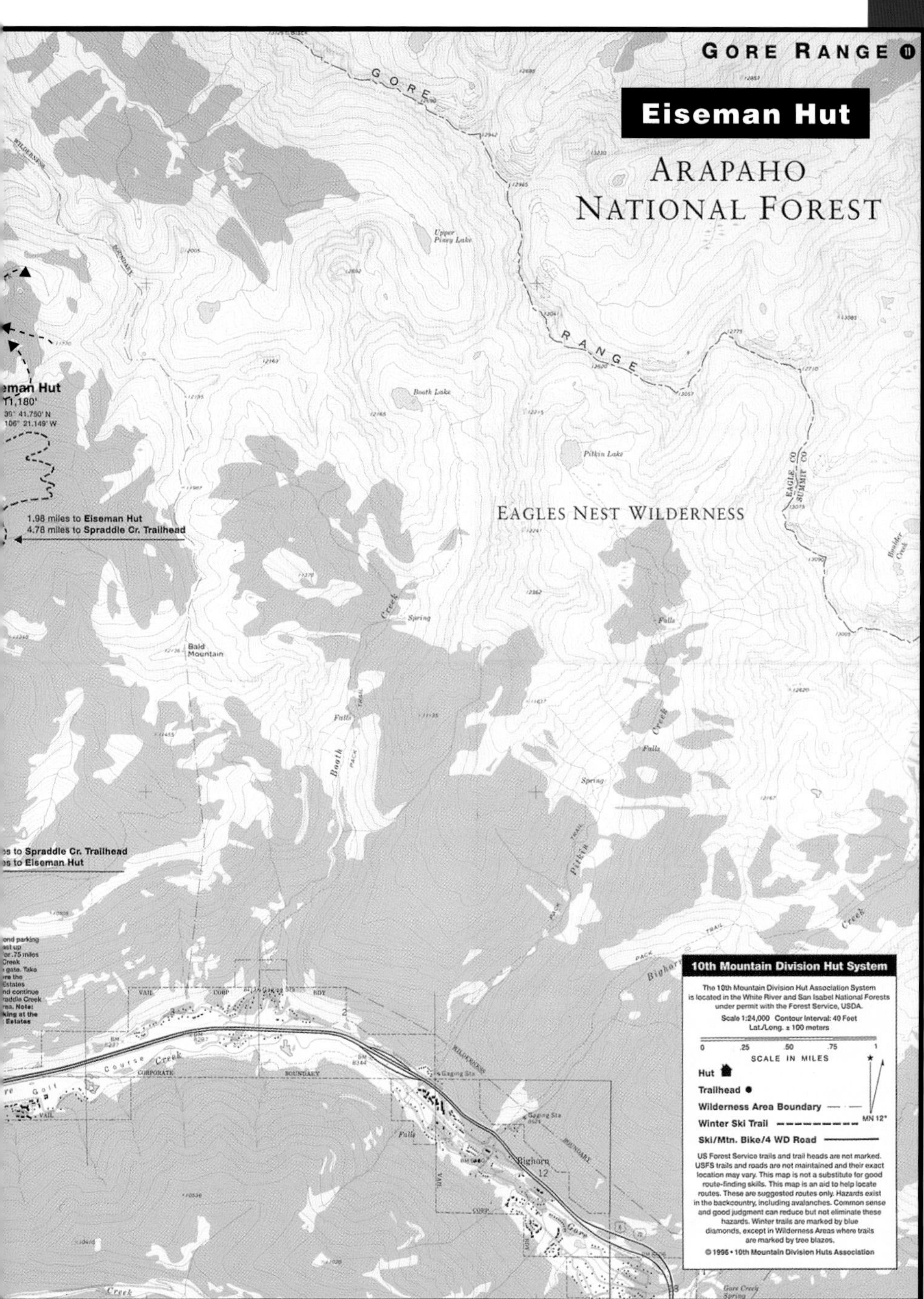
GORE RANGE 11
Eiseman Hut
ARAPAHO NATIONAL FOREST
EAGLES NEST WILDERNESS
GORE RANGE
Upper Piney Lake
Booth Lake
Pitkin Lake
Bald Mountain
Booth Creek
Pitkin
Spring
Falls
EAGLE CO
SUMMIT CO
Boulder Creek
Bighorn Creek
Bighorn
Gore Creek
Gore Creek Spring
Gaging Sta
WILDERNESS BOUNDARY
VAIL CORPORATE BOUNDARY
eman Hut
11,180'
1.98 miles to Eiseman Hut
4.78 miles to Spraddle Cr. Trailhead
s to Spraddle Cr. Trailhead
s to Eiseman Hut
10th Mountain Division Hut System
The 10th Mountain Division Hut Association System is located in the White River and San Isabel National Forests under permit with the Forest Service, USDA.
Scale 1:24,000 Contour Interval: 40 Feet
Lat./Long. ± 100 meters
0 .25 .50 .75 1
SCALE IN MILES
MN 12°
Hut
Trailhead
Wilderness Area Boundary
Winter Ski Trail
Ski/Mtn. Bike/4 WD Road
US Forest Service trails and trail heads are not marked. USFS trails and roads are not maintained and their exact location may vary. This map is not a substitute for good route-finding skills. This map is an aid to help locate routes. These are suggested routes only. Hazards exist in the backcountry, including avalanches. Common sense and good judgment can reduce but not eliminate these hazards. Winter trails are marked by blue diamonds, except in Wilderness Areas where trails are marked by tree blazes.
© 1996 • 10th Mountain Division Huts Association

ADVANCED

TOUR

# 17b Red Sandstone Creek Trailhead to Eiseman Hut

SEE MAP PAGES 124–125 AND 130–131

TIME 6 to 9 hours

DISTANCE 8.93 miles

ELEVATIONS TRAILHEAD: 8,620′ HUT: 11,180′ GAIN: +2,980′

AVALANCHE Minimal danger

MAPS 10th Mountain Division: Gore Range
USGS 7.5′: Vail West, 1987; Vail East, 1987
National Forest: Arapaho, White River
Trails Illustrated: Map #108 (Vail/Frisco/Dillon)

**TOUR OVERVIEW:** Red Sandstone Creek Road is the longer but less technical and less demanding path to the Eiseman Hut. If you are carrying big loads, are not super strong, or are on waxable touring skis, consider this trail. This route can also be a better alternative for returning to civilization. Much of its upper portions are on north-facing terrain and can have better skiing conditions than the lower stretches, which, though south-facing, are wide and easy to tour and snowplow down. Also note that at times snowmobiles and snowcats travel this road. This means it is often packed and may offer a less "wild" experience than Spraddle Creek.

**DIRECTIONS TO TRAILHEAD:** Drive on I-70 to the main exit for central Vail (Exit 176). Take the north frontage road west for 1 mile to the Red Sandstone Creek Road. Turn onto this road and drive 0.35 mile to the recommended parking area on the left. From here you will have to walk up the road through the houses to the point where the summer dirt road veers off to the west/northwest. This intersection is marked. There is some parking closer to the point where the roads split, but it is not always usable.

**THE ROUTE:** Begin the plod up Red Sandstone Creek (Forest Road 700), using wax or skins. Remain on the road for 3 miles until you reach a major intersection with another road (Forest Road 786), which comes in from the right (north/northeast) at 9,325 feet. Take the right fork and ski another 1.34 miles to yet another intersection. Take the right fork (northeast again) onto Forest Road 719. This road leads east up into the South Fork of Red Sandstone Creek and the nearby timber-logging areas. Ski along this road for several miles.

Throughout this stretch of the route, the key is to not be led astray by any of the many clear-cuts and logging trails you'll encounter; keep a map, compass, and altimeter handy. It is also important not to miss the major switchback that wraps to the south for the final ascent to the saddle below the hut—if you are in a Zen state and miss the turn, you can end up far in the head of the drainage.

Once you have passed through the switchback at roughly 10,740 feet, climb up to the saddle, where you can fashion a route up the ridge-crest to the northeast and on to the hut.

If you are heading out by this route, you can ski a beeline directly down from the hut to the lower logging road. Just make sure you don't drop too far.

# 18 Shrine Mountain Inn (Jay's, Chuck's, and Walter's Cabins)

| JAY'S CABIN | |
|---|---|
| HUT ELEVATION | 11,209' |
| DATE BUILT | 1987 |
| SEASONS | Year-round |
| CAPACITY | 12 |
| HUT LAYOUT | 1 room with double bed, 1 room with 2 singles, 1 single in hall upstairs; 1 room with queen bed on main floor; 5 single beds in communal area downstairs |
| HUT ESSENTIALS | Woodstove for heat, propane cookstove and oven, all kitchenware, indoor flush toilets, tub and shower, generator-powered electric lights |
| OTHER GOODIES | Communal sauna, hot and cold running water |

| CHUCK'S CABIN | |
|---|---|
| HUT ELEVATION | 11,209' |
| DATE BUILT | 1988 |
| SEASONS | Year-round |
| CAPACITY | 12 (6 upstairs and 6 down) |
| HUT LAYOUT | 1 room with queen bed, 1 room with 2 singles, 2 couch-beds in main room upstairs; 1 room with double bed, 1 room with 2 singles, 2 couch-beds in main room downstairs |
| HUT ESSENTIALS | Woodstove for heat, propane cookstove and oven, all kitchenware, indoor flush toilets, tub and shower, generator-powered electric lights |
| OTHER GOODIES | Communal sauna, hot and cold running water |

| WALTER'S CABIN | |
|---|---|
| HUT ELEVATION | 11,209' |
| DATE BUILT | 1997 |
| SEASONS | Year-round |
| CAPACITY | 12 (6 upstairs and 6 down) |
| HUT LAYOUT | 1 room with double bed, 1 room with 2 singles, 2 couch-beds in main room upstairs; 1 room with queen bed, 1 room with 2 singles, 2 couch-beds in main room downstairs |
| HUT ESSENTIALS | Woodstove for heat, propane cookstove and oven, all kitchenware, indoor flush toilets, tub and shower, generator-powered electric lights |
| OTHER GOODIES | Communal sauna, hot and cold running water |

The Shrine Mountain Inn, above Shrine Pass and a few miles west of Vail Pass, is a perfect overnight weekend getaway or base camp for day tours in the area. There are plenty of powdery glades, airy ridges, and backcountry roads to explore nearby. The rolling landscape features open meadows with thick stands of trees. The area is a great choice for skiers of all abilities, especially those new to the sport. The short, easy approach (though still not trivial) is accessible to all skiers, hikers, and bikers. Skiing to the inn is ideally suited to traditional cross-country touring gear.

The Shrine Mountain Inn is actually three distinctive structures. The main structure, Jay's Cabin, was built in memory of Jay Utter. It is a magnificent lodge that sleeps 12. Guests share two indoor bathrooms and a kitchen, a beautiful potbellied stove, and a large, south-facing porch with great views of the Gore and Tenmile Ranges.

*Frank Penniciaro and Pamela Crane stay hydrated on the trail.*

The second structure, Chuck's Cabin, built in memory of Chuck Anderson, features two separate units; each sleeps six and is equipped with a bath. This cabin's separate upstairs and downstairs quarters can be reserved individually. The upstairs must be reserved entirely by one group, and the lower quarters can (and will) be filled by multiple groups by the 10th Mountain reservationists.

The third and newest structure is Walter's Cabin, built in memory of Walter Kirsch. Walter's Cabin sits a short walk away from the others, on the edge of a sprawling meadow. It is similar to Chuck's Cabin and has the same reservation requirements. All three cabins are open year-round. For reservations, call the 10th Mountain Division Hut Association (see Appendix A).

**RECOMMENDED DAY TRIPS:**

**Black Lakes Ridge** is the treeless ridge directly northeast of the Shrine Pass Road. Leave the inn and return to the road. Turning toward Vail Pass, ski southeast along the road for 0.7 mile, then onto the ridge. This gentle ridge is a great spot to cruise around. Experienced skiers can also drop off the east face into the Black Lakes drainage for some superb telemark skiing. From the ridge, ski south along a road back to the Vail Pass parking area, then return to the inn. The basic ridge tour is suitable for novices; the descent of the east face is recommended for strong intermediate to advanced skiers.

Head south/southwest from Chuck's and Jay's Cabins, bypass Walter's Cabin, and head up toward the trail to **Shrine Mountain**—the route to the Fowler/Hilliard Hut (see Tour 18c). A short tour provides great views to the southeast, which only get better as you ascend.

Between Shrine Pass and the Vail ski area is the notorious **Commando Run**, one of the most difficult tours in the state. This tour drops northwest, down along the Shrine Pass Road, into Turkey Creek for 1.5 miles. Turn north onto the Timber Creek Road (marked) and ski up along this road to the northwest until the road splits on a wooded saddle. Contour west and southwest on the main (left) fork toward Lime Creek. After several hundred feet, begin a steep climb through the woods to the top of Elevation Point 11,611'. Once on top of the ridge, follow it west and then north, rolling along the crest until a long descent deposits you onto Two Elk Pass near the eastern boundary of Vail's famous Back Bowls.

Ascend north across the windswept south face of Red ("Siberia") Peak, then ski down its northeast ridge. Descend west into Mill Creek through unrivaled backcountry terrain and gain the Mill Creek Road. Follow the road to the Vail ski area and, finally, ski to the bottom of the downhill area via the trail of your choice.

This tour is 18.7 miles from Vail Pass to the bottom of the ski area. Gaining over 2,000 feet of elevation and losing over 5,000 feet, it is an advanced run that requires a shuttle car in Vail (fee parking). *Note:* Skiers taking this tour need an additional map, USGS 7.5-minute Vail East, as well as maps necessary for the Redcliff to Shrine Mountain Inn route (Tour 18b).

*Walter's Cabin overlooks the southern Gore Range and the Tenmile Range.*

NOVICE

TOUR **18a**

## Vail Pass Trailhead to Shrine Mountain Inn

SEE MAP PAGES 124–125 AND 142–143

| | |
|---|---|
| TIME | 2 to 4 hours |
| DISTANCE | 2.7 miles |
| ELEVATIONS | TRAILHEAD: 10,580' SM INN: 11,209' GAIN/LOSS: +629'/-20' |
| AVALANCHE | Minimal danger |
| MAPS | 10th Mountain Division: Resolution Mountain<br>USGS 7.5': Vail Pass, 1987<br>National Forest: Arapaho, White River<br>Trails Illustrated: Map #108 (Vail/Frisco/Dillon) |

**TOUR OVERVIEW:** The Shrine Pass Road, which travels between Vail Pass and the town of Red Cliff, has been a popular recreation area for decades. The name comes from views of the Mount of the Holy Cross as seen from several points along the way. At one time, there was interest in building a place of worship near the summit of the pass, but this never came to fruition. In summer the road is pleasant but often crowded.

In winter the route is one of the most popular ski tours in the state. Unfortunately, during the 1990s, Shrine Pass Road also became very popular with snowmobiles. Consequently, as part of a greater Vail Pass area recreation usage plan created by the Vail Pass Task Force, the actual Shrine Road between the Vail Pass parking area and the top of Shrine Pass is now designated as a snowmobile route. A dedicated route for skiers now runs parallel to the road along the south/southwest side and several hundred feet below the road.

In addition, there is now a $5 per-person, per-day fee payable at the parking area to Forest Rangers or at a self-serve kiosk. Money raised through the fee is used to produce usage maps, create signage, groom trails, and pay attendants.

**DIRECTIONS TO TRAILHEAD:** Drive on I-70 to the Vail Pass exit (Exit 190), 15 miles southeast of Vail, or 5 miles west of Copper Mountain. The Colorado Division of Transportation has now designated an overnight parking area for hut users on the west side of the pass, north of the road that wraps around to the solar-powered rest hut and toilets. After you exit and are on the west side of the pass, the parking area is immediately on the right (north) just past the Forest Service shack.

**THE ROUTE:** Leave the parking area, walk west, and gain the well-signed (Forest Service–style) beginning of Shrine Pass Road. Begin skiing and proceed past the first switchback until you reach the apex of the second major switchback. The skier's trail exits the road here and strikes off to the west/northwest and begins a gradual ascent up through the meadows that lie along the northern slopes of West Tenmile Creek. The route snakes its way for 2.4 miles along the border between the meadow and the trees up to the crest of the pass. The trail is well-marked. If you stray too high to the north, you will hit the road; too low and you will reach the creek.

One thing to remember about Shrine Pass itself is that it is rather indistinct. When you reach it, you will generally be in an area with lots of snowmobile tracks in a flat, open meadow. The pass and a summer Forest Service outhouse will be off to the right (north/northeast). The trail to the inn lies off to the left (southwest) in the thick stand of trees.

Turn to the southwest and locate the trail to the hut. If the area is covered with new snow or the weather is stormy, it may take a minute or two to find the snow-covered road that wraps upward 0.3 mile to the inn.

INTERMEDIATE/ADVANCED

TOUR **18b**

## Red Cliff Trailhead to Shrine Mountain Inn

SEE MAP PAGES 124–125 AND 142–143

| | |
|---|---|
| TIME | 5 to 8 hours |
| DISTANCE | 9.3 miles |
| ELEVATIONS | TRAILHEAD: 8,680' SM INN: 11,209' GAIN: +2,529' |
| AVALANCHE | Some avalanche terrain encountered; easily avoided |
| MAPS | 10th Mountain Division: Resolution Mountain<br>USGS 7.5': Red Cliff, 1978; Vail Pass, 1987<br>National Forest: Arapaho, White River<br>Trails Illustrated: Map #108 (Vail/Frisco/Dillon); Map #109 (Breckenridge/Tennessee Pass) |

**TOUR OVERVIEW:** This route follows the western portion of the classic Shrine Pass route. From Shrine Pass the road drops steadily to the town of Red Cliff. If you are descending into Red Cliff, be prepared for the ride of your life, especially if the road has recently been packed by snowmobilers. If you are skiing up to the inn from Red Cliff, expect a long, taxing ascent. As a direct route to the inn, this alternative is not nearly as popular as the Vail Pass route. However, this route works well as a starting point for a round-trip excursion going from the Shrine Mountain Inn to the Fowler/Hilliard Hut and back to Red Cliff.

**DIRECTIONS TO TRAILHEAD:** From the north, take I-70 and exit at Minturn (Exit 171), 5.4 miles west of Vail. Proceed south on US 24, driving 10.3 miles to the bridge at Turkey Creek. From Leadville, drive north on US 24 from the intersection with CO 91 (just north of Leadville) for 22.6 miles to the Turkey Creek bridge. From the north end of this spectacular bridge, turn east and drive into Red Cliff. Look for the Shrine Pass Road (County Road 16). Park along this road or in a parking lot near the marshal's office.

**THE ROUTE:** The Shrine Pass Road up Turkey Creek begins in a deep valley; the actual starting point varies depending on how far the road has been plowed. Initially, the road is on the south side of the creek. Soon the road crosses over the creek and continues climbing below south-facing slopes for 2.5 miles. Pass the turnoff and bridge to Wearyman Creek (the beginning of the Hornsilver Mountain route from Red Cliff to the Fowler/Hilliard Hut, Tour 19a) and follow the road up and across Turkey Creek.

Ascend through thick forest for 1.9 miles, then cross back to the north side of the creek near some old cabin ruins. Continue up the valley for 2.8 miles until you pass the turnoff to the north for the Timber Creek Road. Climb through a steep, tight turn and eventually pass an outhouse on the right before entering a flat, treeless basin 7.3 miles from Red Cliff. Follow the road up the north side of the basin through a steep gully. Then contour to the south, following the less distinct creek up to 11,720-foot Shrine Pass.

You are near the pass when you can look to the southwest to the Tenmile Range. (An altimeter may help if the weather is inclement.) A Forest Service sign also marks the spot. From here, cross the southwest side of the clearing, enter the forest, and follow the well-traveled trail to the inn.

ADVANCED

TOUR **18c**

## Shrine Mountain Inn to Fowler/Hilliard Hut

SEE MAP PAGES 124–125 AND 142–143

| | |
|---|---|
| TIME | 5 to 8 hours |
| DISTANCE | 6.8 miles |
| ELEVATIONS | SM INN: 11,209′ F/H HUT: 11,500′ GAIN/LOSS: +1,211′/-920′ |
| AVALANCHE | Some avalanche terrain encountered; easily avoided |
| MAPS | 10th Mountain Division: Resolution Mountain<br>USGS 7.5′: Pando, 1987; Red Cliff, 1978; Vail Pass, 1987<br>National Forest: Arapaho, White River<br>Trails Illustrated: Map #108 (Vail/Frisco/Dillon); Map #109 (Breckenridge/Tennessee Pass) |

**TOUR OVERVIEW:** The standard trail linking the Shrine Mountain Inn and the Fowler/Hilliard Hut is a scenic route that will test your fitness level and route-finding abilities. Overall, this challenging trail follows the most direct and commonsense route between the huts, but it always seems to take longer than expected—so get an early start. The first half of the trail travels high across the west side of the south ridge of Shrine Mountain near tree line. Consequently, it is exposed to foul weather and wind from the west. If the weather is severe, consider bypassing the high traverse of Shrine Mountain by skiing through Wilder Gulch by way of the Shrine Pass Road (County Road 16).

*Rick Sayre and Liz Klinga bask in the warm, early morning sun at Jay's Cabin/Shrine Mountain Inn.*

**THE ROUTE:** The trail leaves the Shrine Mountain Inn (from near the new Walter's Cabin) and begins a 1.3-mile southwesterly climb onto Shrine Pass. A compass reading may be helpful here; the rock near the summit of the mountain is a handy orientation point. A scattering of blue diamond trail markers helps show the route up through the sparsely timbered slopes and tree stumps. Break out of the trees and ascend west onto the 11,720-foot pass, just south of the summit of Shrine Mountain.

From the pass, turn south and begin a long, gently descending traverse of the west face of the south ridge of Shrine Mountain, just above tree line. Ski through small islands of trees, following the occasional trail marker. As you near the south end of the ridge, contour slightly to the southeast and begin descending steeper slopes into the forest. Continue south down toward the creek through ever-steepening, forested slopes. Eventually, this descent ends in a small meadow near the head of Wearyman Creek.

The trail into the woods on the south side of the creek is probably the hardest section of this route to locate, so take a little time to find the proper point of entry. Ski west through the meadow until the creek leaves the meadow and begins to drop steeply. On the south side of the creek, you will find trail markers for the route to the Fowler/Hilliard Hut. (Avoid the summer road, which continues down the valley to Red Cliff; it heads west above the creek at this same spot.)

Enter the woods and begin a 200-foot descent to a tiny clearing (shown on the USGS topo map). Ski to the southwest until you gain a wide, gentle road. Follow the road for 2 miles on a seemingly interminable low-angled climb until you reach a series of switchbacks heading directly uphill to the southeast. Ascend through these to the 11,460-foot saddle east of the hut. Turn west (near a summer gate) and ski 0.3 mile over a small hill to the Fowler/Hilliard Hut.

If you ski from the Fowler/Hilliard Hut north to Shrine Mountain Inn, remember to climb through the small meadow at the head of Wearyman Creek. Exit the clearing to the northeast to begin the ascent across the west side of the south ridge of Shrine Mountain.

# 19 Fowler/Hilliard Hut

| | |
|---|---|
| **HUT ELEVATION** | 11,500' |
| **DATE BUILT** | 1988 |
| **SEASONS** | Thanksgiving through April 30 (winter); July 1 through September 30 (summer) |
| **CAPACITY** | 16 |
| **HUT LAYOUT** | 1 room with double bed, 1 room with 4 singles, plus 10 single beds in a communal sleeping area, all upstairs |
| **HUT ESSENTIALS** | Woodstove for heat, wood-burning cookstove with oven, propane cookstoves, all kitchenware, outhouse, photovoltaic electric lights |
| **OTHER GOODIES** | Wheelchair-accessible in summer |

The Fowler/Hilliard Hut is one of the most spectacular and historic sites in the 10th Mountain Division system. From atop a ridge on the northeast side of Resolution Mountain, the hut looks south over terrain where ski soldiers of the 10th Mountain Division once trained. Experienced skiers especially love this hut because there are hundreds of acres of skiable terrain in every direction. It is a strenuous day getting to the hut via any route, but those who can manage the trip will be treated to as much skiing as their knees can handle. The hut was built as a memorial to Anne Fowler and Ed Hilliard.

Hikers and mountain bikers should bear in mind that water may be difficult to obtain during the summer because water sources are some distance from the hut. Directions inside the hut will tell you where to find water, which should be treated or boiled before drinking. This hut is wheelchair-accessible, and in summer you can drive directly to it. Make reservations through the 10th Mountain Division Hut Association (see Appendix A).

**RECOMMENDED DAY TRIPS:**

**In every direction of the compass from the Fowler/Hilliard Hut, there are a variety of ski-play areas.** Certainly, one can climb to the top of Resolution Mountain—either by going directly up the ridge or by passing through the Narrows and scooting up the mountain's gentle back side (west). South of the hut are acres of treeless bowls. Depending on conditions, these can range from sun-baked death crust to rapture-inducing powder fields. Be careful of potential avalanche slopes high up under the cornices on the east face of Resolution Mountain. North of the hut, skiers will find sumptuous tree skiing in dark, north-facing glades. To the east and southeast are more stellar glades and ridges that harbor some of the best skiing in the area. And last, the intrepid can climb up onto Machine Gun Ridge above Ptarmigan Pass for an energetic workout.

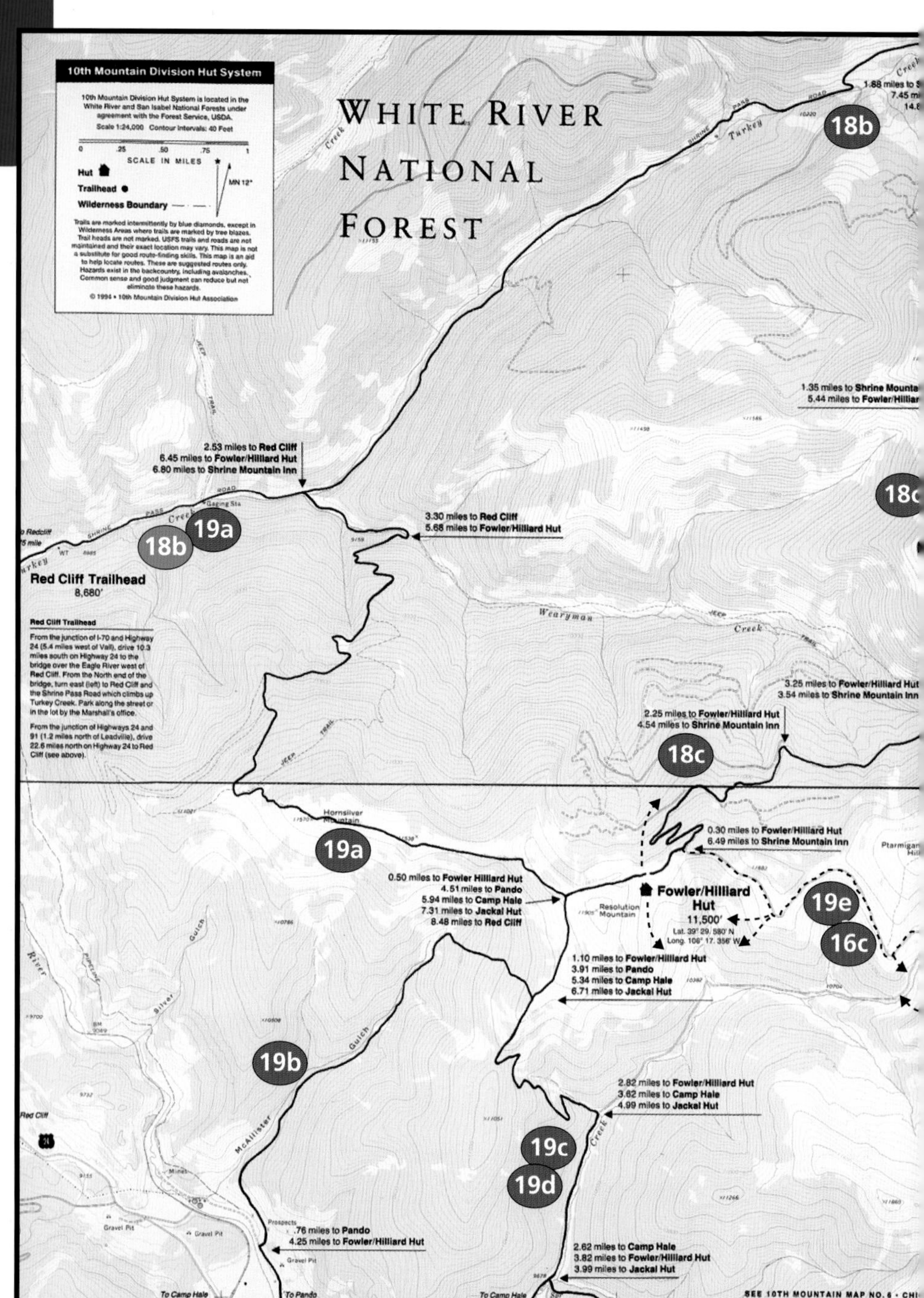

10th Mountain Division Hut System
10th Mountain Division Hut System is located in the White River and San Isabel National Forests under agreement with the Forest Service, USDA.
Scale 1:24,000 Contour Intervals: 40 Feet
0 .25 .50 .75 1
SCALE IN MILES
Hut
Trailhead
Wilderness Boundary
MN 12°
Trails are marked intermittently by blue diamonds, except in Wilderness Areas where trails are marked by tree blazes. Trail heads are not marked. USFS trails and roads are not maintained and their exact location may vary. This map is not a substitute for good route-finding skills. This map is an aid to help locate routes. These are suggested routes only. Hazards exist in the backcountry, including avalanches. Common sense and good judgment can reduce but not eliminate these hazards.
© 1994 • 10th Mountain Division Hut Association
WHITE RIVER NATIONAL FOREST
18b
1.88 miles to S
7.45 mi
1.35 miles to Shrine Mounta
5.44 miles to Fowler/Hilliar
2.53 miles to Red Cliff
6.45 miles to Fowler/Hilliard Hut
6.80 miles to Shrine Mountain Inn
18c
19a
18b
3.30 miles to Red Cliff
5.68 miles to Fowler/Hilliard Hut
Red Cliff Trailhead
8,680'
Red Cliff Trailhead
From the junction of I-70 and Highway 24 (5.4 miles west of Vail), drive 10.3 miles south on Highway 24 to the bridge over the Eagle River west of Red Cliff. From the North end of the bridge, turn east (left) to Red Cliff and the Shrine Pass Road which climbs up Turkey Creek. Park along the street or in the lot by the Marshall's office.
From the junction of Highways 24 and 91 (1.2 miles north of Leadville), drive 22.6 miles north on Highway 24 to Red Cliff (see above).
Wearyman Creek
3.25 miles to Fowler/Hilliard Hut
3.54 miles to Shrine Mountain Inn
2.25 miles to Fowler/Hilliard Hut
4.54 miles to Shrine Mountain Inn
18c
Hornsilver Mountain
19a
0.30 miles to Fowler/Hilliard Hut
6.49 miles to Shrine Mountain Inn
0.50 miles to Fowler Hilliard Hut
4.51 miles to Pando
5.94 miles to Camp Hale
7.31 miles to Jackal Hut
8.48 miles to Red Cliff
Fowler/Hilliard Hut
11,500'
Lat. 39° 29.580' N
Long. 106° 17.356' W
Resolution Mountain
Ptarmigan Hill
19e
16c
1.10 miles to Fowler/Hilliard Hut
3.91 miles to Pando
5.34 miles to Camp Hale
6.71 miles to Jackal Hut
19b
Silver Gulch
McAllister Gulch
2.82 miles to Fowler/Hilliard Hut
3.62 miles to Camp Hale
4.99 miles to Jackal Hut
19c
19d
Red Cliff
.76 miles to Pando
4.25 miles to Fowler/Hilliard Hut
2.62 miles to Camp Hale
3.82 miles to Fowler/Hilliard Hut
3.99 miles to Jackal Hut
Gravel Pit
To Camp Hale
To Pando
To Camp Hale
SEE 10TH MOUNTAIN MAP NO. 6 • CHI

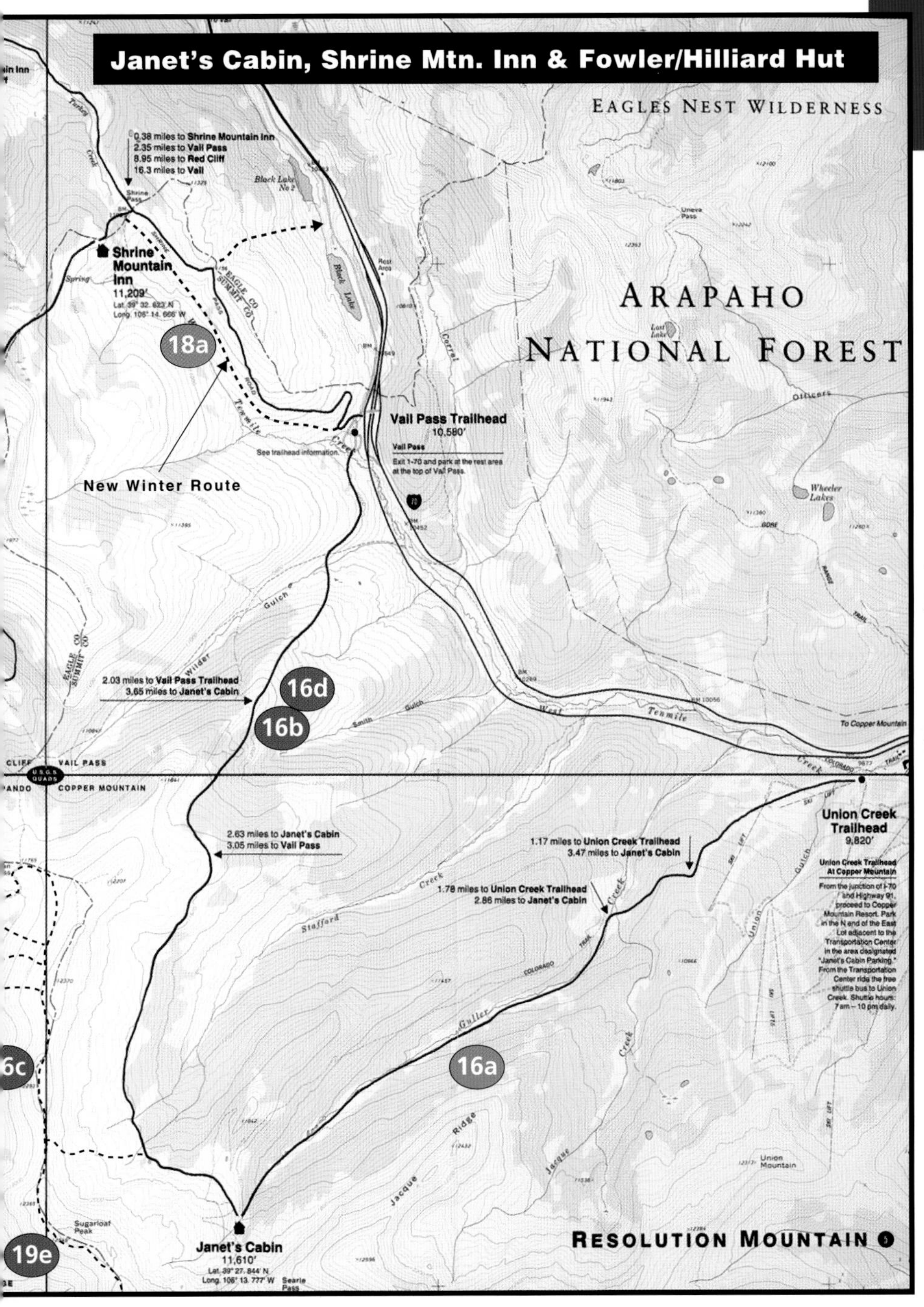
Janet's Cabin, Shrine Mtn. Inn & Fowler/Hilliard Hut
EAGLES NEST WILDERNESS
ARAPAHO NATIONAL FOREST
0.38 miles to Shrine Mountain Inn
2.35 miles to Vail Pass
8.95 miles to Red Cliff
16.3 miles to Vail
Shrine Mountain Inn
11,209'
Lat. 39° 32. 623' N
Long. 106° 14. 666' W
18a
New Winter Route
Vail Pass Trailhead
10,580'
Vail Pass
Exit I-70 and park at the rest area at the top of Vail Pass.
See trailhead information.
2.03 miles to Vail Pass Trailhead
3.65 miles to Janet's Cabin
16d
16b
To Copper Mountain
VAIL PASS
COPPER MOUNTAIN
2.63 miles to Janet's Cabin
3.05 miles to Vail Pass
1.17 miles to Union Creek Trailhead
3.47 miles to Janet's Cabin
1.78 miles to Union Creek Trailhead
2.86 miles to Janet's Cabin
Union Creek Trailhead
9,820'
Union Creek Trailhead At Copper Mountain
From the junction of I-70 and Highway 91, proceed to Copper Mountain Resort. Park in the N end of the East Lot adjacent to the Transportation Center in the area designated "Janet's Cabin Parking." From the Transportation Center ride the free shuttle bus to Union Creek. Shuttle hours: 7am – 10 pm daily.
16a
6c
19e
Janet's Cabin
11,610'
Lat. 39° 27. 844' N
Long. 106° 13. 777' W
Searle Pass
Sugarloaf Peak
Union Mountain
Jacque Ridge
RESOLUTION MOUNTAIN

TOUR

ADVANCED

# 19a Red Cliff Trailhead to Fowler/Hilliard Hut

SEE MAP PAGES 124–125, 142–143, AND 152–153

| | |
|---|---|
| TIME | 7 to 11 hours |
| DISTANCE | 9 miles |
| ELEVATIONS | TRAILHEAD: 8,680' HUT: 11,500' GAIN: +3,170'/-350' |
| AVALANCHE | Some avalanche terrain encountered; easily avoided |
| MAPS | 10th Mountain Division: Resolution Mountain<br>USGS 7.5': Pando, 1987; Red Cliff, 1978<br>National Forest: White River<br>Trails Illustrated: Map #108 (Vail/Frisco/Dillon); Map #109 (Breckenridge/Tennessee Pass) |

**TOUR OVERVIEW:** From Red Cliff, the Hornsilver Mountain route to the Fowler/Hilliard Hut is a long and steep prospect. The 5-mile climb from Wearyman Creek to Resolution Mountain is nothing more than an exercise in high-altitude aerobics—with a pack!

Following marked roads and trails the entire way, you will not have to worry about intricate route-finding. However, when you travel to the hut through Resolution Narrows, you do need to pay attention so you don't end up skiing down into McAllister Gulch or onto any of the potential avalanche slopes on the north side of Resolution Mountain. People headed to Red Cliff from the Fowler/Hilliard Hut will find this the most expedient avenue of egress.

**DIRECTIONS TO TRAILHEAD:** From the north, take I-70 to the Minturn exit (Exit 171), 5.4 miles west of Vail. Proceed south on US 24, driving 10.3 miles to a bridge across Turkey Creek. If you are approaching from the Leadville area, drive north on US 24 from the intersection with CO 91 (just north of Leadville) for 22.6 miles to the Turkey Creek bridge. From the north end of this spectacular bridge, turn east and drive down the narrow road into Red Cliff. Look for the Shrine Pass Road (County Road 16). Park along this road or in a parking lot near the marshal's office.

**THE ROUTE:** The Shrine Pass Road up Turkey Creek begins in a deep valley; the actual starting point of the tour varies depending on how far the road has been plowed. Initially, the road is on the south side of the creek. Soon it crosses the creek and continues climbing below the south-facing slopes for 2.5 miles until you reach the turnoff to Wearyman Creek. Turn south, cross the bridge, and head up into Wearyman Creek along the road. Climb for 0.8 mile to the right (west), then turn into the Hornsilver Mountain Road and begin the 2,270-foot ascent of Hornsilver Mountain. Remain on the marked ski route that follows a four-wheel-drive trail, and continue past a left turn at Elevation Point 10,080' and past several right turns near Elevation Point 10,800'. Traverse up to the west ridge of Hornsilver Mountain, then turn east and ascend along the ridge to the summit.

Continue along the ridge over Hornsilver Mountain. Cross a small hill and a saddle, and ascend the west side of the ridge (there should be signs alerting snowmobilers that they are now at the edge of the nonmotorized bubble that encircles the hut) to the northwest corner of Resolution Mountain. From this flat shoulder, turn east and drop into the large gully, Resolution Narrows, on the north side of the mountain. Ski through this passage, avoiding any potential avalanche slopes on both sides of the gully, and exit up and out of the southeast side of the narrows. After climbing onto the large saddle on the northeast side of Resolution Mountain, it is a quick ski east for several hundred feet to the Fowler/Hilliard Hut.

*Dave Boardman skis on the south-facing front lawn of the Fowler/Hilliard Hut seen on the horizon.*

INTERMEDIATE/ADVANCED

TOUR **19b**

## Pando Trailhead to Fowler/Hilliard Hut

SEE MAP PAGES 124–125, 142–143, AND 152–153

| | |
|---|---|
| TIME | 4 to 7 hours |
| DISTANCE | 5 miles |
| ELEVATIONS | TRAILHEAD: 9,200′ HUT: 11,500′ GAIN/LOSS: +2,500′/-200′ |
| AVALANCHE | Some avalanche terrain encountered; easily avoided |
| MAPS | 10th Mountain Division: Chicago Ridge, Resolution Mountain<br>USGS 7.5′: Pando, 1987<br>National Forest: White River<br>Trails Illustrated: Map #108 (Vail/Frisco/Dillon); Map #109 (Breckenridge/Tennessee Pass) |

**TOUR OVERVIEW:** This tour through McAllister Gulch is the shortest, most direct route to the Fowler/Hilliard Hut. Although it follows a road and is relatively short, it gains a considerable amount of elevation in a short distance, climbing very (repeat, very) steeply through its middle portion near the head of the creek as you approach the southwest ridge of Resolution Mountain. Conversely, for those headed toward Pando and Camp Hale, this route makes for a very fast, thigh-torturing descent. Getting an early start and using climbing skins will help make this tour more manageable. Also, since the trail has a northwest exposure, it normally has better snow than the more south-facing routes, especially important when descending to Camp Hale. Snow conditions can vary widely, though.

**DIRECTIONS TO TRAILHEAD:** From I-70, take the Minturn exit (Exit 171), which is 5.4 miles west of Vail, and proceed south on US 24 for 17 miles. From Leadville drive north on US 24 from the intersection of CO 91 for 16.3 miles over Tennessee Pass to Pando. Park on the east side of the road by the concrete foundations immediately south of the railroad crossing. As there is no bridge, mountain bikers should use the Camp Hale Trailhead.

**THE ROUTE:** From the parking area, ski east and cross the Eagle River via a snow bridge (if there is one) or by fording the stream. Continue toward the mountains, then turn north (left) at the intersection at the foot of the mountain. Ski north along this road for 0.5 mile to a marked trail intersection with McAllister Gulch Road (Forest Road 708). Take the right fork onto McAllister Gulch Road. Continue heading northward toward the forested mouth of McAllister Gulch proper. Eventually the road will swing smartly east/northeast and continue climbing straight up the gut of the gulch along the south side of the creek. After what feels like an eternity, the route veers off and upward from the creek and climbs even more steeply to the southeast toward the southwest ridge of Resolution Mountain. Continue climbing steeply until you leave the trees and intersect the Resolution Creek Trail atop the ridge. Look for trail markers on trees at this intersection.

Follow the trail up the ridge and begin an ascending traverse north across the open west face of Resolution Mountain. (Note views of the Mount of the Holy Cross!) This ascent is 200 to 300 feet beneath the summit of Resolution Mountain through islands of evergreens. Navigation here can be problematic in inclement weather.

From the flat shoulder on the northwest corner of the mountain, turn east and drop into the large cleft, or gully, on the north side of the mountain. This is Resolution Narrows. Ski through this passage, avoiding potential avalanche slopes on both sides, and exit up and out of the southeast side of the narrows. After climbing onto the large saddle on the northeast side of Resolution Mountain, continue several hundred feet east to the hut.

INTERMEDIATE/ADVANCED

TOUR **19c**

## Camp Hale Trailhead to Fowler/Hilliard Hut

SEE MAP PAGES 124–125, 142–143, AND 152–153

TIME 5 to 8 hours

DISTANCE 6.5 miles

ELEVATIONS TRAILHEAD: 9,250' HUT: 11,500' GAIN/LOSS: +2,450'/-200'

AVALANCHE Route crosses avalanche runout zones; can be dangerous during high-hazard periods

MAPS 10th Mountain Division: Chicago Ridge, Resolution Mountain
USGS 7.5': Pando, 1987; Red Cliff, 1978
National Forest: White River
Trails Illustrated: Map #108 (Vail/Frisco/Dillon); Map #109 (Breckenridge/Tennessee Pass)

**TOUR OVERVIEW:** This route leaves Camp Hale and ascends to the Fowler/Hilliard Hut via Resolution Creek. The upper section of this tour is often combined with the Pearl Creek route to the Jackal Hut (Tour 20a) to create the hut-to-hut route between the Jackal Hut and the Fowler/Hilliard Hut. However, when the sun has been at work hardening the south-facing slopes, descending this route can be thrilling, to say the least.

**DIRECTIONS TO TRAILHEAD:** Although all three Camp Hale trailheads are starting points for this trail, only directions from the main Camp Hale parking area are given. From I-70, exit at Minturn (Exit 171), 5.4 miles west of Vail, and proceed south on US 24 for 18.5 miles. From the Leadville area, drive north on US 24 from the intersection with CO 91 for 14.7 miles, across Tennessee Pass to the main Camp Hale Road. Park on the east side of the road.

**THE ROUTE:** There are two possible routes to Resolution Creek. The first goes straight across Camp Hale to the road on the far east side. This entails crossing the Eagle River, which may be simple or difficult, depending on whether there is a snow bridge. Once you have reached the road (Forest Road 714), turn north and proceed to Resolution Creek. If crossing the Eagle River is too difficult, it is also possible to ski to the river, then turn north and ski along the river for 0.8 mile, until you reach the first turn to the east. Follow this road east over the river via a bridge until you reach the Resolution Creek Road, and turn left.

Pass Forest Service signs, then ski up the Resolution Creek Road for 1.4 miles to a fork in the road. Continue along the left fork (the right fork leads to the Jackal Hut), traveling north for 1 mile. The first significant drainage since the Pearl Creek fork is on the left. Turn up this creek and ski along the south side. After climbing 300 feet, the route leaves the creek and ascends a series of switchbacks to the southwest ridge of Resolution Mountain. This climb follows a trail that, at times, is a little difficult to track, for the blue diamond trail markers are spaced far apart. Pay attention.

*Skiers demonstrate "fall-line" skiing on the southern slopes below the Fowler/Hilliard Hut.*

*Note:* Bicyclists should continue straight up Resolution Creek on Forest Road 702 toward Ptarmigan Pass, then turn west 400 feet below the pass onto Forest Road 751, which leads up to the forested pass directly east of the hut.

When you reach a tiny forested saddle on top of the ridge, turn northeast and climb 360 feet directly up the ridge through thinning stands of trees and clearings, passing the McAllister Gulch Trail at 11,300 feet. Continue up the ridge via the trail through ever more open terrain, gaining another 100 feet of elevation. Ascend north across the open west face of Resolution Mountain. The trail heads through large clearings, stands of evergreens, and wind-tortured trees about 250 feet below the summit.

From the flat shoulder on the northwest corner of the mountain, turn east and drop into the large gully, Resolution Narrows, on the north side of the mountain. Ski through this passage, avoiding potential avalanche slopes on either side. Exit out of the southeast side of the narrows. After climbing onto the large saddle on the northeast side of Resolution Narrows, continue east for several hundred feet to the Fowler/Hilliard Hut.

ADVANCED

TOUR
# 19d Fowler/Hilliard Hut to Jackal Hut

SEE MAP PAGES 124–125, 142–143, AND 152–153

| | |
|---|---|
| TIME | 6 to 9 hours |
| DISTANCE | 7.8 miles |
| ELEVATIONS | F/H HUT: 11,500' J HUT: 11,610' GAIN/LOSS: +2,202'/-2,022' |
| AVALANCHE | Route crosses avalanche runout zones; can be dangerous during high-hazard periods |
| MAPS | 10th Mountain Division: Chicago Ridge, Resolution Mountain<br>USGS 7.5': Pando, 1987<br>National Forest: White River<br>Trails Illustrated: Map #109 (Breckenridge/Tennessee Pass) |

**TOUR OVERVIEW:** This classic route combines the Camp Hale to Fowler/Hilliard Hut via Resolution Creek route (Tour 19c) and Camp Hale to Jackal Hut via Pearl Creek route (Tour 20a) into a long hut-to-hut day. Because this route requires several thousand feet of descent and ascent (in either direction), it is a very challenging tour. Skiers must be able to descend long, steady drops wearing backpacks. The climb to the hut adds a final kicker to the day.

**THE ROUTE:** Described from north to south, this trail starts from the Fowler/Hilliard Hut and heads west through Resolution Narrows, the gully due west of the hut on the north side of Resolution Mountain. From the northwest shoulder of Resolution Mountain, the trail then traverses gradually down across the west face of the mountain through sparse islands of trees, following the occasional blue diamond trail marker. The route then follows the southwest ridge of the mountain down past the marked right turn (blue and orange diamonds) to McAllister Gulch.

Continue dropping down the ridge until you reach a small, wooded saddle. Turn to the southeast and begin a long and treacherous descent into the Resolution Creek drainage. Follow a somewhat obscure trail as it switchbacks wildly down through the forest. There are blue trail markers, but you must keep an eye out for them. This descent stays on the southwest side of the creek all the way to the Resolution Creek Road. *Note:* Those less skilled at descending steep, switchbacking trails should consider keeping skins on for the descent.

Drop down the Resolution Creek Road (Forest Road 702) for 1 mile until you reach the turnoff to Pearl Creek, marked by a bridge and mileage sign. Cross the bridge and follow the road south on a gradual climb. After a few hundred feet, the road divides into two logging roads. Take the road that veers sharply to the southeast and heads upstream past old logging cuts. Stay on the south side of the stream, and after a few hundred feet begin an ascending traverse above the creek. Watch for blue trail markers. Do not follow any of the trails that lead down to the creek.

The road climbs steadily, then begins to steepen and turn south along a tiny creek. Follow the road uphill until you spot a road branching sharply to the east/southeast. Cross the creek and follow this road 1 mile to a creek crossing in a small, willow-filled bog. This stretch of trail from Resolution Road to the creek crossing makes for a joyous descent.

Cross to the north side of the creek and follow a distinct trail 0.3 mile upstream to a faint trail crossing to the south of the creek. This poorly marked crossing is in a large clearing along the creek, at a point where the drainage begins to contour to the northeast. From this point, you start to see Sugarloaf Peak high to the northeast. There is also a small stream flowing in from the south, usually marked by old ski tracks and face-plant auger marks. Be careful, though, as many of the descent tracks from previous skiers may wander around from the true trail.

Cross the creek and ski up along its west side, keeping an eye out for blue markers. Skins are recommended for the climb to the hut. After a few hundred feet, the trail climbs steeply to the right, then becomes well-defined. After 800 feet, the gradient relaxes as you reach a picturesque ridge. Ski west through the woods. Continue west into a ridgetop clearing, ascend over the last 200-foot climb, then glide easily to the Jackal Hut.

ADVANCED

TOUR

## 19e Fowler/Hilliard Hut to Jackal Hut via High Traverse

SEE MAP PAGES 124–125, 142–143, AND 152–153

**TIME** 7 to 9 hours

**DISTANCE** 9 miles

**ELEVATIONS** F/H HUT: 11,500′ J HUT: 11,610′ GAIN/LOSS: +2060′/-1,700′

**AVALANCHE** Route crosses avalanche slopes; prone to skier-triggered avalanches during high-hazard periods

**MAPS** 10th Mountain Division: Chicago Ridge, Resolution Mountain
USGS 7.5′: Copper Mountain, 1988; Pando, 1987
National Forest: Arapaho, White River
Trails Illustrated: Map #108 (Vail/Frisco/Dillon)

**TOUR OVERVIEW:** This unofficial 10th Mountain Division route is a high-altitude ridge traverse between the Fowler/Hilliard Hut and the Jackal Hut. The High Traverse is an experience that is more ski mountaineering than cross-country skiing. It is one of the most scenic tours in the state, with unobstructed 360-degree views of central Colorado's mountains, including the Gore Range to the north, the Tenmile Range to the east, the Sawatch Range to the south, and 14,005-foot Mount of the Holy Cross to the west. If you have done the Resolution Creek/Pearl Creek hut-to-hut route one too many times, give this super alternative a try.

Competent, experienced groups will find the route-finding straightforward, the technical difficulty minimal, and the avalanche hazard low under normal conditions.

Parties interested in doing this tour will need a clear day, because most of the route follows a treeless, and therefore unprotected, ridge that is exposed to the full fury of storms coming out of the west or north.

The snowpack is usually scoured by westerly winds, so most of the route travels over either hard sastrugi with occasional patches of talus or grass. Keep an eye out for cornices overhanging the eastern flank, small wind-deposited pockets, and the steep traverse around the western and southern slopes of 12,545-foot Sugarloaf Peak. Be sure to carry safety equipment.

*Rick Sayre skis in the 10th Mountain system.*

**THE ROUTE:** Leave the Fowler/Hilliard Hut and head east over a small hill to the main trail. Turn to the east and follow the roadbed around the southern flank of 12,143-foot Ptarmigan Hill. Ski down to a switchback, where the road swings to the south and west down into Resolution Creek. Leave the road at the apex of the switchback and ski northwest up to Ptarmigan Pass.

From the pass, climb to the southeast, toward the top of the ridge. It is not necessary to climb straight up to the ridge; you can take a long traverse across the moderate and windswept west slopes below Elevation Point 12,370', gaining the ridge at the flat saddle immediately south of this point.

From the saddle, travel south along the crest of the ridge, steering clear of any avalanche hazards, especially the cornices overhanging the eastern aspect of the ridge. Exercise caution on the exposed western and southern flanks of Sugarloaf Peak. Generally, this slope is wind-scoured and requires a walk across stones and crusty snow, so be careful.

Continue southeast along the ridge up and over the high point of the trip, 12,693-foot Elk Mountain. From the summit of this peak, drop south to the first minor saddle at 12,540 feet, then begin a descent southwest across a broad, moderate slope to the saddle immediately northeast of Pearl Peak. From here, ascend directly up the ridge and over Pearl Peak, staying well away from the huge cornices that often form on the southeastern aspect of this peak. Descend west/southwest along the broad ridge-crest to the intersection with the Jackal Hut Trail. Continue west on the trail for 0.6 mile to the hut.

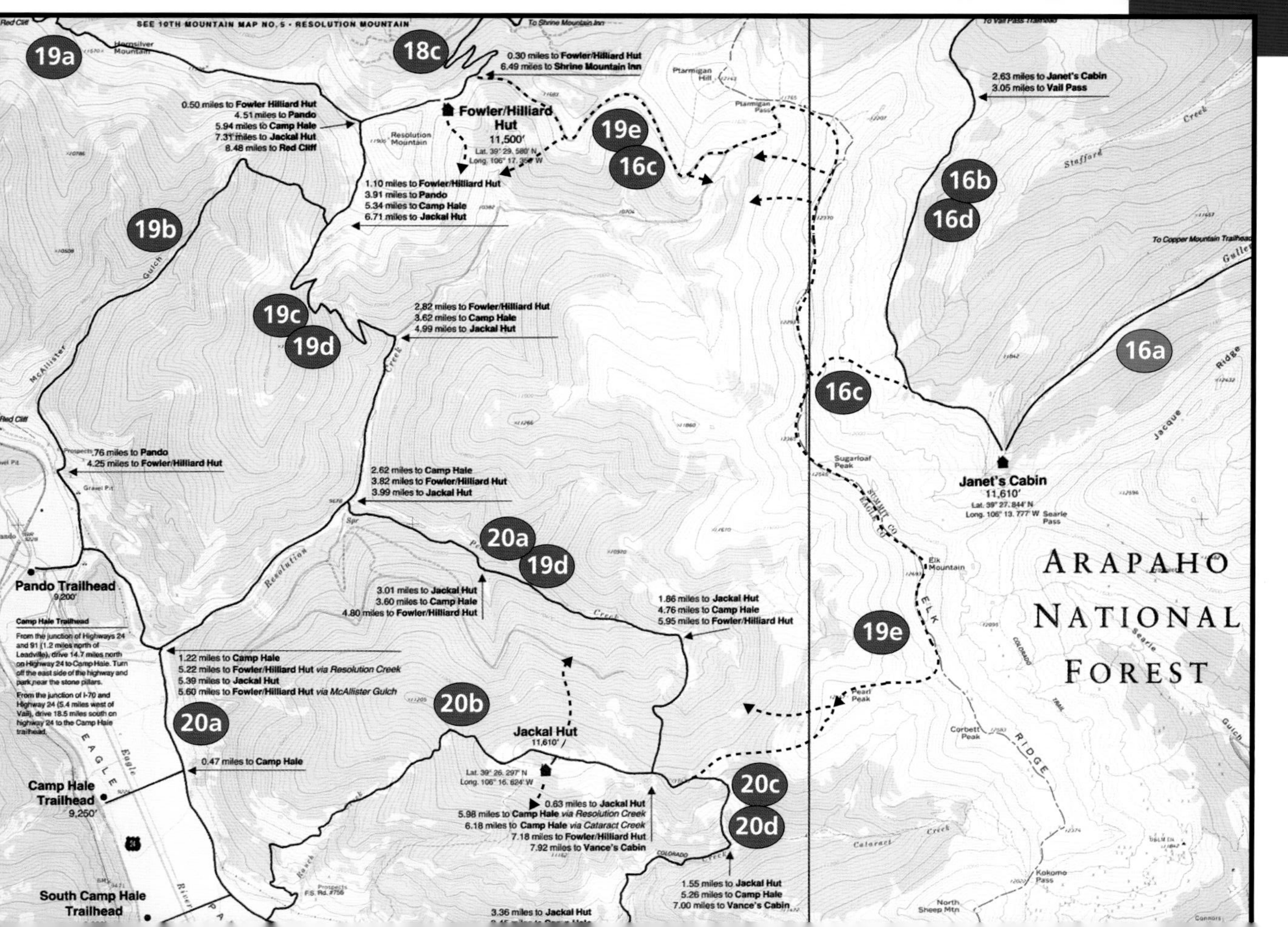

SEE 10TH MOUNTAIN MAP NO. 5 - RESOLUTION MOUNTAIN
Red Cliff
Hornsilver Mountain
To Shrine Mountain Inn
To Vail Pass Trailhead
0.30 miles to Fowler/Hilliard Hut
6.49 miles to Shrine Mountain Inn
0.50 miles to Fowler Hilliard Hut
4.51 miles to Pando
5.94 miles to Camp Hale
7.31 miles to Jackal Hut
8.48 miles to Red Cliff
Fowler/Hilliard Hut
11,500'
Lat. 39° 29. 580' N
Long. 106° 17.
Resolution Mountain
Ptarmigan Hill
Ptarmigan Pass
1.10 miles to Fowler/Hilliard Hut
3.91 miles to Pando
5.34 miles to Camp Hale
6.71 miles to Jackal Hut
2.63 miles to Janet's Cabin
3.05 miles to Vail Pass
To Copper Mountain Trailhead
Stafford Creek
2.82 miles to Fowler/Hilliard Hut
3.62 miles to Camp Hale
4.99 miles to Jackal Hut
McAllister Gulch
.76 miles to Pando
4.25 miles to Fowler/Hilliard Hut
Gravel Pit
Prospects
2.62 miles to Camp Hale
3.82 miles to Fowler/Hilliard Hut
3.99 miles to Jackal Hut
Jacque Ridge
Janet's Cabin
11,610'
Lat. 39° 27. 844' N
Long. 106° 13. 777' W
Searle Pass
Sugarloaf Peak
SUMMIT CO
EAGLE CO
Elk Mountain
ARAPAHO
NATIONAL
FOREST
Pando Trailhead
9,200'
Camp Hale Trailhead
From the junction of Highways 24 and 91 (1.2 miles north of Leadville), drive 14.7 miles north on Highway 24 to Camp Hale. Turn off the east side of the highway and park near the stone pillars.
From the junction of I-70 and Highway 24 (5.4 miles west of Vail), drive 18.5 miles south on highway 24 to the Camp Hale trailhead.
Resolution Creek
3.01 miles to Jackal Hut
3.60 miles to Camp Hale
4.80 miles to Fowler/Hilliard Hut
1.86 miles to Jackal Hut
4.76 miles to Camp Hale
5.95 miles to Fowler/Hilliard Hut
1.22 miles to Camp Hale
5.22 miles to Fowler/Hilliard Hut via Resolution Creek
5.39 miles to Jackal Hut
5.60 miles to Fowler/Hilliard Hut via McAllister Gulch
Jackal Hut
11,610'
Lat. 39° 26. 297' N
Long. 106° 16. 624' W
0.63 miles to Jackal Hut
5.98 miles to Camp Hale via Resolution Creek
6.18 miles to Camp Hale via Cataract Creek
7.18 miles to Fowler/Hilliard Hut
7.92 miles to Vance's Cabin
0.47 miles to Camp Hale
Camp Hale Trailhead
9,250'
EAGLE
Eagle River
Pearl Peak
Corbett Peak
ELK RIDGE
COLORADO TRAIL
Searle Gulch
Cataract Creek
Kokomo Pass
North Sheep Mtn
F.S. Rd. #756
1.55 miles to Jackal Hut
5.26 miles to Camp Hale
7.00 miles to Vance's Cabin
3.36 miles to Jackal Hut
South Camp Hale Trailhead
19a
18c
19e
16c
19b
16b
16d
19c
19d
16a
20a
20b
20c
20d

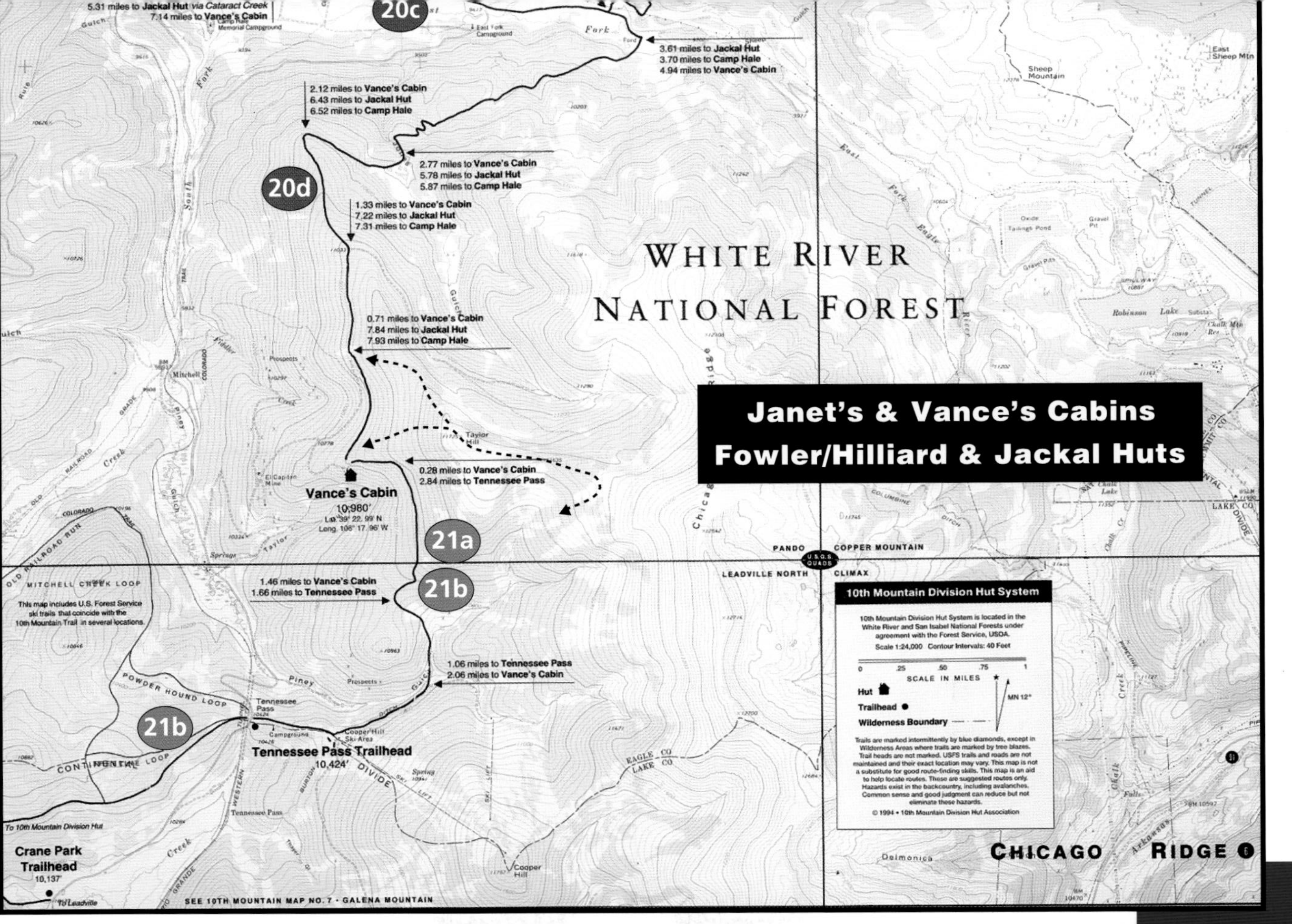
Janet's & Vance's Cabins
Fowler/Hilliard & Jackal Huts
WHITE RIVER NATIONAL FOREST
CHICAGO RIDGE
5.31 miles to Jackal Hut via Cataract Creek
7.14 miles to Vance's Cabin
3.61 miles to Jackal Hut
3.70 miles to Camp Hale
4.94 miles to Vance's Cabin
2.12 miles to Vance's Cabin
6.43 miles to Jackal Hut
6.52 miles to Camp Hale
2.77 miles to Vance's Cabin
5.78 miles to Jackal Hut
5.87 miles to Camp Hale
1.33 miles to Vance's Cabin
7.22 miles to Jackal Hut
7.31 miles to Camp Hale
0.71 miles to Vance's Cabin
7.84 miles to Jackal Hut
7.93 miles to Camp Hale
0.28 miles to Vance's Cabin
2.84 miles to Tennessee Pass
1.46 miles to Vance's Cabin
1.66 miles to Tennessee Pass
1.06 miles to Tennessee Pass
2.06 miles to Vance's Cabin
20c
20d
21a
21b
21b
Vance's Cabin
10,980'
Lat. 39° 22.99' N
Long. 106° 17.96' W
Tennessee Pass Trailhead
10,424'
Crane Park Trailhead
10,137'
To 10th Mountain Division Hut
To Leadville
MITCHELL CREEK LOOP
This map includes U.S. Forest Service ski trails that coincide with the 10th Mountain Trail in several locations.
POWDER HOUND LOOP
CONTINENTAL DIVIDE
OLD RAILROAD RUN
SEE 10TH MOUNTAIN MAP NO. 7 · GALENA MOUNTAIN
PANDO
COPPER MOUNTAIN
LEADVILLE NORTH
CLIMAX
10th Mountain Division Hut System
10th Mountain Division Hut System is located in the White River and San Isabel National Forests under agreement with the Forest Service, USDA.
Scale 1:24,000 Contour Intervals: 40 Feet
0 .25 .50 .75 1
SCALE IN MILES
Hut
Trailhead
Wilderness Boundary
MN 12°
Trails are marked intermittently by blue diamonds, except in Wilderness Areas where trails are marked by tree blazes. Trail heads are not marked. USFS trails and roads are not maintained and their exact location may vary. This map is not a substitute for good route-finding skills. This map is an aid to help locate routes. These are suggested routes only. Hazards exist in the backcountry, including avalanches. Common sense and good judgment can reduce but not eliminate these hazards.
© 1994 • 10th Mountain Division Hut Association

# 20 Jackal Hut

| | |
|---|---|
| **HUT ELEVATION** | 11,610' |
| **DATE BUILT** | 1988 |
| **SEASONS** | Thanksgiving through April 30 (winter); July 1 through September 30 (summer) |
| **CAPACITY** | 16 |
| **HUT LAYOUT** | 1 room with double bed, 1 room with 4 singles, plus 10 single beds in a communal sleeping area, all upstairs |
| **HUT ESSENTIALS** | Woodstove for heat, wood-burning cookstove with oven, propane cookstoves, all kitchenware, outhouse, photovoltaic electric lights |

Perched on the edge of a towering ridge, the Jackal Hut is like an eagle's nest overlooking the Eagle River Valley, Tennessee Pass, and nearly the entire length of the Sawatch Range to the south and west. The view from its porch is one of the finest of any hut in the state. The view you get by climbing directly north onto the hill behind the hut gets even better: a 360-degree panorama that includes the Gore Range to the north and the Tenmile Range to the east and southeast.

Every route to the hut gains over 2,000 feet; there are no easy ways to get here. However, with an early start, most skiers, even novice backcountry skiers with good endurance, can reach the hut.

The Jackal Hut was formerly called the Schuss/Zesiger Hut. Now it bears the monikers of a man named Jack (Schuss) and a man named Al (Zesiger). Get it?

The hut is laid out on the same basic floor plan as its sister hut, the Fowler/Hilliard. The sleeping areas, which include several private rooms and an assortment of sleeping benches, are all upstairs. The view out of the upstairs window rivals the one from the front porch. Whether you are sipping tea on the deck or curled up in a sleeping bag inside near the picture windows, don't miss watching the sun set behind Homestake Peak. Make reservations through the 10th Mountain Division Hut Association (see Appendix A).

**RECOMMENDED DAY TRIPS:**

**When the powder is fresh, there is great telemark skiing right out the front door on the south-facing slopes.** Be careful not to drop too far down! On the north side of the hut, ski over Elevation Point 11,716' where there is tree skiing on advanced downhill descents of 1,400 vertical feet. Winter mountaineers will delight in traversing the ridge to the east and climbing Pearl Peak, Elk Peak, or Corbett Peak.

INTERMEDIATE/ADVANCED

TOUR
# 20a Camp Hale Trailhead to Jackal Hut via Pearl Creek

SEE MAP PAGES 124–125 AND 152–153

| | |
|---|---|
| TIME | 5 to 8 hours |
| DISTANCE | 6.6 miles |
| ELEVATIONS | TRAILHEAD: 9,250′ HUT: 11,610′ GAIN/LOSS: +2,360′/-40′ |
| AVALANCHE | Minimal danger |
| MAPS | 10th Mountain Division: Chicago Ridge<br>USGS 7.5′: Pando, 1987<br>National Forest: White River<br>Trails Illustrated: Map #109 (Breckenridge/Tennessee Pass) |

**TOUR OVERVIEW:** The trail up Pearl Creek is my preferred tour to the Jackal Hut. Though each route to the hut has its own advantages and disadvantages, this one is special for one reason: good snow. Pearl Creek lies deep in a valley, far below and to the north of the Jackal Hut. This route tends to harbor better snow for longer periods of time because it receives less direct sun than its southern counterparts. This is especially noticeable when you are descending from the hut.

This route covers the first 2.6 miles of the Fowler/Hilliard via Resolution Creek route (Tour 19c) to the bridge over Resolution Creek and the last 4 miles of the Fowler/Hilliard-to-Jackal Hut route (Tour 19d). Refer to those routes for detailed descriptions and directions.

*The Jackal Hut maintains vigil at dusk.*

INTERMEDIATE/ADVANCED

TOUR **20b**

## South Camp Hale Trailhead to Jackal Hut via Ranch Creek

SEE MAP PAGES 124–125 AND 152–153

| | |
|---|---|
| TIME | 4 to 6 hours |
| DISTANCE | 4 miles |
| ELEVATIONS | TRAILHEAD: 9,280' HUT: 11,610' GAIN: +2,330' |
| AVALANCHE | Some avalanche terrain encountered; easily avoided |
| MAPS | 10th Mountain Division: Chicago Ridge<br>USGS 7.5': Pando, 1987<br>National Forest: White River<br>Trails Illustrated: Map #109 (Breckenridge/Tennessee Pass) |

**TOUR OVERVIEW:** The Ranch Creek trail is the straight shot to the Jackal Hut. Gaining over 2,300 feet of elevation in 4 miles, this route holds very few surprises. Although the tour is described as starting from South Camp Hale, a start from Camp Hale works just as well, although it does lengthen the trip by roughly 0.6 mile and increase the elevation gain by a formidable 30 feet.

**DIRECTIONS TO TRAILHEAD:** From I-70, exit at Minturn (Exit 171), 5.4 miles west of Vail, and proceed south on US 24 for 19.3 miles. From Leadville, drive north on US 24 from the intersection with CO 91 for 13.9 miles, across Tennessee Pass to the main Camp Hale Road. Park on the east side in a plowed turnout near a fishing pond marked by a sign reading "Fisherman Parking."

**THE ROUTE:** Leave the parking area and drop down a few feet onto the main valley floor. Travel directly across the valley on an east/northeast course, aiming for the south side of a rocky cliff that has power lines running over it. On the south side of the cliff is a low-angled, fan-shaped slope, covered only with shrubs. This is where the trail begins its climb. After crossing the Eagle River by locating a snow bridge or by fording the stream, continue across the valley until you reach a road (Forest Road 714) below the mountainside. Turn south and follow the road for 0.25 mile until you reach a marked left turn (northeast) onto the Ranch Creek Road.

Begin the ascent into Ranch Creek; switchback up the road west and then due north. Climb 200 feet, then turn east and traverse up through a large clearing, heading back toward the creek. From here to the top of the ridge is fairly straightforward, though a steady climb, as the route simply ascends along the bottom of the drainage heading, to the northwest through clearings and trees.

Near the 11,000' level, the trail approaches the head of the drainage and the ridge above; search for the trail leading up to the east/southeast onto the crest of the ridge. Follow the trail into a large meadow, change your direction to east/northeast, then exit the meadow and climb back to the crest of the ridge. From here the trail ascends on a moderate traversing climb to the hut, which is below and south of Elevation Point 11,716'. If you miss any turns, the easiest route to the hut would be to ski north directly onto the ridge-crest and follow it to Elevation Point 11,716'. From there, it is easy to locate the hut by descending south off the top into the large meadow on the southeast side.

INTERMEDIATE/ADVANCED

TOUR **20c**

# South Camp Hale Trailhead to Jackal Hut via Cataract Creek

SEE MAP PAGES 124–125 AND 152–153

TIME 5 to 7 hours

DISTANCE 6 miles

ELEVATIONS TRAILHEAD: 9,280' HUT: 11,610' GAIN/LOSS: +2,440'/-40'

AVALANCHE Some avalanche terrain encountered; easily avoided

MAPS 10th Mountain Division: Chicago Ridge
USGS 7.5': Pando, 1987
National Forest: White River
Trails Illustrated: Map #109 (Breckenridge/Tennessee Pass)

**TOUR OVERVIEW:** This is the most scenic trail to the Jackal Hut. It is south-facing, so the sun can develop a hearty crust on the snow. Some sections may even be rocky. With a deep snowpack or new snow, this route is as good as the other Jackal Hut routes. It is also the most direct route from the Jackal Hut to Vance's Cabin.

**DIRECTIONS TO TRAILHEAD:** From I-70, exit at Minturn (Exit 171), which is 5.4 miles west of Vail, and proceed south on US 24 for 19.3 miles. From Leadville, drive north on US 24 for 13.9 miles across Tennessee Pass to the South Camp Hale parking area. Park in a plowed turnout near a fishing pond, marked by a sign reading "Fisherman Parking."

**THE ROUTE:** Leave the parking area and drop down onto the main valley floor. Travel across the valley on an east/northeast course, aiming for the south side of a rocky cliff with power lines running over it. Cross the Eagle River via a snow bridge or by fording the stream. Continue across the valley to a road (Forest Road 714). Turn south and follow the road for 2 miles.

Uphill to the north, a road leads into Cataract Creek. This road, marked by a sign, climbs almost continuously to the Jackal Hut. (It also joins with the Colorado Trail for 1.8 miles.) Climb the road as it gains altitude rapidly, switchback around a rocky promontory, then switchback again and head north to Cataract Creek. Cross the creek, climb around another large switchback, then traverse northeast across a wide, south-facing slope.

Traverse into the moderately steep, forested upper valley, then search for a narrow, rocky, treeless swath that runs directly uphill to the north. Begin the laborious task of climbing this hill and up a drainage through a series of clearings. Follow the clearings back to the northwest to the top of the ridge. Ski west through the forest, following the crest of the ridge. Pass over a small saddle (where the Pearl Creek route, Tour 20a, attains the ridge from the north). Continue west along the crest of the ridge, then begin climbing the last 260 feet through a large ridgetop clearing. The Jackal Hut is 0.6 mile away from this saddle. As you near Elevation Point 11,716', gently traverse downward toward the southwest and the Jackal Hut.

INTERMEDIATE/ADVANCED

TOUR

# 20d Jackal Hut to Vance's Cabin

SEE MAP PAGES 124–125 AND 152–153

| | |
|---|---|
| TIME | 6 to 9 hours |
| DISTANCE | 8.6 miles |
| ELEVATIONS | J HUT: 11,610' V CABIN: 10,980' GAIN/LOSS: +1,700'/-2,275' |
| AVALANCHE | Some avalanche terrain encountered; easily avoided |
| MAPS | 10th Mountain Division: Chicago Ridge<br>USGS 7.5': Pando, 1987<br>National Forest: White River<br>Trails Illustrated: Map #109 (Breckenridge/Tennessee Pass) |

**TOUR OVERVIEW:** The northern 3.6 miles of this tour follow the Cataract Creek Jackal Hut route (Tour 20c) down the steep south face from Elevation Point 11,716' through Cataract Creek. South of the East Fork of the Eagle River, this trail enters the forest, following a sinuous trail. This route can be longer than you anticipate, particularly when new snow forces you to break trail.

**THE ROUTE:** From the Jackal Hut, ski east along the ridge and make the 260-foot drop to the 11,400-foot saddle. Pass the north turn to Pearl Creek and continue east through the trees. Ski 0.4 mile along the south side of the ridge until the forest opens into a broad, treeless, bowl-shaped drainage. Contour southeast through the meadow, dropping to Cataract Creek.

Ski downstream along the Cataract Creek Road/Colorado Trail for 1.8 miles to the east fork of the Eagle River Road (Forest Road 714). Turn upstream and ski southeast 0.25 mile along the road to the Eagle River. Cross the river, leave the road, and head for the forest, following a south/southwest course. Enter the forest via a marked trail. For the next 2.2 miles, ski through the woods, following a secluded trail up to Jones Gulch. As the trail nears the gulch, it climbs steeply south along the creek until it reaches a beautiful and remote willow-filled meadow.

Follow the trail west, returning to the forest along the meadow's northern edge to an old road. (There are old logging roads in the area that do not appear on the latest USGS topo maps, so be careful and remain alert.) Traverse west on a moderate climb for 0.4 mile and gain the forested, north ridge of Taylor Hill. Turn sharply uphill and follow a distinct trail (the old Trail of the 10th) straight up the ridge for roughly 400 feet to a junction with a road at 11,033 feet. Turn right onto this road and ski along it for 0.6 mile to a tiny clearing and a fork in the trail. Continue on the left, higher trail and ski the last 0.7 mile to Vance's Cabin, which is near the top of a clearing and faces west.

*Doug Seyb takes in a stormy sunset from the deck of the Jackal Hut.*

# Vance's Cabin

| | |
|---|---|
| **HUT ELEVATION** | 10,980' |
| **DATE BUILT** | 1981; renovated for hut use in 1988 |
| **SEASONS** | August 20 through April 30 (fall through winter) |
| **CAPACITY** | 16 |
| **HUT LAYOUT** | 6 beds in upstairs loft, 10 single bunk beds in lower-level communal sleeping area |
| **HUT ESSENTIALS** | Woodstove for heat, wood-burning cookstove with oven, propane cookstoves, all kitchenware, outhouse, photovoltaic electric lights |
| **OTHER GOODIES** | Indoor sauna |

Vance's Cabin, built in honor of Vance Falkenberg, is an unusual 10th Mountain Division structure in that it is privately owned and resembles a hunting lodge. Constructed of logs and featuring a large, south-facing deck, the cabin overlooks the Ski Cooper ski area. It has a tri-level design, with a sleeping loft above the main floor, a large sleeping area in the basement, and a main floor for hanging out and cooking. The basement also contains a sauna fired by a wood-burning stove.

As of summer 2000, Vance's Cabin and the surrounding land is for sale. It is possible that the 10th Mountain Division Association or another private party will purchase it intact and continue running it as is. There also has been talk of the 10th possibly building a new hut higher up to the east, atop Taylor Hill. Stay tuned and stay aware of changes. Make reservations through the 10th Mountain Division Hut Association (see Appendix A).

**RECOMMENDED DAY TRIPS:**

**The skiing immediately around the cabin is somewhat limited.** One possibility is to climb up behind the cabin and into the woods on the west side of Taylor Hill. Another choice is to explore an older cross-country trail, called the Trail of the 10th. From the Ski Cooper parking lot, this trail ascends Piney Gulch to Taylor Hill. From Taylor Hill, the trail travels down the northwest ridge to the Taylor Hill Road at 11,033 feet. From this point, skiers can return south 1.3 miles to Vance's Cabin. From the top of Taylor Hill, it is also quite reasonable to climb onto Chicago Ridge, where there's great skiing after snowstorms.

NOVICE/INTERMEDIATE

TOUR
# 21a Tennessee Pass Trailhead to Vance's Cabin

SEE MAP PAGES 124–125 AND 152–153

| | |
|---|---|
| TIME | 3 to 4 hours |
| DISTANCE | 3.1 miles |
| ELEVATIONS | TRAILHEAD: 10,424' CABIN: 10,980' GAIN/LOSS: +776'/-200' |
| AVALANCHE | Minimal danger |
| MAPS | 10th Mountain Division: Chicago Ridge<br>USGS 7.5': Leadville North, 1970; Pando, 1987<br>National Forest: White River<br>Trails Illustrated: Map #109 (Breckenridge/Tennessee Pass) |

**TOUR OVERVIEW:** From Tennessee Pass, the Piney Gulch Trail to Vance's Cabin is one of the shortest routes to a 10th Mountain Division hut. It is a great introduction to hut skiing. Skiers attempting this trail should still be prepared for winter weather; at times, skiers have had to spend the night on the trail.

**DIRECTIONS TO TRAILHEAD:** From I-70, exit at Minturn (Exit 171), 5.4 miles west of Vail. Drive south on US 24 for 24.4 miles to the top of Tennessee Pass. From Leadville, drive north on US 24 from the junction of CO 91 for 8.8 miles to the top of Tennessee Pass. Park on the west side of the road.

**THE ROUTE:** From the Ski Cooper parking lot, walk to the Nordic center office. Begin skiing east along a snow-packed aqueduct road. This is the start of the Piney Gulch/Cooper Loop Nordic Center trails, so don't get confused. After 0.6 mile, search for a trail and a marker to the north. Cross the creek and begin climbing through a clearing on the west side of Piney Creek, following the north branch of the creek 0.3 mile. Look northeast for an uphill clearing and ascend through it. If you begin to contour northeast along the creek, you've missed the turn. After gaining 300 feet in elevation, the trail reaches a saddle north of Elevation Point 10,963'. Begin climbing northeast into the forest. Watch for the blue diamond markers to confirm that you are on course. Soon the trail starts traversing north at about 11,120 feet. Ski due north and then west. Vance's Cabin is 0.3 mile west and 200 feet down a short but thrilling descent.

*Note:* Occasionally, a snowcat may operate in the area. Be careful not to be led astray by the cat.

INTERMEDIATE

TOUR
# 21b Vance's Cabin to 10th Mountain Division Hut

SEE MAP PAGES 124–125 AND 152–153

TIME 6 to 8 hours

DISTANCE 8.9 miles

ELEVATIONS V CABIN: 10,980' 10TH MTN. HUT: 11,370' GAIN/LOSS: +1,410'/-1,066'

AVALANCHE Minimal danger

MAPS 10th Mountain Division: Chicago Ridge, Galena Mountain
USGS 7.5': Homestake Reservoir, 1970; Leadville North, 1970; Pando, 1987
National Forest: San Isabel, White River
Trails Illustrated: Map #109 (Breckenridge/Tennessee Pass); Map #126 (Holy Cross/Ruedi Reservoir)

**TOUR OVERVIEW:** This is the only game in town for skiers wishing to ski from Vance's Cabin to the 10th Mountain Division Hut. This trail combines the Tennessee Pass Trailhead to Vance's Cabin route (Tour 21a) and the Tennessee Pass Trailhead to the 10th Mountain Division Hut route (Tour 23a). The route is long but not difficult—mostly long stretches of pleasant touring. The trail west of Tennessee Pass utilizes 2.6 miles of a well-used Forest Service Nordic trail (the Mitchell Creek/Old Railroad Run). Summer bicyclists will want to descend south on US 24 for 1.8 miles to Crane Park, then follow Tour 23a.

*Scott Toepfer gives a snowpit analysis course on a "Babes in the Backcountry" winter skills weekend at Francie's Cabin.*

*Opposite: Rick Sayre shows off his climbing skins, essential for forward and upward mobility on modern backcountry skis.*

# Sangree M. Froelicher Hut

| | |
|---|---|
| **HUT ELEVATION** | 11,630' |
| **DATE BUILT** | 1998 |
| **SEASONS** | Thanksgiving through April 30 (winter); July 1 through September 30 (summer) |
| **CAPACITY** | 16 |
| **HUT LAYOUT** | 1 room with a double bed, 1 room with 4 single beds, in addition to 10 single beds in a communal sleeping area, all upstairs |
| **HUT ESSENTIALS** | Woodstove for heat, wood-burning cookstove with oven, propane cookstoves, all kitchenware, outhouse, photovoltaic electric lights |

*The Sangree M. Froelicher Hut north of Leadville has a nice, short approach tour, excellent vistas, and great day tours.*

The Sangree M. Froelicher Hut, formerly the Belvedere Hut, has all of the ingredients for a fine hut outing for skiers of all persuasions. It has a splendid, relatively short approach tour. It offers an expansive panorama of the Collegiate Peaks of the Sawatch Range from its front deck and windows. It is surrounded by varied terrain with nearby telemark slopes, and there are short tours that quickly take you up onto safe ridges above tree line with even better views. And finally, north of the hut is gentle Buckeye Peak, a great introductory challenge for ski mountaineers. All this—along with its close proximity to Summit County, Vail, and the Front Range—accounts for Sangree M. Froelicher's newfound celebrity among Colorado's huts.

Sangree M. Froelicher is located at the southern tail end of the Gore Range, north of Leadville on the eastern aspect of Chicago Ridge, which divides the Fremont Pass/Climax Mine road (CO 91) and the Tennessee Pass road (US 24).

From the ridge above the hut, you can look down onto the Ski Cooper ski area and Tennessee Pass. Presently, there is only one trail to the hut. In the future, additional trails may connect this hut with Ski Cooper and Vance's Cabin.

**RECOMMENDED DAY TRIPS:**

**The entire area around the hut is ideal for exploration**—just be careful of the steep slope east of the hut and the cornice-laden headwall above Buckeye Lake and Gulch. The slopes at the head of the valley, west and southwest of the hut, above the large switchback in the trail near 11,400 feet, cradle excellent telemark terrain. This includes the north-facing glades dropping off Elevation Point 11,577'. The top of the ridge west/northwest above the hut is a quick jaunt for skiers of all abilities.

And finally, consider climbing Buckeye Peak. Climb northwest from the hut and pass between Elevation Points 12,254' and 12,156', then head north along the crest of the ridge to the peak. This area is generally wind-scoured in winter and is almost free of avalanche hazard, but beware of potential slabby pockets of wind-worked snow between 12,200 and 12,400 feet. Consider traversing upward to the west below 12,200 feet along the contour line to the top of the small ridge that runs to the west. Then climb back to the north/northwest to the summit. The view from the summit includes the Gore Range, the Front Range, the Tenmile Range, the Mosquito Range, the Sangre de Cristos, the Sawatch Range, and the Elk Mountains—something not to be missed on a clear day!

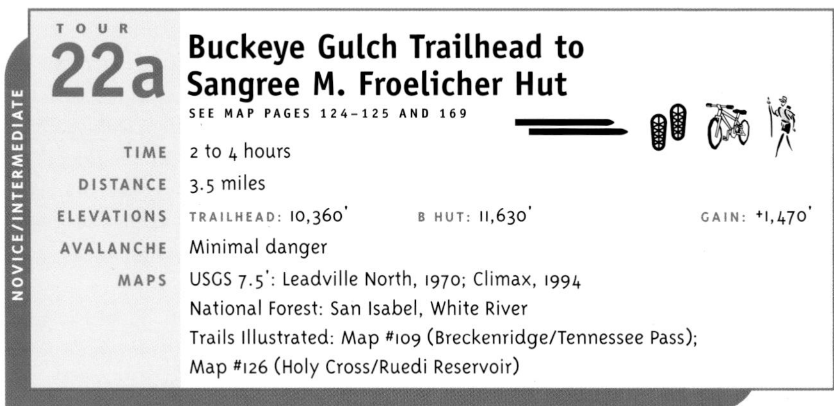

TOUR

# 22a Buckeye Gulch Trailhead to Sangree M. Froelicher Hut

SEE MAP PAGES 124–125 AND 169

NOVICE/INTERMEDIATE

| | |
|---|---|
| TIME | 2 to 4 hours |
| DISTANCE | 3.5 miles |
| ELEVATIONS | TRAILHEAD: 10,360' B HUT: 11,630' GAIN: +1,470' |
| AVALANCHE | Minimal danger |
| MAPS | USGS 7.5': Leadville North, 1970; Climax, 1994<br>National Forest: San Isabel, White River<br>Trails Illustrated: Map #109 (Breckenridge/Tennessee Pass); Map #126 (Holy Cross/Ruedi Reservoir) |

**TOUR OVERVIEW:** Buckeye Gulch makes for a wonderful tour. Within minutes of escaping the parking area and the rush of the highway, you enter a quiet, secluded valley that seems miles from civilization. The ascent is steady, though never overwhelming. Route-finding will keep you on your toes while never being labyrinthine. Descending this trail is a blast and can go quickly. Once our group made it out in just over 20 minutes, at "normal" speed.

**DIRECTIONS TO TRAILHEAD:** The trailhead is located on CO 91 between Copper Mountain and Leadville on the southern side of Fremont Pass. It is 4.3 miles north/northeast of the intersection of US 24 (Tennessee Pass) and CO 91 (Fremont Pass) on the very northern end of Leadville and 7.25 miles west of the actual summit of Fremont Pass on the west side of CO 91 near some homes and cabins. There is a signed parking area for 10th Mountain visitors.

**THE ROUTE:** The trail is divided into three distinct sections, the first being the climb from the highway up through the lower narrow, steeper, southerly exposed canyon. At the 0.95-mile mark, an obvious and signed canyon-trail intersection is reached. From this point, take the left fork (the right fork goes to Buckeye Lake area) and ski almost due west up through the less taxing valley. In some areas the trail is a bit harder to follow, but in general it remains on the left (southern) side of the creek and drainage and travels along the edge of the steeper, wooded slopes.

The upper section of the tour travels in and out of stands of spruce and fir trees and is not too difficult to follow. At around 11,040 feet, the trail escapes the confines of the creek and switchbacks up through a lightly wooded clearing. This area and the north- and east-facing slopes above to the west and south are great for making turns. At around 11,400 feet the trail follows the contours of the valley and contours around the head of the valley in one large switchback that leaves you heading east/northeast on the final moderate ascent to the hut.

ADVANCED/EXPERT

TOUR
# 22b Sangree M. Froelicher Hut to Chalk Creek Traverse

SEE MAP PAGES 124–125 AND 169

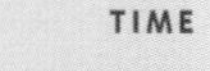

**TIME** 3 to 6 hours

**DISTANCE** 4.5 miles

**ELEVATIONS** B HUT: 11,630' CHALK CREEK TH: 10,600' GAIN/LOSS: +1,237'/-2,267'

**AVALANCHE** Route crosses avalanche slopes; prone to skier-triggered avalanches during high-hazard periods

**MAPS** USGS 7.5': Leadville North, 1970; Climax, 1994
National Forest: San Isabel, White River
Trails Illustrated: Map #109 (Breckenridge/Tennessee Pass); Map #126 (Holy Cross/Ruedi Reservoir)

**TOUR OVERVIEW:** John Scahill and friends, who skied this route as an egress from the Sangree M. Froelicher Hut, suggested this sensational, adventure-packed tour and supplied the information about it. The tour could be skied as a route to the hut, though this is not recommended because you travel over short stretches of avalanche terrain that are best descended, not ascended.

Overall, this is a classic high-mountain tour with great views that extend the Buckeye Peak day tour into a high mountain ridge traverse that finishes with a powder descent through knockout glades.

Be forewarned, though, that this relatively short route at times walks a tightrope on ridges that are difficult to escape. The steep, unskiable terrain is exposed to the elements for much of its length, requiring skiers to do some thoughtful route-finding—and the cornices don't make the task any easier. As a kicker, the route forces you to descend a short, unavoidable avalanche slope. Obviously, clear weather conditions and stability in the snowpack are desirable. Sound fun? For the right group, this is a superb excursion.

**DIRECTIONS TO TRAILHEAD:** The parking area for shuttle cars is on the west (Leadville) side of Fremont Pass on CO 91, 8.4 miles north/northeast of the CO 91/US 24 intersection. At 3.15 miles downhill from the pass is a small valley off to the northwest. Park off the highway along the northwestern side of the road near the plowed Chalk Creek Trailhead parking area (marked with a sign). If you are driving downhill, this is to the right.

**THE ROUTE:** The tour begins with an ascent of 12,867' Buckeye Peak. This is a straightforward ascent accomplished by climbing up from the hut over easy terrain onto the ridge to the west. Once on the ridge, follow it over gentle alpine terrain north to the summit. This area is generally windblown and may require walking. Of greatest concern to skiers on this ascent are wind-deposited pockets of snow that form between 12,200' and 12,400'. Often, the best way to avoid these is to traverse out to the northwest around them, but be careful.

From Buckeye's summit, descend along the ridge toward Elevation Point 12,684'. Pass Elevation Point 12,684' and make a right turn to the east. The route follows the crest of an east/west–running finger ridge off Elevation Point 12,684'.

To quote Scahill, "The easterly route along this ridge is fairly obvious; however, it should be noted that there is no escape off of this ridge. The terrain is rather steep on both the north and south sides, and likely prone to avalanche hazard."

Eventually, the narrow ridge metamorphoses into a broad, gladed, triangular face that cascades down to the highway. This transition point is probably the single most hazardous spot on the tour. Scahill continues, "The nose at the far eastern edge of the ridge must also be negotiated carefully as it drops about 60-80 feet into the trees. The best line we found was slightly north of east. As one descends, there are a few small, scraggly trees that can be used as guideposts." A word to the wise—ski through this area as expeditiously and as gingerly as possible.

Now that you have paid your dues, you get your reward in the form of 800 feet of sublime powder glade skiing. Work the terrain trending along the northern half of the triangular face down to around 11,000 feet.

The final challenge is found in choosing the right path from the 11,000-foot level to the trailhead. You cannot ski directly down through the creek drainages in this area, as the bottoms of the drainages tend to be gorgelike in their narrowness and possess impassable cliff bands—especially near the waterfall—that bar easy passage to the highway. The best route, according to Scahill, traverses north across the left (west) fork of Chalk Creek right around 11,000 feet. This may entail a short scramble up the south-facing slopes on the far side of the creek until gaining a heavily treed slope that gently feeds you down in an east/southeast direction.

*Two skiers are dwarfed by the landscape above the hut.*

After a few hundred yards of tree bashing, this opens up in flats where the power line runs through. Continue east, passing under the power line until you reach the gorge of main Chalk Creek. Turn upstream (north) and continue roughly 200 to 300 feet until you reach an obvious, gently sloping section leading down to the creek. A group of trees across the creek from this access point permits safe passage up the northeastern banks of the creek. Once across Chalk Creek, continue east until you gain the old four-wheel-drive road that leads back down to the highway and the trailhead.

An alternative descent route is to drop from the 11,000-foot level continuously down the densely timbered ski slopes until you reach the power line, which can be followed south to the highway—downstream of the parking area several hundred yards. This entails skiing down through heavy timber.

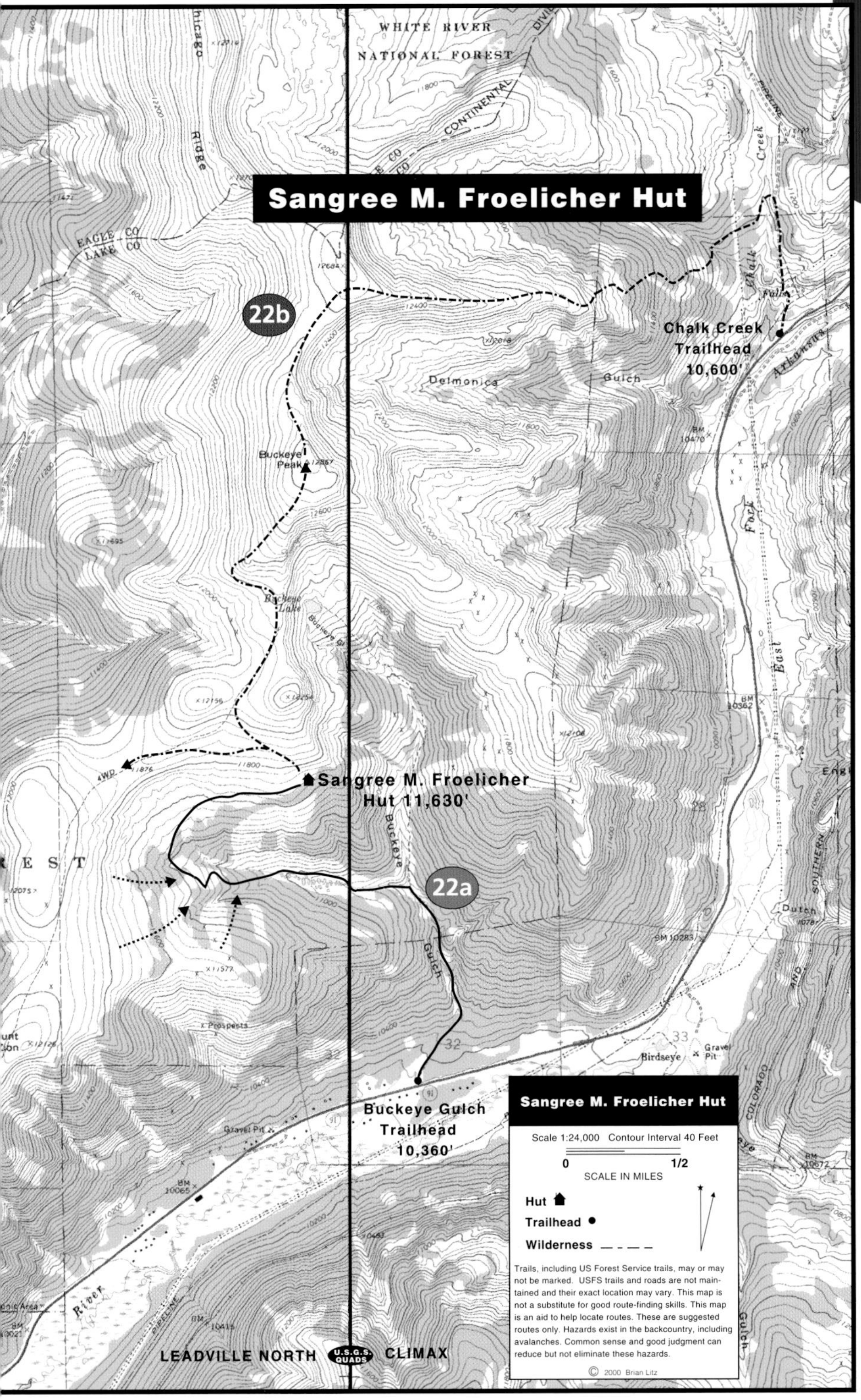

Sangree M. Froelicher Hut
22b
Chalk Creek
Trailhead
10,600'
Buckeye Peak
Sangree M. Froelicher
Hut 11,630'
22a
Buckeye Gulch
Trailhead
10,360'
LEADVILLE NORTH
U.S.G.S. QUADS
CLIMAX
Sangree M. Froelicher Hut
Scale 1:24,000 Contour Interval 40 Feet
0
1/2
SCALE IN MILES
Hut
Trailhead
Wilderness
Trails, including US Forest Service trails, may or may not be marked. USFS trails and roads are not maintained and their exact location may vary. This map is not a substitute for good route-finding skills. This map is an aid to help locate routes. These are suggested routes only. Hazards exist in the backcountry, including avalanches. Common sense and good judgment can reduce but not eliminate these hazards.
© 2000 Brian Litz

# 10th Mountain Division Hut

| | |
|---|---|
| **HUT ELEVATION** | 11,370' |
| **DATE BUILT** | 1989 |
| **SEASONS** | Thanksgiving through April 30 (winter); July 1 through September 30 (summer) |
| **CAPACITY** | 16 |
| **HUT LAYOUT** | 1 room with 6 single beds, 1 room with 4 single beds, in addition to 1 double bed and 4 single beds in a communal sleeping area, all upstairs |
| **HUT ESSENTIALS** | Woodstove for heat, wood-burning cookstove with oven, propane cookstoves, all kitchenware, outhouse, photovoltaic electric lights |

When the first edition of *Colorado Hut to Hut* was published, the 10th Mountain Division Hut and Uncle Bud's Hut were the new kids on the block. Along with the Skinner Hut and the Betty Bear, these huts created the link that finally connected the Camp Hale/Vail Pass huts with the Aspen/Edwards huts—a bridge between east and west. The 10th Mountain Division Hut, although now a bit weathered, remains very popular and is the quintessential hut. It was built and named in collective honor of the 10th Mountain Division soldiers.

The trails to the hut, while suitable for strong beginners, are classic intermediate trails. Novice skiers who are ready to push their limits a little and folks who are ready to lead their own trip would do well to head for this hut. The surroundings are magnificent. Above the hut to the west is Homestake Peak and a glacially carved cirque. There really is something for everyone here—including those who want to just kick back in the sun on the porch and enjoy the vista of the Collegiate Peaks of the Sawatch Range or dream about bottomless powder. Make reservations through the 10th Mountain Division Hut Association (see Appendix A).

**RECOMMENDED DAY TRIPS:**

**There are three good choices for day trips here.** A gem of a trail follows the Slide Lake four-wheel-drive road 0.6 mile to Slide Lake. If you get up early and ski to the lake, you'll enjoy a special treat at sunrise.

Industrious backcountry skiers will want to climb Homestake Peak, which is often covered with fine snow perfect for carving turns. By skiing southwest from the hut, it is possible to traverse up onto the east ridge. Once on the ridge, simply head straight up 1,400 feet to the top. This ridge is normally free of avalanche danger—though you need to exercise caution while climbing out of the trees and gaining the ridge. The glades to the west of the hut make for fun runs close to the cabin.

And finally, the eastern end of the high alpine ridge north of the hut boasts fine slopes for telemarking. Many people never explore this area—their loss!

INTERMEDIATE

TOUR

# 23a Tennessee Pass Trailhead to 10th Mountain Division Hut

SEE MAP PAGES 124–125, 180–181, AND 186–187

**TIME** 5 to 7 hours

**DISTANCE** 5.7 miles

**ELEVATIONS** TRAILHEAD: 10,424′ HUT: 11,370′ GAIN/LOSS: +1,210′/–140′

**AVALANCHE** Minimal danger

**MAPS** 10th Mountain Division: Galena Mountain
USGS 7.5′: Homestake Reservoir, 1970; Leadville North, 1970
National Forest: San Isabel, White River
Trails Illustrated: Map #109 (Breckenridge/Tennessee Pass); Map #126 (Holy Cross/Ruedi Reservoir)

**TOUR OVERVIEW:** This trail begins on the summit of Tennessee Pass and heads west along a Forest Service Nordic trail and the Colorado Trail into the massive West Fork of the Tennessee Creek drainage. After the route meets the Crane Park/Slide Lake Trail, the trails merge and climb to the hut. This trail is not as popular as the Crane Park Trailhead and is generally used as an interconnect route with Vance's Cabin.

**DIRECTIONS TO TRAILHEAD:** From I-70, take the Minturn exit (Exit 171), 5.4 miles west of Vail, and drive on US 24 south 24.4 miles to the top of Tennessee Pass. Approaching from Leadville, drive north on US 24 from the junction with CO 91 for 8.8 miles to the summit of Tennessee Pass. Park on the west side of US 24.

**THE ROUTE:** From the parking area, begin traveling southwest on the Nordic trail that joins the Colorado Trail. Begin a long, descending traverse to the southwest, into the West Fork of the Tennessee Creek drainage. After 2.3 miles the trail crosses a creek, then turns south and climbs to the Wurt's Ditch Road. The intersection is marked with trail signs for the 10th Mountain Trail, Colorado Trail, and Mitchell Creek.

Cross the road, following the Colorado and 10th Mountain trails south and west over a hill and down a quick descent to another junction. The left (southeast) trail heads to the gravel pit; the trail to the south/southwest heads up West Tennessee Creek to Uncle Bud's Hut; and the right (west/northwest) trail heads to the 10th Mountain Division Hut. Take the righthand trail, which then leaves the Colorado Trail and heads toward Lily Lake.

Go northwest through the woods into a creek drainage, eventually crossing the creek. Ascend along the southern side of the creek to another trail junction between the north side of Lily Lake and the south edge of a large meadow. Follow the trail that crosses northwest through a willow bog.

Climb a steep but short hill (around 200 feet of elevation gain) on the far side, then begin the long but moderate ascent along the north side of Slide Creek. This climb travels through open clearings and among occasional tree stumps and evergreen trees for 1.6 miles until you reach a flat meadow. Veer right (north) into the meadow and to the 10th Mountain Division Hut.

The greatest challenge on this route is to avoid turning off onto one of the many well-traveled, and errant, trails in the area. Pay close attention to map, compass, and trail markers, especially at intersections.

INTERMEDIATE

TOUR 23b

## Crane Park Trailhead to 10th Mountain Division Hut

SEE MAP PAGES 124–125, 180-181, AND 186–187

TIME 4 to 6 hours

DISTANCE 4.4 miles

ELEVATIONS TRAILHEAD: 10,137' HUT: 11,370' GAIN/LOSS: +1,343'/-140'

AVALANCHE Minimal danger

MAPS 10th Mountain Division: Galena Mountain,
USGS 7.5': Homestake Reservoir, 1970; Leadville North, 1970
National Forest: San Isabel, White River
Trails Illustrated: Map #109 (Breckenridge/Tennessee Pass);
Map #126 (Holy Cross/Ruedi Reservoir)

**TOUR OVERVIEW:** Crane Park/Slide Lake Trail is the most popular route to the 10th Mountain Division Hut, gaining 1,300 feet in 4.4 miles. Initially, this route weaves through a network of plowed and unplowed back roads, so keep your map and compass handy. Note that the first mile of trail has been relocated and more stringent parking rules apply. The designated plowed parking area is near the main highway on the left (south) side of the road. Formerly the trail left the parking area and followed the plowed gravel road west through a small group of houses. Now the trail exits the road just west of the parking area, on the north side of the road (near a 10th Mountain sign) and parallels the road on the north through a meadow along the creek. Eventually, it ascends up into the woods, where it meets Wurt's Ditch Road (Tennessee Pass/10th Mountain Hut Trail; also the Colorado Trail). From there the trail turns left (south) and proceeds over a hill to the cabin. Refer to the shared Tennessee Pass route (see Tour 23a) for a description of the trail between Wurt's Ditch Road and the hut.

**DIRECTIONS TO TRAILHEAD:** From I-70, exit at Minturn (Exit 171), 5.4 miles west of Vail, and go south on US 24 for 24.4 miles to the top of Tennessee Pass. Continue 1.6 miles to the Crane Park turnoff (Forest Road 100), turning west at a large curve in the road. Traveling north from Leadville, drive from the junction of CO 91 on US 24 for 7.2 miles to the Crane Park turnoff (FR 100). A yellow piece of machinery marks the turn. Park near US 24, being careful not to block the road.

**THE ROUTE:** Ski west along the road from the official parking area. After a few hundred feet, you'll see a 10th Mountain trailhead on the right. Leave the road and ski into the meadow. The trail heads west and follows the creek until it reaches the Tennessee Pass/10th Mountain Hut Trail. Turn left (south), following the Colorado Trail and 10th Mountain trails south and west over a hill to another junction. The left (southeast) junction heads to a gravel pit; the south/southwest trail heads up West Tennessee Creek to Uncle Bud's Hut; and the right (west/northwest) trail heads to the 10th Mountain Division Hut. Take the righthand trail, which then leaves the Colorado Trail and heads to Lily Lake and the Slide Lake four-wheel-drive road. Follow Tour 23a for the last 2.7 miles to the hut.

*Note:* As this book goes to print, the 10th Mountain Division maps do not reflect the trail changes. These will be corrected in the future.

*The 10th Mountain Division Hut is the quintessential hut.*

INTERMEDIATE

TOUR **23c**

# 10th Mountain Division Hut to Uncle Bud's Hut

SEE MAP PAGES 124–125, 180–181, AND 186–187

| | |
|---|---|
| TIME | 5 to 8 hours |
| DISTANCE | 7.2 miles |
| ELEVATIONS | 10TH MTN. HUT: 11,370' UB HUT: 11,380' GAIN/LOSS: +1,520'/-1,500' |
| AVALANCHE | Some avalanche terrain encountered; easily avoided |
| MAPS | 10th Mountain Division: Galena Mountain, Continental Divide<br>USGS 7.5': Homestake Reservoir, 1970<br>National Forest: San Isabel, White River<br>Trails Illustrated: Map #109 (Breckenridge/Tennessee Pass); Map #126 (Holy Cross/Ruedi Reservoir) |

**TOUR OVERVIEW:** The trail between the 10th Mountain Division Hut and Uncle Bud's is a spectacular and geologically compelling route—one of the most scenic in the system. Running north-south, parallel to the Continental Divide on the east side of the Sawatch Range, the trail passes through an area that was heavily scoured during the Pleistocene glacial period (around 3 million years ago), and it's a stone's throw from textbook cirques, alpine tarns, and rock outcrops shaped and smoothed by the massive weight of glacial ice. The many creeks, descents, and climbs make for interesting and enjoyable route-finding. This route crosses the Holy Cross Wilderness Area and is closed to bikes.

**THE ROUTE:** From the 10th Mountain Hut, the trail heads south through a meadow, past a dead tree with a trail marker. Ski up over a flat ridge with a tiny, snow-covered pond, then drop into the North Fork of West Tennessee Creek below the east ridge of Homestake Peak. Continue south up and over a small, forested ridge and down to West Tennessee Creek. At the clearing in the valley bottom, correct your direction of travel and head slightly southwest. Cross the creek and pick up the trail as it climbs south into the forest along the west side of a small creek. Enter a flat meadow, turn east, cross the clearing, and re-enter the woods.

Follow the trail east and then south over another ridge with a tiny lake, then begin a distinct drop into a marshy creek. Head south/southeast from this marsh past a trail junction (joining the Colorado Trail), then ski around the east scarp of Elevation Point 11,375' and begin a long, traversing descent to the southwest into Long's Gulch. Follow the creek upstream past the wilderness boundary (1.5 miles west of the trail junction), then begin ascending out of the valley to the southwest.

The trail climbs through rocky terrain onto a promontory that overlooks the valley and the peaks to the west. Contour to the east and easily drop down and across Porcupine Gulch. Begin the 600-foot ascent of the steepest and most demanding 1 mile of trail. From here, the route switchbacks up a steep and at times rocky trail until it gains the east ridge of Galena Mountain, near tree line. (For those headed north to the 10th Mountain Division Hut, this portion of the route presents very difficult telemark skiing; you may wish to leave climbing skins on to slow the descent.) Make a gentle traverse east down to a forested saddle. Descend to the hut by curving sharply to the southwest, following trail markers through a drainage and into a clearing. After dropping 400 feet, the trail leaves the creek and traverses southeast along the Colorado Trail up to Uncle Bud's Hut.

*Beth Smith takes in the view near Uncle Bud's Hut.*

# Uncle Bud's Hut

| | |
|---|---|
| **HUT ELEVATION** | 11,380' |
| **DATE BUILT** | 1989 |
| **SEASONS** | Thanksgiving through April 30 (winter);<br>July 1 through September 30 (summer) |
| **CAPACITY** | 16 |
| **HUT LAYOUT** | 1 room with 6 beds, 1 room with 4 beds, in addition to 1 double bed and 4 single beds in a communal sleeping area, all upstairs |
| **HUT ESSENTIALS** | Woodstove for heat, wood-burning cookstove with oven, propane cookstoves, all kitchenware, outhouse, photovoltaic electric lights |

This hut is named for Burdell "Bud" Winter, a 10th Mountain Division soldier killed in action in the Italian Alps during World War II. A display tells the story of a man who died young, already a seasoned mountaineer.

Uncle Bud's Hut is unique in that the first level is constructed of stone, with a traditional wood-sided second story. Day skiing around the hut is extensive and varied, with a little bit of everything for everyone. Uncle Bud's Hut works well in conjunction with trips to the Skinner Hut to the southwest and the 10th Mountain Division Hut to the north, and as a destination in its own right. Make reservations through the 10th Mountain Division Hut Association (see Appendix A).

### RECOMMENDED DAY TRIPS:

**The area near Uncle Bud's Hut offers several options.** To the west of the hut is a large basin between Saint Kevin, Galena, and Bear Lakes. It is easy to drop down from the hut and spend a full day touring up and down this gully. Behind the hut to the north, skiers can climb back to the east ridge of Galena Mountain and ascend west to Elevation Point 12,313' for a brief introduction to winter mountaineering. Around the northeast corner of the hut is Saint Kevin Gulch, which has many acres of treeless terrain offering nice and easy telemark skiing, especially after a storm.

Finally, Galena Mountain's south ridge makes for a very safe, classic winter climb. From the hut, the route drops down to the Colorado Trail/Skinner Hut Trail, then west to the foot of the south ridge of Galena Mountain and a safe route up and out of the forest. Once on the south ridge, the route is straightforward and ascends north up a broad ridge to the 12,893-foot summit. If you attempt this route, although it's easy for a climb to a 12,000-foot peak, it does require commitment.

INTERMEDIATE

TOUR

# 24a Turquoise Lake Trailhead to Uncle Bud's Hut

SEE MAP PAGES 124–125, 180–181, AND 186–187

TIME 4 to 7 hours

DISTANCE 5.8 miles

ELEVATIONS TRAILHEAD: 9,760' HUT: 11,380' GAIN/LOSS: +1,620'/-40'

AVALANCHE Minimal danger

MAPS 10th Mountain Division: Continental Divide, Galena Mountain
USGS 7.5': Homestake Reservoir, 1970; Leadville North, 1970
National Forest: San Isabel, White River
Trails Illustrated: Map #109 (Breckenridge/Tennessee Pass); Map #126 (Holy Cross/Ruedi Reservoir)

**TOUR OVERVIEW:** Because of acts of vandalism at the traditional trailhead, the trailhead was moved down the road 2.1 miles into the main Tennessee Creek/Arkansas River Valley. Located on the eastern side of the river and the railroad tracks, this new parking lot is more open and lighted. Still, try not to leave valuables in your car—or valuable cars—here.

The trail now gains an additional 270 feet of elevation and is 5.8 miles long. It is still an easy-to-follow road for the entire distance. Novice skiers will be challenged by the climb to the hut but will enjoy cranking turns (or snowplowing!) back down to the parking area. For skiers, bikers, and hikers, this steep route climbs continuously from the parking area to the hut and features nice views of the Mosquito Range to the east.

**DIRECTIONS TO TRAILHEAD:** The Turquoise Lake Trailhead is a little difficult to locate, so follow the directions closely. The road to the trailhead begins on the north end of Leadville near Safeway. From the junction of US 24 and Mountain View Drive, turn west and drive 2.8 miles to a T junction. Turn north (right), cross a fork of the Arkansas River, and proceed to the parking lot, which is near the place where the road veers west to cross the main river and the railroad tracks.

**THE ROUTE:** Ski or walk west over the railroad tracks. Cross the main stem of the Arkansas River, then head west past the entrance to Turquoise Lake. When you reach another intersection, turn north again. Follow Forest Road 104, passing a picnic area, campgrounds, and boat ramps on the left between the road and the lake. Continue along the road, above the lake on the northeast, to a fork in the road.

Take the north fork onto Forest Road 107 and start climbing. Pass a right turn to Saint Kevin Gulch after 0.3 mile. Continue climbing north, ski under a power line, and then contour west up to a flat shoulder and small clearing with great views of the Arkansas Valley. Traverse west along the south aspect of the ridge for another 0.3 mile, then gain another flat shoulder.

Follow the trail north across gentle terrain, then begin the final 340-foot climb to the hut. Head northwest up a forested ridge and across a clearing, eventually leaving the road near Elevation Point 11,285'. Ski northwest through thinning trees to Uncle Bud's Hut.

ADVANCED

TOUR

# 24b Uncle Bud's Hut to Skinner Hut

SEE MAP PAGES 124–125, 180–181, AND 186–187

| | |
|---|---|
| TIME | 6 to 9 hours |
| DISTANCE | 7 miles |
| ELEVATIONS | UB HUT: 11,380' S HUT: 11,620' GAIN/LOSS: +1,985'/-1,760' |
| AVALANCHE | Some avalanche terrain encountered; easily avoided |
| MAPS | 10th Mountain Division: Continental Divide, Galena Mountain<br>USGS 7.5': Homestake Reservoir, 1970<br>National Forest: San Isabel, White River<br>Trails Illustrated: Map #126 (Holy Cross/Ruedi Reservoir) |

**TOUR OVERVIEW:** This route climbs to the Skinner Hut via one of the steepest and most physically taxing sections of trail in the 10th Mountain Division system. The ascent of Glacier Creek seems to catch people off guard and pushes them to the limit. Get an early start so you can travel at a comfortable pace.

**THE ROUTE:** Leave Uncle Bud's and descend into the basin west of the hut, called Bud's Gulch. Proceed to the Wilderness Area boundary sign and intercept the Colorado Trail. Follow the trail west over a small rise, then drop down across the Bear Creek drainage. Cross the basin north of Galena and Bear Lakes and ski southwest for 0.5 mile. Climb a series of switchbacks to tree line, across a shoulder of Galena Mountain.

Traverse west for a few hundred feet, then begin the long, switchbacking descent into Lake Fork Valley through a clearing. After descending roughly 150 feet,

*Skiers disembark from 10th Mountain Division Hut heading for Uncle Bud's Hut.*

traverse west through the trees, below a large ridge south of Galena Mountain. Continue on switchbacks near Mill Creek, then head southeast under the power lines, and finally turn west into the Lake Fork Valley.

The fun begins when you start the ascent to the Skinner Hut. Finding the trail can be a little tricky. Basically, the arduous ascent begins about 500 feet south of several Forest Service/Colorado Trail signs, located in a clearing near Lake Fork Creek, west of Turquoise Lake. (If you happen to be coming from the Turquoise Lake Trailhead, follow that road west until it turns south to cross the creek. From this spot, ski west along the creek on a trail through the woods. After a few hundred feet you will see several signs.)

From the signs, ski southwest, following the trail into the woods and across the creek to a trail junction. The right fork is the Timberline Lake Trail. Take the left fork, which heads south through some tightly spaced trees and begins climbing immediately.

*Beth Smith sits on the porch of Uncle Bud's Hut.*

From here, the trail switchbacks to the southwest without respite as it heads up and into Glacier Creek. The trail, marked by blue diamonds, remains on the west side of the creek. After climbing nearly 600 feet, the trail enters a flat basin below large cliffs and avalanche slopes to the west. The Skinner Hut is on top of the ridge to the south.

Ski directly up the valley along the creek and enter the woods on the far southwest end. Climb the west side of the creek, gaining an impressive 400 feet in elevation, and enter a second, smaller basin. Ski past the east edge of the meadow and follow the trail southwest, gaining approximately 160 feet in elevation. Turn to the southeast and climb the last grueling 200-foot slope to the ridgetop. Once gaining the ridge, turn to the northeast and traverse its crest for 0.3 mile to the Skinner Hut.

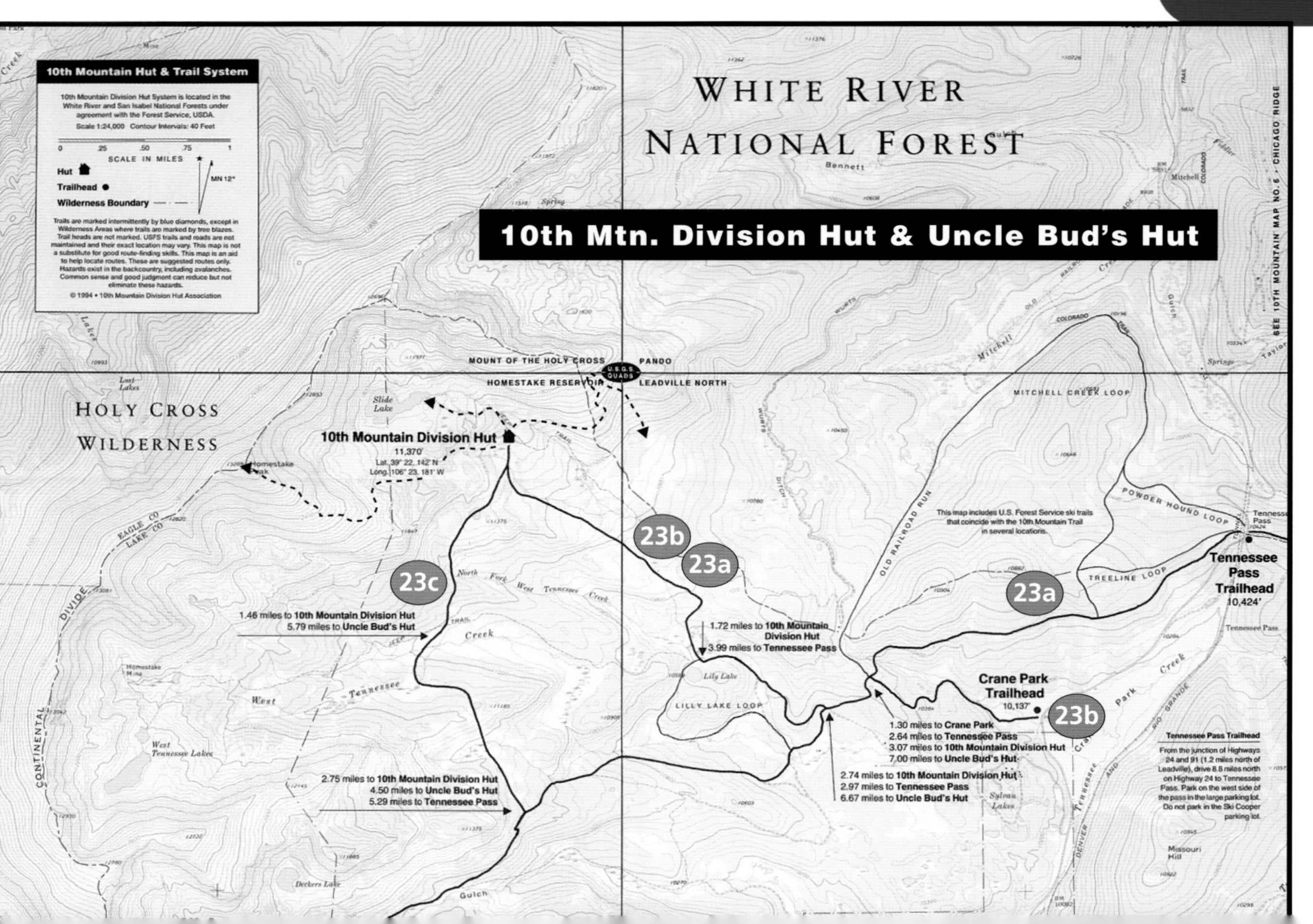
10th Mtn. Division Hut & Uncle Bud's Hut
WHITE RIVER NATIONAL FOREST
HOLY CROSS WILDERNESS
10th Mountain Hut & Trail System
10th Mountain Division Hut System is located in the White River and San Isabel National Forests under agreement with the Forest Service, USDA.
Scale 1:24,000 Contour Intervals: 40 Feet
0 .25 .50 .75 1
SCALE IN MILES
MN 12°
Hut
Trailhead
Wilderness Boundary
Trails are marked intermittently by blue diamonds, except in Wilderness Areas where trails are marked by tree blazes. Trail heads are not marked. USFS trails and roads are not maintained and their exact location may vary. This map is not a substitute for good route-finding skills. This map is an aid to help locate routes. These are suggested routes only. Hazards exist in the backcountry, including avalanches. Common sense and good judgment can reduce but not eliminate these hazards.
© 1994 • 10th Mountain Division Hut Association
MOUNT OF THE HOLY CROSS
PANDO
HOMESTAKE RESERVOIR
LEADVILLE NORTH
U.S.G.S. QUADS
10th Mountain Division Hut
11,370'
Lat. 39° 22. 142' N
Long. 106° 23. 181' W
Homestake Peak
Slide Lake
23a
23b
23c
1.46 miles to 10th Mountain Division Hut
5.79 miles to Uncle Bud's Hut
1.72 miles to 10th Mountain Division Hut
3.99 miles to Tennessee Pass
2.75 miles to 10th Mountain Division Hut
4.50 miles to Uncle Bud's Hut
5.29 miles to Tennessee Pass
1.30 miles to Crane Park
2.64 miles to Tennessee Pass
3.07 miles to 10th Mountain Division Hut
7.00 miles to Uncle Bud's Hut
2.74 miles to 10th Mountain Division Hut
2.97 miles to Tennessee Pass
6.67 miles to Uncle Bud's Hut
Crane Park Trailhead
10,137'
Tennessee Pass Trailhead
10,424'
This map includes U.S. Forest Service ski trails that coincide with the 10th Mountain Trail in several locations.
Tennessee Pass Trailhead
From the junction of Highways 24 and 91 (1.2 miles north of Leadville), drive 8.8 miles north on Highway 24 to Tennessee Pass. Park on the west side of the pass in the large parking lot. Do not park in the Ski Cooper parking lot.
MITCHELL CREEK LOOP
OLD RAILROAD RUN
POWDER HOUND LOOP
TREELINE LOOP
LILLY LAKE LOOP
Lily Lake
North Fork West Tennessee Creek
CONTINENTAL DIVIDE
EAGLE CO
LAKE CO
West Tennessee Lakes
Sylvan Lakes
Missouri Hill
Deckers Lake
SEE 10TH MOUNTAIN MAP NO. 6 • CHICAGO RIDGE

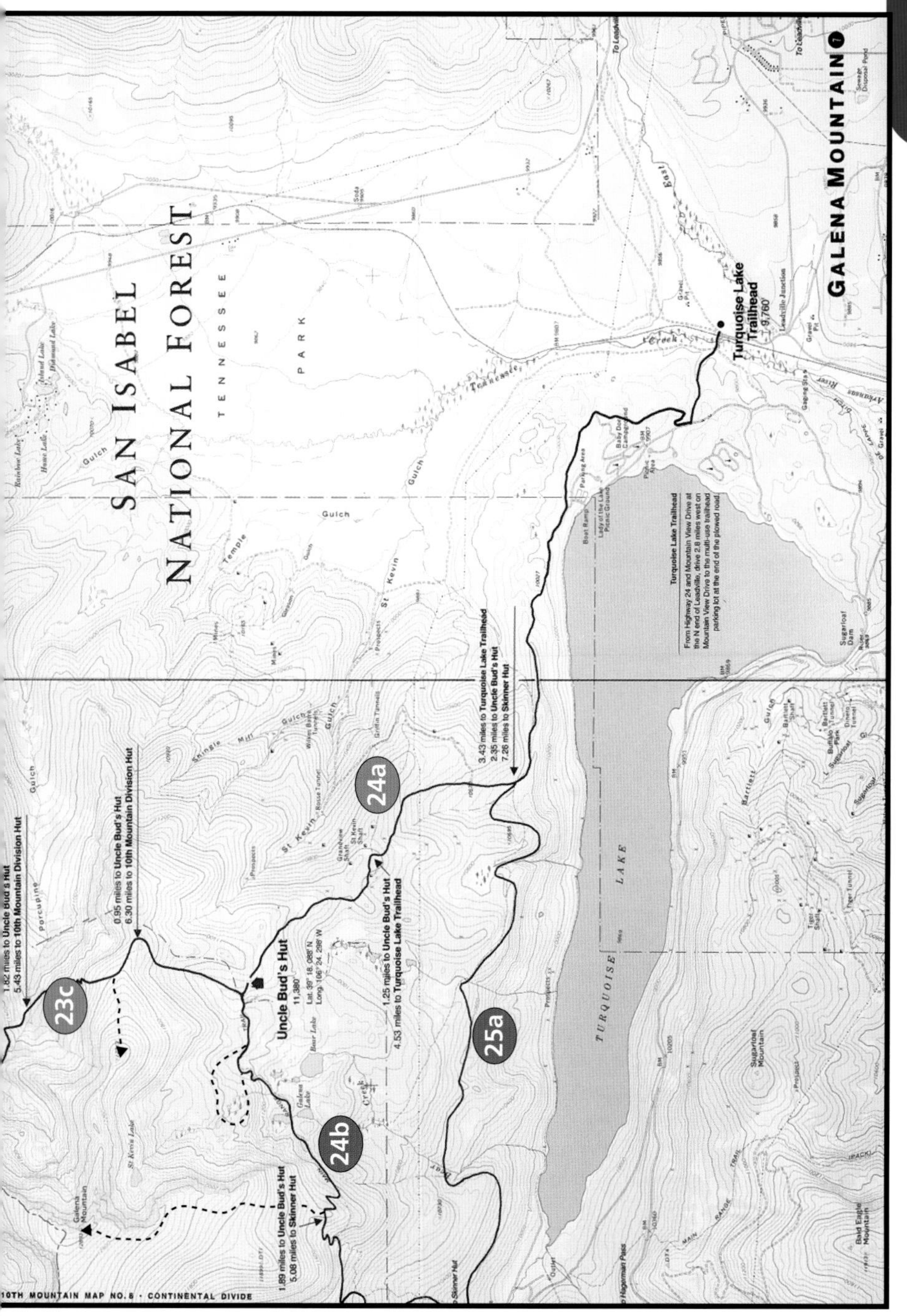

SAN ISABEL
NATIONAL FOREST
TENNESSEE
PARK
GALENA MOUNTAIN
Turquoise Lake Trailhead
9,760'
Uncle Bud's Hut
11,380'
Lat. 39° 18.088' N
Long. 106° 24.298' W
23c
24a
24b
25a
1.82 miles to Uncle Bud's Hut
5.43 miles to 10th Mountain Division Hut
0.95 miles to Uncle Bud's Hut
6.30 miles to 10th Mountain Division Hut
1.25 miles to Uncle Bud's Hut
4.53 miles to Turquoise Lake Trailhead
3.43 miles to Turquoise Lake Trailhead
2.35 miles to Uncle Bud's Hut
7.28 miles to Skinner Hut
1.89 miles to Uncle Bud's Hut
5.08 miles to Skinner Hut
Turquoise Lake Trailhead
From Highway 24 and Mountain View Drive at the N end of Leadville, drive 2.8 miles west on Mountain View Drive to the multi-use trailhead parking lot at the end of the plowed road.
TURQUOISE LAKE
Sugarloaf Mountain
Bald Eagle Mountain
Galena Mountain
10TH MOUNTAIN MAP NO. 8 · CONTINENTAL DIVIDE

# 25 Skinner Hut

| | |
|---|---|
| **HUT ELEVATION** | 11,620' |
| **DATE BUILT** | 1990 |
| **SEASONS** | Thanksgiving through April 30 (winter);<br>July 1 through September 30 (summer) |
| **CAPACITY** | 16 |
| **HUT LAYOUT** | 3 small rooms with double beds, 10 single beds in communal sleeping area, all on 1 floor |
| **HUT ESSENTIALS** | Woodstove for heat, wood-burning cookstove with oven, propane cookstoves, all kitchenware, outhouse, photovoltaic electric lights |

Balanced on the apex of a craggy, precipitous ridge, the Skinner Hut is on one of the most vertigo-inducing sites of any hut in the state. This hut is the most remote and hardest to reach in the system—and probably responsible for the most unplanned bivouacs. But those able to get here are in for a treat.

Protected from the wind by stands of rugged spruce trees, the handsome one-story stone building appears to have been carved from the underlying rock, and it blends well with the high alpine landscape. This shelter has a decidedly European flavor.

Inside the hut the living/cooking area is set apart from the sleeping quarters. Numerous windows provide abundant light, and views of Leadville and the Arkansas River Valley are especially pretty at night with the twinkling lights of town far below. Make reservations through the 10th Mountain Division Hut Association (see Appendix A).

**SUMMER NOTE:** During the summer, bikers can reach the Skinner Hut directly from the Fryingpan River drainage (west) and from Turquoise Lake (east) by riding up the Hagerman Pass Road (Forest Road 105).

To reach the hut from the Leadville area, proceed to the east entrance to Turquoise Lake. See Tour 24a for directions to the entrance. Turn left (south) and follow the road over the dam. Proceed 5 miles to the turnoff to the Hagerman Pass Road. Park and bike up toward the pass for 7 miles and a gain of 1,400 feet. The Skinner Hut is directly on top of a spectacular ridge above the final, sharp switchback. It is roughly 100 feet north of the road, marked by a dirt driveway and rock cairn. Keep an eye out, as this shelter can be difficult to see from the road. This optional summer-only route makes for strenuous, intermediate bike touring.

From the Fryingpan River, leave from the trailhead for the Betty Bear Hut via Forest Road 505. See Tour 26a for directions to the trailhead. From the parking area, bike along Hagerman Pass Road for 14.7 miles to the top of Hagerman Pass (be sure to follow the road above Ivanhoe Lake to the north). From there, drop for 1 mile down the east side of the pass to the left turn. Ride out on the ridge 0.3 mile to the hut.

**RECOMMENDED DAY TRIPS:**

**Skiing around the Skinner Hut is more alpine than the skiing around most other huts.** Since the hut is so high and exposed to the westerly winds over Hagerman Pass, the surrounding snowpack tends to be less forgiving. Intermediate and advanced skiers can tour up to Hagerman Pass and onto the Continental Divide. From the pass, you can climb to the north and south onto the surrounding peaks. Telemark skiing near the summit is limited because of the steepness of the terrain. The skiing in this area improves in the spring, when thicker, heavier snow allows for more touring above tree line.

ADVANCED

TOUR **25a**

## Turquoise Lake Trailhead to Skinner Hut

SEE MAP PAGES 124–125, 186–187, AND 192–193

**TIME** 7 to 11 hours

**DISTANCE** 8.6 miles

**ELEVATIONS** TRAILHEAD: 9,760' HUT: 11,620' GAIN/LOSS: +2,170'/-580'

**AVALANCHE** Some avalanche terrain encountered; easily avoided

**MAPS** 10th Mountain Division: Continental Divide, Upper Fryingpan
USGS 7.5': Homestake Reservoir, 1970; Leadville North, 1970
National Forest: San Isabel, White River
Trails Illustrated: Map #109 (Breckenridge/Tennessee Pass); Map #126 (Holy Cross/Ruedi Reservoir)

**TOUR OVERVIEW:** This is the standard trail to the Skinner Hut. The first 7.7 miles, which follow the Turquoise Lake Road, pass easily. Near the end of the road, at Lake Fork Creek, the character of the route changes dramatically, climbing directly up to the hut via Glacier Creek. Gaining over 1,500 feet of elevation in just under 3 miles, this route provides navigation and route-finding challenges, giving the trail its advanced rating. The route should be attempted only by skiers who are physically prepared to work hard at high altitudes. Get an early start! This trail shares the climb to the hut with the Uncle Bud's to Skinner Hut route.

**DIRECTIONS TO TRAILHEAD:** The Turquoise Lake Trailhead is a little difficult to locate, so follow directions closely. The road to the trailhead begins on the north end of Leadville, near Safeway. From the junction of US 24 and Mountain View Drive, turn west and drive toward Mount Massive (on the horizon). After 2.8 miles, you'll reach a T road junction. Turn north (right), cross a fork of the Arkansas River, and proceed to the parking lot, which is near where the road veers west to cross the main river and the railroad tracks.

**THE ROUTE:** Ski or walk west over the railroad tracks. Cross the main stem of the Arkansas River, then head west, past the entrance to Turquoise Lake. When you reach another intersection, turn north again. Follow Forest Road 104, passing a picnic area, campgrounds, and boat ramps that are on the left between the road and the lake. Continue along the road, above the lake on the northeast. Ski west along the Turquoise Lake Road (FR 104/105) for 7.7 miles, passing the right (north) turn to Uncle Bud's Hut at 3.4 miles.

Basically, the first part of the tour just follows this popular summer road. It is very obvious and traverses through the woods above the lake, gradually climbing for the first half, then beginning a long descent into the Lake Fork Creek Valley. Just be careful not to turn off into any of the campgrounds or boat ramps.

At 7.7 miles, where the road turns sharply and heads southeast back along the creek, leave the road and ski west into the woods, following a trail that leads to a small clearing and a large Forest Service sign. Refer to Tour 24b for a detailed description of the trail between the sign and the hut.

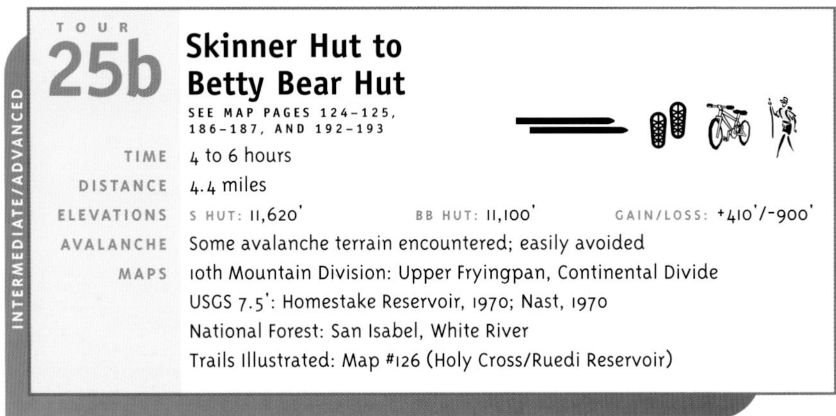

INTERMEDIATE/ADVANCED

TOUR 25b

## Skinner Hut to Betty Bear Hut

SEE MAP PAGES 124–125, 186–187, AND 192–193

TIME 4 to 6 hours

DISTANCE 4.4 miles

ELEVATIONS S HUT: 11,620' BB HUT: 11,100' GAIN/LOSS: +410'/-900'

AVALANCHE Some avalanche terrain encountered; easily avoided

MAPS 10th Mountain Division: Upper Fryingpan, Continental Divide
USGS 7.5': Homestake Reservoir, 1970; Nast, 1970
National Forest: San Isabel, White River
Trails Illustrated: Map #126 (Holy Cross/Ruedi Reservoir)

**TOUR OVERVIEW:** The trail between the Skinner Hut and the Betty Bear Hut is significant because it is one of only two points in the 10th Mountain Division system where a hut-to-hut route crosses the Continental Divide, connecting the eastern and western sections of the system. (Vance's Cabin to 10th Mountain Division Hut is the other.)

This trail crosses Hagerman Pass at an elevation of 11,925 feet and is exposed to mountain storms. Fifty percent of the total mileage is above tree line. Under settled skies, skilled skiing parties can successfully complete this route in a few hours, while those with less route-finding experience could easily wander about much longer. Navigation can be very difficult in blizzards and whiteouts. Compass bearings and altimeters are especially helpful on this tour.

**THE ROUTE:** Leave the Skinner Hut and return southwest along the ridge to the Hagerman Pass Road. Follow the road west, above tree line, on an ascent around the north side of a low, rocky hill. Contour southwest on the road to a narrow passage overlooking Busk Creek and Mount Massive. Turn west and ascend moderate terrain to Hagerman Pass, which is marked by a large wooden Forest Service sign.

Ski west from the sign and begin to descend gradually to the south/southwest. Either follow the summer road down to the first sharp switchback, losing 150 feet of elevation, or ski across the tundra toward the trees and the roadbed (the Hagerman Tunnel grade) that traverses west around the upper Lake Ivanhoe drainage at 11,450 feet.

At the road, ski west 0.7 mile until the road crosses the earthen bridge, or saddle, separating Lily Pad Creek from the Ivanhoe drainage. Follow a well-traveled trail that drops off the road to the west into the Lily Pad drainage. Proceed west through the center of a long meadow for 1.2 miles, crossing Lily Pad Creek. Continue along the south edge of the meadow until you reach the junction of the Forest Road 505 trail. Turn left (south) and descend a short distance to the Betty Bear Hut.

Many skiers take a workable but unofficial alternate route that exits the meadow a little prematurely and follows the Lily Pad Creek Road around the south side of Lily Pad Lake, then down a steep hill to a switchback. From there, it is possible to turn north and ski up to the Betty Bear Hut via a short climb. If you descend too far down, however, this road begins to drop into the Fryingpan River on a long series of switchbacks. During the winter, the descent to the Fryingpan River becomes an avalanche deathtrap—do not descend this way! This hazard is why the marked ski route drops to the Fryingpan River via the more protected Lily Pad Creek to the west of the Betty Bear Hut.

*Kirk Watson watches the day begin at Skinner Hut.*

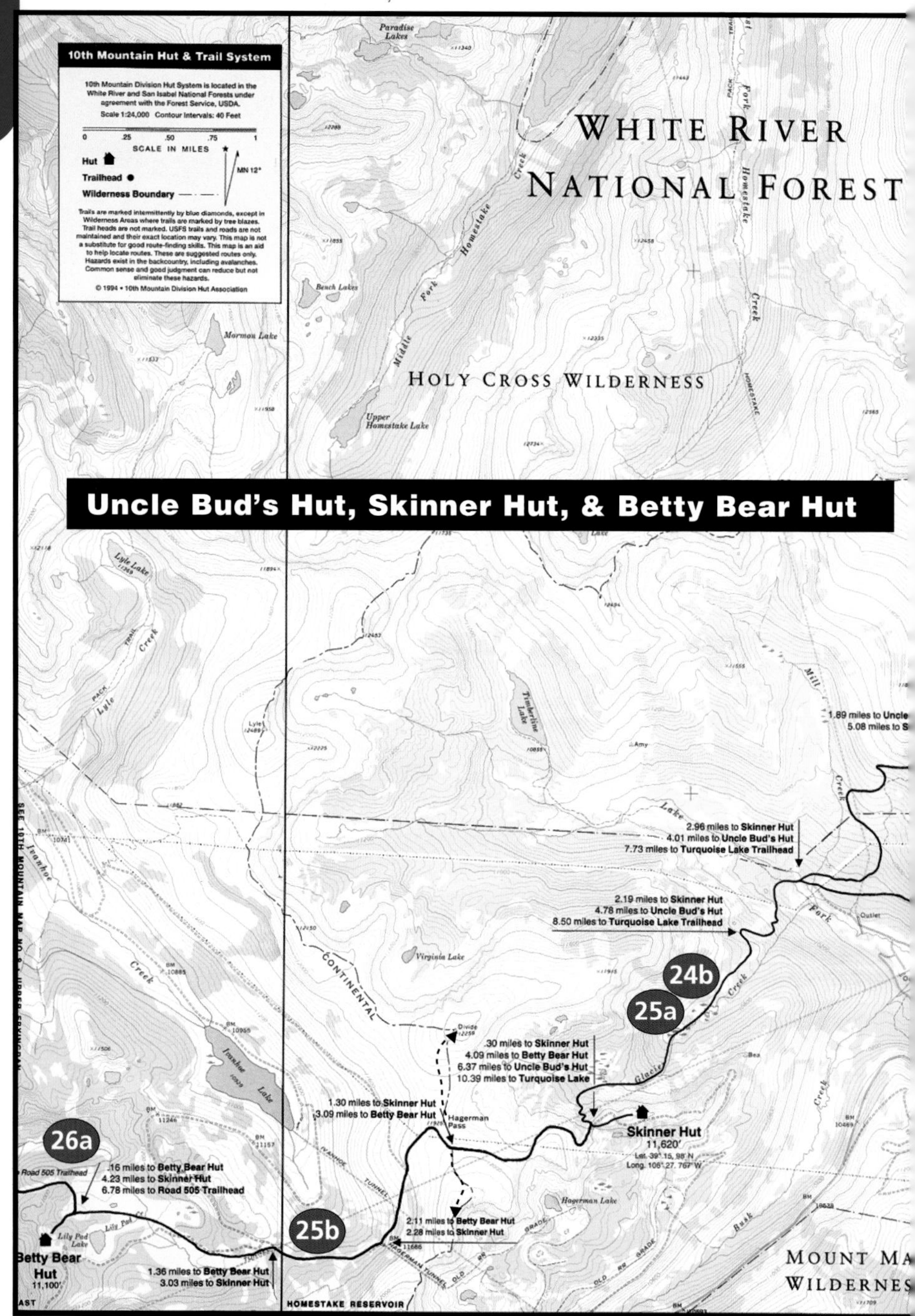

10th Mountain Hut & Trail System
10th Mountain Division Hut System is located in the White River and San Isabel National Forests under agreement with the Forest Service, USDA.
Scale 1:24,000 Contour Intervals: 40 Feet
0 .25 .50 .75 1
SCALE IN MILES
Hut
Trailhead
Wilderness Boundary
MN 12°
Trails are marked intermittently by blue diamonds, except in Wilderness Areas where trails are marked by tree blazes. Trail heads are not marked. USFS trails and roads are not maintained and their exact location may vary. This map is not a substitute for good route-finding skills. This map is an aid to help locate routes. These are suggested routes only. Hazards exist in the backcountry, including avalanches. Common sense and good judgment can reduce but not eliminate these hazards.
© 1994 • 10th Mountain Division Hut Association
WHITE RIVER
NATIONAL FOREST
HOLY CROSS WILDERNESS
Uncle Bud's Hut, Skinner Hut, & Betty Bear Hut
Paradise Lakes
Mormon Lake
Upper Homestake Lake
Middle Fork Homestake Creek
Lyle Lake
Timberline Lake
Virginia Lake
CONTINENTAL
Hagerman Pass
Hagerman Lake
Ivanhoe Lake
Lily Pad Lake
1.89 miles to Uncle
5.08 miles to S
2.96 miles to Skinner Hut
4.01 miles to Uncle Bud's Hut
7.73 miles to Turquoise Lake Trailhead
2.19 miles to Skinner Hut
4.78 miles to Uncle Bud's Hut
8.50 miles to Turquoise Lake Trailhead
24b
25a
.30 miles to Skinner Hut
4.09 miles to Betty Bear Hut
6.37 miles to Uncle Bud's Hut
10.39 miles to Turquoise Lake
1.30 miles to Skinner Hut
3.09 miles to Betty Bear Hut
Skinner Hut
11,620'
Lat. 39° 15. 98' N
Long. 106° 27. 767' W
26a
Road 505 Trailhead
.16 miles to Betty Bear Hut
4.23 miles to Skinner Hut
6.78 miles to Road 505 Trailhead
25b
2.11 miles to Betty Bear Hut
2.28 miles to Skinner Hut
Betty Bear Hut
11,100'
1.36 miles to Betty Bear Hut
3.03 miles to Skinner Hut
HOMESTAKE RESERVOIR
MOUNT MA
WILDERNES

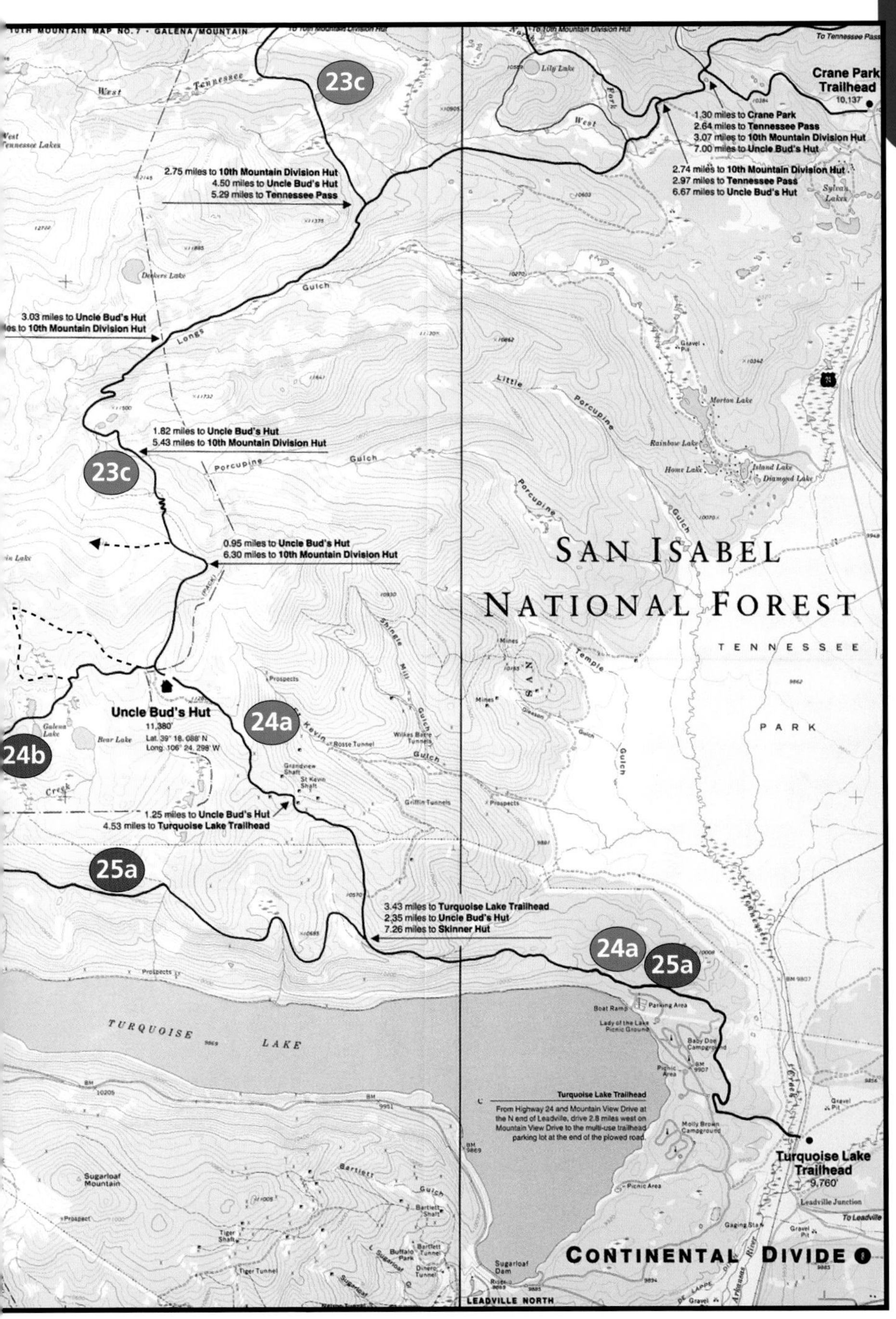
10TH MOUNTAIN MAP NO. 7 · GALENA MOUNTAIN
To 10th Mountain Division Hut
To Tennessee Pass
Crane Park Trailhead
10,137'
1.30 miles to Crane Park
2.64 miles to Tennessee Pass
3.07 miles to 10th Mountain Division Hut
7.00 miles to Uncle Bud's Hut
2.74 miles to 10th Mountain Division Hut
2.97 miles to Tennessee Pass
6.67 miles to Uncle Bud's Hut
23c
2.75 miles to 10th Mountain Division Hut
4.50 miles to Uncle Bud's Hut
5.29 miles to Tennessee Pass
3.03 miles to Uncle Bud's Hut
1.82 miles to Uncle Bud's Hut
5.43 miles to 10th Mountain Division Hut
23c
0.95 miles to Uncle Bud's Hut
6.30 miles to 10th Mountain Division Hut
SAN ISABEL
NATIONAL FOREST
TENNESSEE
PARK
Uncle Bud's Hut
11,380'
Lat. 39° 18. 088' N
Long. 106° 24. 298' W
24a
24b
1.25 miles to Uncle Bud's Hut
4.53 miles to Turquoise Lake Trailhead
25a
3.43 miles to Turquoise Lake Trailhead
2.35 miles to Uncle Bud's Hut
7.26 miles to Skinner Hut
24a
25a
TURQUOISE LAKE
Turquoise Lake Trailhead
From Highway 24 and Mountain View Drive at the N end of Leadville, drive 2.8 miles west on Mountain View Drive to the multi-use trailhead parking lot at the end of the plowed road.
Turquoise Lake Trailhead
9,760'
CONTINENTAL DIVIDE
LEADVILLE NORTH

# 26 Betty Bear Hut

| | |
|---|---|
| **HUT ELEVATION** | 11,100' |
| **DATE BUILT** | 1991 |
| **SEASONS** | Thanksgiving through April 30 (winter); July 1 through September 30 (summer) |
| **CAPACITY** | 16 |
| **HUT LAYOUT** | 3 bedrooms with double beds, 1 bunk bed with singles, 8 beds in communal sleeping room, all on bottom floor |
| **HUT ESSENTIALS** | Woodstove for heat, wood-burning cookstove with oven, propane cookstoves, all kitchenware, outhouse, photovoltaic electric lights |
| **OTHER GOODIES** | Wheelchair-accessible in summer |

Named for Betty Schuss and Bear Zesiger, the wives of Jack Schuss and Al Zesiger, this hut gets my vote for having the best panorama in the system. From the second-story deck, you can see the magnificent Hunter-Fryingpan Wilderness and the glacially carved gorge of Marten Creek.

The standard two-story floor plan is inverted: The sleeping quarters are on the first level; the spacious upper level serves as the lounging, cooking, and eating area. The second story has a very open feel, thanks to a cathedral ceiling and a long bank of windows along its south side. During the day the upper level warms up considerably from the sunlight. A final nicety of the second level is a glassed-in dining nook, which provides an intimate vista to the south and west. Make reservations through the 10th Mountain Division Hut Association (see Appendix A).

*Upstairs at the Betty Bear Hut.*

**RECOMMENDED DAY TRIPS:**

**There are many fine cross-country ski routes and mountain biking tours in the upper Lily Pad Creek and Ivanhoe drainages.** Feel free to explore and even climb to Hagerman Pass for a high-altitude lunch. The non-aerobically challenged can strike out for the high peaks lying south of Hagerman Pass.

*Mary Kay (Litz) Buckner bikes to the Betty Bear Hut.*

Marmot
Marmot

INTERMEDIATE/ADVANCED

TOUR

# 26a Forest Road 505 Trailhead to Betty Bear Hut

SEE MAP PAGES 124–125, 186–187, AND 192–193

| | |
|---|---|
| TIME | 6 to 8 hours |
| DISTANCE | 6.9 miles |
| ELEVATIONS | TRAILHEAD: 9,120' HUT: 11,100' GAIN/LOSS: +1,980'/-40' |
| AVALANCHE | Route crosses avalanche runout zones; can be dangerous during high-hazard periods |
| MAPS | 10th Mountain Division: Upper Fryingpan, Continental Divide<br>USGS 7.5': Nast, 1970<br>National Forest: White River<br>Trails Illustrated: Map #126 (Holy Cross/Ruedi Reservoir) |

**TOUR OVERVIEW:** This route is as straightforward as they come. After leaving the trailhead, it follows Forest Road 505 for 4.7 miles to the Lily Pad Creek drainage. The ascent along the road is very gradual, but the climb up Lily Pad Creek is steep and abrupt. This trail was laid out this way to avoid the dangerous avalanche slopes along the Lily Pad Lake Trail (Forest Road 1907). The hazardous slopes are southeast of the cabin, directly above the gauging station and the Fryingpan Lakes Trailhead, where the trail climbs to Lily Pad Lake.

The new winter trail ascends steeply through the forest along the east side of the creek, thereby avoiding any potential threat. In summer, the Lily Pad Lake Trail is the recommended route for mountain bikes.

**DIRECTIONS TO TRAILHEAD:** Drive east from the town of Basalt on Forest Road 105 for 32.2 miles, passing Ruedi Reservoir en route. Drive carefully on this slow, twisting road, as the surrounding hillsides consist of structurally unsound bedrock that often falls onto the road. This road may also be very slick, and the drive can take 45 minutes or more. Drive past the turnoff to FR 505 to the winter road closure, and park.

**THE ROUTE:** Walk back to the FR 505 junction. Follow FR 505 down across Ivanhoe Creek and begin the long ascent into the upper Fryingpan River drainage. Continue 4.7 miles up the valley along the road to the spot where it crosses Lily Pad Creek immediately east of the second rock outcrop on the south side of the road.

Search for a trail marker on the uphill side of the road. Climb a steep series of south-facing switchbacks along the east side of Lily Pad Creek. Watch for trail markers. After gaining roughly 500 feet in elevation, enter a clearing near the creek. Follow the trail eastward on a 500-foot climb to the west edge of the Lily Pad Creek meadow. After entering the clearing, turn to the south and follow the trail 300 yards to the hut.

When returning to the trailhead, ski in control (possibly even using skins) on the descent from Lily Pad Creek to FR 505.

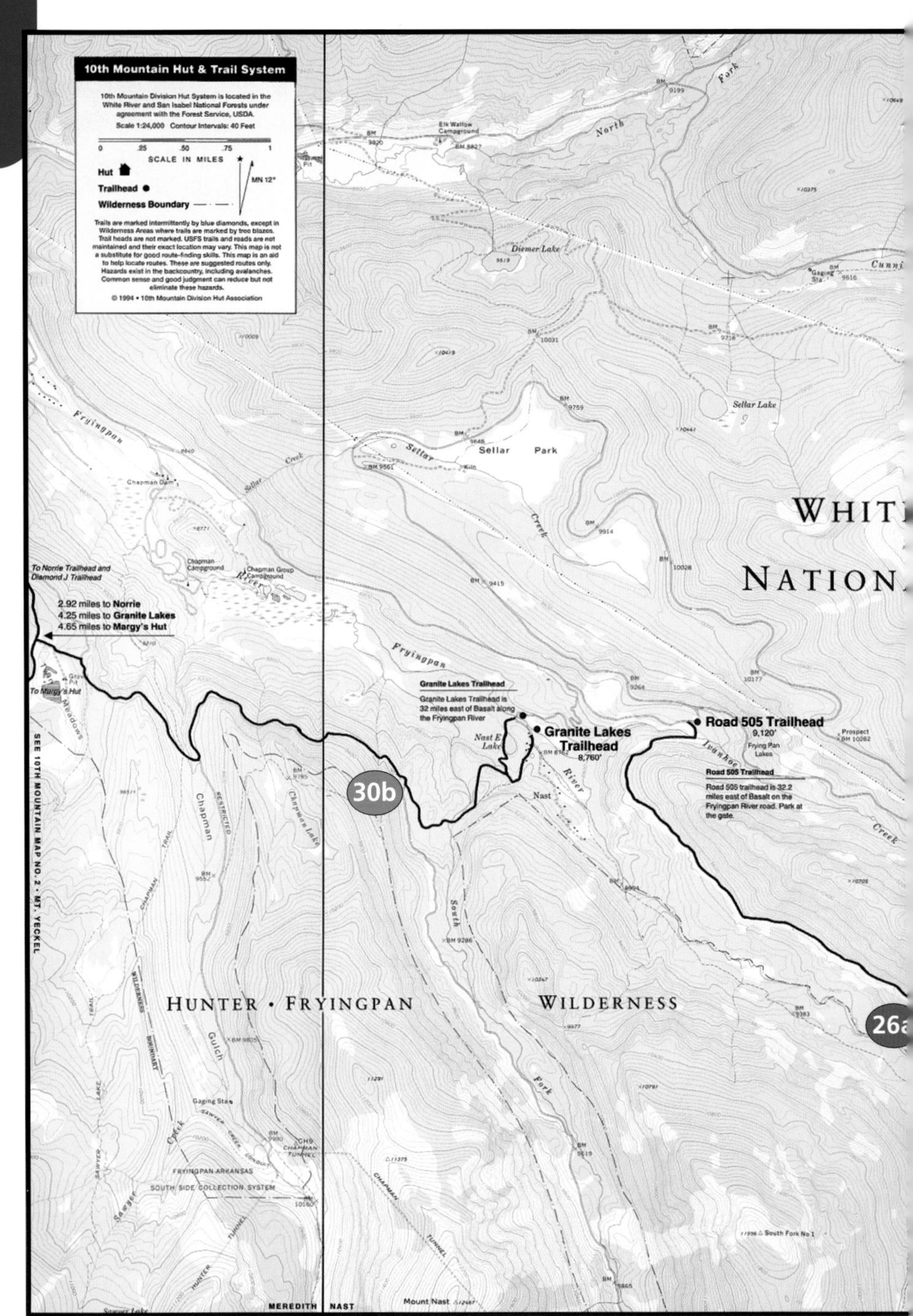
10th Mountain Hut & Trail System
10th Mountain Division Hut System is located in the White River and San Isabel National Forests under agreement with the Forest Service, USDA.
Scale 1:24,000 Contour Intervals: 40 Feet
SCALE IN MILES
Hut
Trailhead
Wilderness Boundary
MN 12°
Trails are marked intermittently by blue diamonds, except in Wilderness Areas where trails are marked by tree blazes. Trail heads are not marked. USFS trails and roads are not maintained and their exact location may vary. This map is not a substitute for good route-finding skills. This map is an aid to help locate routes. These are suggested routes only. Hazards exist in the backcountry, including avalanches. Common sense and good judgment can reduce but not eliminate these hazards.
© 1994 • 10th Mountain Division Hut Association
To Norrie Trailhead and Diamond J Trailhead
2.92 miles to Norrie
4.25 miles to Granite Lakes
4.65 miles to Margy's Hut
To Margy's Hut
SEE 10TH MOUNTAIN MAP NO. 2 • MT. YECKEL
Granite Lakes Trailhead
Granite Lakes Trailhead is 32 miles east of Basalt along the Fryingpan River
Granite Lakes Trailhead
8,760'
Road 505 Trailhead
9,120'
Road 505 Trailhead
Road 505 trailhead is 32.2 miles east of Basalt on the Fryingpan River road. Park at the gate.
30b
26a
WHITE
NATION
HUNTER • FRYINGPAN
WILDERNESS
Sellar Park
Sellar Lake
Diemer Lake
Elk Wallow Campground
North Fork
Fryingpan
Sellar Creek
Chapman Dam
Chapman Campground
Chapman Group Campground
Chapman Gulch
Nast
South Fork
Ivanhoe Creek
Frying Pan Lakes
Gaging Sta
FRYINGPAN-ARKANSAS
SOUTH SIDE COLLECTION SYSTEM
CHAPMAN TUNNEL
HUNTER TUNNEL
Mount Nast
South Fork No 1
Sawyer Creek
MEREDITH
NAST

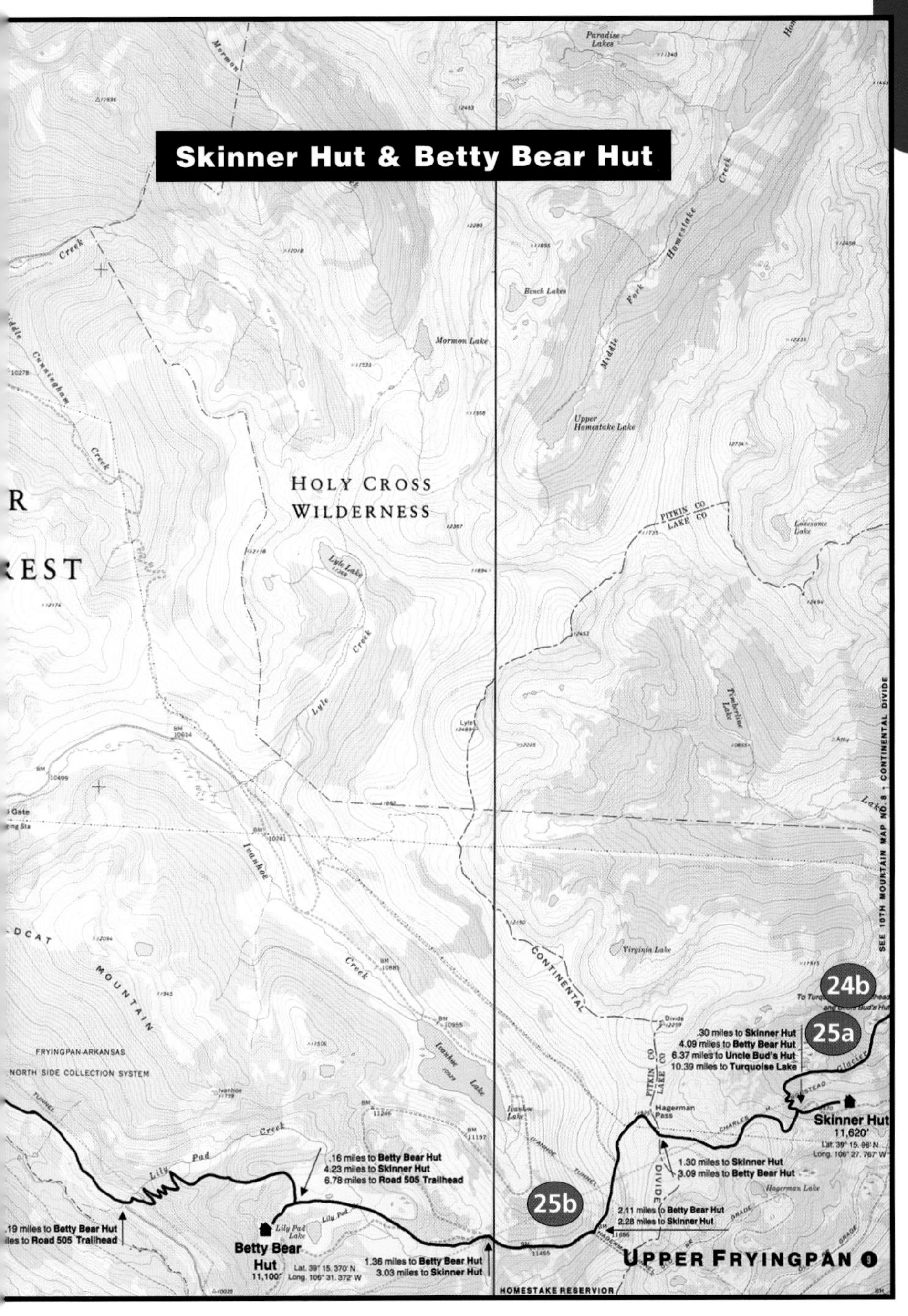

Skinner Hut & Betty Bear Hut
HOLY CROSS WILDERNESS
Mormon Lake
Bench Lakes
Paradise Lakes
Upper Homestake Lake
Lyle Lake
Lyle Creek
Ivanhoe Creek
Ivanhoe Lake
Lily Pad Creek
Lily Pad Lake
Virginia Lake
Timberline Lake
Lonesome Lake
Hagerman Lake
Hagerman Pass
PITKIN CO
LAKE CO
CONTINENTAL DIVIDE
FRYINGPAN-ARKANSAS NORTH SIDE COLLECTION SYSTEM
.30 miles to Skinner Hut
4.09 miles to Betty Bear Hut
6.37 miles to Uncle Bud's Hut
10.39 miles to Turquoise Lake
24b
25a
25b
Skinner Hut
11,620'
Lat. 39° 15. 98' N
Long. 106° 27. 767' W
1.30 miles to Skinner Hut
3.09 miles to Betty Bear Hut
2.11 miles to Betty Bear Hut
2.28 miles to Skinner Hut
.16 miles to Betty Bear Hut
4.23 miles to Skinner Hut
6.78 miles to Road 505 Trailhead
.19 miles to Betty Bear Hut
iles to Road 505 Trailhead
Betty Bear Hut
11,100'
Lat. 39° 15. 370' N
Long. 106° 31. 372' W
1.36 miles to Betty Bear Hut
3.03 miles to Skinner Hut
UPPER FRYINGPAN
HOMESTAKE RESERVIOR
SEE 10TH MOUNTAIN MAP NO. 8 : CONTINENTAL DIVIDE

# Polar Star Inn and Carl's Cabin

| POLAR STAR INN | |
|---|---|
| HUT ELEVATION | 11,040' |
| DATE BUILT | 1987 |
| SEASONS | Thanksgiving through April 30 (winter);<br>July 1 through September 30 (summer) |
| CAPACITY | 17 |
| HUT LAYOUT | Semiprivate rooms upstairs, communal sleeping area,<br>1 bedroom with single bunk bed |
| HUT ESSENTIALS | Woodstove for heat, wood-burning cookstove with oven, propane cookstoves and oven, all kitchenware, outhouse, photovoltaic electric lights |
| OTHER GOODIES | Indoor sauna; year-round potable well water |

| CARL'S CABIN | |
|---|---|
| HUT ELEVATION | 11,040' |
| DATE BUILT | 1993 |
| SEASONS | November 15 through April 30 (winter);<br>July 1 through September 30 (summer) |
| CAPACITY | 6 (entire hut must be booked by same group) |
| HUT LAYOUT | 2 rooms with double beds plus 2 single beds in main room |
| HUT ESSENTIALS | Woodstove for heat, propane cookstoves, all kitchenware, outhouse, photovoltaic electric lights; there is no oven |

The Polar Star Inn is like a "stretch" version of a typical 10th Mountain Division hut. Named after a local mine, the Polar Star Inn is equipped with a muscle-melting sauna and has running spring water and a propane barbecue. Conveniently located on the northwest corner of New York Mountain, the inn, which is privately owned, fits well into the overall 10th Mountain Division scheme. It is often combined with the Peter Estin Hut and the Harry Gates Hut for great hut-to-hut ski and mountain bike trips.

Carl's Cabin is a satellite hut a very short walk from the Polar Star Inn. This diminutive shelter is completely equipped for a group of six—the idea being to provide a structure that can easily be rented by a single group. This cozy cabin costs slightly more per person than a typical 10th Mountain hut fee, but it is a small price to pay to enjoy the privacy of your own hut. Make reservations through the 10th Mountain Division Hut Association (see Appendix A).

**RECOMMENDED DAY TRIPS:**

**The area around the Polar Star Inn is laced with many old logging and mining roads that offer many days of skiing and mountain biking.** A recommended day trip climbs New York Mountain by the north ridge. The route up the mountain is quite direct. Leave the inn and ascend east to the ridge. Follow the crest of the north ridge, just south to the summit. A great mountaineering trip, this is one of the most straightforward climbs to a 12,000-foot peak available to hut skiers. Carry appropriate safety equipment and be wary of snow cornices overhanging the northeast face.

*The Polar Star Inn is named after a local mine.*

INTERMEDIATE/ADVANCED

TOUR **27a**

## West Lake Creek Trailhead to Polar Star Inn and Carl's Cabin

SEE MAP PAGES 124–125 AND 202–203

| | |
|---|---|
| TIME | 6 to 9 hours |
| DISTANCE | 7 miles |
| ELEVATIONS | TRAILHEAD: 8,220' INN/CABIN: 11,040' GAIN/LOSS: +2,820'/-200' |
| AVALANCHE | Minimal danger |
| MAPS | 10th Mountain: New York Mountain<br>USGS 7.5': Fulford, 1987; Grouse Mountain, 1987<br>National Forest: White River<br>Trails Illustrated: Map #121 (Eagle/Avon) |

**TOUR OVERVIEW:** The route from West Lake Creek Trailhead is the longest way to the Polar Star Inn and is a textbook exercise in gear hauling. Many skiers use this trailhead as a jumping-off point for a multiday traverse of the western half of the system, ending their trip in Aspen. Other skiers choose to begin in Aspen and end their expedition at the inn. Without question, it is easier to ski out than to ski in via this route because of the considerable gain in elevation. This route is not open to mountain bikers because it crosses the Holy Cross Wilderness Area.

**DIRECTIONS TO TRAILHEAD:** Turn off I-70 at the Edwards exit (Exit 163). Head south across the Eagle River to US 6. Turn west for 0.7 mile to Lake Creek Road. Turn south on Lake Creek Road for 1.8 miles to a fork in the road. Take the right

*Carl's Cabin is a beacon in the night.*

fork onto West Lake Creek Road and proceed 2.8 miles to a sharp hairpin curve. Park at the apex of the turn, where Forest Road 423 heads south. The road is marked with a National Forest welcome sign and a sign for East Lake Trail Baryetta Cabins.

**THE ROUTE:** From the parking area, ski south along the east side of the creek on FR 423, then cross a bridge and make a rising traverse across the steeply angled slopes on the west side of the creek. At the 1-mile mark, the road heads back across the creek to the east, to a trail junction. Stay on the right fork as it climbs up and around to the west. From here, the road contours east through a meadow past some old cabins and then begins the climb straight south along a forested ridge.

Eventually the trail reaches an intersection at 9,370 feet, near an old, faded Forest Service trail sign attached to a tree. Take the Card Springs Trail, which is the right fork and is marked with a blue diamond. It leaves the main trail and crosses south, then west into a forested basin. Keep a compass handy.

Follow the trail west, cross into the Wilderness boundary near the creek, and continue ascending along a road until it fades out in an aspen forest. The route switchbacks cross-country, heading west, straight up through aspen trees to a small meadow on the Card Creek Saddle at 9,980 feet. Finding the proper route through this stretch is probably the trickiest section of the tour, although it is usually marked with a few pieces of colored plastic flagging. Don't be misled by ski trails left by skiers coming downhill through the aspen trees or ski trails by an old road that heads directly north through the aspen trees just before you climb onto the Card Creek Saddle.

Once at the small, protected meadow (a nice break or lunch spot), ski straight through it to the west, re-enter the woods, and begin a descending traverse into Squaw Creek. The trail contours into the Squaw Creek drainage and ascends all the way up it, first along the west side, then, after making a very sharp dogleg turn at 9,980 feet, on the east. After crossing the creek, the trail climbs steadily through the forest and exits the Wilderness Area and the Squaw Creek drainage near a sign at 10,700 feet.

Continue heading south/southeast to an intersection with a switchback on a logging road. The trail follows the road for a short while, then strikes off through the woods above the road along its northeast side. It eventually regains the road and follows it the last few hundred yards to the Polar Star Inn. This last few hundred yards of trail travels through open meadows and sporadic trees and can be a little bit difficult to navigate during snowstorms.

For those leaving the inn, ski north to the road, past a tree with a blue diamond. Keep an eye out for the places where the trail deviates from the switchbacking road during the first mile and don't be surprised by the abrupt dogleg turn at the 2.1-mile mark. This is a very fast descent for most of its length, so exercise caution.

TOUR **27b**

INTERMEDIATE

# Yeoman Park Trailhead to Polar Star Inn and Carl's Cabin via Fulford Road

SEE MAP PAGES 124–125 AND 202–203

| | |
|---|---|
| TIME | 5 to 7 hours |
| DISTANCE | 6.2 miles |
| ELEVATIONS | TRAILHEAD: 9,060' INN/CABIN: 11,040' GAIN/LOSS: +2,033'/-140' |
| AVALANCHE | Minimal danger |
| MAPS | 10th Mountain Division: New York Mountain<br>USGS 7.5': Fulford, 1987<br>National Forest: White River<br>Trails Illustrated: Map #121 (Eagle/Avon) |

**TOUR OVERVIEW:** There are two routes from the Yeoman Park Trailhead to the Polar Star Inn: Fulford Road and Newcomer Spring. Both routes ascend through similar terrain, switchback and traverse a great deal, and gain roughly the same amount of elevation. What differentiates the two is that the Fulford Road route follows a wide, well-traveled road for the initial 4.4 miles while the Newcomer Spring route is a trail through the forest. After the two routes converge, they ascend more steeply to the inn. Fulford Road is better for folks who want to follow an obvious road and like lots of space for snowplow turns, although it is traveled by snowmobilers.

**DIRECTIONS TO TRAILHEAD:** Drive on I-70 to the Eagle exit (Exit 147). Head south across the Eagle River, then turn right onto US 6. Proceed into Eagle and turn left on Broadway. Drive to the intersection of Broadway and 5th Street and turn left onto 5th Street. Continue on 5th Street to Capitol; turn right. From Capitol, turn right onto Brush Creek Road (FR 307). Drive about 0.4 mile and make another right turn to remain on Brush Creek Road. Drive about 9 miles (passing signs for Sylvan Lake State Park) to where the pavement ends and a fork in the road appears. Take the left fork to East Brush Creek Road (to Fulford and Yeoman Park) and proceed 5.6 miles, then turn right, cross the creek, and turn into an obvious plowed parking area.

**THE ROUTE:** Leave the parking lot, return to East Brush Creek Road, and head southeast. Ski or walk along the road for 0.4 mile to the turnoff to Fulford Road (Forest Road 418). Follow Fulford Road for 4.2 miles as it gradually traverses, switchbacks, and climbs to the isolated, tiny community of Fulford.

There are two sections where skiers can deviate from the road to avoid snowmobile traffic. The first is near the 1.4-mile mark after the road veers back to the southeast into a creek drainage. Here, skiers can parallel the road down near the creek. The second alternative is found where the main road switchbacks sharply to the west at the 1.7-mile mark. At this point, a logging road heads southeast across the upper stretches of the creek. Turn onto it and climb along the creek, heading southeast. Cross the creek and tour through a switchback. Follow the logging road several hundred yards south until it switchbacks sharply to the north and makes an ascending traverse across the head of the previous creek before connecting with Fulford Road southeast of the little forested hill marked 9,953 feet. Both of these alternatives are marked with blue diamonds. *Note:* Be careful of the misleading tracks of confused skiers who have strayed onto other old logging trails that lace the area around the second shortcut.

From here, the route contours around a sharp, northwest-running ridge before it traverses into the Nolan Creek drainage. The route intersects another road just upstream from the community of Fulford, near an outhouse and a sign that reads "Upper Town & Nolan Lake." Turn here at a blue diamond into Nolan Creek and take a short but steep ascent to a clearing with several cabin ruins.

Head straight east past the ruins to a trail marked with blue diamonds. This is where the Newcomer Spring route meets this trail. From here, the route leaves the road and switchbacks up through the aspen forest, gaining elevation quickly. Watch for diamonds on the trees here. At 5.3 miles the trail intercepts another road, the New York Mountain jeep road, at 10,520 feet. Switchback onto this trail and head south, then east on the final approach to the hut. Climb steadily up the road for 0.5 mile until you reach another intersection with signs for the Polar Star Mine and New York Mountain. Take the left (northeast) fork and follow this marked trail for the last 0.5 mile to the Polar Star Inn and Carl's Cabin.

*Note:* At the aforementioned intersection, be careful of tracks that lead off to the right. These go up to the Hidden Treasure Yurt (see Tours 39a and 39b).

INTERMEDIATE/ADVANCED

TOUR **27c**

## Yeoman Park Trailhead to Polar Star Inn and Carl's Cabin via Newcomer Spring

SEE MAP PAGES 124–125 AND 202–203

| | |
|---|---|
| TIME | 5 to 7 hours |
| DISTANCE | 6 miles |
| ELEVATIONS | TRAILHEAD: 9,060' INN/CABIN: 11,040' GAIN/LOSS: +2,180'/-160' |
| AVALANCHE | Minimal danger |
| MAPS | 10th Mountain Division: New York Mountain<br>USGS 7.5': Crooked Creek Pass, 1987; Fulford, 1987<br>National Forest: White River<br>Trails Illustrated: Map #121 (Eagle/Avon)<br>Map #126 (Holy Cross/Ruedi Reservoir) |

**TOUR OVERVIEW:** Of the two Yeoman Park routes to the Polar Star Inn, Newcomer Spring is slightly more challenging, avoids snowmobile traffic, and is the route of choice, when combined with the Ironedge Trail (Tour 28a), for traveling between the inn and the Peter Estin Hut. The Newcomer Spring route shares the last 1.8 miles with Fulford Road route and also shares the same trailhead and parking area. Refer to the Yeoman Park Trailhead to Polar Star Inn via Fulford Road route (Tour 27b) for trailhead directions.

**THE ROUTE:** Leave the parking area, return to the East Brush Creek Road, and head southeast. Ski or walk up the road, past the turnoff to Fulford, for 1 mile to the Newcomer Spring Trailhead, which is indicated by a trail marker. Begin the steep initial climb by leaving the road and following the trail up through a series of large switchbacks.

*Skis take the night off.*

After you gain 600 feet of elevation, the angle of ascent begins to lessen and the trail, beginning on a road, traverses due north for 1 mile on a very gradual climb. This stretch of trail provides the most challenging route-finding as it leads through nondescript forests interspersed with clearings and woods. At 10,160 feet, it also crosses a logging road that is occasionally plowed and can add to the confusion. Keep map, compass, and altimeter at the ready here, and watch closely for trail markers.

Switchback to the southeast around a sharp, forested ridge and then descend to Nolan Creek. The trail contours across the head of this creek and descends slightly to a road above the cabin ruins on the Fulford Road route. From here, follow the route to the inn as described in Tour 27b.

ADVANCED

TOUR
# 27d Polar Star Inn to Peter Estin Hut

SEE MAP PAGES 124–125 AND 202–203

| | |
|---|---|
| TIME | 6 to 8 hours |
| DISTANCE | 8.3 miles |
| ELEVATIONS | PS INN: 11,040′ PE HUT: 11,200′ GAIN/LOSS: +2,120′/-2,080′ |
| AVALANCHE | Minimal danger |
| MAPS | 10th Mountain Division: New York Mountain<br>USGS 7.5′: Crooked Creek Pass, 1987; Fulford, 1987<br>National Forest: White River<br>Trails Illustrated: Map #121 (Eagle/Avon);<br>Map #126 (Holy Cross/Ruedi Reservoir) |

**TOUR OVERVIEW:** This route makes a large V down and across East Brush Creek. Whether you're heading south from the Polar Star Inn or north from the Peter Estin Hut, there is considerable elevation gain and loss. Get an early start, for this passage can take more time than one would expect. Skiers without minimal experience descending steep and narrow trails should consider substituting either the Hat Creek Trail or the Fulford Road Trail, which are much easier to descend.

**THE ROUTE:** This route is a combination of the Newcomer Spring Trail and the Ironedge Trail, which meet on the East Brush Creek Road, 1 mile upstream from the Yeoman Park Trailhead. Refer to the Newcomer Spring route (Tour 27c) and the Ironedge Trail route (Tour 28a) for specific directions.

*Two skiers contemplate the trail ahead en route from the Polar Star Inn to New York Peak.*

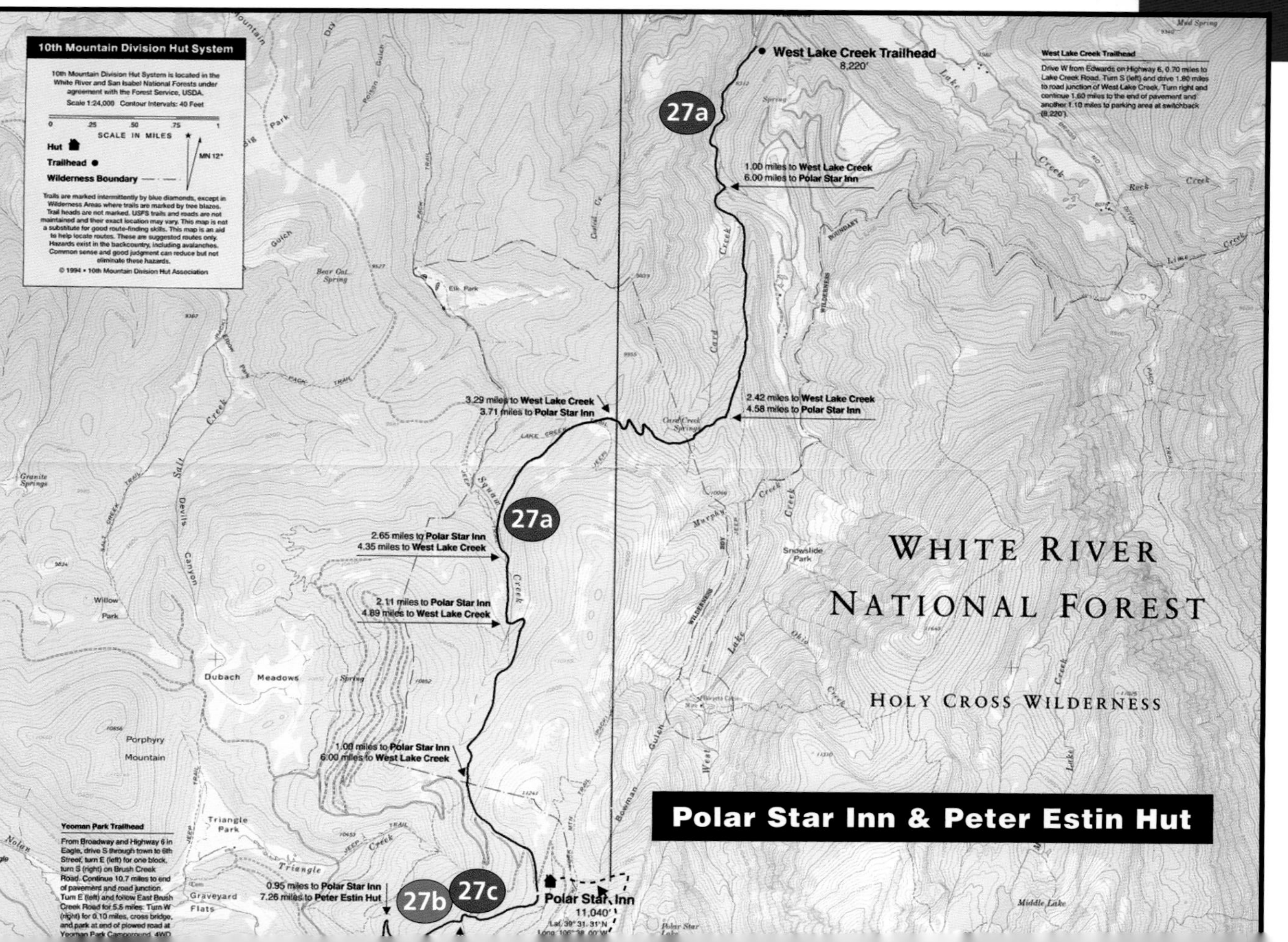
10th Mountain Division Hut System
10th Mountain Division Hut System is located in the White River and San Isabel National Forests under agreement with the Forest Service, USDA.
Scale 1:24,000 Contour Intervals: 40 Feet
SCALE IN MILES
Hut
Trailhead
Wilderness Boundary
MN 12°
Trails are marked intermittently by blue diamonds, except in Wilderness Areas where trails are marked by tree blazes. Trail heads are not marked. USFS trails and roads are not maintained and their exact location may vary. This map is not a substitute for good route-finding skills. This map is an aid to help locate routes. These are suggested routes only. Hazards exist in the backcountry, including avalanches. Common sense and good judgment can reduce but not eliminate these hazards.
© 1994 • 10th Mountain Division Hut Association
West Lake Creek Trailhead
8,220'
West Lake Creek Trailhead
Drive W from Edwards on Highway 6, 0.70 miles to Lake Creek Road. Turn S (left) and drive 1.80 miles to road junction of West Lake Creek. Turn right and continue 1.60 miles to the end of pavement and another 1.10 miles to parking area at switchback (8,220').
27a
1.00 miles to West Lake Creek
6.00 miles to Polar Star Inn
3.29 miles to West Lake Creek
3.71 miles to Polar Star Inn
2.42 miles to West Lake Creek
4.58 miles to Polar Star Inn
27a
2.65 miles to Polar Star Inn
4.35 miles to West Lake Creek
2.11 miles to Polar Star Inn
4.89 miles to West Lake Creek
1.00 miles to Polar Star Inn
6.00 miles to West Lake Creek
0.95 miles to Polar Star Inn
7.26 miles to Peter Estin Hut
27b
27c
Polar Star Inn
11,040'
Lat 39° 31.31'N
White River National Forest
Holy Cross Wilderness
Polar Star Inn & Peter Estin Hut
Elk Park
Bear Cat Spring
Granite Springs
Devils Canyon
Willow Park
Dubach Meadows
Porphyry Mountain
Triangle Park
Graveyard Flats
Snowslide Park
Middle Lake
Yeoman Park Trailhead
From Broadway and Highway 6 in Eagle, drive S through town to 6th Street, turn E (left) for one block, turn S (right) on Brush Creek Road. Continue 10.7 miles to end of pavement and road junction. Turn E (left) and follow East Brush Creek Road for 5.5 miles. Turn W (right) for 0.10 miles, cross bridge, and park at end of plowed road at Yeoman Park Campground. 4WD

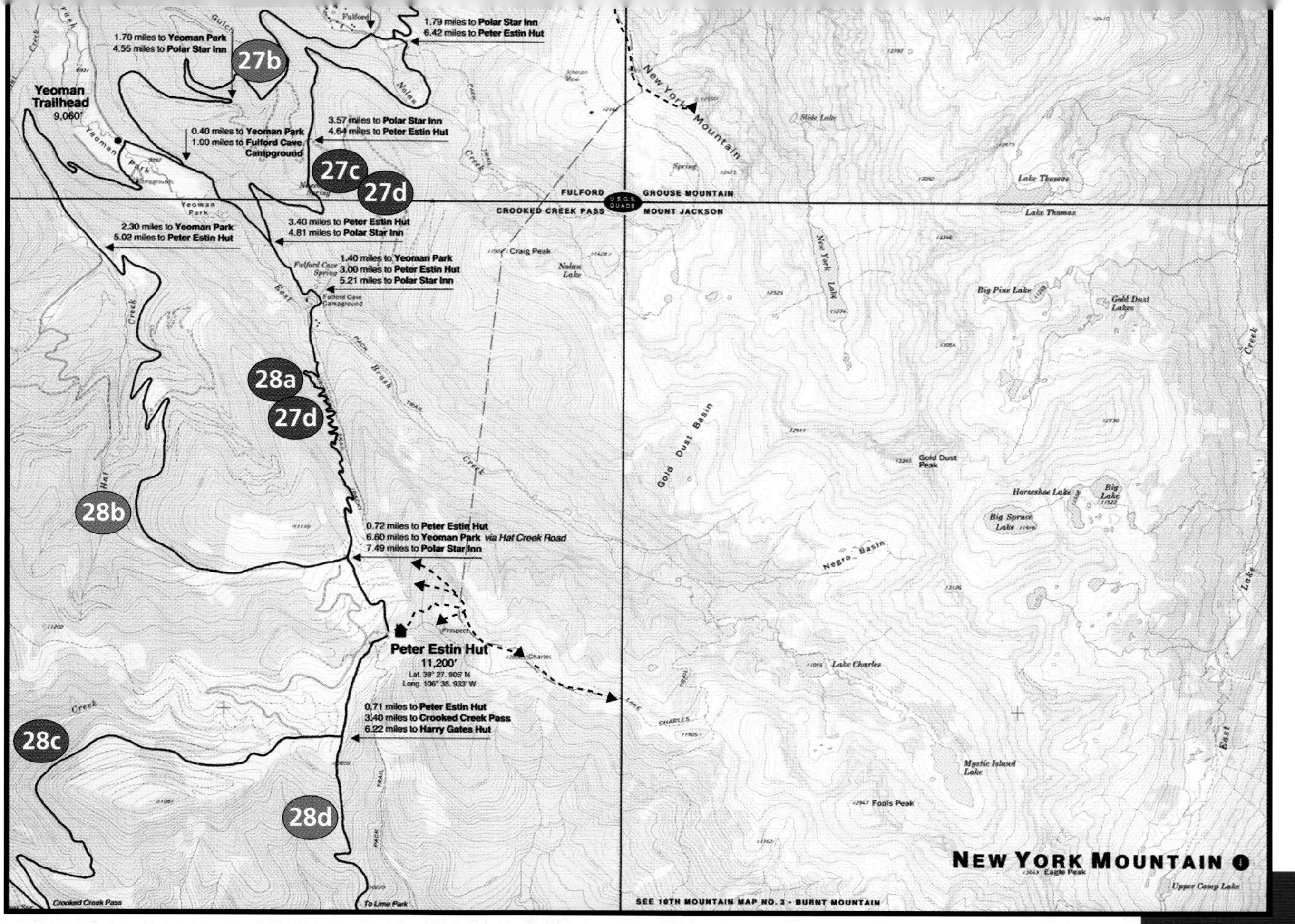
Yeoman Trailhead
9,060'
1.70 miles to Yeoman Park
4.55 miles to Polar Star Inn
1.79 miles to Polar Star Inn
6.42 miles to Peter Estin Hut
0.40 miles to Yeoman Park
1.00 miles to Fulford Cave Campground
3.57 miles to Polar Star Inn
4.64 miles to Peter Estin Hut
27b
27c
27d
FULFORD
GROUSE MOUNTAIN
CROOKED CREEK PASS
MOUNT JACKSON
2.30 miles to Yeoman Park
5.02 miles to Peter Estin Hut
3.40 miles to Peter Estin Hut
4.81 miles to Polar Star Inn
1.40 miles to Yeoman Park
3.00 miles to Peter Estin Hut
5.21 miles to Polar Star Inn
Fulford Cave Campground
Craig Peak
Nolan Lake
New York Mountain
Slide Lake
Lake Thomas
New York Lake
Big Pine Lake
Gold Dust Lakes
28a
27d
Gold Dust Basin
Gold Dust Peak
Horseshoe Lake
Big Lake
Big Spruce Lake
28b
0.72 miles to Peter Estin Hut
6.60 miles to Yeoman Park via Hat Creek Road
7.49 miles to Polar Star Inn
Negro Basin
Peter Estin Hut
11,200'
Lat. 39° 27. 905' N
Long. 106° 38. 933' W
Lake Charles
0.71 miles to Peter Estin Hut
3.40 miles to Crooked Creek Pass
6.22 miles to Harry Gates Hut
28c
Mystic Island Lake
Fools Peak
28d
NEW YORK MOUNTAIN 4
Eagle Peak
Upper Camp Lake
Crooked Creek Pass
To Lime Park
SEE 10TH MOUNTAIN MAP NO. 3 - BURNT MOUNTAIN

# Peter Estin Hut

| | |
|---|---|
| **HUT ELEVATION** | 11,200' |
| **DATE BUILT** | 1985 |
| **SEASONS** | Thanksgiving through April 30 (winter);<br>July 1 through September 30 (summer) |
| **CAPACITY** | 16 |
| **HUT LAYOUT** | 2 rooms with double beds, plus 8 single beds in communal room upstairs; 4 single beds in main room on main floor |
| **HUT ESSENTIALS** | Woodstove for heat, wood-burning cookstove with oven, propane cookstoves, all kitchenware, outhouse, photovoltaic electric lights |

The Peter Estin Hut, one of the oldest huts in the system, is one of the most popular—for good reasons. The hut is on a forested ridge and looks south over Lime Park and the Elk Mountains. Telemark skiing around the hut is first-rate, with thinly forested glades dominating the landscape. There are also many north- and west-facing slopes to explore. Beginners and expert skiers alike will find a staggering selection of possible downhill runs.

Above the hut to the east is a treeless slope on the northwest ridge of Charles Peak. The skiing along the ridge is outstanding. Individuals interested in a little ridge running can traverse the spine of the ridge all the way to Fool's Peak. In addition, a variety of itineraries connecting with the Gates Hut and the Polar Star Inn can be schemed for skiers of all abilities. Make reservations through the 10th Mountain Division Hut Association (see Appendix A).

## RECOMMENDED DAY TRIPS:

**The area north of the hut was once logged and today is covered with a thin forest, perfectly suited for intermediate-level tree skiing.** Ski north and west from the hut along the Ironedge Trail. By remaining east of the trail, it is possible to drop 400 to 600 feet across rolling, stepped topography, crossing a series of old logging roads in the process. When the drainage begins to constrict, it is very easy to traverse west to the upper part of the Ironedge Trail and return to the hut.

**From the hut, ski south to the edge of the steep drainage.** Contour east around the edge of the trees, then begin climbing into the forest. Follow the path of least resistance up to the east until you reach a clearing. Switchback up to tree line and the top of the ridge. Be sure to catch the view into East Brush Creek and the Holy Cross Wilderness before you telemark back down through the clearing to the hut.

*Joe Burleson and Gene White head for the powder stashes above the Peter Estin Hut on Charles Ridge.*

TOUR

# 28a Yeoman Park Trailhead to Peter Estin Hut via Ironedge Trail

INTERMEDIATE/ADVANCED

SEE MAP PAGES 124–125, 202–203, AND 210–211

| | |
|---|---|
| TIME | 4 to 7 hours |
| DISTANCE | 4.4 miles |
| ELEVATIONS | TRAILHEAD: 9,060' HUT: 11,200' GAIN/LOSS: +2,140'/-80' |
| AVALANCHE | Minimal danger |
| MAPS | 10th Mountain Division: New York Mountain<br>USGS 7.5': Crooked Creek Pass, 1987; Fulford, 1987<br>National Forest: White River<br>Trails Illustrated: Map #121 (Eagle/Avon); Map #126 (Holy Cross/Ruedi Reservoir) |

**TOUR OVERVIEW:** The Ironedge Trail is the direct route to the Peter Estin Hut. The trail ascends a moderate road before beginning a stiff climb to the hut. Skiers with climbing skins and well-developed lungs and calves will make quick work of this trail. Returning, however, is a different matter. The route down is steep and narrow and has many switchbacks. Competent skiers will enjoy this route; skiers with less experience should consider the Hat Creek Trail (Tour 28b) as an alternative.

**DIRECTIONS TO TRAILHEAD:** For directions to the Yeoman Park Trailhead, see Tour 27b.

**THE ROUTE:** Leave the parking lot and ski onto the East Brush Creek Road (Forest Road 415) and head southeast. Ski up the road, past the turnoff to Fulford at 0.4 mile and the Newcomer Spring Trailhead near the 1-mile mark until you finally reach the Fulford Cave Campground at 1.4 miles. Continue past the campground and a small lake, following the road as it turns west and passes some cabins, until it finally crosses East Brush Creek.

Enter the deep forest and begin climbing a seemingly interminable series of short switchbacks heading south. Eventually, the narrow "valley of the switchbacks" begins to open up into a logged area near the 10,400-foot level. The trail soon widens into a road that climbs south through open terrain up to the 11,100-foot ridge immediately west of the hut. At the ridge, turn east and follow a Peter Estin Hut sign as you ski through a stand of spruce trees to the hut.

INTERMEDIATE

TOUR

# 28b Yeoman Park Trailhead to Peter Estin Hut via Hat Creek Trail

SEE MAP PAGES 124–125, 202–203, AND 210–211

| | |
|---|---|
| TIME | 6 to 8 hours |
| DISTANCE | 7.4 miles |
| ELEVATIONS | TRAILHEAD: 9,060' HUT: 11,200' GAIN/LOSS: +2,180'/-40' |
| AVALANCHE | Minimal danger |
| MAPS | 10th Mountain Division: New York Mountain<br>USGS 7.5': Crooked Creek Pass, 1987; Fulford, 1987<br>National Forest: White River<br>Trails Illustrated: Map #121 (Eagle/Avon); Map #126 (Holy Cross/Ruedi Reservoir) |

**TOUR OVERVIEW:** Although it is several miles longer than the Ironedge Trail, the Hat Creek Trail is the recommended Peter Estin Hut tour for strong novice and intermediate skiers as well as for mountain bikers, especially for the return run down to Yeoman Park. The route follows a road and should present very few navigation problems.

**DIRECTIONS TO TRAILHEAD:** For directions to the Yeoman Park Trailhead, see Tour 27b.

**THE ROUTE:** From the parking area, this route heads to the southwest, away from East Brush Creek. Begin skiing (or riding, as the case may be) southwest, then southeast along Forest Road 416, past a campground. Begin climbing in earnest by ascending to Hat Creek via a long traverse to the northwest. After gaining about 400 feet of elevation, the road switchbacks sharply to the southeast into the Hat Creek drainage. Climb along the east side of Hat Creek, passing a right (southwest) turn onto Forest Road 436 at the 5-mile mark.

Remain on the northeast side of Hat Creek, enter a logged area, and climb through one series of switchbacks. Continue traversing upward, then go through another, much larger series of switchbacks. Contour around the south flank of Elevation Point 11,110' and intersect the Ironedge Trail on a saddle at 6.6 miles. Turn south onto the top of the 11,200-foot ridge, gaining 400 feet of elevation from the trail junction. Once you have reached the top of the ridge, turn east and follow a Peter Estin Hut sign as you ski through a stand of spruce trees to the hut.

INTERMEDIATE/ADVANCED

TOUR

# 28c Sylvan Lake Trailhead to Peter Estin Hut via Crooked Creek Pass

SEE MAP PAGES 124–125, 202–203, AND 210–211

TIME 7 to 10 hours

DISTANCE 9.5 miles

ELEVATIONS TRAILHEAD: 8,558' HUT: 11,200' GAIN/LOSS: +2,702'/-60'

AVALANCHE Minimal danger

MAPS 10th Mountain Division: Burnt Mountain, New York Mountain
USGS 7.5': Crooked Creek Pass, 1987
National Forest: White River
Trails Illustrated: Map #126 (Holy Cross/Ruedi Reservoir)

**TOUR OVERVIEW:** This is the longest route to the Peter Estin Hut. It is the preferred route for people who are skiing between this hut and the Harry Gates Hut and want to return to a common trailhead. Most of the route follows a moderate road and features typical intermediate skiing. Although the technical difficulty of the skiing is not great, this tour covers a lot of ground and much gain in elevation, which makes it a touch more difficult than the average intermediate tour. The trail jaunts 1 mile cross-country up to the hut via the last bit of the Lime Ridge Trail, which connects the Peter Estin Hut to the Harry Gates Hut.

**DIRECTIONS TO TRAILHEAD:** Take I-70 to the Eagle exit (Exit 147). Drive south across the Eagle River, then turn right onto US 6. Proceed into Eagle and turn left on Broadway. Drive to the intersection of Broadway and 6th Street and turn left onto 6th Street. Drive one block, then turn right onto the Brush Creek Road (Forest Road 400). Drive to a fork in the road near the end of the pavement. Take the right fork to Sylvan Lake and proceed 4.7 miles along West Brush Creek to a parking area on the east side of the lake.

**THE ROUTE:** Ski from the parking area, following the West Brush Creek Road around the east side of Sylvan Lake, then southeast up into Brush Creek. Follow FR 400 up through Brush Creek on a long, steady 5.3-mile climb to the top of the pass, skiing around several switchbacks en route.

From the top of the pass, leave the main road and follow a road (Forest Road 428) that switchbacks sharply up toward the northwest across a clearing. Reaching the crest of a ridge, switchback to the southeast around the top of a drainage (Spine Creek). Follow the trail as it traverses west and north above Spine Creek. Enter a logged area and continue due east, dropping across a flat depression, or pass, until you reach a switchback along a creek where the road heads back to the northeast.

Exit the road at the switchback and follow the shallow drainage east on a moderate climb to the top of Lime Ridge. Turn left (north) and follow the Lime Ridge Trail through sparse timber along the crest of the ridge, with a steep drainage on the east. Contour slightly to the northeast to reach the Peter Estin Hut, which is set back several hundred feet from the edge of the clearing at the head of the drainage.

*Laura Caruso and Joe Burleson approach the Peter Estin Hut from the south, with the High Elk Mountains in the distance.*

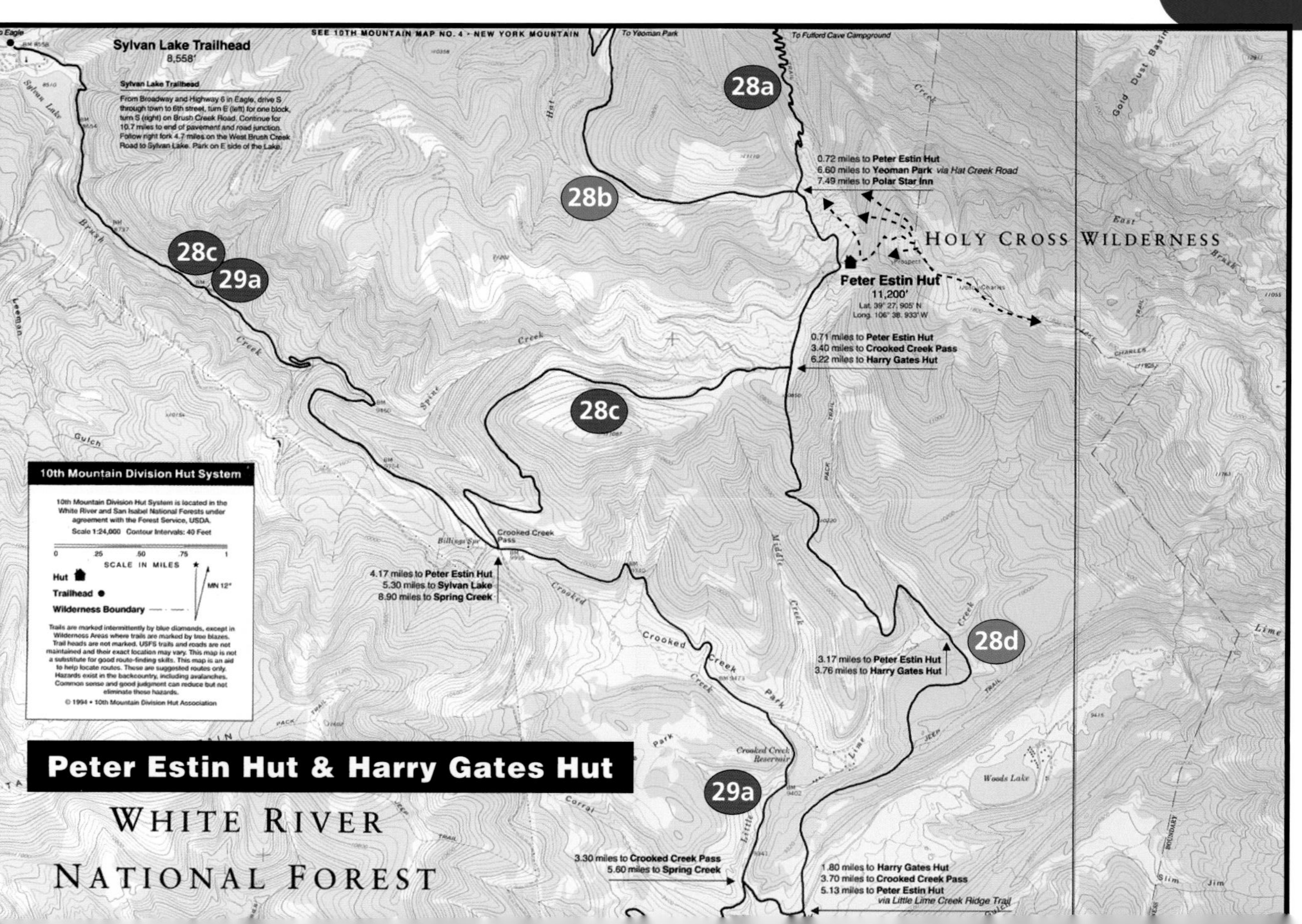

SEE 10TH MOUNTAIN MAP NO. 4 - NEW YORK MOUNTAIN
To Eagle
To Yeoman Park
To Fulford Cave Campground
Sylvan Lake Trailhead
8,558'
Sylvan Lake Trailhead
From Broadway and Highway 6 in Eagle, drive S through town to 6th street, turn E (left) for one block, turn S (right) on Brush Creek Road. Continue for 10.7 miles to end of pavement and road junction. Follow right fork 4.7 miles on the West Brush Creek Road to Sylvan Lake. Park on E side of the Lake.
28a
28b
28c
29a
28c
28d
29a
0.72 miles to Peter Estin Hut
6.60 miles to Yeoman Park via Hat Creek Road
7.49 miles to Polar Star Inn
HOLY CROSS WILDERNESS
Peter Estin Hut
11,200'
Lat. 39° 27.905' N
Long. 106° 38.933' W
0.71 miles to Peter Estin Hut
3.40 miles to Crooked Creek Pass
6.22 miles to Harry Gates Hut
Crooked Creek Pass
4.17 miles to Peter Estin Hut
5.30 miles to Sylvan Lake
8.90 miles to Spring Creek
3.17 miles to Peter Estin Hut
3.76 miles to Harry Gates Hut
3.30 miles to Crooked Creek Pass
5.60 miles to Spring Creek
1.80 miles to Harry Gates Hut
3.70 miles to Crooked Creek Pass
5.13 miles to Peter Estin Hut
via Little Lime Creek Ridge Trail
Gold Dust Basin
East Brush
Sylvan Lake
Brush Creek
Leeman Gulch
Spruce Creek
Hat Creek
Middle Creek
Crooked Creek
Crooked Creek Park
Crooked Creek Reservoir
Woods Lake
Corral
Lime Creek
10th Mountain Division Hut System
10th Mountain Division Hut System is located in the White River and San Isabel National Forests under agreement with the Forest Service, USDA.
Scale 1:24,000 Contour Intervals: 40 Feet
0 .25 .50 .75 1
SCALE IN MILES
MN 12°
Hut
Trailhead
Wilderness Boundary
Trails are marked intermittently by blue diamonds, except in Wilderness Areas where trails are marked by tree blazes. Trail heads are not marked. USFS trails and roads are not maintained and their exact location may vary. This map is not a substitute for good route-finding skills. This map is an aid to help locate routes. These are suggested routes only. Hazards exist in the backcountry, including avalanches. Common sense and good judgment can reduce but not eliminate those hazards.
© 1994 • 10th Mountain Division Hut Association
Peter Estin Hut & Harry Gates Hut
WHITE RIVER
NATIONAL FOREST

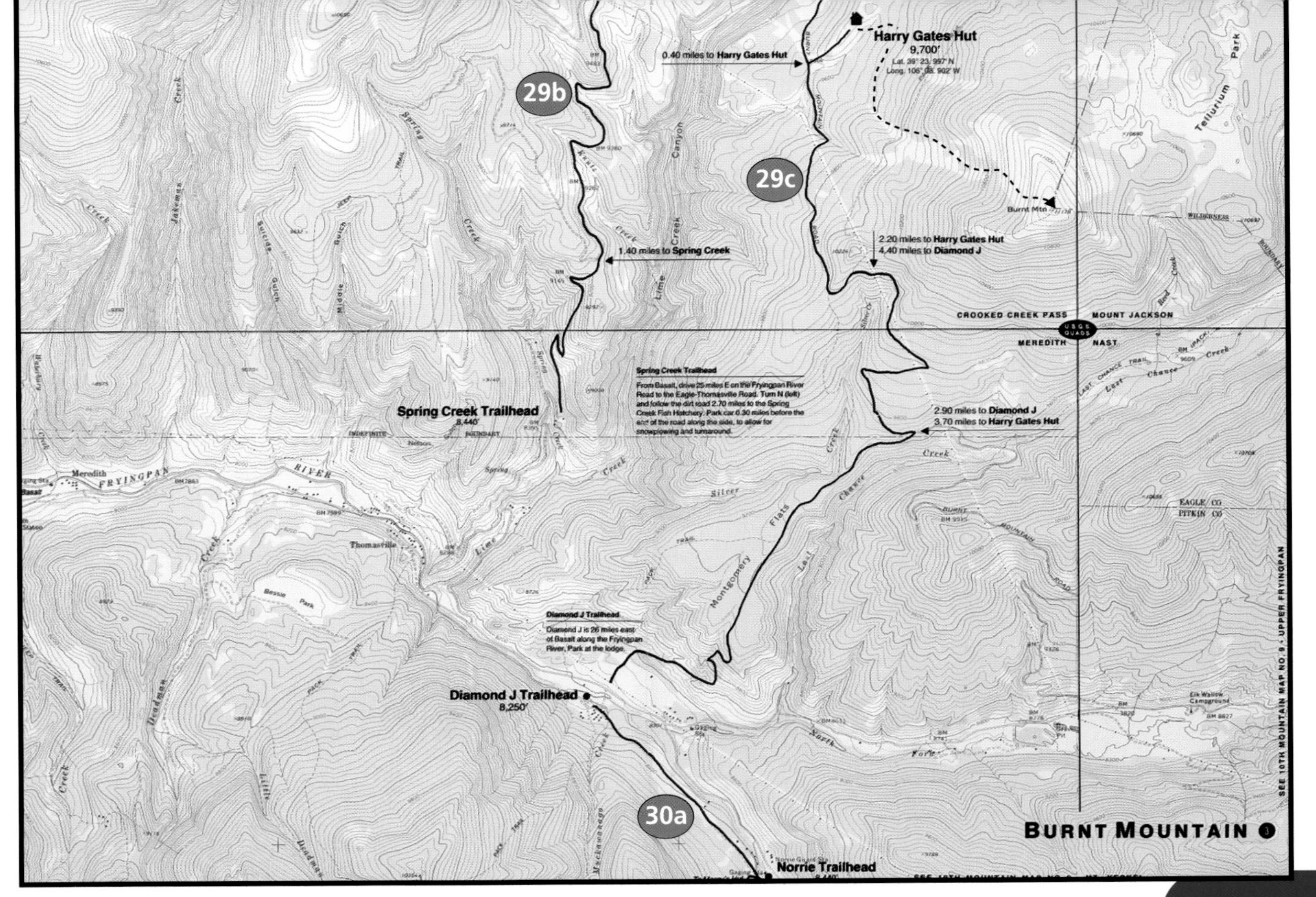

Harry Gates Hut
9,700'
Lat. 39° 23.997' N
Long. 106° 38.902' W
0.40 miles to Harry Gates Hut
29b
29c
1.40 miles to Spring Creek
2.20 miles to Harry Gates Hut
4.40 miles to Diamond J
CROOKED CREEK PASS
MOUNT JACKSON
MEREDITH
NAST
Spring Creek Trailhead
From Basalt, drive 25 miles E on the Fryingpan River Road to the Eagle-Thomasville Road. Turn N (left) and follow the dirt road 2.70 miles to the Spring Creek Fish Hatchery. Park car 0.30 miles before the end of the road along the side, to allow for snowplowing and turnaround.
Spring Creek Trailhead
8,440'
2.90 miles to Diamond J
3.70 miles to Harry Gates Hut
Diamond J Trailhead
Diamond J is 26 miles east of Basalt along the Fryingpan River. Park at the lodge.
Diamond J Trailhead
8,250'
30a
Norrie Trailhead
BURNT MOUNTAIN
SEE 10TH MOUNTAIN MAP NO. 9 - UPPER FRYINGPAN

INTERMEDIATE

TOUR

# 28d Peter Estin Hut to Harry Gates Hut

SEE MAP PAGES 124–125, 202–203, AND 210–211

TIME 5 to 7 hours

DISTANCE 7 miles

ELEVATIONS PE HUT: 11,200′ HG HUT: 9,700′ GAIN/LOSS: +734′/-2,180′

AVALANCHE Minimal danger

MAPS 10th Mountain Division: Burnt Mountain
USGS 7.5′: Crooked Creek Pass, 1987
National Forest: White River
Trails Illustrated: Map #126 (Holy Cross/Ruedi Reservoir)

**TOUR OVERVIEW:** This is the most direct path connecting these huts. The route is long but not too severe. With a net loss of 2,180 feet from the Peter Estin Hut (on the north) to the Harry Gates Hut (on the south), the most taxing portion of the trail is descending the ridge between Lime Creek and the Peter Estin Hut. And vice versa, if you are traveling from the Gates Hut to the Estin Hut, ascending this ridge late in the day can drain the tanks of tired skiers. Also, the route crosses the wide and treeless Lime Park, which may present navigation difficulties during blizzards and whiteouts. Keep navigation tools handy. Because of the elevation gain, skiing north from the Gates Hut to the Estin Hut is more difficult.

**THE ROUTE:** From the Peter Estin Hut, begin skiing southwest into the trees above the steep drainage to the south. Follow a marked trail that descends straight south through sparse timber along the ridge that forms the east boundary of Middle Creek. Some skiers may want to bypass this ridge completely by dropping straight down from the hut through the unnamed tributary on the east side of the ridge along the summer pack trail. Attempt this only when avalanche danger is low! (*Note:* Bikes are not allowed on the ridge.)

After dropping 1,300 feet to the very steep terrain and aspen trees directly above Lime Creek, the trail switchbacks north into an unnamed tributary of Lime Creek and then south across the Lime Creek basin. Cross the creek and ascend southeast to a flat, low ridge. Turn right and follow the four-wheel-drive road to the southwest along the forested ridge-crest (very narrow at times). Finally the ridge begins to spread out, and the trail eventually enters a meadow. Head due south across the clearing on a slight descent to the intersection with the Woods Lake Road (Forest Road 507) and Burnt Mountain Road (Forest Road 506). This intersection is in wide-open meadow, so keep an eye out for signs and trail markers and keep maps and compass handy.

From the intersection of Burnt Mountain and Woods Lake Roads, turn sharply south onto the Burnt Mountain Road and descend across the Lime Creek drainage. Follow the Burnt Mountain Road south for 1.4 miles to a small clearing in the midst of evergreen and aspen trees on top of a tiny ridge. Exit the road to the northeast onto a trail that follows the ridge, ski through stands of aspen trees, and continue 0.4 mile to the Harry Gates Hut, which is hidden in the trees.

*Note:* Bicyclists should consider descending into Lime Park via Crooked Creek Pass (see Tour 28c) and continuing to the Harry Gates Hut via the route described in Tour 29a.

*Craig Snowden skis below the Peter Estin Hut to the north.*

# 29 Harry Gates Hut

| | |
|---|---|
| **HUT ELEVATION** | 9,700' |
| **DATE BUILT** | 1986 |
| **SEASONS** | Thanksgiving through April 30 (winter); July 1 through September 30 (summer) |
| **CAPACITY** | 16 |
| **HUT LAYOUT** | 2 rooms with double beds, plus 6 single beds in communal room upstairs; 6 single beds in main room on main floor |
| **HUT ESSENTIALS** | Woodstove for heat, wood-burning cookstove with oven, propane cookstoves, all kitchenware, outhouse, photovoltaic electric lights |

The Harry Gates Hut is one of the lower-elevation destinations in this guidebook, which makes it a nice choice for beginning hut-to-hut travelers. Aside from Lime Park, which can present a few possible route-finding problems, all of the trails follow wide roads.

The Harry Gates Hut is the quintessential log cabin. It is slightly larger than other system huts, which affords occupants plenty of room to spread out and relax. What the surrounding terrain lacks in advanced telemark skiing, it makes up for with lots of options for classic long Nordic tours. For reservations, call the 10th Mountain Division Hut Association (see Appendix A).

**RECOMMENDED DAY TRIPS:**

**Day skiing around the hut consists mostly of long, moderate trail excursions into Lime Park and Tellurium Park.** The exception is the tour up **Burnt Mountain**, the 11,178-foot peak southeast of the cabin. The top of Burnt Mountain provides a great panorama and many acres of glade skiing. It is recommended for intermediate and advanced skiers. Leave from the porch of the hut and ski across the creek drainage, heading first southeast across the drainage, then climb due south until you reach the inverted Y-shaped clearing shown on the topo map. Work straight up the clearing, heading slightly southeast at first and then more or less due east. Pass through sparse trees and continue up to the summit.

*Above: Holy Cross Wilderness as seen from summit of Mount Yeckel.*

INTERMEDIATE/ADVANCED

TOUR
# 29a Sylvan Lake Trailhead to Harry Gates Hut

SEE MAP PAGES 124–125, 210–211, AND 220–221

| | |
|---|---|
| TIME | 8 to 11 hours |
| DISTANCE | 10.7 miles |
| ELEVATIONS | TRAILHEAD: 8,558' HUT: 9,700' GAIN/LOSS: +2,140'/-895' |
| AVALANCHE | Minimal danger |
| MAPS | 10th Mountain Division: Burnt Mountain, Mount Yeckel<br>USGS 7.5': Crooked Creek Pass, 1987<br>National Forest: White River<br>Trails Illustrated: Map #126 (Holy Cross/Ruedi Reservoir) |

**TOUR OVERVIEW:** At 10.7 miles, this is a marathon route across Crooked Creek Pass to the Harry Gates Hut and is recommended only if you intend to travel back to Sylvan Lake, to Yeoman Park (via the Peter Estin Hut), or possibly to the West Lake Trailhead. Car shuttles are necessary if you plan to ski to the north or south end of the system.

This trail follows secondary roads for its entire length. As long as you pay attention to your surroundings and keep your map and compass handy for routine checks, you should have very little trouble navigating. But beware of skiing this route after a major dump of snow when you are forced to break trail for the duration of the trip, as it would test your endurance in an absolute way. The first 8.6 miles of this route simply climb up and over Crooked Creek Pass into Lime Park.

**DIRECTIONS TO TRAILHEAD:** Take 1-70 to the Eagle exit (Exit 147). Head south across the Eagle River and turn right onto US 6 in Eagle. Turn left on Broadway. Drive to the intersection of Broadway and 6th Street and turn left onto 6th Street. Drive for one block, then turn right onto the Brush Creek Road (Forest Road 400). Drive to a fork in the road near the end of the pavement and take the right fork to Sylvan Lake, proceeding 4.7 miles along West Brush Creek to a parking area on the east side of the lake.

**THE ROUTE:** From the parking lot, ski along FR 400, following it around the east side of Sylvan Lake and then southeast up into the Brush Creek drainage. Follow the road along Brush Creek on a steady 5.3-mile climb to the top of Crooked Creek Pass via several switchbacks.

Cross directly over the pass and continue on a southeast course down the other side through scenic aspen forests. Skirt the west side of Crooked Creek Reservoir and head south for 0.7 mile downstream to an intersection. Take the left (southeast) fork onto Burnt Mountain Road (Forest Road 506), climb over a small rise, then drop down to a second junction with the Woods Lake Road (Forest Road 507).

From the Burnt Mountain Road/Woods Lake Road intersection, remain on Burnt Mountain Road through a sharp south turn and head across the Lime Creek drainage. Follow the Burnt Mountain Road for 1.4 miles to a small clearing in the midst of evergreen and aspen trees on top of a tiny knoll. Exit via the road to the northeast onto a trail along the ridge through stands of aspen, skiing 0.4 mile to the Harry Gates Hut.

*Note:* Do not shortcut across Lime Park; there are many hidden cliffs along the creek that can be very dangerous in whiteout conditions.

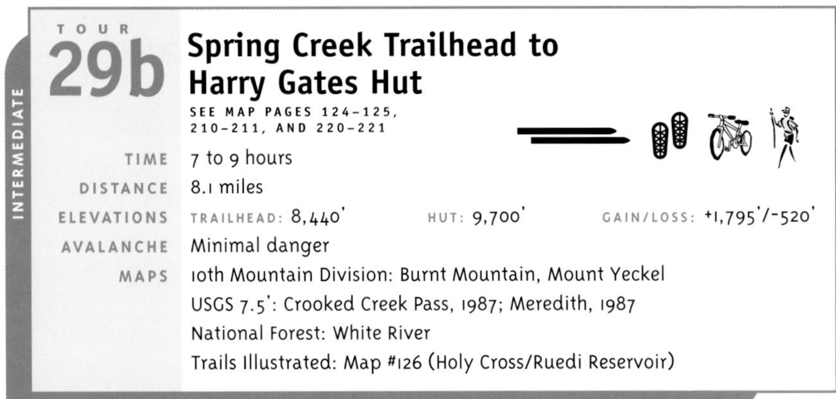

INTERMEDIATE

TOUR **29b**

## Spring Creek Trailhead to Harry Gates Hut

SEE MAP PAGES 124–125, 210–211, AND 220–221

| | |
|---|---|
| TIME | 7 to 9 hours |
| DISTANCE | 8.1 miles |
| ELEVATIONS | TRAILHEAD: 8,440′ HUT: 9,700′ GAIN/LOSS: +1,795′/-520′ |
| AVALANCHE | Minimal danger |
| MAPS | 10th Mountain Division: Burnt Mountain, Mount Yeckel<br>USGS 7.5′: Crooked Creek Pass, 1987; Meredith, 1987<br>National Forest: White River<br>Trails Illustrated: Map #126 (Holy Cross/Ruedi Reservoir) |

**TOUR OVERVIEW:** The Spring Creek Trail begins downriver from the Diamond J Ranch. After an initial steep climb, the Spring Creek/Crooked Creek Pass Road becomes gentler, allowing for moderate Nordic skiing through Lime Park.

**DIRECTIONS TO TRAILHEAD:** Drive 25 miles east from Basalt on the Fryingpan/Ruedi Reservoir Road (Forest Road 105). Take your time on FR 105 because the narrow, twisting road is often snow-packed and littered with fallen rocks. Turn left (north) onto the Eagle/Thomasville Road (Forest Road 400) and drive 2.7 miles to a parking area near the Spring Creek Fish Hatchery. Park about 300 yards below the hatchery, leaving room for snowplows and vehicles turning around.

**THE ROUTE:** Get ready to work. Begin by skiing around a switchback, past the fish hatchery buildings, and proceed uphill for 1.4 miles until the grade begins to level out. Continue climbing north along the road toward Lime Park, passing under power lines at the 3.6-mile mark. Begin descending to Lime Park at 4.3 miles.

Drop 300 feet to the junction of Burnt Mountain and Crooked Creek Pass roads. Take the right fork onto Burnt Mountain Road (Forest Road 506) over a small rise, then drop down to a second junction with the Wood Lake Road. From this intersection, turn sharply south onto the Burnt Mountain Road and head down across the Lime Creek drainage. Follow the Burnt Mountain Road south for 1.4 miles to a small clearing on top of a tiny ridge in the midst of evergreen and aspen trees. Exit the road to the northeast onto a trail that follows the ridge. Ski through stands of aspen for 0.4 mile to the Harry Gates Hut, which is hidden among the trees.

*Skiers disembark from Harry Gates Hut.*

INTERMEDIATE

TOUR **29c**

## Diamond J Trailhead/Montgomery Flats to Harry Gates Hut

SEE MAP PAGES 124–125, 210–211, AND 220–221

| | |
|---|---|
| TIME | 5 to 7 hours |
| DISTANCE | 6.6 miles |
| ELEVATIONS | TRAILHEAD: 8,250′ HUT: 9,700′ GAIN/LOSS: +1,930′/-480′ |
| AVALANCHE | Minimal danger |
| MAPS | 10th Mountain Division: Burnt Mountain, Mount Yeckel<br>USGS 7.5′: Crooked Creek Pass, 1987; Meredith, 1987<br>National Forest: White River<br>Trails Illustrated: Map #126 (Holy Cross/Ruedi Reservoir) |

**TOUR OVERVIEW:** Formerly known as the Mountain Haven Trailhead, the Diamond J Trailhead provides skiers with a relatively direct and less technically difficult route to the Harry Gates Hut. It is not an easy trail, however, as this road tour still gains a sizeable amount of elevation. This trail works well for travelers continuing through to Aspen and for those spending the night in the upper Fryingpan River Valley before heading north to the Yeoman Park/Edwards area.

*John Oates engages in some white-collar work.*

**DIRECTIONS TO TRAILHEAD:** Drive east from Basalt for 26 miles on the Fryingpan/Ruedi Reservoir Road (Forest Road 105). Take your time on FR 105, for this narrow, twisting road is often snow-packed and littered with fallen rocks. At the entrance to the Diamond J Ranch, turn right (south) into the ranch, cross the river, and park in the plowed area on the left.

**THE ROUTE:** Return to the road from the parking area. Cross the road, go through a fence, and begin ascending to the northeast for 0.3 mile to a road above the Diamond J Trailhead, passing under a power line en route. Once you have reached the road, follow it uphill onto Montgomery Flats, gaining 750 feet of elevation. Ski to the northeast along the southeast edge of Montgomery Flats above Last Chance Creek until you cross a constriction between Silver Creek (to the northwest) and Last Chance Creek (to the southeast). After crossing the constriction, traverse off the ridge, heading east toward the Burnt Mountain Road (Forest Road 506), which you will intercept 1.4 miles from the south edge of Montgomery Flats.

*Vicious winter weather can descend on skiers with little warning.*

From here, the route climbs the road for 1.5 miles, crossing back and forth under the power lines, until you begin descending and pass around the southwest ridge of Elevation Point 10,224'. Continue descending northerly for a little under 2 miles, crossing two tributaries of Lime Creek en route. After crossing the second tributary, climb onto a tiny clearing on a ridge surrounded by evergreen and aspen trees. Exit the road to the northeast onto a trail that follows the ridge, skiing through stands of aspen for 0.4 mile to the Harry Gates Hut.

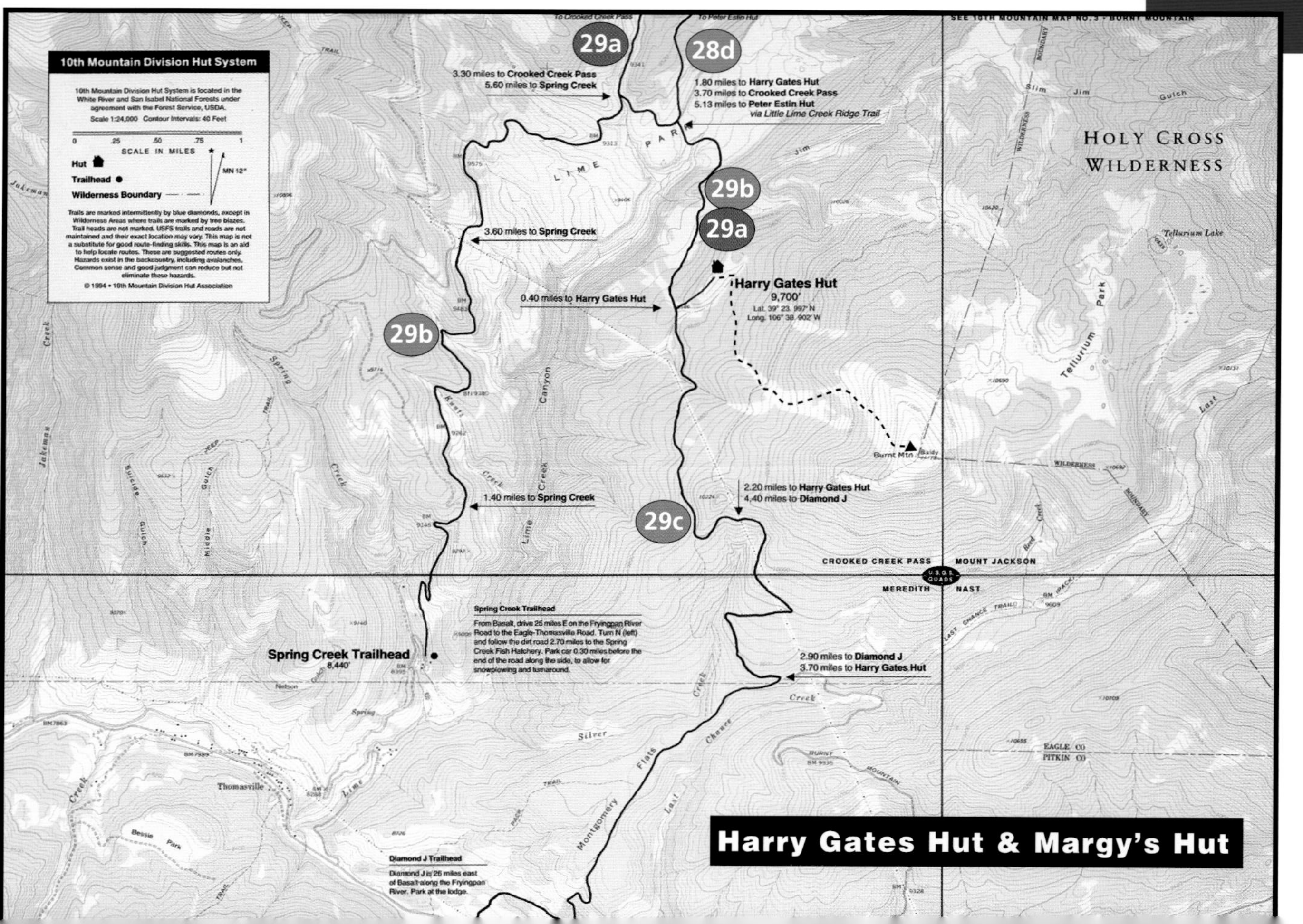
Harry Gates Hut & Margy's Hut
10th Mountain Division Hut System
10th Mountain Division Hut System is located in the White River and San Isabel National Forests under agreement with the Forest Service, USDA.
Scale 1:24,000 Contour Intervals: 40 Feet
0 .25 .50 .75 1
SCALE IN MILES
Hut
Trailhead
Wilderness Boundary
MN 12°
Trails are marked intermittently by blue diamonds, except in Wilderness Areas where trails are marked by tree blazes. Trail heads are not marked. USFS trails and roads are not maintained and their exact location may vary. This map is not a substitute for good route-finding skills. This map is an aid to help locate routes. These are suggested routes only. Hazards exist in the backcountry, including avalanches. Common sense and good judgment can reduce but not eliminate these hazards.
© 1994 • 10th Mountain Division Hut Association
SEE 10TH MOUNTAIN MAP NO. 3 • BURNT MOUNTAIN
To Crooked Creek Pass
To Peter Estin Hut
29a
28d
3.30 miles to Crooked Creek Pass
5.60 miles to Spring Creek
1.80 miles to Harry Gates Hut
3.70 miles to Crooked Creek Pass
5.13 miles to Peter Estin Hut
via Little Lime Creek Ridge Trail
HOLY CROSS
WILDERNESS
29b
29a
3.60 miles to Spring Creek
Harry Gates Hut
9,700'
Lat. 39° 23. 997' N
Long. 106° 38. 902' W
0.40 miles to Harry Gates Hut
29b
Telluride Lake
Tellurium Park
Burnt Mtn
1.40 miles to Spring Creek
2.20 miles to Harry Gates Hut
4.40 miles to Diamond J
29c
CROOKED CREEK PASS
MOUNT JACKSON
U.S.G.S. QUADS
MEREDITH
NAST
Spring Creek Trailhead
From Basalt, drive 25 miles E on the Fryingpan River Road to the Eagle-Thomasville Road. Turn N (left) and follow the dirt road 2.70 miles to the Spring Creek Fish Hatchery. Park car 0.30 miles before the end of the road along the side, to allow for snowplowing and turnaround.
Spring Creek Trailhead
8,440'
2.90 miles to Diamond J
3.70 miles to Harry Gates Hut
EAGLE CO
PITKIN CO
Thomasville
Bessie Park
Montgomery Flats
Diamond J Trailhead
Diamond J is 26 miles east of Basalt along the Fryingpan River. Park at the lodge.

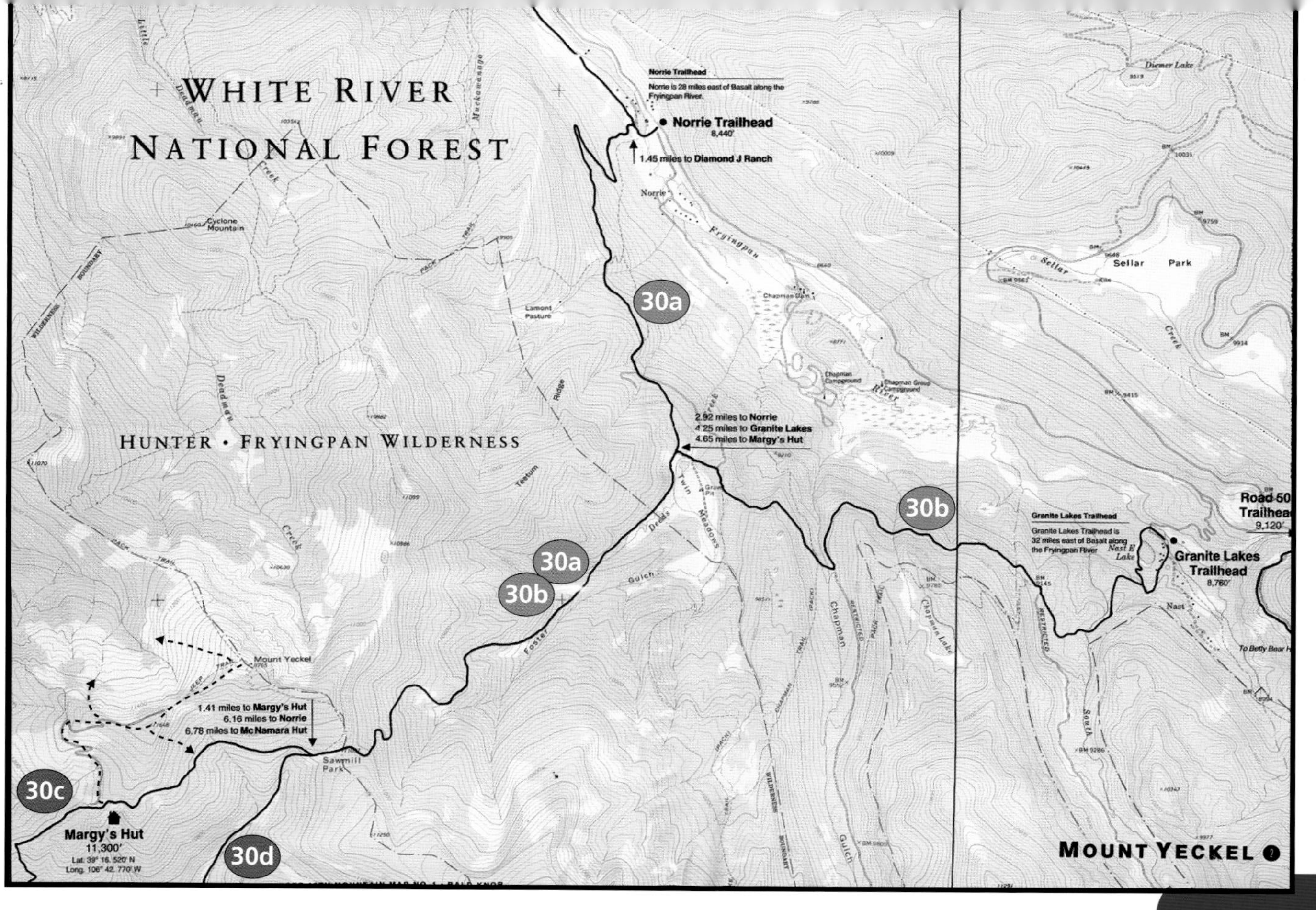
WHITE RIVER
NATIONAL FOREST
HUNTER • FRYINGPAN WILDERNESS
Norrie Trailhead
Norrie is 28 miles east of Basalt along the Fryingpan River.
Norrie Trailhead
8,440'
1.45 miles to Diamond J Ranch
2.92 miles to Norrie
4.25 miles to Granite Lakes
4.65 miles to Margy's Hut
Granite Lakes Trailhead
Granite Lakes Trailhead is 32 miles east of Basalt along the Fryingpan River
Granite Lakes Trailhead
8,760'
Road 505 Trailhead
9,120'
Mount Yeckel
1.41 miles to Margy's Hut
6.16 miles to Norrie
6.78 miles to McNamara Hut
Margy's Hut
11,300'
Lat. 39° 16.520' N
Long. 106° 42.770' W
30a
30b
30a
30b
30c
30d
Cyclone Mountain
Lamont Pasture
Sellar Park
Diemer Lake
Chapman Campground
Chapman Group Campground
Twin Meadows
Sawmill Park
Chapman Gulch
Chapman Lake
Nast Lake
To Betty Bear Hut
MOUNT YECKEL

# 30 Margy's Hut

| | |
|---|---|
| **HUT ELEVATION** | 11,300' |
| **DATE BUILT** | 1982 |
| **SEASONS** | Thanksgiving through April 30 (winter); July 1 through September 30 (summer) |
| **CAPACITY** | 16 |
| **HUT LAYOUT** | 1 room with double bed plus 10 single beds in a communal room upstairs; 4 single beds in bunkroom on main floor |
| **HUT ESSENTIALS** | Woodstove for heat, wood-burning cookstove with oven, propane cookstoves, all kitchenware, outhouse, photovoltaic electric lights |

Margy's Hut and McNamara Hut were the first two huts constructed by the 10th Mountain Division Hut Association. Both were created and named to honor Margaret McNamara, the late wife of former Secretary of Defense Robert McNamara.

Margy's Hut occupies one of the loveliest sites in Colorado. High on the south ridge of Mount Yeckel at the edge of the Hunter-Fryingpan Wilderness, this hut has all of the qualities that make Colorado hut-to-hut skiing a special experience. It can be reached by several intermediate-rated tours; there is excellent telemark skiing directly below the front porch and on Mount Yeckel; and, finally, the hut overlooks the Williams, Sawatch, and Elk Mountains.

Margy's Hut can be reached from the community of Lenado, from Aspen via the McNamara Hut, or from the north, out of the Fryingpan River Valley. This hut, along with other huts situated on the west side of the Holy Cross Wilderness, tends to receive less traffic than it used to because of the increase in popularity of the Vail Pass/Tennessee Pass area huts. Make reservations through the 10th Mountain Division Hut Association (see Appendix A).

**RECOMMENDED DAY TRIPS:**

**A nice south-facing slope directly below the front porch of the hut is perfect for practicing free-heel skiing.** Some of the finest backcountry powder skiing in the 10th Mountain Division system is on **Mount Yeckel.** A large, open meadow lies northwest of the hut on the west ridge of the mountain. The road that leads across this clearing begins on the west side of the cabin and travels northwest, past the turnoff to Lenado. Skiers can follow this road to the summit ridge of Mount Yeckel. The northwest face of Mount Yeckel offers supreme telemark skiing. It is easy to spend a full "rest" day cutting fresh tracks down into this bowl. Anyone skiing off Mount Yeckel should be well-versed in avalanche-terrain travel.

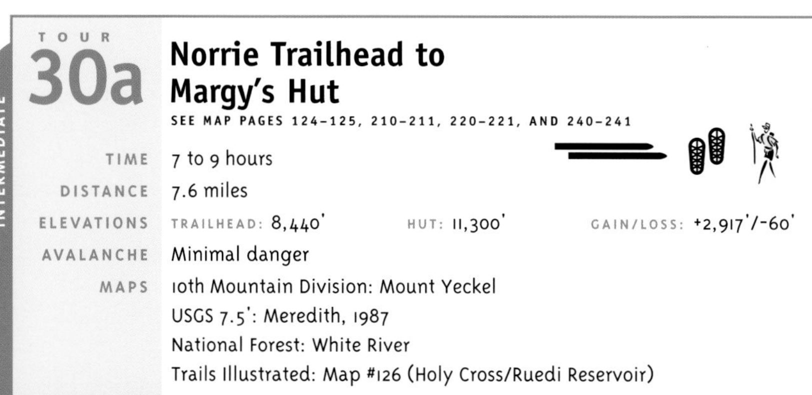


**TOUR OVERVIEW:** This trail has an elevation gain of nearly 3,000 feet, making for a very long, steady climb to the hut or a long cruise if you are leaving the hut and descending north into the Fryingpan River Valley. Though there are a few critical trail junctions that must be negotiated, overall this is a straightforward route. The stout amount of elevation gain on this route makes it a bit harder than the standard intermediate-grade route. This route crosses the Hunter-Fryingpan Wilderness and is closed to bike travel.

**DIRECTIONS TO TRAILHEAD:** Drive 28 miles east from Basalt on the Fryingpan/Ruedi Reservoir Road (Forest Road 105). Take your time driving on FR 105, because the narrow, twisting road is often snow-packed and littered with fallen rocks. Pass the Diamond J Ranch entrance at 26 miles, then arrive at the well-marked right turn into Norrie. Proceed a few hundred feet, crossing the river, and drive to the end of the plowed road to park.

**THE ROUTE:** The route ascends an obvious and unplowed section of road (Forest Road 504) as it switchbacks above the valley to the southwest for the first 2.5 miles. Begin skiing along the road, gaining elevation immediately as you climb around a switchback. After two switchbacks, the road begins a long, ascending traverse to the trail to Twin Meadows, which is obvious and marked by a blue diamond. Nevertheless, it is possible to ski past it while climbing the road. Bear in mind that the trail is on the right after the third drainage crossing. If you miss the trail, the road does continue up into the meadow, but it is not as direct a route.

Once on the trail, climb a few hundred feet into the north edge of Twin Meadows. After entering the meadows, you will need to pay attention in order to locate the exit point to Deed's Creek and the Hunter-Fryingpan Wilderness Area. From the meadows' north edge, ski due south along the west edge of the meadows, passing to the west of a tiny pond and a road that meets the trail from the east. (Both of these features may be partially obscured by snow.) Continue for a few hundred yards until the trail exits into the forest and Deed's Creek drainage, the first drainage on the west.

Pass a large Wilderness Area information sign and begin a long, steep climb. Ski up Deed's Creek for about a mile, then follow the trail into Foster Gulch. Continue upward on a well-traveled trail that ascends Foster Gulch along its northwest bank, then up through the forest for a final steep climb through several switchbacks. After 4.2 miles, you will reach the flat saddle of Sawmill Park.

From here, it is important to accurately locate the trail to the hut. To find it, continue over the Sawmill Park saddle, skiing along the right (north) edge of the forest on a very gradual descent. Keep searching on the edge of the trees for old ski tracks or for trail markers, but also be careful that you do not mistake someone's day-touring telemark tracks for the trail. If you begin dropping into Spruce Creek, you have gone too far.

After finding the trail, ski to the hut via a 1.4-mile gradual traverse. This section of trail is heavily used, but you still need to keep an eye out for trail markers. Margy's Hut sits near the top of a low-angled clearing just below the northwest ridge of Mount Yeckel.

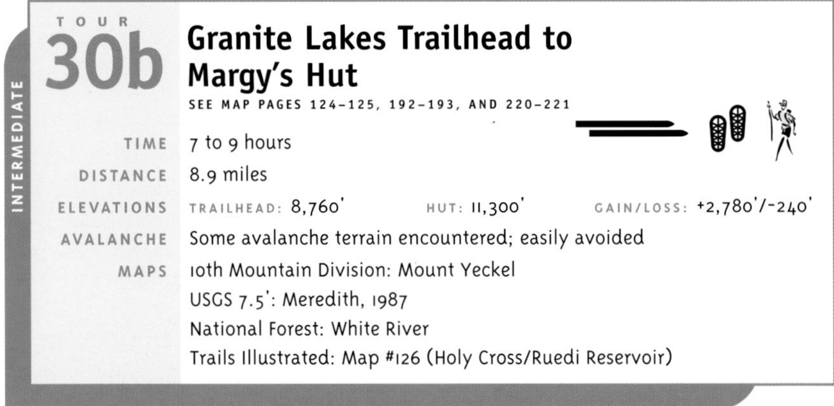

INTERMEDIATE

TOUR 30b

## Granite Lakes Trailhead to Margy's Hut

SEE MAP PAGES 124–125, 192–193, AND 220–221

TIME: 7 to 9 hours

DISTANCE: 8.9 miles

ELEVATIONS: TRAILHEAD: 8,760' HUT: 11,300' GAIN/LOSS: +2,780'/-240'

AVALANCHE: Some avalanche terrain encountered; easily avoided

MAPS: 10th Mountain Division: Mount Yeckel
USGS 7.5': Meredith, 1987
National Forest: White River
Trails Illustrated: Map #126 (Holy Cross/Ruedi Reservoir)

**TOUR OVERVIEW:** The Granite Lakes Trailhead is 6 miles upstream from the Diamond J Ranch. It is essentially an alternate start from the Norrie Trailhead and is often used by people staying at the Fryingpan River Ranch or by those descending from the Betty Bear Hut. Frankly, this route sees little activity.

**DIRECTIONS TO TRAILHEAD:** From the town of Basalt, drive east on the Fryingpan/Ruedi Reservoir Road (Forest Road 105). Take your time on FR 105, for the narrow, twisting road is often snow-packed and littered with fallen rocks. Pass the Diamond Joy Retreat at 26 miles, turn right at the fork in the road, pass Norrie at 28 miles, and turn right into the ranch at 32 miles, which is well-marked. Proceed down the curvy road past the main buildings to the south end of the retreat, near the last cabins. Park in assigned visitors' spots.

**THE ROUTE:** Begin skiing up the trail through dense forest on a curving climb into the South Fork of the Fryingpan River, crossing a creek via a small bridge en route. Ski west across the South Fork and continue up to a wide road (Forest Road 504) by contouring slightly to the northwest. Once on this road, follow it west/northwest, traversing high above the Fryingpan River (to the north) toward Twin Meadows. Intercept the Norrie Trailhead route on the north edge of the meadows and follow that route 4.6 miles to the hut. See Tour 30a for directions to the hut.

*Rick Sayre (rear) and Cully Culbreth (front) tour up to Mount Yeckel near Margy's Hut.*

INTERMEDIATE/ADVANCED

TOUR

# 30c Lenado Trailhead to Margy's Hut

SEE MAP PAGES 124–125, 220–221, AND 240–241

| | |
|---|---|
| TIME | 5 to 7 hours |
| DISTANCE | 6.3 miles |
| ELEVATIONS | TRAILHEAD: 9,640' HUT: 11,300' GAIN: +2,660' |
| AVALANCHE | Route crosses avalanche slopes; prone to skier-triggered avalanches during high-hazard periods |
| MAPS | 10th Mountain Division: Smuggler Mountain (replaces Bald Knob)<br>USGS 7.5': Meredith, 1987<br>National Forest: White River<br>Trails Illustrated: Map #126 (Holy Cross/Ruedi Reservoir) |

**TOUR OVERVIEW:** The route from the Lenado Trailhead up Johnson Creek is the most direct route to Margy's Hut. The trail climbs steadily, gaining over 2,600 feet in elevation in a little over 6 miles. Be prepared for some labored breathing when you ski to the hut and some exciting schusses on the way back down. The lower portion of the trip follows a distinct road, while the latter sections of the trail require a bit of heads-up navigation as the route tours through clearings and scattered, less dense woods.

*Margy's Hut.*

**DIRECTIONS TO TRAILHEAD:** Drive on CO 82 to the Woody Creek Canyon turn, 6.5 miles northwest of Aspen. Cross the Roaring Fork River and continue to an intersection. Turn left (north) and drive on County Road 17 for 1 mile to the Woody Creek Tavern. Drive another 0.25 mile and take a sharp right turn (east) onto the Woody Creek Road (County Road 18/Forest Road 103). Proceed 8.5 miles to Lenado and park near the end of the plowed road. This road is narrow and often snow-packed, so drive carefully.

The turnoff onto the Woody Creek Road (CR 18/FR 103) is north of the Woody Creek Tavern and may also be reached from Glenwood Springs or Basalt by turning onto Lower River Road at Old Snowmass or a little farther upstream across from the Aspen Village Trailer Park. From here drive across to the Lower River Road, on the north side of the Roaring Fork River. Now, follow Lower River Road upstream to the Woody Creek turn.

**THE ROUTE:** Leave the parking area and start climbing east on the unplowed road (FR 103). Follow the road as it crosses Woody Creek and contours to the northwest. After gaining roughly 100 feet of elevation, search for a marked trail to the north. Follow this trail up the Silver Creek drainage. The trail switchbacks sharply to the southeast and begins to climb generally eastward, up and into the Johnson Creek drainage. Climb the drainage until you reach a road near Johnson Creek, gaining a steep 1,200 feet.

Follow this road east, then north on a 2.3-mile traverse around Elevation Point 11,376'. Pass a clearing above the road, take a left turn, and climb onto a saddle near the top of Elevation Point 11,376'. Upon reaching an intersection, turn northeast, following this road 0.7 mile up to a point where the road begins to turn out into a massive, low-angled, south-facing meadow. Turn east, then ski through a stand of spruce trees and descend to the backside of Margy's Hut. If you miss this turn down to the hut, you will be on your way across the meadow toward the west ridge of Mount Yeckel.

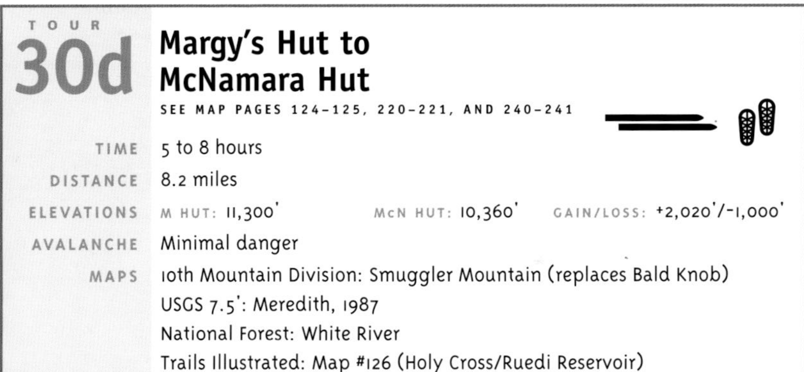

INTERMEDIATE/ADVANCED

TOUR **30d**

## Margy's Hut to McNamara Hut

SEE MAP PAGES 124–125, 220–221, AND 240–241

TIME 5 to 8 hours

DISTANCE 8.2 miles

ELEVATIONS M HUT: 11,300' McN HUT: 10,360' GAIN/LOSS: +2,020'/-1,000'

AVALANCHE Minimal danger

MAPS 10th Mountain Division: Smuggler Mountain (replaces Bald Knob)
USGS 7.5': Meredith, 1987
National Forest: White River
Trails Illustrated: Map #126 (Holy Cross/Ruedi Reservoir)

**TOUR OVERVIEW:** The section of trail between these two huts was the first hut-to-hut trail in the 10th Mountain Division system. It is generally well-traveled and, because the route follows a well-marked and obvious path, navigation is not too difficult. This is one of the longer hut interconnect trails in the system, so plan accordingly and get an early start. The McNamara Hut is closed in summer.

**THE ROUTE:** Leave Margy's Hut and traverse east/northeast down to Sawmill Park via the last section of the Norrie/Margy's Hut Trail. Enter this tiny clearing, swing sharply to the southwest, and begin the long and treacherous drop down to Spruce Creek. Follow the trail along the creek for 3.3 miles, remaining on the northwest side of Spruce Creek all the way down to the confluence of Woody Creek and Spruce Creek. This spot is marked by the obvious narrowing of the two drainages; make sure you do not drop down into Woody Creek here.

Cross Spruce Creek via a quick, steep drop. Ski south, traversing up across steep, timbered slopes above the precipitous confluence. Pass some trail signs, then contour sharply east into the Woody Creek drainage. Climb Woody Creek for 0.8 mile. Switchback across the creek and begin climbing due west for a few hundred yards, then due south upward along Woody Creek. Follow the trail across this creek, then traverse west (crossing two more tributaries) until you cross a large drainage. Follow the trail south, then west across this creek, and continue 0.4 mile to the McNamara Hut, which is on the north side of the trail.

*John Fielder skis the trail in the 10th Mountain Division Hut system. Note the nonmotorized diamond on the tree to the right.*

# 31 McNamara Hut

| | |
|---|---|
| **HUT ELEVATION** | 10,360' |
| **DATE BUILT** | 1982 |
| **SEASONS** | Thanksgiving through April 30 |
| **CAPACITY** | 16 |
| **HUT LAYOUT** | 1 room with double bed plus 10 single beds in a communal room upstairs; 4 single beds in bunkroom on main floor |
| **HUT ESSENTIALS** | Woodstove for heat, wood-burning cookstove with oven, propane cookstoves, all kitchenware, outhouse, photovoltaic electric lights |

The McNamara Hut is one of the first two huts built in the system. Like Margy's Hut, it is a memorial to Margaret McNamara, the wife of former Secretary of Defense Robert McNamara. The closest hut to Aspen, it was one of the most frequently used huts in the early days of the 10th Mountain Division system, and it still provides access to classic cross-country ski adventures.

The hut is set back in the woods below and north of 11,092-foot Bald Knob. Skiers can climb to the summit of Bald Knob for a 360-degree top-of-the-world panorama of Colorado's most famous peaks, including the Maroon Bells. Telemark skiing on the slopes between the hut and Bald Knob can be excellent.

McNamara Hut is open only for winter use. The area is closed in the summer because it is a calving area for elk. Make reservations through the 10th Mountain Division Hut Association (see Appendix A).

*A commemorative plaque for Margaret McNamara marks the hut named in her honor.*

**RECOMMENDED DAY TRIPS:**

Day touring in the area is limited relative to other huts in the system. **The classic day trip ascends Bald Knob,** takes in the panorama from the top, and then returns down through ideal terrain for making turns. Leave the hut, regain the trail, and follow it to the southwest for a few hundred feet to the creek drainage. Ascend this drainage to the southwest and as you gain elevation, begin to contour to the southeast up toward the summit. There is no best or exact route. Take your camera—and lots of film!

INTERMEDIATE

TOUR

# 31a Hunter Creek Trailhead to McNamara Hut

SEE MAP PAGES 124–125 AND 240–241

TIME 5 to 8 hours

DISTANCE 5.7 miles

ELEVATIONS TRAILHEAD: 8,380' HUT: 10,360' GAIN/LOSS: +1,980'/-40'

AVALANCHE Minimal danger

MAPS 10th Mountain Division: Smuggler Mountain (replaces Bald Knob)
USGS 7.5': Aspen, 1987; Thimble Rock, 1987
National Forest: White River
Trails Illustrated: Map #127 (Aspen/Independence Pass)

**TOUR OVERVIEW:** This tour begins at Hunter Creek on the north edge of Aspen. The trail is spectacular, overlooking the town of Aspen, the downhill ski areas, and the Elk Mountains. If you can find the parking area and the trailhead (in the middle of a hillside residential area), you should have no problem navigating this route.

**DIRECTIONS TO TRAILHEAD:** Locate the intersection of Mill Street and Main Street in Aspen. Go north on Mill Street and proceed across the Roaring Fork River. Turn left onto Red Mountain Road and climb north for roughly 1 mile to an intersection on a flat bench. Turn sharply right (downhill) on the Hunter Creek Road. Drive south, then east for 0.25 mile to a left turn before a stone gate. Turn left and drive a few hundred feet to a parking area near a water tank. From this point, walk back to the Hunter Creek Road and continue along it to the northeast (toward the creek). Walk up and around a steep switchback to the trailhead on the right. Watch for traffic on this road!

**THE ROUTE:** After locating the trailhead, ski or walk along this south-facing trail (which is a popular walking area for locals and is often without snow for the first few hundred feet) as it travels above Hunter Creek and below some houses. Follow the trail as it turns east and crosses the creek via a bridge. Now climb a very steep trail deep into the woods along the south side of Hunter Creek. Follow this trail for roughly 0.9 mile until you can cross Hunter Creek via the 10th Mountain Division Bridge. Be sure not to cross the creek on any of several private bridges, as these lead to large homes with even larger dogs. Ski well past these estates as you look for route markers.

Cross the bridge and climb north, away from the creek and around a curve to the west. Pass a large Forest Service information sign near barbed-wire fences. Follow the steep road on a rising traverse to the northeast, eventually crossing Lenado Creek. Just before you reach the creek, you'll pass an obvious left turn, marked by a wooden sign that reads "Red Mountain/Lenado to the left and Van Horn Park to the right."

Turn sharply right and ski to the northeast, passing through a gate before entering Van Horn Park. Climb through the treeless park, following a road on the northwest side. Continue following the road as it leads into the woods at the northeast corner of the park. From here, follow the steep, well-traveled trail through the forest for 1.9 miles to the McNamara Hut.

*"Eat my dust!"*

# 32 Benedict Huts: Fritz's and Fabi's Cabins

| | |
|---|---|
| **FRITZ'S CABIN** | |
| **HUT ELEVATION** | 10,970' |
| **DATE BUILT** | 1997 |
| **SEASONS** | Thanksgiving through April 30 |
| **CAPACITY** | 10 |
| **HUT LAYOUT** | 3 compact bedrooms with double beds; 3 single beds and 1 couch-bed in main room |
| **HUT ESSENTIALS** | Woodstove for heat, propane cookstoves and oven, all kitchenware, outhouse, photovoltaic electric lights |
| **FABI'S CABIN** | |
| **HUT ELEVATION** | 10,970' |
| **DATE BUILT** | 1997 |
| **SEASONS** | Thanksgiving through April 30 |
| **CAPACITY** | 6 (entire hut must be booked by same group) |
| **HUT LAYOUT** | 1 bedroom with double bed; 2 single beds and 1 double in main room |
| **HUT ESSENTIALS** | Woodstove for heat, propane cookstoves and oven, all kitchenware, outhouse, photovoltaic electric lights |

The Benedict Huts were built in honor of the late Fritz Benedict, the father of the 10th Mountain Division Hut system, and his wife, Fabi. Fritz and Fabi passed away in 1995 and 1997, respectively. Certainly the 10th Mountain Division hut system itself is the greatest lasting recognition of the enormous talent and vision of Fritz Benedict. The steady stream of grinning, frosty hut converts who return each year to the 10th Mountain huts is a tribute to Fritz's love of Colorado's high country. However, Colorado's hut scene would seem incomplete without a memorial bearing the names of this noted Colorado couple.

Standing side by side, Fritz's and Fabi's Cabins are unique in the 10th Mountain Division system in that they were designed as complementary cabins that can be booked alone or together. The idea was to build two cabins, rather than one big hut, that could serve two separate groups and provide a more intimate experience for each group. Fritz's can be reserved wholly or in part; Fabi's can only be reserved by one group.

The huts themselves are a stunning blend of contemporary angles and lines and old-world materials (including wood recycled from a nearby barn). Wooden logs, corrugated metal, and large windows have been used judiciously along with compact floor plans to provide coziness without sacrificing streaming sunlight or room to spread out and relax. For my money, these are the most beautiful huts in the system.

The skiing near the huts has a more Nordic, or cross-country, bent to it. You will not find steep tree skiing or high peaks to ascend. Instead, the area is well-suited for long, flat tours out onto the snow-covered peat bogs and up onto the small knolls that dot the landscape. Also, because of the huts' location and the nearby Wilderness Area, hut-to-hut travel is not readily available. The only close hut destination is the McNamara Hut, which requires choosing between one of two very arduous route options to reach it. The first option is a very committing passage directly through the Wilderness Area; the other is a reversal of the route to the Benedict Huts added onto almost the entire approach route to the McNamara Hut. This latter combo is well-traveled and well-marked, though very long and taxing. Consequently, many visitors to the Benedict Huts make the trip into a round-trip affair, allotting several days to relax, enjoy the magnificent views of the Elk Range, and tip a cup of tea in honor of two great Colorado pioneers.

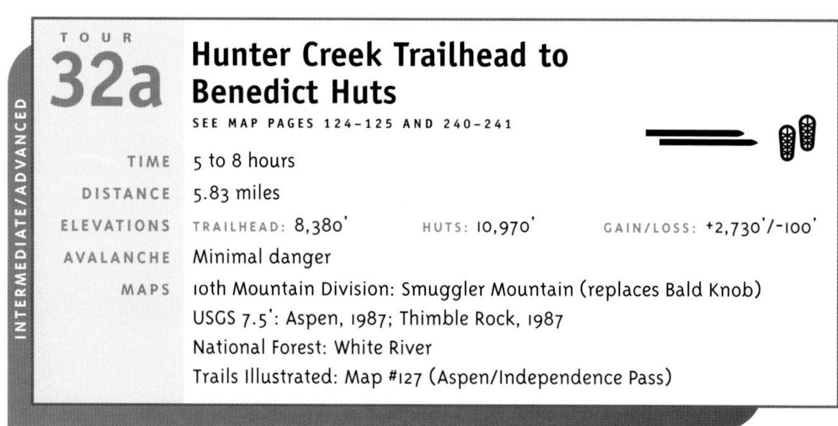

INTERMEDIATE/ADVANCED

TOUR 32a

## Hunter Creek Trailhead to Benedict Huts

SEE MAP PAGES 124–125 AND 240–241

| | |
|---|---|
| TIME | 5 to 8 hours |
| DISTANCE | 5.83 miles |
| ELEVATIONS | TRAILHEAD: 8,380' HUTS: 10,970' GAIN/LOSS: +2,730'/-100' |
| AVALANCHE | Minimal danger |
| MAPS | 10th Mountain Division: Smuggler Mountain (replaces Bald Knob)<br>USGS 7.5': Aspen, 1987; Thimble Rock, 1987<br>National Forest: White River<br>Trails Illustrated: Map #127 (Aspen/Independence Pass) |

**TOUR OVERVIEW:** The primary route to the Benedict Huts shares the same trailhead and first 0.75 mile of trail with the Van Horn Park route to the McNamara Hut. After this point, the arduous trail strikes off on its journey up the west flank of Smuggler Mountain via Smuggler Mountain Road. This trail has a split personality. The first third to half of the route climbs steeply—in fact, very steeply—after the 2-mile mark as it follows a road/trail and crawls directly onto a ridge with few respites. Eventually, the trail gains the undulating, hummocky plateau of upper Smuggler Mountain. Here, the terrain is more moderate, while navigation becomes a bit more difficult as the trail rolls along nicely through forests and meadows. The steep climbs offer views down the Roaring Fork Valley and Aspen and across the valley to the Aspen Mountain ski area and the high Elks to keep your mind off the task at hand.

**DIRECTIONS TO TRAILHEAD:** Locate the intersection of Mill Street and Main Street in Aspen. Go north on Mill Street and proceed across the Roaring Fork River. Turn left onto Red Mountain Road and climb north for roughly 1 mile to an intersection on a flat bench. Turn sharply right (downhill) on the Hunter Creek Road. Drive south, then east, for 0.25 mile to a left turn before a stone gate. Turn left and drive a few hundred feet to a parking area near a water tank. From this point, walk back to the Hunter Creek Road and continue along it to the northeast (toward the creek). Walk up and around a steep switchback to the trailhead on the right. Watch for traffic on this road!

**THE ROUTE:** After locating the trailhead, ski or walk along this south-facing trail (which is often without snow for the first few hundred feet) as it travels above Hunter Creek and below some houses. Follow the trail as it turns east and crosses the creek via a bridge. Now climb a very steep trail deep into the woods along the south side of Hunter Creek. Follow this trail for roughly 0.75 mile until you approach the meadow where the Van Horn Park trail to the McNamara Hut strikes off to the north across the creek and the clearing. Be sure not to cross the creek on any of several private bridges in the area; these lead to large homes with even larger dogs. Ski well past these estates as you look for route markers.

*John Fielder relaxes in Fritz's Cabin.*

Search for markers that head southeast away from the Van Horn Trail and begin to follow a road up into the north-facing woods. This steady climb continues for just over a mile until you reach an area where you can begin to see off the south side of the ridge. Here, the tempo of the ascent increases. Follow the distinct road as it climbs incessantly straight east along the ridge-crest. You will pass a telecommunications facility on the right. Do not confuse this with the "radio tower" marked on the topo maps, which sits to the west well below the route on lower Smuggler Mountain Road.

Eventually, the trail begins to contour north/northeast as you approach the upper half of the route and the more moderate terrain. At around 10,100 feet, the road makes a little switchback and then heads directly east, ascending more gradually. Now the trail heads to the east and southeast following the road, which can be obscured by deep snow in the more open clearings and meadows. Keep navigation tools handy here.

At the 5.26-mile mark, Smuggler Mountain Road veers to the south along the eastern side of a meadow/wetland area. To the east are steeper slopes. Leave the trail and follow an ascending traverse south/southeast to the huts, which sit on the south-facing slopes near the top of Elevation Point 10,977'.

ADVANCED/EXPERT

TOUR

# 32b Benedict Huts to McNamara Hut via Thimble Rock

SEE MAP PAGES 124–125 AND 240–241

| | |
|---|---|
| TIME | 7 to 12 hours |
| DISTANCE | 8.03 miles |
| ELEVATIONS | B HUTS: 10,970' M HUT: 10,360' GAIN/LOSS: +2,012'/-2,632' |
| AVALANCHE | Minimal danger |
| MAPS | 10th Mountain Division: Smuggler Mountain (replaces Bald Knob)<br>USGS 7.5': Aspen, 1987; Thimble Rock, 1987<br>National Forest: White River<br>Trails Illustrated: Map #127 (Aspen/Independence Pass) |

**TOUR OVERVIEW:** The Benedict Huts and the McNamara Hut are separated by Hunter Creek and the protected wildlands of the Hunter-Fryingpan Wilderness Area. The chasm formed by Hunter Creek makes this route a physically demanding trail. The presence of the wilderness means that there cannot be a flagged, signed, or "improved" route connecting the huts. Even if the route were marked and a trail cut, the elevation loss and gain alone add up to a long, taxing day for the average skier.

In 25-plus years of backcountry skiing, this is the only route that forced me into an unplanned bivouac. Obviously, if other parties have completed this route and have left a broken trail, the tour can be substantially easier. On our epic trip, the Benedict Huts had just opened and no one had yet skied the route that winter. Combine 8 miles of trail-breaking—with snow ranging from nearly nonexistent to 3 feet of early-season granular "sugar snow" (known as "depth hoar") underlain with willows and logs—and thought-provoking navigation (though we never strayed from the recommended route), and you end up with 13-plus hours on an 8-mile trail. So be forewarned—this route is not to be trifled with.

On the other hand, this is a challenging sojourn into true wilderness skiing in a beautiful setting. Just get an early start and keep your map, compass, and altimeter handy.

**THE ROUTE:** Leave the Benedict Huts and drop east off Elevation Point 10,970' into the meadow below. Once on the flats, head east/southeast around the small forest knob east of the huts. Ski around the south side and strike off east/northeast

*Above: Fritz's Cabin wears a commemorative plaque.*

across the next, large meadow. Pass south of the craggy summit of Elevation Point 11,140'. Wander east/northeast through the woods toward the descent into No Name Creek. This area is nondescript; aim for the depression and drainage that lie just northeast of the "u" in Smuggler on the topo map.

Slowly the forest gives way to the more open western slopes of No Name Creek. There is much room for creative route-finding here. The goal is to reach the creek bottom in one piece. We switchbacked down thin, crusty snow through sporadic aspen trees and scattered evergreens—in an area strewn with boulders. Though slow, our descent was straightforward, and generally open views across the valley allowed for orientation.

Once down in the creek bottom, head due north along the creek. As you approach the steeper slopes that eventually lead down to Hunter Creek, you will pass large concrete structures that are part of a water-diversion project. There is no reason to follow No Name Creek. Rather, below this point the best path begins to head northeast away from No Name Creek down difficult cross-country terrain over a boulder field.

*John Fielder and Cully Culbreth head from the Benedict Huts on the traverse to the McNamara Hut.*

Welcome to the nasty bottom of Hunter Creek—filled with downed trees and boulders, depending on the snowpack. Using Thimble Rock as a landmark (in the truest sense), head upstream a few hundred feet until open, south-facing, aspen-covered slopes appear around 9,100 feet. The second half of the trip begins with an ascent directly north up these slopes. Near the top of this ascent, the angle begins to lessen as you regain evergreen forests.

The next section of trail up through and over Hunter Flats has some of the trickiest route-finding on the tour. The trail wanders north through subtle, rolling terrain mottled with stands of trees and clearings—though there are fine views to the high peaks, which can aid in navigation. Ski north following old tracks, your nose, or, better yet, a compass, along the western perimeter of Hunter Flats. Eventually, the topography begins to close in and narrow into a drainage corridor as you approach a small pass separating the Hunter Flats area and Slab Park and the head of the tributary of Hunter Creek.

Once over the "pass," the terrain and the forest begin to open up once again. Follow the terrain and a compass bearing and skirt across the head of the drainage. Continue north/northwest following a subtle, willow-filled drainage that appears as the long, narrow clearing straddling the trail marked on the 10th Mountain map (between Slab Park and "Hut"). From here, the "trail" stays the course and climbs through thick, nondescript woods toward the northeast ridge of Bald Knob. Here the route is not particularly exact. Rather, follow the terrain and a compass until you reach the ridge-crest.

*Cully Culbreth is about to throw another log on the fire during an unplanned bivouac en route from Benedict Huts to McNamara Hut.*

Now the "official" route turns and climbs south/southwest to the summit of Bald Knob. From there, ski west off the summit, then immediately veer northwest following the day-trip route in reverse down to the hut. Basically, the route here follows the terrain northwest down into the drainage on the northwest side of Bald Knob and spits you out immediately southwest of the hut.

Frankly, it is not absolutely necessary to make the ascent over Bald Knob. A shorter route passes directly over the northeast ridge of Bald Knob and descends down nice, skiable slopes directly to the Spruce Creek/Margy's Hut trail. A descent of about 500 feet deposits you onto the distinct trail several hundred yards east of the McNamara Hut. Turn left (west) and tour easily to the hut.

INTERMEDIATE/ADVANCED

TOUR
# 32c Benedict Huts to McNamara Hut via Van Horn Park

SEE MAP PAGES 124–125 AND 240–241

TIME 5 to 8 hours
DISTANCE 10 miles
ELEVATIONS B HUTS: 10,970' M HUT: 10,360' GAIN/LOSS: +1,800'/-2,430'
AVALANCHE Minimal danger
MAPS 10th Mountain Division: Smuggler Mountain (replaces Bald Knob)
USGS 7.5': Aspen, 1987; Thimble Rock, 1987
National Forest: White River
Trails Illustrated: Map #127 (Aspen/Independence Pass)

**TOUR OVERVIEW:** This is the other route connecting these huts. It is essentially a combination of the two primary routes to both huts; it is long and loses and gains considerable elevation. Consequently, while being a route that is well-traveled, signed "trade" routes, it still adds up to a stout day of travel.

**THE ROUTE:** The game plan reverses the Smuggler Mountain Road route (Tour 32a) to the Benedict Huts all the way back down to Hunter Creek. From there, follow the Van Horn Park Trail to McNamara Hut (Tour 31a).

*Nancy Coulter-Parker enjoys the morning sun from Fabi's Cabin at the Benedict Huts.*

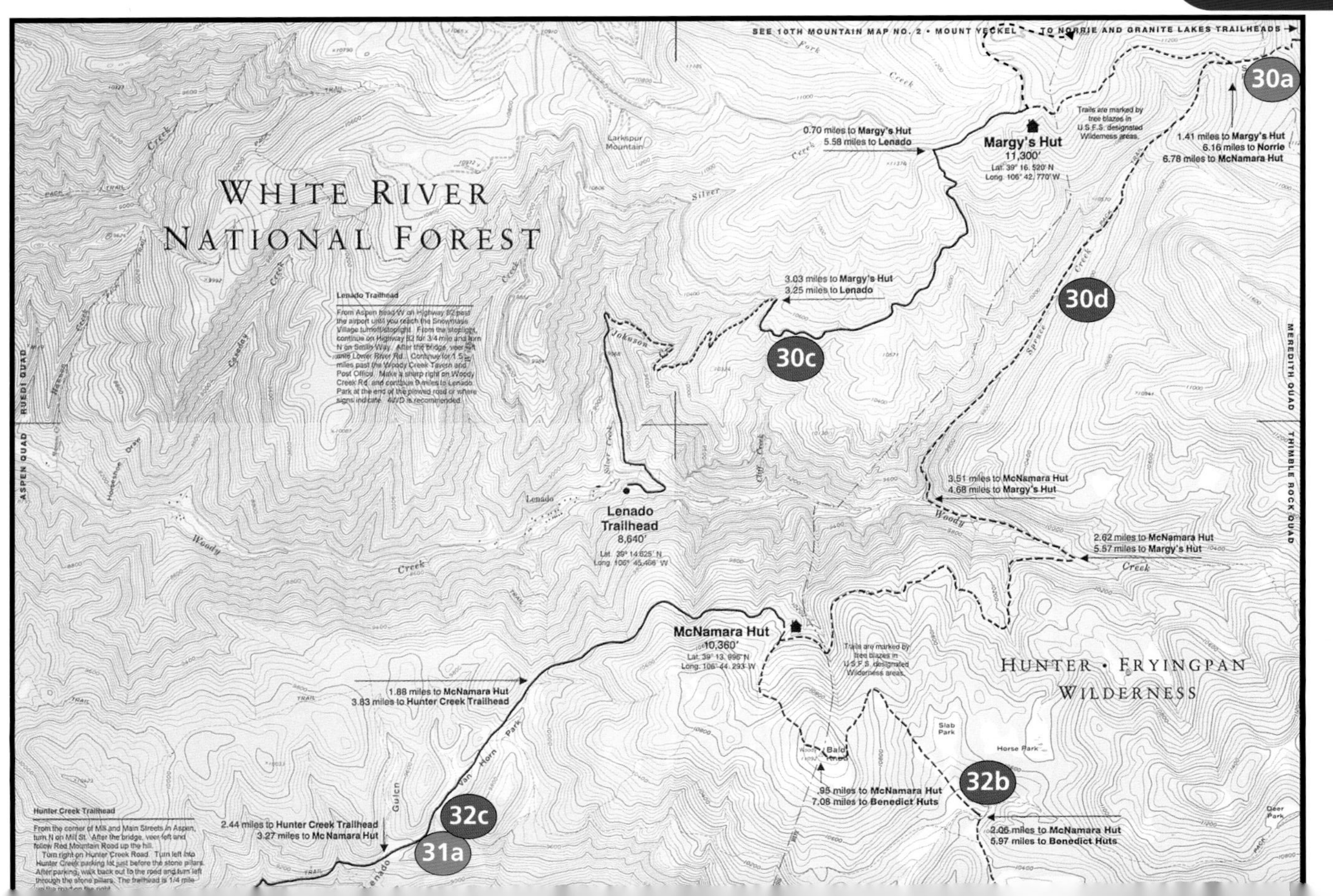
SEE 10TH MOUNTAIN MAP NO. 2 • MOUNT YECKEL • TO NORRIE AND GRANITE LAKES TRAILHEADS
RUEDI QUAD
ASPEN QUAD
MEREDITH QUAD
THIMBLE ROCK QUAD
WHITE RIVER
NATIONAL FOREST
Lenado Trailhead
From Aspen head W on Highway 82 past the airport until you reach the Snowmass Village turnoff/stoplight. From the stoplight, continue on Highway 82 for 3/4 mile and turn N on Smith Way. After the bridge, veer left onto Lower River Rd. Continue for 1.5 miles past the Woody Creek Tavern and Post Office. Make a sharp right on Woody Creek Rd. and continue 9 miles to Lenado. Park at the end of the plowed road or where signs indicate. 4WD is recommended.
Larkspur Mountain
0.70 miles to Margy's Hut
5.58 miles to Lenado
Margy's Hut
11,300'
Lat: 39° 16.520' N
Long: 106° 42.770' W
Trails are marked by tree blazes in U.S.F.S. designated Wilderness areas.
30a
1.41 miles to Margy's Hut
6.16 miles to Norrie
6.78 miles to McNamara Hut
3.03 miles to Margy's Hut
3.25 miles to Lenado
30c
30d
3.51 miles to McNamara Hut
4.68 miles to Margy's Hut
2.62 miles to McNamara Hut
5.57 miles to Margy's Hut
Lenado
Lenado
Trailhead
8,640'
Lat: 39° 14.825' N
Long: 106° 45.468' W
McNamara Hut
10,360'
Lat: 39° 13.996' N
Long: 106° 44.293' W
Trails are marked by tree blazes in U.S.F.S. designated Wilderness areas.
HUNTER • FRYINGPAN
WILDERNESS
1.88 miles to McNamara Hut
3.83 miles to Hunter Creek Trailhead
Slab Park
Horse Park
Bald Knob
Deer Park
.95 miles to McNamara Hut
7.08 miles to Benedict Huts
32b
2.05 miles to McNamara Hut
5.97 miles to Benedict Huts
Hunter Creek Trailhead
From the corner of Mill and Main Streets in Aspen, turn N on Mill St. After the bridge, veer left and follow Red Mountain Road up the hill.
Turn right on Hunter Creek Road. Turn left into Hunter Creek parking lot just before the stone pillars. After parking, walk back out to the road and turn left through the stone pillars. The trailhead is 1/4 mile
2.44 miles to Hunter Creek Trailhead
3.27 miles to Mc Namara Hut
32c
31a

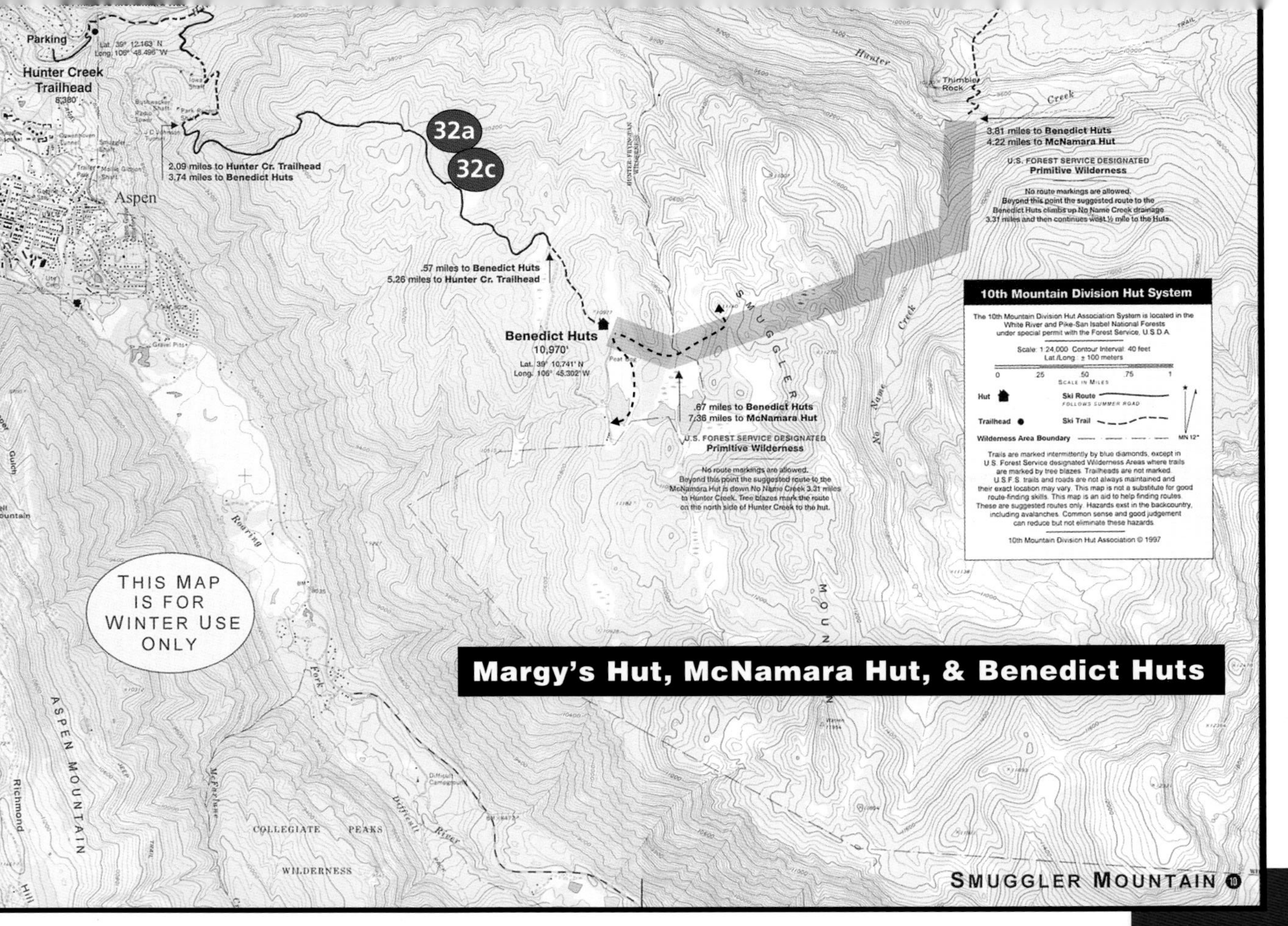

Margy's Hut, McNamara Hut, & Benedict Huts
SMUGGLER MOUNTAIN
10th Mountain Division Hut System
The 10th Mountain Division Hut Association System is located in the White River and Pike-San Isabel National Forests under special permit with the Forest Service, U.S.D.A.
Scale: 1:24,000 Contour Interval: 40 feet
Lat./Long.: ± 100 meters
Hut
Trailhead
Ski Route
Ski Trail
Wilderness Area Boundary
Trails are marked intermittently by blue diamonds, except in U.S. Forest Service designated Wilderness Areas where trails are marked by tree blazes. Trailheads are not marked. U.S.F.S. trails and roads are not always maintained and their exact location may vary. This map is not a substitute for good route-finding skills. This map is an aid to help finding routes. These are suggested routes only. Hazards exist in the backcountry, including avalanches. Common sense and good judgement can reduce but not eliminate these hazards.
10th Mountain Division Hut Association © 1997
THIS MAP IS FOR WINTER USE ONLY
Parking
Hunter Creek Trailhead
8,380'
Aspen
32a
32c
2.09 miles to Hunter Cr. Trailhead
3.74 miles to Benedict Huts
.57 miles to Benedict Huts
5.26 miles to Hunter Cr. Trailhead
Benedict Huts
10,970'
.67 miles to Benedict Huts
7.36 miles to McNamara Hut
U.S. FOREST SERVICE DESIGNATED
Primitive Wilderness
No route markings are allowed.
Beyond this point the suggested route to the McNamara Hut is down No Name Creek 3.31 miles to Hunter Creek. Tree blazes mark the route on the north side of Hunter Creek to the hut.
3.81 miles to Benedict Huts
4.22 miles to McNamara Hut
U.S. FOREST SERVICE DESIGNATED
Primitive Wilderness
No route markings are allowed.
Beyond this point the suggested route to the Benedict Huts climbs up No Name Creek drainage 3.31 miles and then continues west ½ mile to the Huts.
SMUGGLER
MOUN
Thimble Rock
Hunter
Creek
No Name Creek
Roaring
Fork
Difficult
River
COLLEGIATE PEAKS WILDERNESS
McFarlane
ASPEN MOUNTAIN
Richmond
Hill
Copper
Gulch
Bell Mountain

## Alfred A. Braun Memorial Hut System

The Alfred A. Braun Memorial Hut System was the first backcountry-shelter system in Colorado created specifically for ski mountaineers and Nordic skiers. Pitkin County residents Jay Laughlin and Stuart and Isabel Mace are credited with the idea for the system: a network of cabins providing outdoor enthusiasts the opportunity to live in Colorado's winter wilderness in relative comfort and safety.

Work on the first huts, the early Tagert and the Lindley, began in the 1940s and 1950s; construction on the present Tagert Hut and on additional huts began in 1963. The huts are a wonderfully eclectic collection, ranging from small A-frames to log cabins. Each one is unique.

The Braun hut system—named in honor of the man who managed it for many years—recently changed hands and is now run by a local Aspen-based non-profit group. With new energy and vision, the group intends to refurbish and remodel all of the huts during the next few years and may build a limited number of new huts in the future. Simple architectural modifications, such as relocating outhouses away from the main structures and creating new windows, will greatly enhance the ambiance and livability of these classic backcountry shelters. Since renovation work will be ongoing over the next four to five years, do not be surprised if things change relative to the information in this edition of *Colorado Hut to Hut.*

Thankfully, what will not change are the five-star vistas found at the huts and the superlative, diverse selection of ski trails and routes connecting these huts (the original planners did their homework when choosing the hut sites). The Braun hut system is located in the Elk Mountains, in the midst of some of Colorado's most scenic and most photographed peaks. Ancient red sedimentary rocks have weathered into precipitous, crumbling cliffs, delicately balanced towers, and graceful peaks. Outstanding Nordic trails, unparalleled tree-line bowls, and a seemingly endless array of 13,000- and 14,000-foot mountains offer enough skiing and mountaineering challenges to fill many vacations.

The skiing, especially off trail, is for more experienced skiers. All skiers using this system should have substantial experience traveling in the mountains in winter; the Elk Mountains contain ever-present avalanche danger because of their steep topography. Ideally, each skier heading into this hut system will have completed at least an introductory-level avalanche class. Less experienced skiers are encouraged to join a group of advanced skiers or to employ one of the many excellent guide services operating in the area (see Appendix D).

All of the Braun huts are fully stocked with the usual assortment of hut accoutrements: woodstoves, matches, propane stoves, electric lights, cookware, axes, outhouse facilities, and beds and mattresses. It is highly recommended that skiers bring shovels, transceivers, probes, compasses, bivouac gear, and altimeters.

The routes to the huts are not marked, although some trails do have old hiking, skiing, and even snowmobile markers that may aid in navigation. Plan on route-finding.

*Sunrise wakes up Castle Peak and Cathedral Peak in the Elk Range.*

**RESERVATION NOTE:** Because of the remoteness and degree of serious skiing within the Braun system, a minimum of four skiers is required to reserve a hut. The huts are rented exclusively to one group of four or more skiers, and each visitor must pay the nightly fee. Multiple groups are not booked together in a hut. (The Lindley Hut requires a minimum of six skiers for exclusive occupancy.) To reserve a Braun hut, call the 10th Mountain Division Hut Association (see Appendix A).

*Note:* This edition of *Colorado Hut to Hut* is split into two volumes. Volume I covers the northern and central huts, and Volume II covers the southern huts exclusively. The line of demarcation is the crest of the Elk Range and the Monarch Pass area. The Friends Hut technically would fall into Volume II, but it is the pivotal hut connecting the huts south of the crest of the Elk Mountains and the Alfred Braun huts on the north side of the range. Because many (if not most) people ski to the Friends Hut via Pearl Pass and the Braun Huts, the Friends Hut will be included in both volumes. The rest of the Crested Butte–area huts (which were formerly in the Central section) are in Volume II.

**DIRECTIONS TO TRAILHEADS:** All of the Braun hut trails share the same parking area in Ashcroft, a defunct mining community that has been a favorite Nordic ski area for decades. To reach Ashcroft, turn south off CO 82 and onto Maroon Creek Road (County Road 13/Forest Road 125). This is a marked intersection at a stoplight on the west edge of Aspen. After turning onto Maroon Creek Road, immediately turn left onto the Castle Creek Road (County Road 15/Forest Road 102) and drive 11 miles along this winding and often snow-packed road. The overnight parking lot in Ashcroft is across the road from the Toklat Gallery. It is the first lot on the east (or left) side of the road and is marked by a sign.

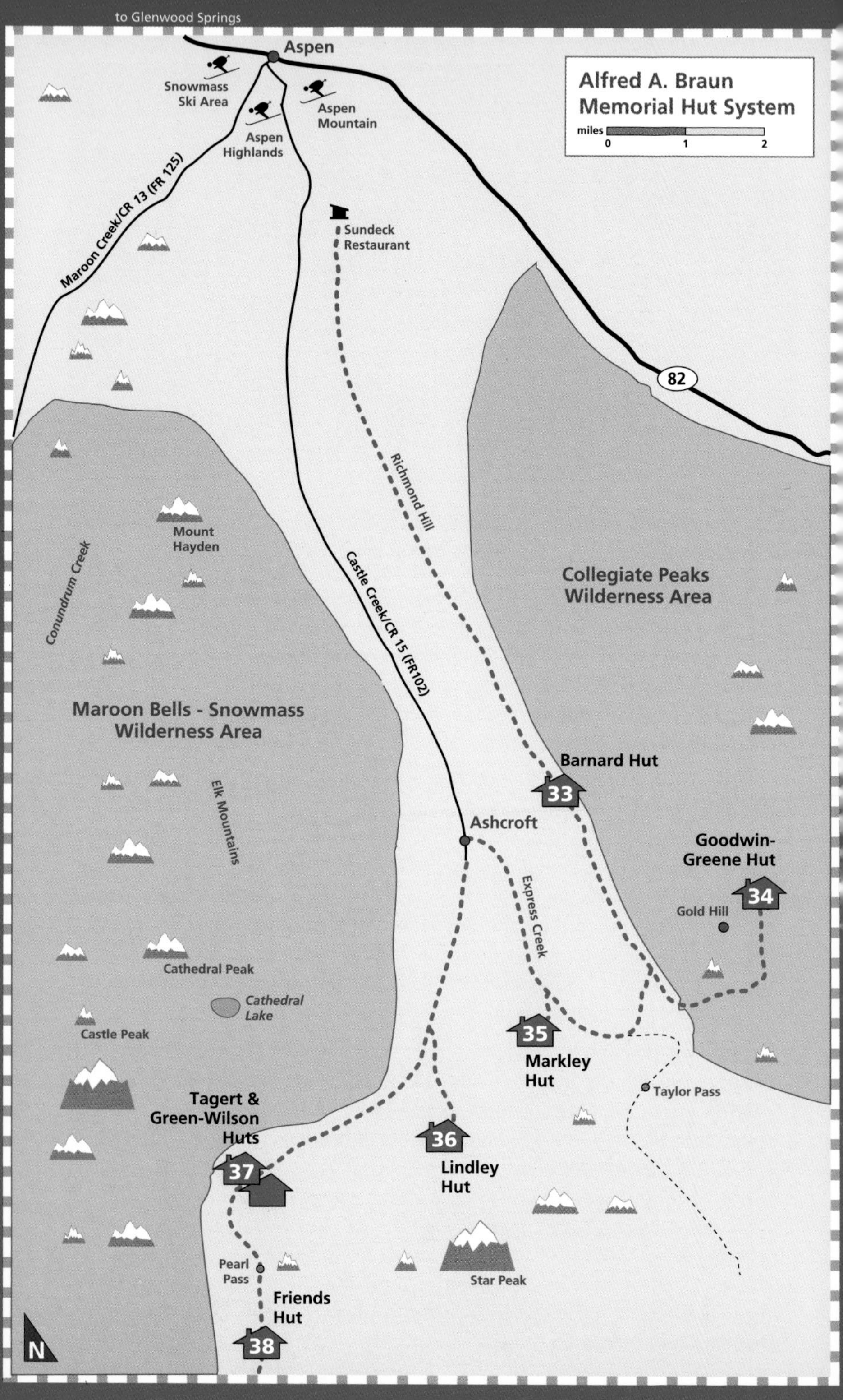

to Glenwood Springs

## Alfred A. Braun Memorial Hut System

miles 0 1 2

Aspen
Snowmass Ski Area
Aspen Highlands
Aspen Mountain
82
Maroon Creek/CR 13 (FR 125)
Sundeck Restaurant
Richmond Hill
Castle Creek/CR 15 (FR102)
Collegiate Peaks Wilderness Area
Mount Hayden
Conundrum Creek
Maroon Bells - Snowmass Wilderness Area
Elk Mountains
Barnard Hut
33
Ashcroft
Goodwin-Greene Hut
34
Gold Hill
Express Creek
Cathedral Peak
Cathedral Lake
Castle Peak
35
Markley Hut
Taylor Pass
Tagert & Green-Wilson Huts
37
36
Lindley Hut
Pearl Pass
Star Peak
Friends Hut
38
N

# 33 Barnard Hut

| | |
|---|---|
| **HUT ELEVATION** | 11,480' |
| **DATE BUILT** | 1960s |
| **SEASONS** | Thanksgiving through end of May |
| **CAPACITY** | 8 |
| **HUT LAYOUT** | This hut is slated for a major renovation during summer 2000; it will lose the sleeping room, leaving one great room |
| **HUT ESSENTIALS** | Woodstove for heat, propane cookstoves, all kitchenware, outhouse, photovoltaic electric lights |

The rustic Barnard Hut, named in memory of Marsh Barnard, is hidden in a glade of evergreens on Richmond Hill, which is more of a ridge than a hill. The northern end of Richmond Hill terminates at Aspen Mountain (still called Ajax Mountain by longtime locals). The southern end blends into alpine uplands near Taylor Pass, Gold Hill, and the head of Express Creek and a tributary of Taylor Creek. To the west and east are dramatic drops into the Castle Creek Valley on the west and the Difficult Creek Valley to the east. Skiers and photographers alike will find Richmond Hill a delight.

Whether you ski to the Barnard Hut from the north (Aspen Mountain) or from the south and west (Ashcroft), be prepared for a long journey. Many skiers ride the gondola to the top of Aspen Mountain, ski to the Barnard and Goodwin-Greene huts, and then to Ashcroft via Express Creek (returning to Aspen by car shuttle). Skiers from Ashcroft might consider spending the first night at the Markley Hut, reducing the first day's mileage. For information on reservations and riding the Aspen Mountain gondola, refer to Appendix A.

**RECOMMENDED DAY TRIPS:**

**The area surrounding Barnard Hut is good for exploring.** A great slope for telemark skiing drops off below and to the west of the southwest-facing front porch of the hut. Due south, the 12,139-foot summit of McArthur Mountain is a nice destination for day skiers experienced in ski mountaineering, route-finding, and avalanche protocol. Feel free to tour to the north along Richmond Ridge and explore the knolls and hills that harbor fun terrain and great vistas of Mount Hayden.

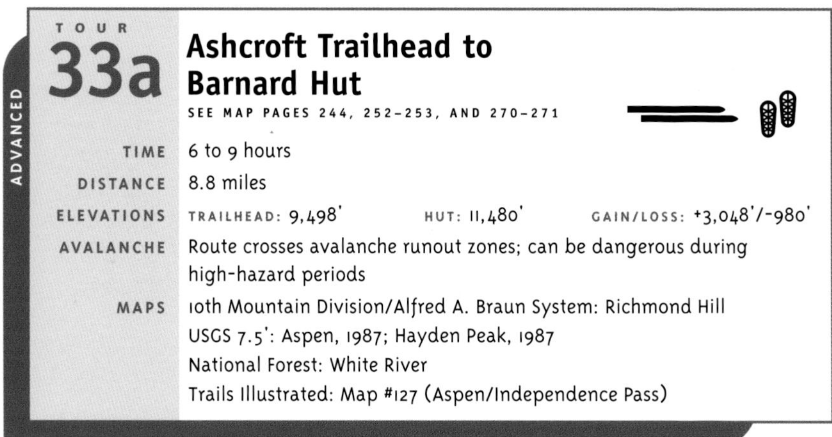

TOUR

# 33a Ashcroft Trailhead to Barnard Hut

ADVANCED

SEE MAP PAGES 244, 252–253, AND 270–271

**TIME** 6 to 9 hours

**DISTANCE** 8.8 miles

**ELEVATIONS** TRAILHEAD: 9,498' HUT: 11,480' GAIN/LOSS: +3,048'/-980'

**AVALANCHE** Route crosses avalanche runout zones; can be dangerous during high-hazard periods

**MAPS** 10th Mountain Division/Alfred A. Braun System: Richmond Hill
USGS 7.5': Aspen, 1987; Hayden Peak, 1987
National Forest: White River
Trails Illustrated: Map #127 (Aspen/Independence Pass)

**TOUR OVERVIEW:** Ashcroft is the traditional trailhead for the Barnard Hut. This route is very long and gains considerable elevation through the Express Creek Valley; however, it is the most desirable trail if you wish to start and finish your tour in Ashcroft. Express Creek has incredible views of Castle Peak and the high summits around Taylor Pass.

Be aware that this valley has conspicuous avalanche runs, which the trail crosses several times. Thankfully though, the crossings are low down, near the runout zones. Also, since the slopes face west into the prevailing winds, they are often scoured to the ground and nonthreatening. After periods of heavy snowfall, though, be extremely careful and travel prudently. Remember to call for information concerning current avalanche conditions and exercise proper avalanche protocol when traveling through this gorgeous valley (see Appendix E).

**DIRECTIONS TO TRAILHEAD:** Park across from the Toklat Gallery in Ashcroft. For directions, see the Alfred A. Braun Memorial Hut System introductory text on page 243.

**THE ROUTE:** The road to Express Creek is visible from the parking lot as it traverses southeast up through aspen forests. There are two ways to this road. You can leave the northeast corner of the parking lot (near a tiny, wooden building) by climbing over snow piles and crossing the field to the northeast to the Taylor Pass/Express Creek Road (Forest Road 122). Or you can walk north along the Castle Creek Road for a few hundred feet to the summer turnoff to the Taylor Pass/Express Creek Road. This area is part of the Ashcroft Ski Touring Center, so please respect the center's trails and skiers.

The Taylor Pass/Express Creek Road angles to the southeast, crosses Castle Creek via a bridge, and then begins to traverse upward. The initial 5 miles of the tour follow this road until reaching a distinct pass above and to the east of the turnoff for Taylor Pass.

Avalanche paths are plentiful along the east side of Express Creek. There are three obvious avalanche paths within the first mile, with many more upstream, including a massive system of slide paths around the 3-mile mark. If conditions warrant, skiers can avoid the upper two avalanche paths by dropping down to the bottom of Express Creek Valley and skiing up through the relative safety of the forested drainage. This ascent is steep and climbing skins are recommended.

Once at the unnamed 11,900-foot pass at the head of Express Creek (marked as the intersection to the Barnard and Goodwin-Greene huts), turn due north and ascend along the boundary of Pitkin and Gunnison Counties to the unnamed summit immediately west of Gold Hill. At the top of this knoll is one of the most commanding views of the Elk Mountains in the Braun system. *Note:* The route to the hut doesn't go anywhere near the real Taylor Pass.

The rest of the route to the hut follows a popular snowmobile trail that normally is marked by four-inch-square wooden poles driven into the ground every few hundred feet. However, the area is exposed to storms and high winds, which may obliterate the snowmobile tracks. Do not plan on navigating by connecting the poles or following old snowmobile tracks because they may or may not be there.

*Craig Fournier and Beth Smith kick back at the Goodwin-Greene Hut.*

Rather, descend northwest and follow the crest of the ridge toward McArthur Mountain, aiming for the flat shoulder on the southeast side. The main route drops from this shoulder down a low-angle drainage below the east face of the mountain. This gully runs below several potential avalanche slopes. When conditions are questionable, drop down to the small, forested ridge immediately east of the creek bed—rather than down the gully itself—to avoid possible danger from the slopes above.

The gully opens into a flat meadow. Cross the meadow by skiing north, following the natural path of the clearing. Within 0.5 mile, the meadow narrows between two forested knobs. To the west, hidden in the trees on a tiny knob, is the Barnard Hut. The turnoff is usually marked by a small sign reading "Hut Touring Area." The brown building is just beyond the edge of the meadow and can be difficult to spot.

INTERMEDIATE/ADVANCED

TOUR

# 33b Sundeck Trailhead to Barnard Hut

SEE MAP PAGES 244 AND 252–253

TIME 5 to 7 hours

DISTANCE 7.2 miles

ELEVATIONS TRAILHEAD: 11,212' HUT: 11,480' GAIN/LOSS: +1,260'/-1,050'

AVALANCHE Route crosses avalanche runout zones; can be dangerous during high-hazard periods

MAPS 10th Mountain Division/Alfred A. Braun System: Richmond Hill
USGS 7.5': Aspen, 1987; Hayden Peak, 1987
National Forest: White River
Trails Illustrated: Map #127 (Aspen/Independence Pass)

**TOUR OVERVIEW:** The mileage on this tour may seem daunting, but the route is actually quite manageable for most skiers. Except for the long drop in the Difficult Creek drainage, most of the touring is moderate and pleasant.

The trailhead atop Aspen Mountain starts at the ski area's Sundeck Restaurant. The key to completing this tour successfully is to get an early start via Aspen's gondola. The logistics involved in leaving a shuttle vehicle in Ashcroft, finding parking in Aspen, getting one-way lift tickets, and riding up the gondola can consume a great deal of time. However, this is the easiest way to gain 3,000 feet of elevation between Aspen and Richmond Hill. Skiers must be equipped for a serious backcountry trip and prepared for complicated route-finding if the weather turns bad or if trail markers are obscured. (For information on gondola tickets, see Appendix A.)

**THE ROUTE:** From immediately behind the top of the gondola, two roads head south. One drops steeply to the south/southwest, while the other leads off to the south/southeast. Avoid the first road to Little Annie Basin. The second choice, the Richmond Hill Road, is relatively flat and remains on the ridge. Traveled by skiers and snowmobilers alike and marked by orange snowmobile diamonds, this trail is generally a straightforward trip, though at times snowmobile and ski trails criss-cross, which can be confusing. Keep maps, compasses, and thinking caps handy and remember to watch for the orange markers all the way to the hut.

Follow the Richmond Hill Road south, eventually passing several private cabins along the top of the ridge. The views here include Pyramid, Hayden, Cathedral, and Castle Peaks to the west, with the Sawatch Range to the east and the Holy Cross Wilderness far off to the northeast.

Approaching the 2-mile mark, the trail traverses down along the east side of Elevation Point 11,534', then contours to the southwest on a fun and moderate descent. Pleasant ski touring dominates as you follow the obvious road on a gentle ascent south through the forest for several miles. Eventually, the road enters a flat,

*Two skiers cross the wide-open ridge-crest near Gold Hill en route from the Goodwin-Greene Hut to the Ashcroft Trailhead; Castle Peak is in the distance.*

wide clearing on top of the ridge. Continue southeast until the road approaches the forest.

At this point the trail drops abruptly into the woods to the head of the Difficult Creek drainage. This very steep section of road has several blind curves, is traveled by snowmobilers, and often has a washboard surface. Solid intermediate skiers and advanced skiers will encounter little trouble on this descent, while those weak in downhill snowplows might consider walking or wearing skins.

The descent ends at Difficult Creek, 1.5 miles from the Barnard Hut. Once you enter the drainage, turn uphill and ascend along the west side of the creek via the snow-covered road. (Do not take the left fork, marked by an orange diamond, which splits off to the east at the bottom of the drop.) Ski a few hundred yards up the creek to a point where the terrain steepens and becomes forested. Climb through a series of switchbacks (not well-indicated on maps) to the west of the creek, taking time to enjoy the great view of Hayden Peak to the west.

Follow the trail markers south, noting small clearings. Ski through rolling terrain, in and out of trees on a less distinct path. Pass two small hills, drop down and across the head of a Castle Creek tributary, and ascend gently into the north edge of a large, flat meadow. Snowmobilers often travel in this meadow, obscuring old Nordic trails. However, the turnoff to the hut is usually marked by a sign reading "Hut Touring Area." The Barnard Hut is 100 feet farther in the trees, facing south on a small, forested knob.

ADVANCED

TOUR **33c**

## Barnard Hut to Goodwin-Greene Hut

SEE MAP PAGES 244, 252–253, AND 270–271

**TIME** 5 to 7 hours

**DISTANCE** 4.5 miles

**ELEVATIONS** B HUT: 11,480′ G-G HUT: 11,680′ GAIN/LOSS: +1,100′/-910′

**AVALANCHE** Route crosses avalanche runout zones; can be dangerous during high-hazard periods

**MAPS** 10th Mountain Division/Alfred A. Braun System: Richmond Hill
USGS 7.5′: Aspen, 1987; Hayden Peak, 1987
National Forest: White River
Trails Illustrated: Map #127 (Aspen/Independence Pass)

**TOUR OVERVIEW:** This high-altitude traverse is spectacular. Like many of the routes on and around Richmond Hill, this one is exposed to high-country weather patterns. While the distance between the Barnard Hut and the Goodwin-Greene Hut is not great, inclement weather can drastically increase the difficulty of this tour.

Most of the route follows the upper portion of the trail from Ashcroft to Barnard Hut (Tour 33a). Snowmobilers also use this route, and there generally are tracks to follow, as well as a series of four-inch-square posts and orange trail diamonds.

The Goodwin-Greene Hut is at the head of Difficult Creek/Bruin Creek and lies at tree line northeast and below Gold Hill. Skiers must traverse south around Gold Hill. Be careful not to confuse a private cabin that lies on the northwest shoulder of Gold Hill with the Goodwin-Greene Hut. This private cabin sits in a very prominent spot, and many people have skied to it in error.

**THE ROUTE:** From the Barnard Hut, return east into the large, flat meadow and turn south. Ski through the center of the meadow, heading south/southeast following the natural contour of this subtle drainage. Continue south into a treeless corridor that marks the creek bed. Ascend a gully below the east face of McArthur Mountain and cross over a small, flat shoulder on the northeast corner of the mountain. This gully traverses below possible avalanche slopes; during periods of high avalanche danger, ascend past McArthur Mountain by climbing along the forested ridge immediately to the east of the gully.

From the top of the shoulder, you can see the rest of the route. Continue south/southeast along the crest of the ridge, then begin the 500-foot climb to an unnamed point immediately west of Gold Hill. There are incredible vistas along this entire stretch. If you plan to descend to Express Creek when your trip is over, this is a good spot for orientation in case clouds and/or snow enshroud the area when you are ready to depart.

From here, head east toward Gold Hill. Drop down across a saddle, then begin a short climb up and over the gentle, south flank of Gold Hill. Once past the crest of this broad ridge, gradually contour slightly to the northeast as you drop 200 feet to a small pass immediately east of Gold Hill. Descend the north side of the pass and cross a small, flat bowl spilling into steeper slopes that drop to Bruin/Difficult Creek.

The Goodwin-Greene Hut is at the base of these final, steep slopes, tucked in a grove of spruce trees. The steeps may be bypassed in favor of more gradual terrain by traversing down to the northeast. Remember to avoid the avalanche slopes that cover the upper aspects of Gold Hill.

*Note:* In years past (and in out-of-print guidebooks from the 1970s), a straighter, more direct route was used to connect these huts. Though it has fallen out of favor, it avoids the high-altitude circumnavigation of the southern flanks of Gold Hill and the accompanying exposure to weather in that broad, treeless area.

Though I do not give a full written description of the route, people may want to consider heading cross-country from near McArthur Mountain more or less directly to the hut. This entails passing through the notch between the hill that sits above the cluster of ponds shown on the USGS topo maps near the 11,800-foot contour mark and Gold Hill before dropping down into the tributary of Difficult Creek that is immediately north of Gold Hill. Once in the creek drainage, devise a route up to the hut. Be very careful to stay well away from the avalanche paths that spill off the northern face of Gold Hill as this route travels across the lowest reaches of the runout zones of these slide paths.

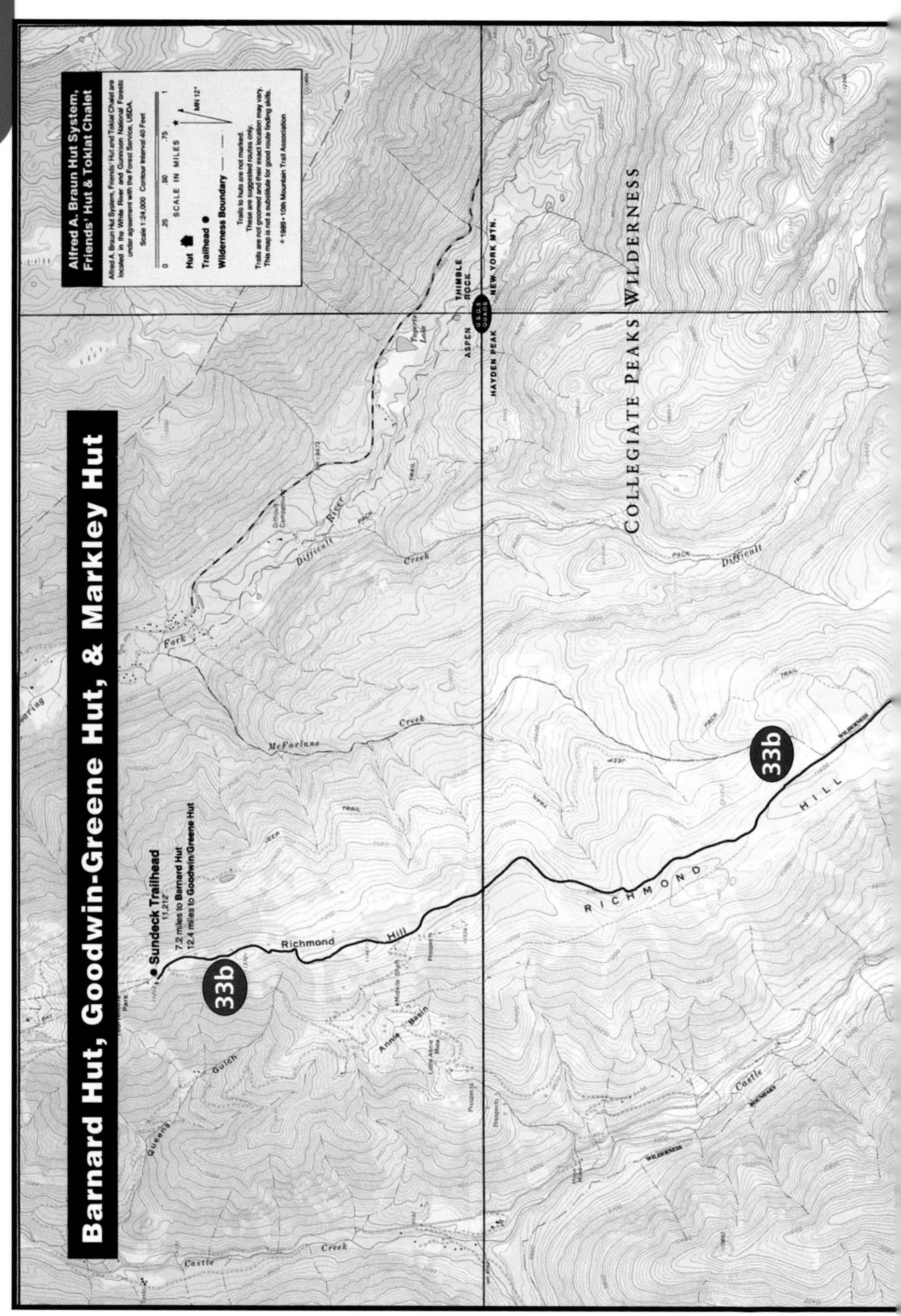
Barnard Hut, Goodwin-Greene Hut, & Markley Hut
Alfred A. Braun Hut System, Friends' Hut & Toklat Chalet
Alfred A. Braun Hut System, Friends' Hut and Toklat Chalet are located in the White River and Gunnison National Forests under agreement with the Forest Service, USDA.
Scale 1:24,000 Contour Interval 40 Feet
0 .25 .50 .75 1
SCALE IN MILES
Hut
Trailhead
Wilderness Boundary
MN 12°
Trails to huts are not marked. These are suggested routes only.
Trails are not groomed and their exact location may vary.
This map is not a substitute for good route finding skills.
© 1989 • 10th Mountain Trail Association
Sundeck Trailhead
11,212'
7.2 miles to Barnard Hut
12.4 miles to Goodwin/Greene Hut
33b
33b
Richmond
Hill
RICHMOND
HILL
COLLEGIATE PEAKS WILDERNESS
ASPEN
HAYDEN PEAK
THIMBLE ROCK
NEW YORK MTN.
U.S.G.S. QUADS
McFarlane
Creek
Difficult
Creek
River
Fork
Queens
Gulch
Annie
Basin
Castle
Creek
WILDERNESS
BOUNDARY
PACK
TRAIL
JEEP

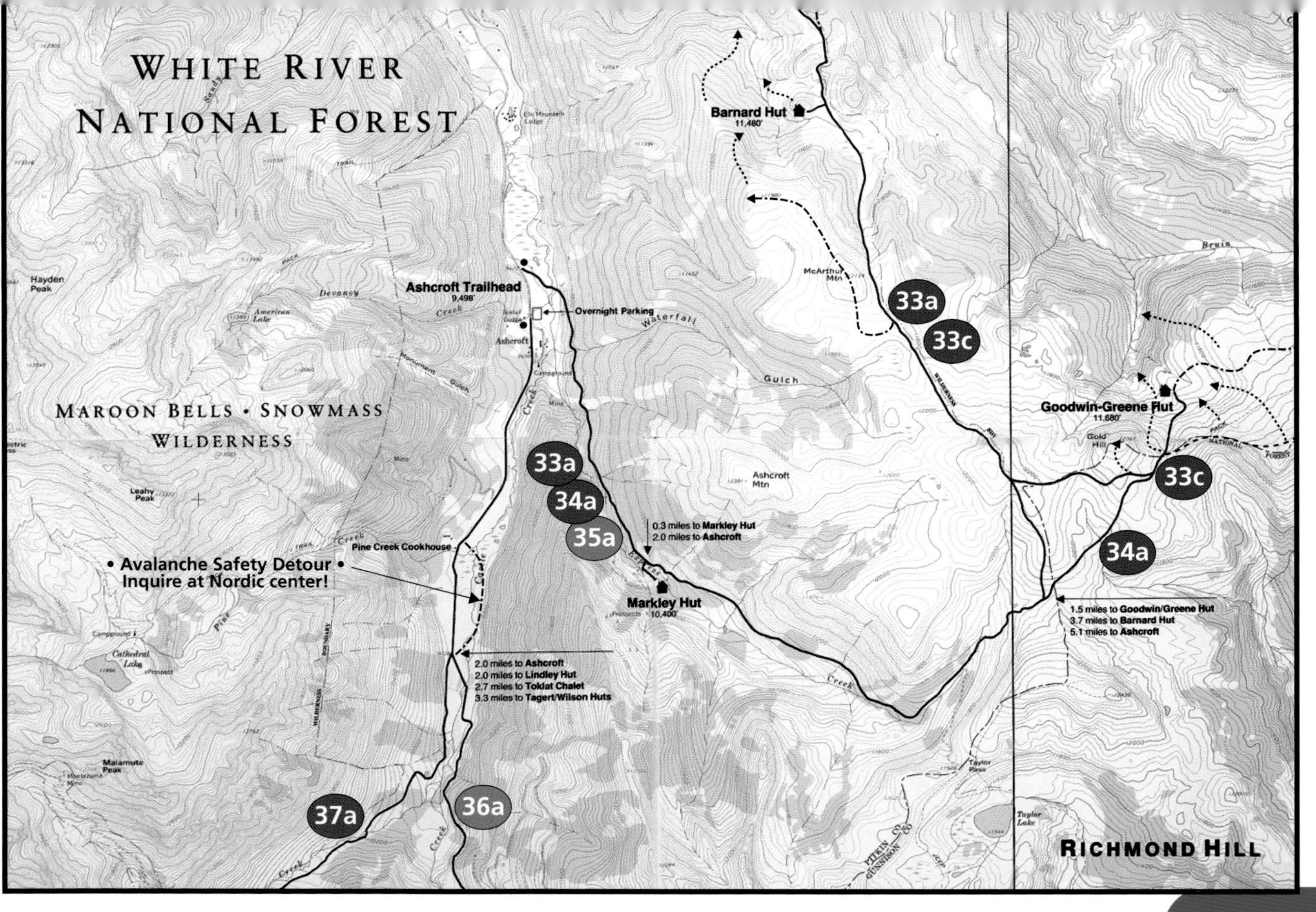

WHITE RIVER
NATIONAL FOREST
MAROON BELLS • SNOWMASS
WILDERNESS
Barnard Hut
11,480'
Hayden Peak
American Lake
Ashcroft Trailhead
9,498'
Overnight Parking
Ashcroft
Waterfall
Gulch
McArthur Mtn
33a
33c
Goodwin-Greene Hut
11,680'
Gold Hill
33c
Leahy Peak
33a
34a
35a
Ashcroft Mtn
0.3 miles to Markley Hut
2.0 miles to Ashcroft
Pine Creek Cookhouse
• Avalanche Safety Detour •
Inquire at Nordic center!
Markley Hut
10,400'
34a
1.5 miles to Goodwin/Greene Hut
3.7 miles to Barnard Hut
5.1 miles to Ashcroft
Cathedral Lake
2.0 miles to Ashcroft
2.0 miles to Lindley Hut
2.7 miles to Toklat Chalet
3.3 miles to Tagert/Wilson Huts
Creek
Malamute Peak
Taylor Pass
Taylor Lake
37a
36a
RICHMOND HILL

# 34 Goodwin-Greene Hut

| | |
|---|---|
| **HUT ELEVATION** | 11,680' |
| **DATE BUILT** | 1970s |
| **SEASONS** | Thanksgiving through end of May |
| **CAPACITY** | 8 |
| **HUT LAYOUT** | 1-story log cabin with 2 single beds in main room, separate sleeping room with 1 double bunk and 1 single bunk (will be renovated in the next few years) |
| **HUT ESSENTIALS** | Woodstove for heat, propane cookstoves and oven, all kitchenware, outhouse, photovoltaic electric lights |

The Goodwin-Greene Hut is in one of the most extraordinary backcountry locations in Colorado and is one of my favorite ski destinations. One trip to this hut was made memorable by copious amounts of fresh powder and sunshine each morning. This is truly a special place!

*The Goodwin-Greene Hut.*

The cozy cabin was built as a memorial to two young men, Peter Goodwin and Carl Greene, who perished in a mountaineering accident. Situated at the head of Difficult Creek, it is surrounded by a treeless bowl. Rolling alpine terrain dominates the southern and eastern horizons. These bowls and ridges provide thousands of acres of glorious ski terrain. Make reservations through the 10th Mountain Division Hut Association (see Appendix A).

### RECOMMENDED DAY TRIPS:

**The bowls surrounding this hut provide unsurpassed backcountry skiing.** The high ridges to the east, as well as Gold Hill, make fine destinations for day trips. Immediately north of the hut, there are knockout slopes for skiing, plunging down into upper Difficult Creek and Bruins Creek. Excellent long runs drop off the southeast shoulder of Gold Hill, which can be worked all the way down into the Difficult Creek drainage below the north face of Gold Hill. Stay well away from the steeper potential slide paths that guard all of the eastern and northern flanks of Gold Hill.

ADVANCED

TOUR

# 34a Ashcroft Trailhead to Goodwin-Greene Hut

SEE MAP PAGES 244, 252–253, AND 270–271

| | |
|---|---|
| TIME | 5 to 7 hours |
| DISTANCE | 6.6 miles |
| ELEVATIONS | TRAILHEAD: 9,422' HUT: 11,680' GAIN/LOSS: +2,838'/-580' |
| AVALANCHE | Route crosses avalanche runout zones; can be dangerous during high-hazard periods |
| MAPS | 10th Mountain Division/Alfred A. Braun System: Richmond Hill<br>USGS 7.5': Hayden Peak, 1987; New York Mountain, 1987<br>National Forest: White River<br>Trails Illustrated: Map #127 (Aspen/Independence Pass) |

**TOUR OVERVIEW:** You can ski to the Goodwin-Greene Hut from the Barnard Hut (Tour 33c) or from Ashcroft via Express Creek. The most direct route, though quite strenuous, is from Ashcroft.

It is possible to break the tour into two shorter days by skiing into the Markley Hut for the first night, then on to the Goodwin-Greene Hut on the second day. This itinerary works especially well if you are planning to arrive at the trailhead and ski the same day (rather than staying in Aspen or Glenwood Springs the night before you start). Compass bearings are very useful on this tour, as on any route above tree line.

**DIRECTIONS TO TRAILHEAD:** Park across from the Toklat Gallery in Ashcroft. For directions, see the Alfred A. Braun Memorial Hut System introductory text on page 243.

**THE ROUTE:** The first 75 percent of this tour follows the route from the Ashcroft Trailhead to Barnard Hut; follow the directions for Tour 33a to 11,900-foot Taylor Pass.

From Taylor Pass, contour northeast around the south flank of a blunt ridge connecting the saddle and an unnamed point immediately west of Gold Hill. Drop down across the creek drainage, then begin a short climb up and over the gentle south flank of Gold Hill. Once past the crest of the south ridge, begin to gradually contour slightly to the northeast as you drop 200 feet to a small pass immediately east of Gold Hill.

Drop off the north side of the pass and cross a small, flat bowl that spills into steeper slopes down to the Bruin Creek/Difficult Creek drainage. The hut is at the base of these slopes, tucked into a grove of spruce trees on a small shelf. The steeper slopes may be bypassed in favor of more gradual terrain by traversing to the northeast. Be sure to avoid the avalanche slopes on the east and north aspects of Gold Hill.

# 35 Markley Hut

| | |
|---|---|
| **HUT ELEVATION** | 10,400' |
| **DATE BUILT** | Mid-1960s; acquired by Braun in 1967 |
| **SEASONS** | Thanksgiving through end of May |
| **CAPACITY** | 8 |
| **HUT LAYOUT** | A-frame with 6 single beds in upstairs sleeping loft and 1 double bed on the main floor (will be renovated in the next few years) |
| **HUT ESSENTIALS** | Woodstove for heat, propane cookstoves and oven, all kitchenware, outhouse, photovoltaic electric lights |

Deep in the Express Creek forest, the Markley Hut is a secluded A-frame set among evergreens. It is not hard to reach, although the route to it gains almost 1,000 feet of elevation and crosses a few avalanche gullies. Strong beginners can enjoy this tour and get a taste of skiing the Elk Mountains. All skiers should be able to recognize avalanche terrain.

*Markley Hut*

Touring around the cabin is somewhat limited. The steep topography of Express Creek is better suited to tours along the valley bottom or to longer excursions up the road toward Taylor Pass. This hut can be a stopover en route to the Barnard or Goodwin-Greene Hut.

The Markley is one of the older backcountry shelters in the state and is a memorial to Mrs. Edna Markley. Make reservations through the 10th Mountain Division Hut Association (see Appendix A).

NOVICE/INTERMEDIATE

TOUR

# 35a Ashcroft Trailhead to Markley Hut

SEE MAP PAGES 244, 252–253, AND 270–271

| | |
|---|---|
| TIME | 2 to 4 hours |
| DISTANCE | 2.3 miles |
| ELEVATIONS | TRAILHEAD: 9,422' HUT: 10,400' GAIN: +978' |
| AVALANCHE | Route crosses avalanche runout zones; can be dangerous during high-hazard periods |
| MAPS | 10th Mountain Division/Alfred A. Braun System: Richmond Hill, Star Peak<br>USGS 7.5': Hayden Peak, 1987<br>National Forest: White River<br>Trails Illustrated: Map #127 (Aspen/Independence Pass) |

**TOUR OVERVIEW:** The route to the Markley Hut follows the Taylor Pass/Express Creek Road.

**DIRECTIONS TO TRAILHEAD:** Park across from the Toklat Gallery in Ashcroft. For directions, see the Alfred A. Braun Memorial Hut System introductory text on page 243.

**THE ROUTE:** The road to Express Creek is visible from the parking lot as it traverses southeast up through the aspen forest. There are two ways to the road: Skiers can leave the northeast corner of the parking lot (near a tiny wooden building) by climbing over the piled-up snow and crossing the field northeast to the Taylor Pass/Express Creek Road (Forest Road 122); or they can walk north back along the Castle Creek Road for a few hundred feet to the summer turnoff to the Taylor Pass/Express Creek Road. This area is part of the Ashcroft Ski Touring Center, so please respect its trails and skiers.

The hut is located below Express Creek Road, very near and to the west of the creek. The turnoff to the hut is at the 2-mile point. This intersection is usually tracked, but can be somewhat difficult to spot, especially if you are moving fast along Express Creek Road. At the marked intersection, cross the creek and follow small painted circles on trees as you enter the forest. The Markley Hut is nearly impossible to see until you ski up to its front porch.

Avalanche paths are numerous throughout the Express Creek drainage. Three major slide paths are crossed within the first mile of the trail. Under normal conditions these paths are blown clear of snow by the winds, but you should always exercise caution. Bent trees indicate relatively recent slide activity. Call the Colorado Avalanche Information Center (see Appendix E) before you leave, or stop at the Ashcroft Ski Touring Center to inquire about the latest avalanche activity.

# 36 Lindley Hut

| | |
|---|---|
| **HUT ELEVATION** | 10,440' |
| **DATE BUILT** | Original Lindley, 1957 (burned down); current hut, late 1960s |
| **SEASONS** | Thanksgiving through end of May |
| **CAPACITY** | 14 |
| **HUT LAYOUT** | Cinderblock hut with cathedral ceiling; sleeping loft with 5 single mattresses; first-floor bedroom with 3 bunk beds (double lower bunks and single upper bunks) |
| **HUT ESSENTIALS** | Woodstove for heat, propane cookstoves, wood-burning cookstove with oven, all kitchenware, outhouse, photovoltaic electric lights |

The Lindley Hut is located in the Cooper Creek drainage and is a relatively easy destination (of the Braun huts, it is generally considered the easiest and safest to reach) with magnificent views of the surrounding country. The southern boundary of the Cooper Creek basin is an impressive, impenetrable wall of jagged ridges and summits that includes 13,521-foot Star Peak.

Largest of the Braun huts, the Lindley Hut is spacious and well-equipped. This hut is unique in that it is built of painted cinder blocks. The Lindley Hut can be reserved through the 10th Mountain Division Hut Association (see Appendix A).

**RECOMMENDED DAY TRIPS:**

**Much of upper Cooper Creek is steep and extremely dangerous during high-avalanche-hazard periods.** Consequently, much care is needed for day tours above the hut. Skiing up Cooper Creek to Pearl Pass or into any of the higher cirques is not recommended unless you are highly skilled in traveling through very serious mountain terrain.

Day skiers can climb northeast from the hut, ad-libbing route selection through the glades or following the old roadbed to the mine. There is plenty of turf on these south- and west-facing slopes for great tele skiing if and when snow conditions are favorable. Another attraction is the basin, or cirque, cradled between Star Peak and Taylor Peak. The best way to explore this basin is to bushwhack to the southeast up through the creek drainage to the slopes above tree line. The tantalizing valley directly south of the hut can at times harbor sweet turns, too. These destinations should be visited only during periods of extreme stability, that is, springtime.

NOVICE/INTERMEDIATE

TOUR **36a**

# Ashcroft Trailhead to Lindley Hut

SEE MAP PAGES 244, 252–253, AND 270–271

| | |
|---|---|
| TIME | 2 to 4 hours |
| DISTANCE | 4 miles |
| ELEVATIONS | TRAILHEAD: 9,498' HUT: 10,440' GAIN/LOSS: +1,022'/-80' |
| AVALANCHE | Route crosses avalanche runout zones; can be dangerous during high-hazard periods |
| MAPS | 10th Mountain Division/Alfred A. Braun System: Star Peak<br>USGS 7.5': Hayden Peak, 1987<br>National Forest: White River<br>Trails Illustrated: Map #127 (Aspen/Independence Pass) |

**TOUR OVERVIEW:** Navigation to the hut is straightforward. The first half of the tour crosses the Castle Creek Valley and is essentially flat; the more demanding second half ascends via a moderately steep road.

Avalanche danger is minimal but does exist in several lightly timbered stretches, on slopes east of the road.

**DIRECTIONS TO TRAILHEAD:** Park across from the Toklat Gallery in Ashcroft. For directions, see the Alfred A. Braun Memorial Hut System introductory text on page 243.

*Mark Collen does some late-afternoon day-tripping above Lindley Hut. In the distance are Star Peak and the Cooper Creek drainage.*

**THE ROUTE:** The first 2 miles of the tour cross the Ashcroft Ski Touring Area and cover relatively flat terrain. There are two routes across the ski area. The traditional, shorter route simply follows the snow-covered Castle Creek Road (Forest Road 102) to the large Forest Service information sign. At this spot, a trail marked by a Lindley Hut sign forks to the left (southeast). Turn left and cross the flat valley bottom, ski around a barricade and bridge, and then intercept a groomed Nordic trail near a large timber home tucked into the trees.

While this public access route is obvious and begins next to the ski-touring center, it does have one serious drawback: It crosses the runout zones of some of the largest avalanche paths in the Castle Creek drainage. Most of the time it is safe to ski under these east-facing slide paths. However, after storms and periods of high winds, they can be extremely dangerous. The Castle Creek Road turnoff to the Lindley Hut should be used only when conditions permit.

*Mark Collen exhibits gastronomic greatness at the Green-Wilson Hut.*

For skiers who do not wish to run the gauntlet below dangerous gullies, the Ashcroft Ski Touring Center has created a special avalanche path that avoids this hazardous section. Called the "Avalanche Avoidance Trail," this route follows the Castle Creek Road to the Pine Creek Cookhouse, then turns east at a trail intersection marked with signs warning skiers of avalanche hazards. The road crosses Castle Creek, then continues south along the touring-area trails to a point where it exits the area near the timber home mentioned above.

The Avalanche Avoidance Trail, which is marked by orange discs, is provided as a courtesy by the Nordic center. Complimentary trail passes are required and can be picked up at the Nordic center office, immediately south of the Toklat Gallery. Please inquire at the Nordic center for current information about avalanche conditions in the area. Snowshoes are not allowed on this alternative route. This trail adds a little mileage to the trip, but it avoids the dangerous runout zones and is well worth it.

From the timber home, the trail is straightforward as it steadily climbs the moderate Cooper Creek Road (Forest Road 121) into the Cooper Creek drainage. At the first major switchback, leave the road and ski south, crossing the creek via a snow-covered bridge. The hut is only a few hundred feet away, but is hard to see and not well-marked. Begin a descending traverse across the clearing, heading toward Cooper Creek and stands of evergreen trees. The large, white Lindley Hut sits near the creek.

*Note:* Keep an eye out for potential avalanche slopes on your left, especially near the 2.3- and 3-mile points.

# 37 Tagert and Green-Wilson Huts

| | |
|---|---|
| **TAGERT HUT** | |
| **HUT ELEVATION** | 11,250' |
| **DATE BUILT** | 1963; overhauled 1999 |
| **SEASONS** | Thanksgiving through end of May |
| **CAPACITY** | 7 |
| **HUT LAYOUT** | A-frame with a small 4-mattress sleeping loft; 1 double bed and 1 single bed in main room on first floor |
| **HUT ESSENTIALS** | Woodstove for heat, propane cookstoves, all kitchenware, new large outhouse, photovoltaic electric lights |
| **GREEN-WILSON HUT** | |
| **HUT ELEVATION** | 11,280' |
| **DATE BUILT** | 1978; overhauled 1999 |
| **SEASONS** | Thanksgiving through end of May |
| **CAPACITY** | 8 |
| **HUT LAYOUT** | 1-story log cabin with 1 large room with 1 double bed, 2 singles, and 1 bunk bed with single beds; sleeping loft in entry/wood room with 2 mattresses (heated by vent windows connecting to main room) |
| **HUT ESSENTIALS** | Woodstove for heat, propane cookstoves, all kitchenware, new large outhouse, photovoltaic electric lights |
| **OTHER GOODIES** | A great new deck |

The remote Tagert and Green-Wilson Huts are in the heart of the Elk Mountains and provide a close approximation of the true European alpine hut-trip experience. These diminutive huts—located below Castle, Pearl, and Star Peaks—serve up genuine ski mountaineering. Nowhere in Colorado are such steep, forbidding summits and high-altitude descents so readily accessible from the front door of your hut. Fact is, there is no finer off-piste destination than these two quaint shelters.

Both of these stellar huts were recently gutted and completely overhauled by the new owners. Improvements include large south-facing windows, bright tongue-and-groove paneling, south-facing decks, spacious outhouses, and a full complement of hut amenities on par with other state-of-the-art huts around the state.

This is where it really all began—both for Colorado hut skiing and for many Colorado-bred ski mountaineers who cut their teeth on the bowls above the huts in Pearl Basin (myself included, as this was the site of my first hut trip in January 1977). Above the huts, the skiing potential is truly vast, as are opportunities for winter and spring ski mountaineering—and avalanches!

Built in 1963, the A-frame Tagert Hut is one of the oldest backcountry shelters in the state. It was named for Billy Tagert, who drove stage and freight wagons over Taylor Pass during the silver-mining heyday in the early 20th century and who donated the land upon which the hut was built. Interestingly, the "new" Tagert Hut was constructed by Fred Braun, along with volunteers from the Colorado Rocky Mountain School. The Tagert's sister hut, the Green-Wilson, was named as a memorial to Lu Lynne Green-Wilson.

These huts work well as a place to overnight when skiing on to the Friends Hut or on a longer expedition to Crested Butte via Pearl Pass. The cabins are within walking distance of each other and both may be booked for large groups. Make reservations through the 10th Mountain Division Hut Association (see Appendix A).

*Tagert Hut glows on a beautiful moonlit evening.*

**RECOMMENDED DAY TRIPS:**

**One could easily devote an entire book to the skiing around these huts.** Here are a few suggestions to get you started: Immediately west of the huts, awesome slopes for turns lie at the head of the bowl on the left. Follow the road west from the Green-Wilson Hut and climb up to tree line. The best runs are south of the creek on the north-facing slopes. Also, the whole of Pearl Basin is one giant playground that can take many days to fully exploit. The north face of Pearl Peak, the crown jewel in the range, is a fine ski-mountaineering route under stable conditions. Peak 13,312' (Pearl's sister summit to the northwest) is a textbook ski-mountaineering tour with some thought-provoking avalanche terrain on some of the lower slopes. We found the direct route up the wind-scoured talus slope on the north face of the lower slopes to be the no-nonsense, safe route up onto the upper slopes below the summit.

Castle Peak is a relatively popular, though serious, touring goal, especially in the spring. The unnamed 12,528-foot peak east/southeast of the huts—really more like a long ridge—is known locally as Mace Peak. It bears the name of Ashcroft local Greg Mace, who died in a climbing accident in the range; Greg was the son of Braun Hut System cofounder Stuart Mace. Climb to the west summit for a quick peak bag and great panorama of the basin. The area around Pearl Basin and upper Castle Creek is truly killer terrain—both in the sense that it is some of the best alpine skiing in Colorado, and because its avalanches have killed skiers. So be careful.

INTERMEDIATE/ADVANCED

TOUR

# 37a Ashcroft Trailhead to Tagert/Green-Wilson Huts

SEE MAP PAGES 244, 252–253, AND 270–271

| | |
|---|---|
| TIME | 4 to 7 hours |
| DISTANCE | 5.3 miles |
| ELEVATIONS | TRAILHEAD: 9,498' T/GW HUTS: 11,280' GAIN: +1,767' |
| AVALANCHE | Route crosses avalanche runout zones; can be dangerous during high-hazard periods |
| MAPS | 10th Mountain Division/Alfred A. Braun System: Star Peak<br>USGS 7.5': Hayden Peak, 1987; Pearl Pass, 1961<br>National Forest: White River<br>Trails Illustrated: Map #127 (Aspen/Independence Pass) |

**TOUR OVERVIEW:** The route to the Tagert and Green-Wilson Huts follows the Castle Creek Road through the Ashcroft Ski Touring Center, passing the turnoff to Cooper Creek and the Lindley Hut, and climbs toward upper Castle Creek. The first few miles are easy; the last 3 miles ascend steadily until you arrive at the huts. This stretch can be taxing for skiers with heavy loads. Also, Castle Creek is lined with massive avalanche paths. Groups heading to the huts must exercise all proper avalanche procedures.

**DIRECTIONS TO TRAILHEAD:** To reach the trailhead, park across from the Toklat Gallery in Ashcroft; for directions, see the Alfred A. Braun Memorial Hut System introductory text on page 243. From the parking area, there are two routes: the traditional route and the avalanche-safety path (Ava-Pass) through the Ashcroft Ski Touring Area.

**THE ROUTE:** The traditional route follows the road past the Pine Creek Cookhouse beneath avalanche runout zones. The alternate "Avalanche Avoidance Trail" route parts at the cookhouse on a marked route along the Nordic trails. This route remains farther away from the dangerous slide terrain, usurping some of the Nordic trails in the process. These two routes meet at the south end of the valley in an aspen forest near the turnoff to the Kellogg Cabin, a Nordic area warming hut.

The Avalanche Avoidance Trail, marked by orange discs, is provided as a courtesy by the Nordic center. Complimentary trail passes are required and can be picked up at the Nordic center office, immediately south of the Toklat Gallery. Please inquire at the Nordic center for current information about avalanche conditions in the area. Snowshoes are not allowed on this alternate route. This trail does add a little mileage to the trip, but it avoids the dangerous runout zones and is well worth it.

*Powder skiing in Upper Castle Creek. Can you spot the snow-covered roofs of the Tagert and Green-Wilson Huts? They are just visible in the woods on the right side of the photo.*

From this point, the Castle Creek Road (Forest Road 102) is easy to follow —though steep. The serious climbing begins near the Kellogg Cabin, ascends past a pond, across the lower reaches of several huge avalanche gullies (coming down from the north side of the valley), and through several large switchbacks into lower reaches of the upper valley. The road then drops down and crosses Castle Creek via a bridge. Once on the south side of the creek, more steep climbing through woods eventually brings you into the upper valley. Here, the road can be obscured as it enters a meadow characterized by moderate terrain; sometimes the route through the meadow is marked by wands or road signs. Ski west directly up the valley, staying on the south side of the creek. Cross the large meadow and re-enter the woods. Be careful throughout this tour and keep a watchful eye on the multitude of avalanche runs coming off Mace Peak to the south.

*Sally Moser, Philippe Dunoyer, Bob Moore, and Mark Collen head for Pearl Pass and the Friends Hut across Pearl Basin.*

Re-enter the woods and continue west, passing through several switchbacks on the trail. At 10,580 feet, you will encounter the Mace Hut (or Toklat Chalet, not to be confused with the Toklat Gallery back in Ashcroft), a private cabin by the creek on the north side of the trail. Just past the hut, the trail crosses the lower runout zone of a large avalanche slope (marked by damaged trees) coming off Mace Peak. Cross the runout zone, heading slightly upward to the west/southwest, and follow the road into the woods again. Climb very steeply to the north through two switchbacks near the turnoff to the Montezuma Mine, crossing the creek in the process. After the switchbacks, the trail climbs up into the lowest reaches of Pearl Basin, leaves the road, then wanders southwest across the creek and ascends a small, steep rise to the huts.

ADVANCED/EXPERT

TOUR

# 37b Tagert/Green-Wilson Huts to Friends Hut via Pearl Pass

SEE MAP PAGES 244 AND 270–271

**TIME** 5 to 8 hours

**DISTANCE** 4.2 miles

**ELEVATIONS** T/GW HUTS: 11,280' F HUT: 11,500' GAIN/LOSS: +1,440'/-1,205'

**AVALANCHE** Route crosses avalanche slopes; prone to skier-triggered avalanches during high-hazard periods

**MAPS** 10th Mountain Division/Alfred A. Braun System: Star Peak
USGS 7.5': Hayden Peak, 1987; Pearl Pass, 1961
National Forest: White River, Gunnison
Trails Illustrated: Map #127 (Aspen/Independence Pass);
Map #131 (Crested Butte/Pearl Pass)

**TOUR OVERVIEW:** Crossing Pearl Pass is one of Colorado's most thrilling and challenging hut-to-hut tours. The route, from Ashcroft up Castle Creek and down toward Crested Butte through the Brush Creeks, has long been a favorite winter adventure for experienced skiers. The trail follows the summer Pearl Pass Road that was originally built in 1882 as a direct stage and freight route between Crested Butte and the busy silver mining camp of Ashcroft. At 12,705 feet, Pearl Pass is one of the highest spots covered in this guide. Almost all of the terrain is above tree line. The panoramas are unsurpassed. Rolling benches in large glacial cirques make for strenuous, yet not too technical, skiing.

The distance between the huts is just over 4 miles. However, the elevation gain/loss is considerable. Under ideal conditions, the tour can pass quickly and uneventfully. During storms, the lack of trail markers or a distinct trail can leave ski parties wandering aimlessly below major avalanche slopes. People have perished in this area in such conditions.

Keep in mind that because of the wide-open, rolling terrain, there isn't really an exact trail. It is almost more important to tell people where not to go than it is to tell them where to ski. Avoid dropping into the head of Cooper Creek (going in either direction). Also, be careful not to ski too sharply to the northeast as you drop off Mace Saddle (the low point immediately west of Mace Peak, or Peak 12,528') because this will take you to steep, dangerous terrain. Avoid all of the hazardous slopes that guard the lower flanks of Pearl Peak and Peak 13,312' (Pearl's sister summit to the northwest). And, finally, be very careful on the final approach onto Pearl Pass and below the southern flanks of Star Peak on the Friends Hut side.

*Note:* Rock cairns with wooden sticks occasionally mark the summer road and can be followed or used for navigation. For skiers heading north from the Friends Hut, a better route near Mace Saddle stays slightly to the left of these markers as you get closer to the drop into Castle Creek.

In addition, it is quite possible to cross Pearl Pass under pleasant weather only to be stranded by blizzards, unable to return over the pass to either Ashcroft or Crested Butte. Be sure to check avalanche and weather forecasts before embarking on this journey.

All skiers attempting this route should be knowledgeable about winter travel and should carry shovels, transceivers, and bivouac equipment. Keep maps and compasses handy and consider carrying an altimeter to aid in navigation.

Some skiers travel straight from Ashcroft to the Friends Hut in one push. The less-committing plan calls for spending a night at the Tagert/Green-Wilson huts. This option is described below.

*Green-Wilson Hut*

**THE ROUTE:** From the front door of the Green-Wilson Hut, begin the ascent into Pearl Basin by skiing up the snow-covered Pearl Pass Road. Follow the path of least resistance to the southwest up through the last trees before you reach one of several large, wide, shallow gully systems that climb south through hummocky terrain. Around 11,800 feet, begin heading southeast, winding through small knolls and patches of willows and dwarf evergreen trees until you eventually gain the indistinct, flat saddle (Mace Saddle) west/southwest of Elevation Point 12,528' (Greg Mace Peak)—near the word "jeep" on the USGS 7.5-minute map. Again, there is no exact route here—just head in the general direction. Also, the flat saddle is one of the low points on the indistinct ridge, or crest, that runs from Mace Peak over to 13,312-foot "West Pearl" Peak (see Recommended Day Trips, page 263).

Atop this indistinct ridge is a good spot to take compass bearings and to memorize landmarks. Pearl Pass is one low point on the ridge that forms the southern wall of Cooper Creek and Pearl Basin. Pearl Pass is hidden just to the left behind the rocky, buttressed ridge that forms the left skyline of Pearl Peak from this vantage. From this ridge, people with binoculars or good eyesight can spot the sign that marks the pass.

Initially, as you leave the Mace Saddle area, aim for the toe of the distinct, aforementioned precipitous northeast ridge of Pearl Peak. As you near it, however, be aware of steep, east-facing pockets of snow very near the toe itself (this area is near "trail" on the 7.5-minute topos). Rather, trend a bit to the east toward the Cooper Creek drainage—but do not go into it! Pick a route down onto the shelf that blends up into the bowl directly beneath Pearl Pass. This section along this shelf and up to the pass follows the summer road fairly closely. Watch for wooden markers in rock piles and the rough outline of the summer road in the rocks.

Remember, it is crucial to avoid dropping down into the Cooper Creek drainage. If you are skiing in from the south, the terrain naturally will draw you toward this very steep valley. Keep an eye out for the wooden trail markers along the route.

Continuing our tour over the pass, ski across the moderately undulating terrain below Pearl Peak and begin to make your approach toward Pearl Pass proper through wind-scoured talus fields. When visibility is good, it is possible to see the wooden sign atop the pass. The slope on the north side of the pass is the most dangerous portion of the tour, and astute route-finding is required to ensure a safe crossing. Be prepared to assess the avalanche hazard before climbing this final slope. Also, be ready to turn back if the conditions are questionable.

Many groups make the mistake of traversing too high to the west as they climb the last few hundred feet up to Pearl Pass, placing themselves directly below classic avalanche terrain. Try to ascend to the pass as directly as possible, yet slightly to the right (west). Several small hills facilitate this ascent. Make the final ascent one at a time and follow all avalanche-hazard procedures.

The south side of Pearl Pass is not as treacherous as the north side, but it still possesses its share of hazards. The best route down follows the road for roughly 50 feet, then turns sharply southeast and descends onto a terrace that crosses the basin from the northwest to the southeast. Ski east/southeast across the basin, contouring around the steep slopes above the northwest fork of the creek and staying well away from the steep flanks of Star Peak. Descend into a subtle drainage immediately east of a low ridge covered with stunted trees (and below the steep, rocky buttresses of Star Peak). When you begin to see full-sized trees and the forest, head due south, following the natural contours of the drainage through sparse trees. A few final turns on steeper slopes lead to the flat terrain immediately north of the hut. Cross the northeast branch of East Brush Creek and ski the last few hundred feet up to the hut, which is visible on a small, forested hill at the edge of the forest.

*Cully Culbreth and John Fielder stand atop Pearl Pass en route to the Friends Hut.*

During periods of poor visibility, compass bearings and an altimeter can be invaluable on this passage. Have readings ready before setting out, whether you are skiing north to south or in the reverse direction.

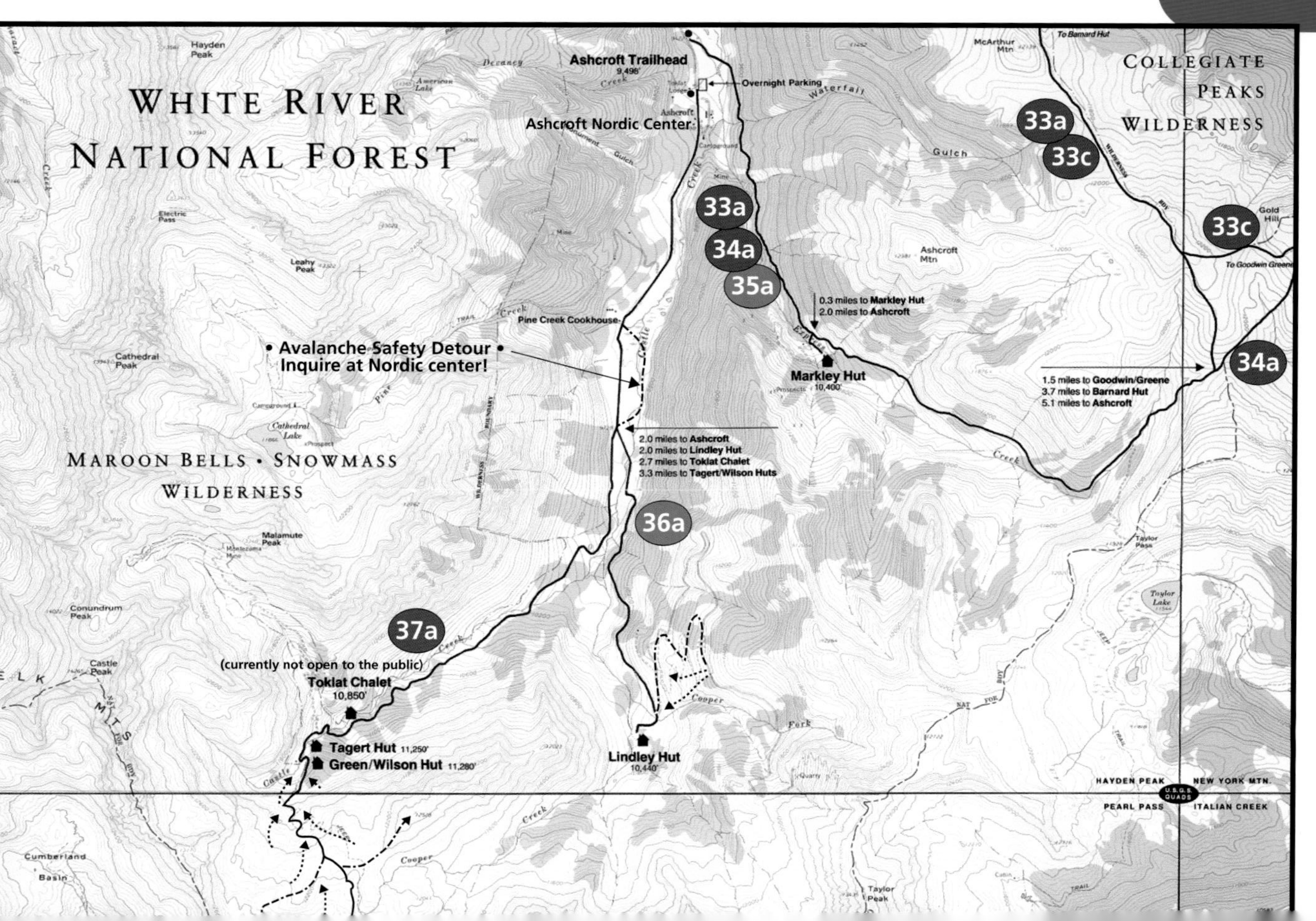

WHITE RIVER NATIONAL FOREST
COLLEGIATE PEAKS WILDERNESS
MAROON BELLS · SNOWMASS WILDERNESS
Ashcroft Trailhead 9,498'
Overnight Parking
Ashcroft Nordic Center
To Barnard Hut
To Goodwin Greene
McArthur Mtn
Gold Hill
Ashcroft Mtn
33a
33c
33a
34a
35a
33c
34a
0.3 miles to Markley Hut
2.0 miles to Ashcroft
Markley Hut 10,400'
1.5 miles to Goodwin/Greene
3.7 miles to Barnard Hut
5.1 miles to Ashcroft
Pine Creek Cookhouse
Avalanche Safety Detour
Inquire at Nordic center!
2.0 miles to Ashcroft
2.0 miles to Lindley Hut
2.7 miles to Toklat Chalet
3.3 miles to Tagert/Wilson Huts
36a
37a
(currently not open to the public)
Toklat Chalet 10,850'
Tagert Hut 11,250'
Green/Wilson Hut 11,280'
Lindley Hut 10,440'
Hayden Peak
Electric Pass
Leahy Peak
Cathedral Peak
Cathedral Lake
Malamute Peak
Conundrum Peak
Castle Peak
ELK MTS
Cumberland Basin
Taylor Pass
Taylor Lake
Taylor Peak
HAYDEN PEAK
NEW YORK MTN.
PEARL PASS
ITALIAN CREEK
U.S.G.S. QUADS

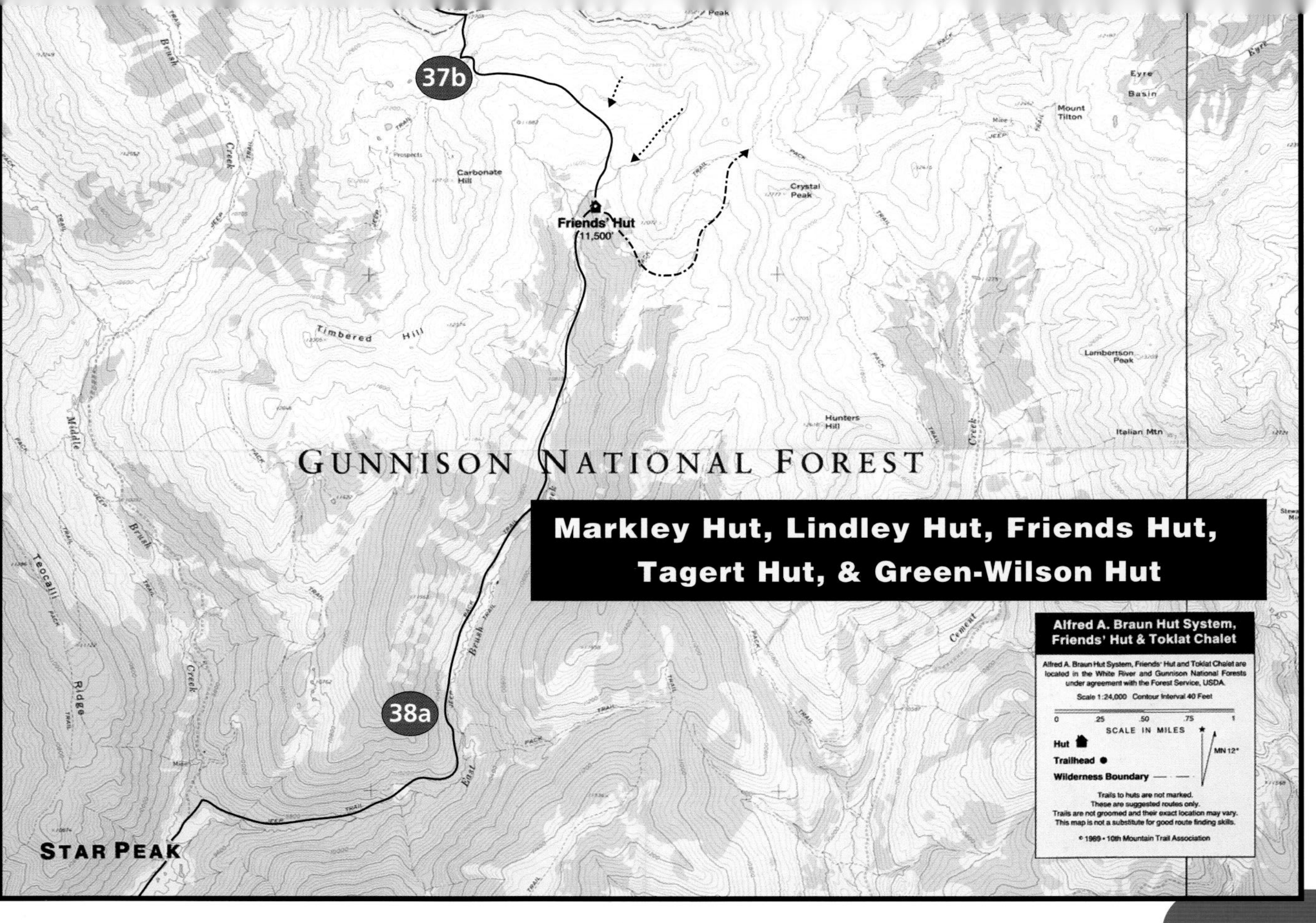
Markley Hut, Lindley Hut, Friends Hut,
Tagert Hut, & Green-Wilson Hut
Alfred A. Braun Hut System,
Friends' Hut & Toklat Chalet
Alfred A. Braun Hut System, Friends' Hut and Toklat Chalet are located in the White River and Gunnison National Forests under agreement with the Forest Service, USDA.
Scale 1:24,000 Contour Interval 40 Feet
0 .25 .50 .75 1
SCALE IN MILES
Hut
Trailhead
Wilderness Boundary
MN 12°
Trails to huts are not marked.
These are suggested routes only.
Trails are not groomed and their exact location may vary.
This map is not a substitute for good route finding skills.
© 1989 • 10th Mountain Trail Association
GUNNISON NATIONAL FOREST
37b
38a
Friends' Hut
11,500'
Carbonate Hill
Prospects
Timbered Hill
Crystal Peak
Hunters Hill
Mount Tilton
Eyre Basin
Lambertson Peak
Italian Mtn
Teocalli
Ridge
Middle
Brush
Creek
East
Cement
STAR PEAK

# 38 Friends Hut

| | |
|---|---|
| **HUT ELEVATION** | 11,500' |
| **DATE BUILT** | 1984–1985 |
| **SEASONS** | Thanksgiving through end of May |
| **CAPACITY** | 8 |
| **HUT LAYOUT** | Log cabin with sleeping loft for 6, and couch/beds for 2 on main floor |
| **HUT ESSENTIALS** | Wood-burning stove for heat, propane cookstove and oven, photovoltaic electric lights, full kitchenware, running water in nearby creek (has to be treated) |

A sign in Friends Hut states that the hut is for serious skiers—and it is! Located below the south faces of Star and Crystal Peaks, this hut provides access to many acres of skiable alpine terrain as well as long, challenging tours.

Friends Hut was constructed as a memorial to 10 residents of Aspen and Crested Butte who died in a plane crash above East Maroon Pass. Volunteers provided the labor to build the hut, which opened during the winter of 1985–1986. Today, the Friends Hut is a backcountry link between Aspen and Crested Butte—a fitting tribute to a group of people who loved the Colorado Rockies.

*The Elk Range hosts a solitary skier.*

Friends Hut is recommended for advanced, self-sufficient skiers who understand the potential severity of backcountry skiing. Strong intermediates can also enjoy this trip if accompanied by experienced partners or guides. Because this cabin is so remote, it is recommended that groups book the hut for a minimum of two nights so skiers can enjoy a full day of rest or day touring. Extra time spent at the hut also provides weather insurance should parties need to re-cross Pearl Pass.

Located 1,000 feet below the summit of Pearl Pass, the Friends Hut completes the hut system across the Elk Mountains. Most skiers tour to the Friends Hut via Pearl Pass; the Braun system's Tagert/Green-Wilson Huts work well as a jumping-off point for crossing the pass. Because skiers depend on windows of settled mountain weather to ensure a safe crossing, this itinerary is very committing. Please refer to the Tagert/Green-Wilson Huts description in the Alfred Braun Hut System.

Approaching Friends Hut from Crested Butte, skiers are faced with a long trek up Brush Creek. This route is less spectacular than skiing from Ashcroft, but it is also considerably less alpine in nature and exposed to far less avalanche danger.

The hut's rough-hewn timbers and wood paneling create a warm winter oasis. Eight people can sleep on beds in a sleeping loft and around the wood-burning stove on the main floor. A large window inspires contemplative thought. Water can be drawn from the creek for most of the winter; notices in the hut direct skiers to the most reliable water sources. Creek water should be treated or boiled before using.

**RESERVATION NOTE:** Friends Hut rents for a flat fee per person with no minimum number in the party size or for number of nights. If all spaces are booked there is a flat fee that reduces the per-person rate slightly. Book reservations through the 10th Mountain Division Hut Association (see Appendix A).

*Note:* Friends Hut appears in both volumes of *Colorado Hut to Hut* because it is the critical link between the two volumes. Also, though it is reserved through the 10th Mountain Division reservation system and often combined with the Braun huts for Elk Mountain hut-to-hut trips, it is actually an independent hut. And because it shares trails with the Braun system, it is included here for continuity.

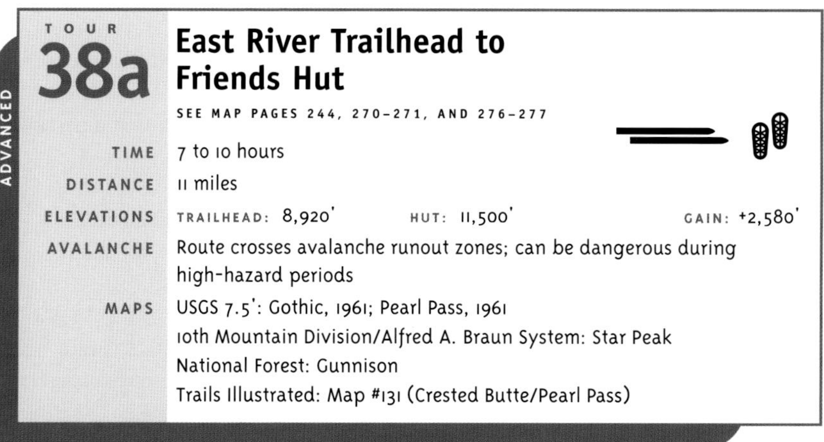

ADVANCED

TOUR **38a**

## East River Trailhead to Friends Hut

SEE MAP PAGES 244, 270–271, AND 276–277

**TIME** 7 to 10 hours

**DISTANCE** 11 miles

**ELEVATIONS** TRAILHEAD: 8,920' HUT: 11,500' GAIN: +2,580'

**AVALANCHE** Route crosses avalanche runout zones; can be dangerous during high-hazard periods

**MAPS** USGS 7.5': Gothic, 1961; Pearl Pass, 1961
10th Mountain Division/Alfred A. Braun System: Star Peak
National Forest: Gunnison
Trails Illustrated: Map #131 (Crested Butte/Pearl Pass)

**TOUR OVERVIEW:** The route to Friends Hut from Crested Butte is one of the longest and most arduous tours to any backcountry hut. Classic cross-country skiing follows Brush Creek Road and then East Brush Creek Road on a consistent climb from the East River near the Cold Spring Ranch to tree line below Star Peak. This route takes a lot of work but is worth the effort. Get an early start and be prepared for a long day if you expect to have to break trail.

The route passes near the runout zones of several large slide paths, especially in upper East Brush Creek. Skiers should be able to assess avalanche danger and make necessary adjustments in route selection. Your group should also be prepared for severe winter conditions. Since the trail lies within deep valleys and is well-marked, route-finding is not too difficult. The trickiest task is locating the hut as you approach it through the woods.

**DIRECTIONS TO TRAILHEAD:** Drive from the town of Crested Butte for 2 miles south on CO 135 to the Skyland Country Club/Airport Road (County Road 738). This turn is immediately southeast of the bridge across the Slate River. Follow the road as it curves past the entrance to Skyland Country Club on the left. Continue along the road as it skirts the southeast flank of Mount Crested Butte. After driving 2.5 miles, you'll arrive at a small plowed parking area on the left. Park here. Do not drive past the Lazy F Bar Outfitters sign, as there is no public parking beyond this point.

**THE ROUTE:** Ski on the road past the Lazy F Bar Outfitters sign and contour north past the ranch on the left. Near the 1.5-mile mark, you'll reach the broad, treeless mouth of Brush Creek. Turn northeast and follow the summer four-wheel-drive road along the left side of the creek. Turn right at the marked intersection of the West Brush Creek Trail (Forest Road 738.2A) and the Brush Creek/Middle Brush Creek Trail (Forest Road 738).

*Leigh Girvin leaves Friends Hut heading toward Ashcroft and Aspen.*

Ski down and across the creek and begin a short ascent to a fork in the trail near the 4-mile mark. Take the left fork on a steep climb high above a narrow and precipitous constriction in the valley bottom. After making a traverse across the toe of lower Teocalli Ridge, drop back down into Brush Creek and ski up the drainage along the broad valley bottom.

The trail eventually crosses the creek via snow bridges in an area filled with willows. Near the end of the valley, ascend east onto East Brush Creek Road (Forest Road 738.2B). Follow the road into thicker spruce forests and continue up the valley. The road in the upper valley is on the west side of the creek and leads directly under several avalanche runout zones. Many skiers cross to the east side of the creek and ski in the relative safety of the thicker trees on that bank. The actual point of creek crossing is left to the discretion of the group.

Friends Hut is above the confluence of the two highest, unnamed forks of East Brush Creek. By traversing upward above the northeast fork of the creek, near the upper limit of the forest, you ski directly to the hut, which sits atop a tiny knoll protected by tall spruce trees.

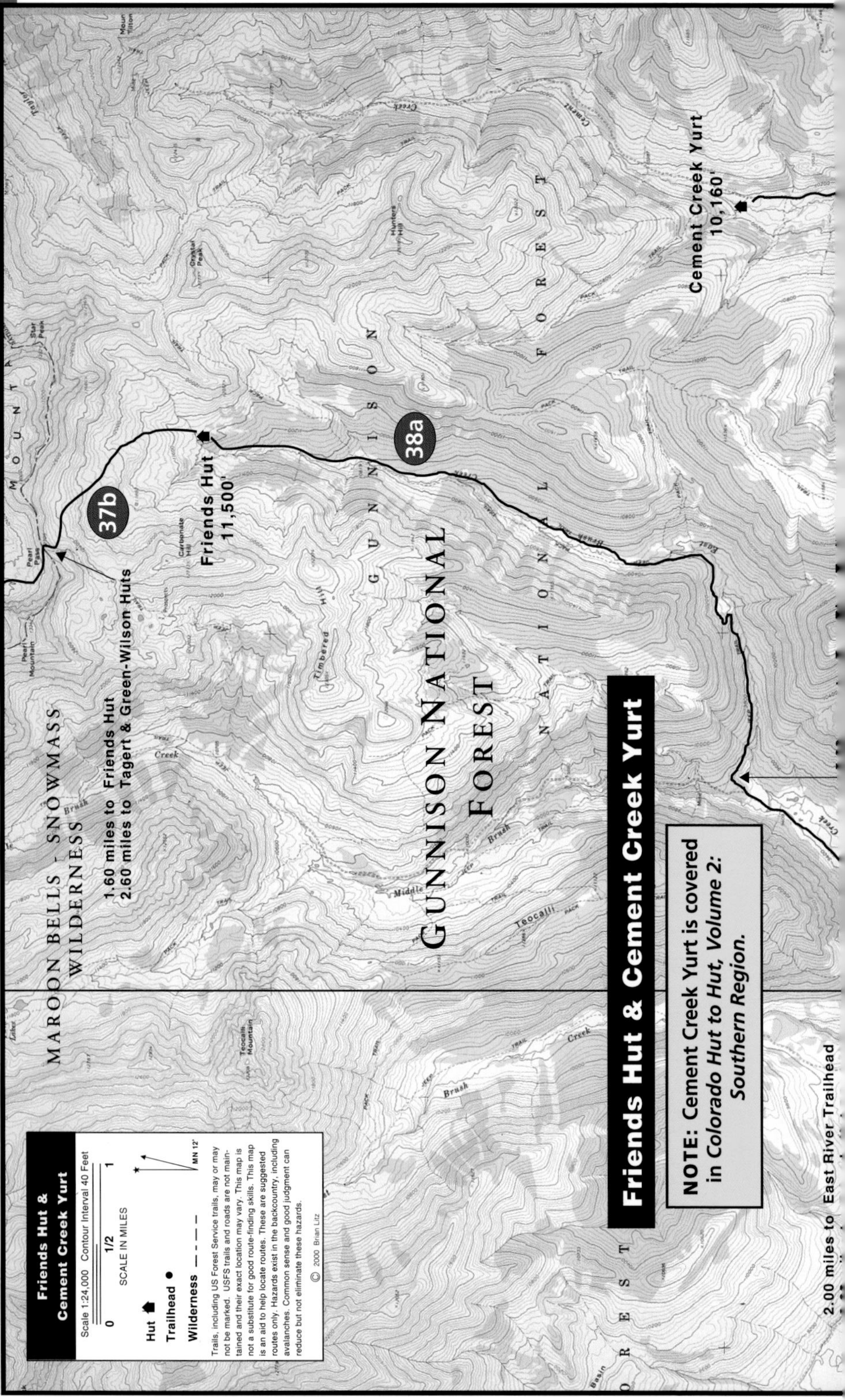

Friends Hut & Cement Creek Yurt
NOTE: Cement Creek Yurt is covered in *Colorado Hut to Hut, Volume 2: Southern Region.*
Friends Hut
11,500'
Cement Creek Yurt
10,160'
37b
38a
1.60 miles to Friends Hut
2.60 miles to Tagert & Green-Wilson Huts
2.00 miles to East River Trailhead
MAROON BELLS - SNOWMASS
WILDERNESS
GUNNISON NATIONAL
FOREST
Pearl Pass
Pearl Mountain
Star Peak
Crystal Peak
Hunters Hill
Carbonate Hill
Timbered Hill
Teocalli Mountain
Teocalli
Middle
Brush
Creek
East
Cement
Friends Hut & Cement Creek Yurt
Scale 1:24,000 Contour Interval 40 Feet
0 1/2 1
SCALE IN MILES
Hut
Trailhead
Wilderness
MN 12°
Trails, including US Forest Service trails, may or may not be marked. USFS trails and roads are not maintained and their exact location may vary. This map is not a substitute for good route-finding skills. This map is an aid to help locate routes. These are suggested routes only. Hazards exist in the backcountry, including avalanches. Common sense and good judgment can reduce but not eliminate these hazards.
© 2000 Brian Litz

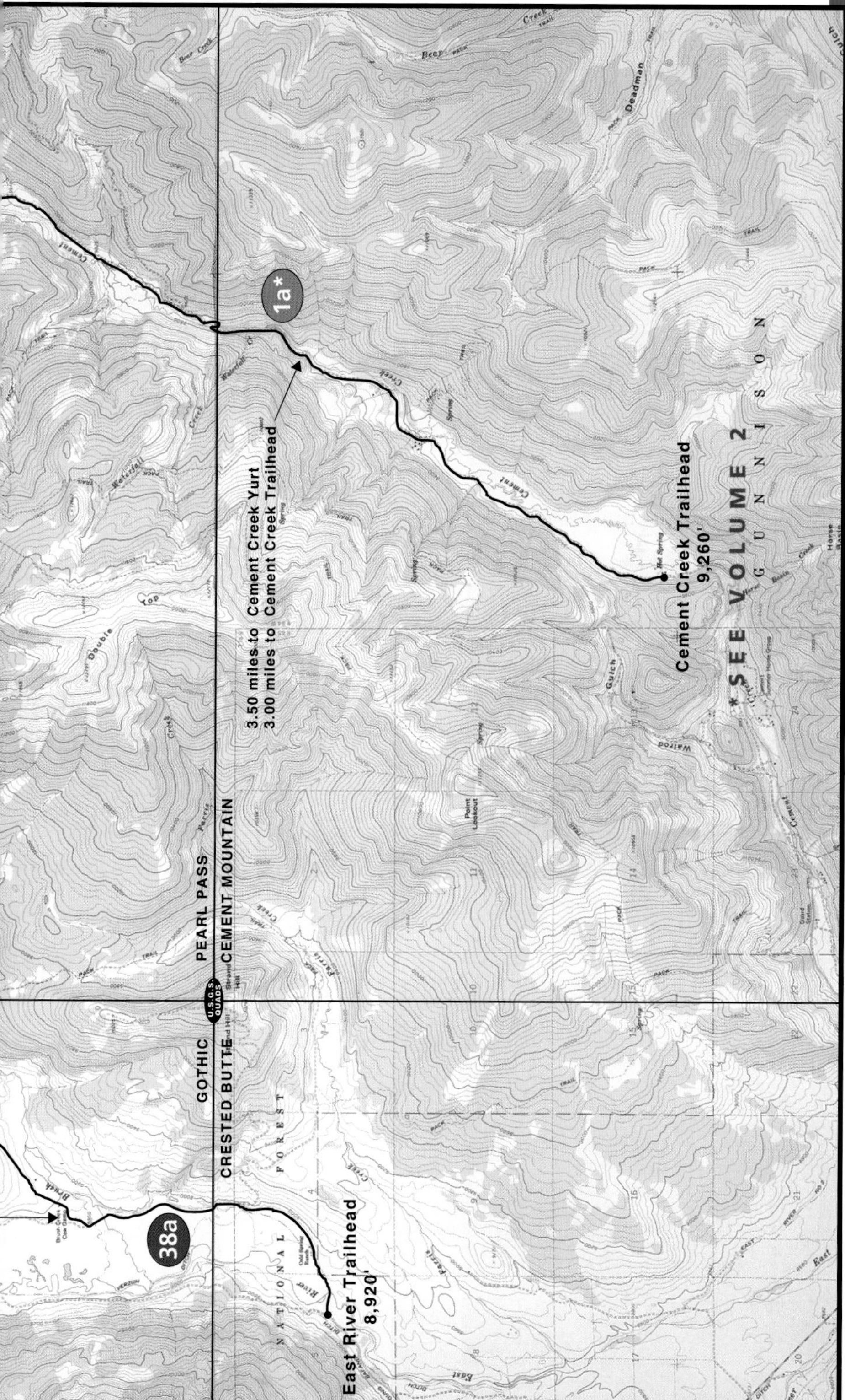

38a
GOTHIC
U.S.G.S. QUADS
PEARL PASS
CRESTED BUTTE
CEMENT MOUNTAIN

NATIONAL FOREST

East River Trailhead
8,920'

3.50 miles to Cement Creek Yurt
3.00 miles to Cement Creek Trailhead

1a*

Cement Creek Trailhead
9,260'

*SEE VOLUME 2
GUNNISON

## Central Independent Huts

This guidebook covers two independently run huts operating in the central mountains of Colorado. The Sunlight Backcountry Cabin, near Glenwood Springs, was featured in past editions of this guide. The new entry is the Hidden Treasure Yurt, which is on the northwestern slopes of New York Mountain. The Hidden Treasure Yurt hides in a thick forest of spruce and fir trees roughly a half-mile from the 10th Mountain Division's (though also privately owned) Polar Star Inn.

*Mark Collen tackles the terrain in Pearl Basin above the Tagert and Green-Wilson Huts.*

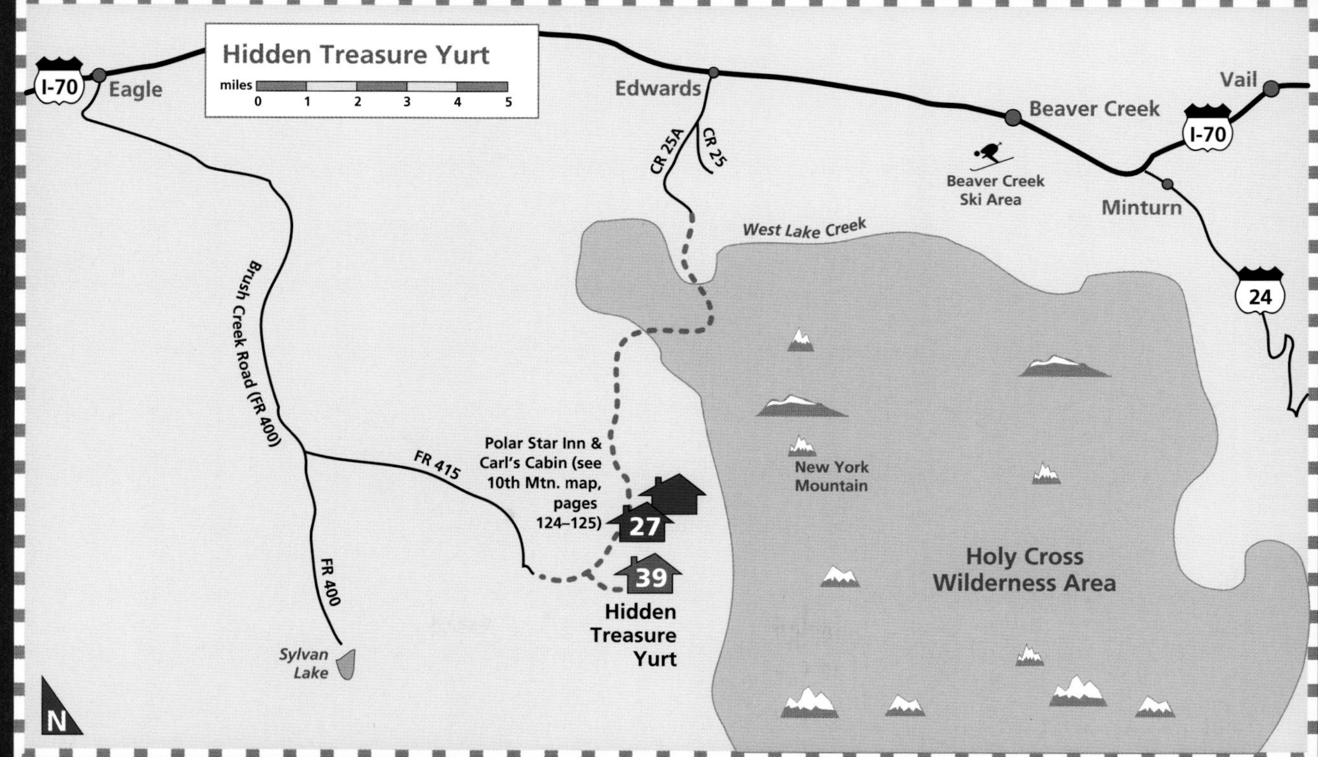

Hidden Treasure Yurt
miles
0
1
2
3
4
5
I-70
Eagle
Edwards
Beaver Creek
I-70
Vail
CR 25A
CR 25
Beaver Creek
Ski Area
Minturn
24
West Lake Creek
Brush Creek Road (FR 400)
FR 415
Polar Star Inn &
Carl's Cabin (see
10th Mtn. map,
pages
124–125)
27
39
Hidden
Treasure
Yurt
New York
Mountain
Holy Cross
Wilderness Area
FR 400
Sylvan
Lake
N

# 39 Hidden Treasure Yurt

| | |
|---|---|
| **HUT ELEVATION** | 11,200' |
| **DATE BUILT** | 1995 |
| **SEASONS** | Year-round |
| **CAPACITY** | 8 |
| **HUT LAYOUT** | 24-foot yurt with futon bunk beds |
| **HUT ESSENTIALS** | Woodstove for heat, propane cookstoves, propane lighting, all kitchenware, outhouse |

The privately owned Hidden Treasure Yurt resides on the slopes of New York Mountain, very close to the Polar Star Inn (see page 279). Guarded on all sides by towering spruce and fir trees, the yurt offers a sense of seclusion. It also provides excellent tree skiing, which is a snowball's throw away. On clear days, the more adventurous should consider a day trip up windswept New York Mountain for a taste of high-altitude winter mountaineering.

Except for the last half-mile or so, the two primary routes to the hut are identical to those for the Polar Star Inn.

**RESERVATION NOTE:** The Hidden Treasure Yurt is reserved on a per-person basis with a minimum fee required on Friday and Saturday nights. Make reservations through Hidden Treasure Adventures (see Appendix A).

*Skiers plunder picture-perfect powder.*

INTERMEDIATE/ADVANCED

TOUR **39a**

## West Lake Creek Trailhead to Hidden Treasure Yurt

SEE MAP PAGES 244, 279, AND 284

TIME 6 to 9 hours
DISTANCE 7 miles
ELEVATIONS TRAILHEAD: 8,220' YURT: 11,200' GAIN/LOSS: +2,980'/-200'
AVALANCHE Minimal danger
MAPS 10th Mountain Division: New York Mountain
USGS 7.5': Fulford, 1987; Grouse Mountain, 1987
National Forest: White River
Trails Illustrated: Map #121 (Eagle/Avon)

**TOUR OVERVIEW:** The route from West Lake Creek Trailhead is the longest way to the Hidden Treasure Yurt and is a textbook exercise in gear hauling. Many skiers use this trailhead as a jumping-off point for a multiday traverse of the western half of the 10th Mountain Division system, ending their trip in Aspen. Other skiers choose to begin in Aspen and end their expedition at the Polar Star Inn or now at the Hidden Treasure Yurt. Without question, it is easier to ski out than to ski in via this route, because of the considerable elevation gain. This route is not open to mountain bikers because it crosses the Holy Cross Wilderness Area.

**DIRECTIONS TO TRAILHEAD:** Turn off I-70 at the Edwards exit (Exit 163). Head south across the Eagle River to US 6. Turn west for 0.7 mile to the Lake Creek Road. Turn south on Lake Creek Road for 1.8 miles to a fork in the road. Take the right fork onto West Lake Creek Road and proceed 2.8 miles to a sharp hairpin curve. Park at the apex of the turn, where Forest Road 423 heads south. The road is marked with a National Forest welcome sign and a sign for East Lake Trail Baryetta Cabins.

**THE ROUTE:** From the parking area, ski south along the east side of the creek on FR 423, then cross a bridge and make a rising traverse across the steeply angled slopes on the west side of the creek. At the 1-mile mark, the road heads back across the creek to the east, to a trail junction. Stay on the right fork as it climbs up and around to the west. From here, the road contours east through a meadow, past some old cabins, and then begins the climb straight south up along a forested ridge.

Eventually the trail reaches an intersection at 9,370 feet, near an old, faded Forest Service trail sign attached to a tree. The Card Springs Trail is the right fork and is marked with a blue diamond. It leaves the main trail and crosses south, then west into a forested basin.

Follow the Card Springs Trail west, cross into the Wilderness Area boundary near the creek, and continue ascending along a road until it fades out in an aspen forest. The route switchbacks cross-country, heading west up through aspen trees to a small meadow on the Card Creek Saddle at 9,980 feet. Although it is usually marked with a few pieces of colored plastic flagging, finding the proper route through this stretch is probably the trickiest section of the tour. Don't be misled by ski trails through the aspen trees or by an old road that heads directly north through the aspen trees just before you climb onto the Card Creek Saddle.

Once at the small, protected meadow (a nice break or lunch spot), ski straight through it to the west, re-enter the woods, then begin a descending traverse into Squaw Creek. The trail contours into the Squaw Creek drainage and ascends all the way up it, first along the west side, then, after making a very sharp dogleg turn at 9,980 feet, on the east. After crossing the creek, the trail climbs steadily through the forest and exits the Wilderness Area and the Squaw Creek drainage near a sign at 10,700 feet.

Continue to the south/southeast to an intersection with a switchback on a logging road. The trail follows the road for a short distance, then strikes off through the woods above the road along its northeast side. It eventually regains the road and follows it the last few hundred yards to the Polar Star Inn and Carl's Cabin. This last few hundred yards of trail travels through open meadows and sporadic trees, which can be a little bit difficult to navigate during snowstorms.

To reach the Hidden Treasure Yurt, search for an old logging road that begins to ascend to the south/southeast above and behind the Polar Star Inn—often you will cross old tracks left by day skiers in this area. Once on the road, follow it south for 0.5 mile to the Hidden Treasure Yurt.

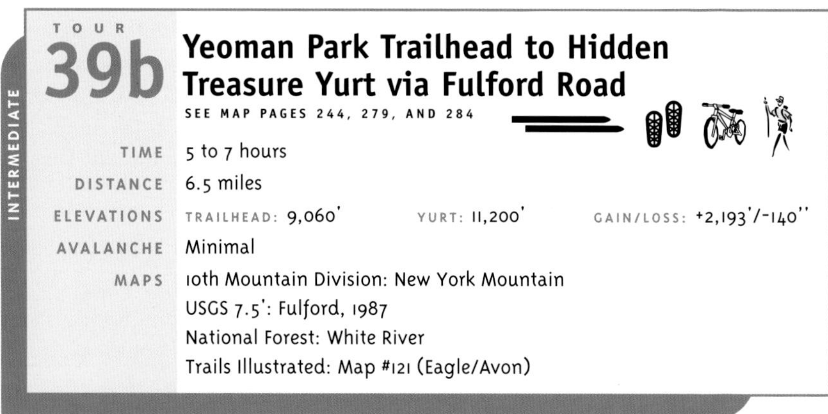

INTERMEDIATE

TOUR **39b**

## Yeoman Park Trailhead to Hidden Treasure Yurt via Fulford Road

SEE MAP PAGES 244, 279, AND 284

TIME 5 to 7 hours

DISTANCE 6.5 miles

ELEVATIONS TRAILHEAD: 9,060' YURT: 11,200' GAIN/LOSS: +2,193'/-140''

AVALANCHE Minimal

MAPS 10th Mountain Division: New York Mountain
USGS 7.5': Fulford, 1987
National Forest: White River
Trails Illustrated: Map #121 (Eagle/Avon)

**TOUR OVERVIEW:** There are two routes from the Yeoman Park Trailhead to the Hidden Treasure Yurt: Fulford Road and Newcomer Spring. Both routes ascend through similar terrain, switchback and traverse a great deal, and gain roughly the same amount of elevation. What differentiates the two is that the Fulford Road route follows a wide, well-traveled road for the initial 4.4 miles, while the Newcomer Spring route is a trail through the forest. After the two routes converge, they ascend together more steeply to the yurt. The Fulford Road is better for folks who want to follow an obvious road and like lots of space for snowplow turns—

although it is traveled by snowmobilers. Only the Fulford route will be described here (for a description of Newcomer Spring tour, please see Polar Star Inn, Tour 27c).

**DIRECTIONS TO TRAILHEAD:** Drive on I-70 to the Eagle exit (Exit 147). Head south across the Eagle River, then turn right onto US 6. Proceed into Eagle and turn left on Broadway. Drive to the intersection of Broadway and 6th Street and turn left onto 6th Street. Drive for one block, then turn right onto the Brush Creek Road (Forest Road 400). Drive to a fork in the road near where the pavement ends. Take the left fork to East Brush Creek Road (to Fulford and Yeoman Park) and proceed 5.6 miles, then turn right, cross the creek, and turn into an obvious plowed parking area.

**THE ROUTE:** Leave the parking lot, return to the East Brush Creek Road, and head southeast. Ski or walk along the road for 0.4 mile to the turnoff to Fulford Road (Forest Road 418). Follow Fulford Road for 4.2 miles as it gradually traverses, switchbacks, and climbs to the isolated, tiny community of Fulford.

There are two sections where skiers can deviate from the road to avoid snowmobile traffic. The first is near the 1.4-mile mark after the road veers back to the southeast into a creek drainage. Here, skiers can parallel the road down near the creek. The second spot is actually a shortcut at the head of this creek, where the main road switchbacks sharply back to the west at the 1.7-mile mark. At this point, a logging road heads southeast up into the upper stretches of the creek. Turn onto it and climb along the creek before regaining the primary route southeast of the little forested hill, marked 9,953 feet. Both of these alternatives are marked with blue diamonds. *Note:* Be careful of misleading tracks made by confused skiers who have strayed onto other old logging trails that lace the area around the second shortcut.

From here, the route contours around a sharp northwest-running ridge before it traverses into the Nolan Creek drainage. The route intersects another road just upstream from the little community of Fulford, near an outhouse and a sign that reads "Upper Town & Nolan Lake." Turn here at a blue diamond into Nolan Creek and make a short but steep ascent to a clearing with several cabin ruins.

Head straight east past the ruins to a trail marked with blue diamonds. This is where the Newcomer Spring route meets this trail. From here, the route leaves the road and switchbacks up through the aspen forest, gaining elevation quickly. Watch for diamonds on the trees here. At 5.3 miles, the trail intercepts another road, the New York Mountain jeep road, at 10,520 feet. Switchback onto this trail and head south, then east on the final approach to the yurt. Climb steadily up the road for 0.5 mile until you reach another intersection with signs for the Polar Star Mine and New York Mountain. Take the right fork (south) and follow this marked trail for the last 0.5 mile to the Hidden Treasure Yurt. The left fork goes 0.45 mile to the Polar Star Inn. Once you have turned onto the final approach road to the Hidden Treasure Yurt, follow it south up through the woods for several hundred yards until it distinctly sweeps east. Continue to climb until you arrive at the yurt.

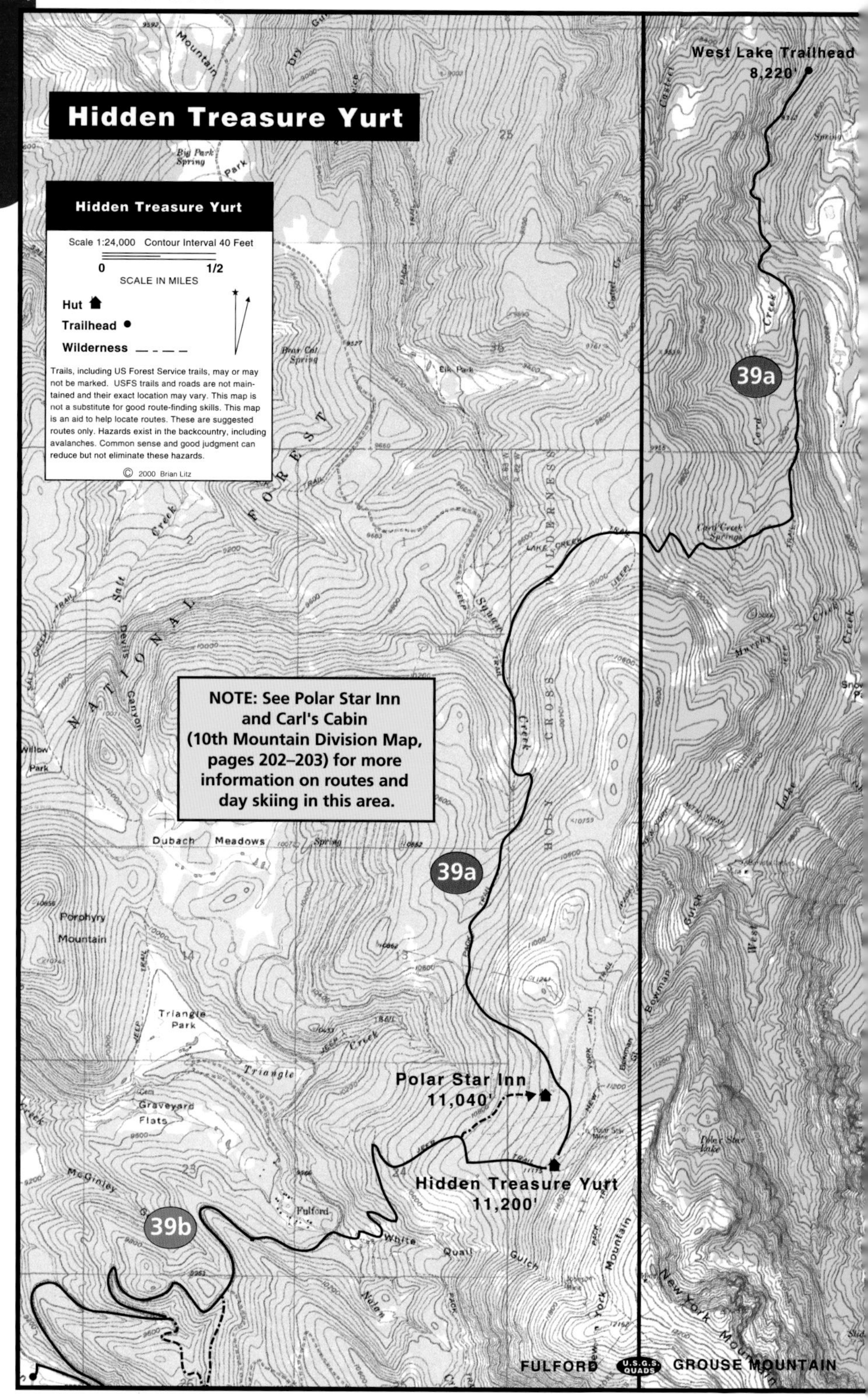

Hidden Treasure Yurt
Hidden Treasure Yurt
Scale 1:24,000 Contour Interval 40 Feet
0 1/2
SCALE IN MILES
Hut
Trailhead
Wilderness
Trails, including US Forest Service trails, may or may not be marked. USFS trails and roads are not maintained and their exact location may vary. This map is not a substitute for good route-finding skills. This map is an aid to help locate routes. These are suggested routes only. Hazards exist in the backcountry, including avalanches. Common sense and good judgment can reduce but not eliminate these hazards.
© 2000 Brian Litz
NOTE: See Polar Star Inn and Carl's Cabin (10th Mountain Division Map, pages 202–203) for more information on routes and day skiing in this area.
West Lake Trailhead
8,220'
39a
39a
39b
Polar Star Inn
11,040'
Hidden Treasure Yurt
11,200'
Dubach Meadows
Porphyry Mountain
Triangle Park
Graveyard Flats
Fulford
White Quail Gulch
NATIONAL FOREST
HOLY CROSS WILDERNESS
New York Mountain
FULFORD
U.S.G.S. QUADS
GROUSE MOUNTAIN

# 40 Sunlight Backcountry Cabin

| | |
|---|---|
| **HUT ELEVATION** | 8,440' |
| **DATE BUILT** | 1880s |
| **SEASONS** | Year-round |
| **CAPACITY** | 8 |
| **HUT LAYOUT** | 1-story log cabin with bunks and foam pads for 8 |
| **HUT ESSENTIALS** | Woodstove for heat, woodstove for cooking (*note:* no propane cookstove; bring your own stove and use it outside), all utensils, outhouse, photovoltaic electric lights |

The Sunlight Backcountry Cabin is truly a historic destination. Moved from its original site, the cabin was built during the 1800s and is thought to have served as the payroll building for a coal mining company that operated in the area. The name Sunlight comes from the town that once supplied the mine. During the intervening years, the cabin has served many purposes, including housing ski-area employees and ranch hands. Now the cabin is part of the Nordic center of the Sunlight Mountain Resort and is open for day use as a warming hut and as a backcountry overnight shelter by reservation.

*Rick Sayre practices his take-off and landings.*

The route to the hut is one of the easiest hut tours in this book and, consequently, this is a great hut for beginning hut skiers and for experienced skiers who want a quick, simple overnight jaunt.

Remember, there is no cookware or propane gear. Visitors are allowed to bring their own backpacking-type stoves to supplement the wood-burning cookstove. For obvious safety reasons, these must be used outside the hut.

**RESERVATION NOTE:** The hut is open year-round and booked for a flat fee. To make reservations, call the Sunlight Mountain Resort Nordic Center (see Appendix A).

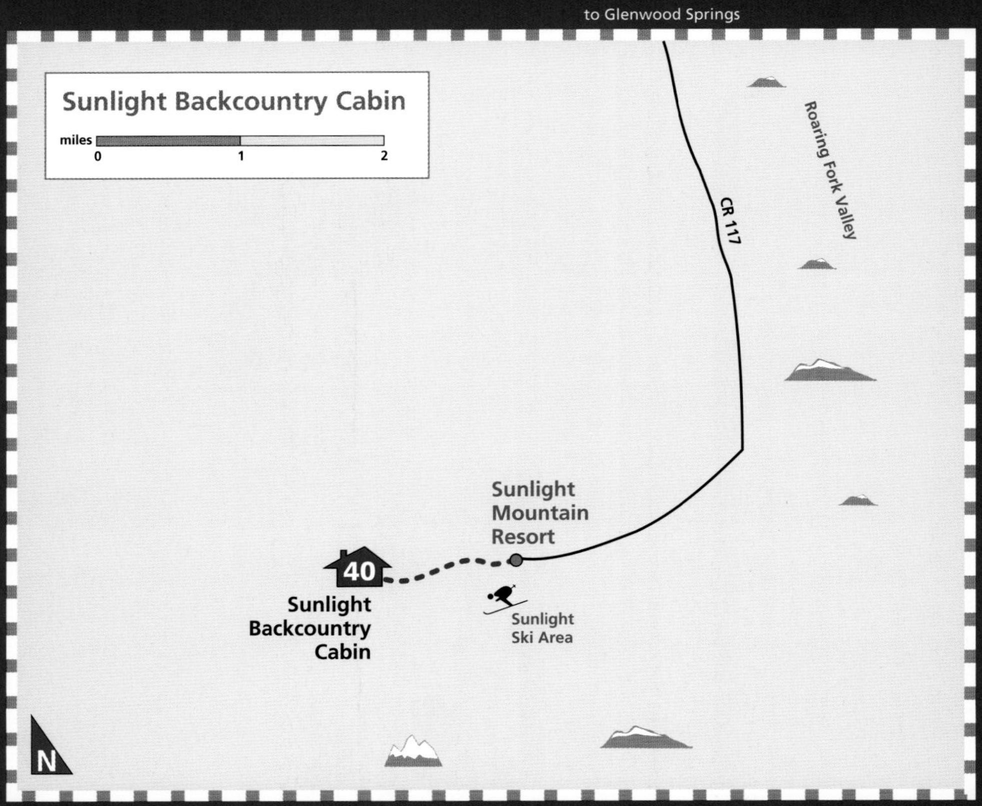

## Sunlight Backcountry Cabin

miles 0 1 2

to Glenwood Springs

CR 117

Roaring Fork Valley

Sunlight Mountain Resort

Sunlight Ski Area

40

Sunlight Backcountry Cabin

N

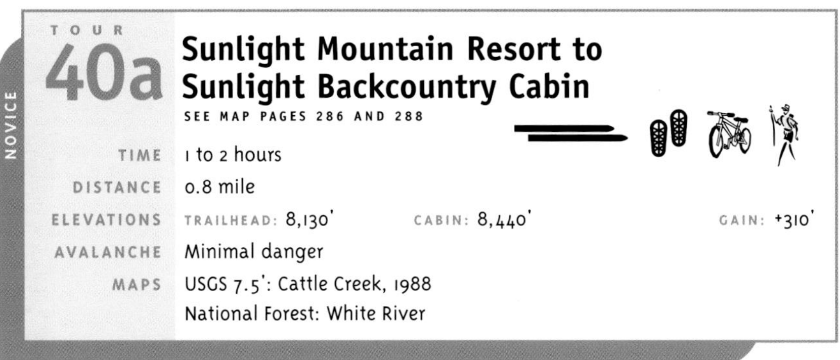

NOVICE

TOUR 40a

## Sunlight Mountain Resort to Sunlight Backcountry Cabin

SEE MAP PAGES 286 AND 288

| | |
|---|---|
| TIME | 1 to 2 hours |
| DISTANCE | 0.8 mile |
| ELEVATIONS | TRAILHEAD: 8,130' CABIN: 8,440' GAIN: +310' |
| AVALANCHE | Minimal danger |
| MAPS | USGS 7.5': Cattle Creek, 1988<br>National Forest: White River |

**DIRECTIONS TO TRAILHEAD:** To reach the Sunlight Mountain Resort and the trailhead, follow signs from the south end of Glenwood Springs on CO 82 to the turnoff for County Road 117. Follow CR 117 for 10 miles. When you reach the turn into the parking-area entrance, look for a small, plowed parking area on the right side of the road. The trail is marked by a gate and a sign saying "Old Four-Mile Road."

**THE ROUTE:** Pass through the gate and follow the road (marked by signs) for 0.8 mile to the cabin, which sits on the south side of Four Mile Creek at the mouth of Babbish Gulch. Babbish Gulch is a nice day-tour destination.

*Jeff Parker skis below the spoils—"West Pearl" Peak near Tagert Hut.*

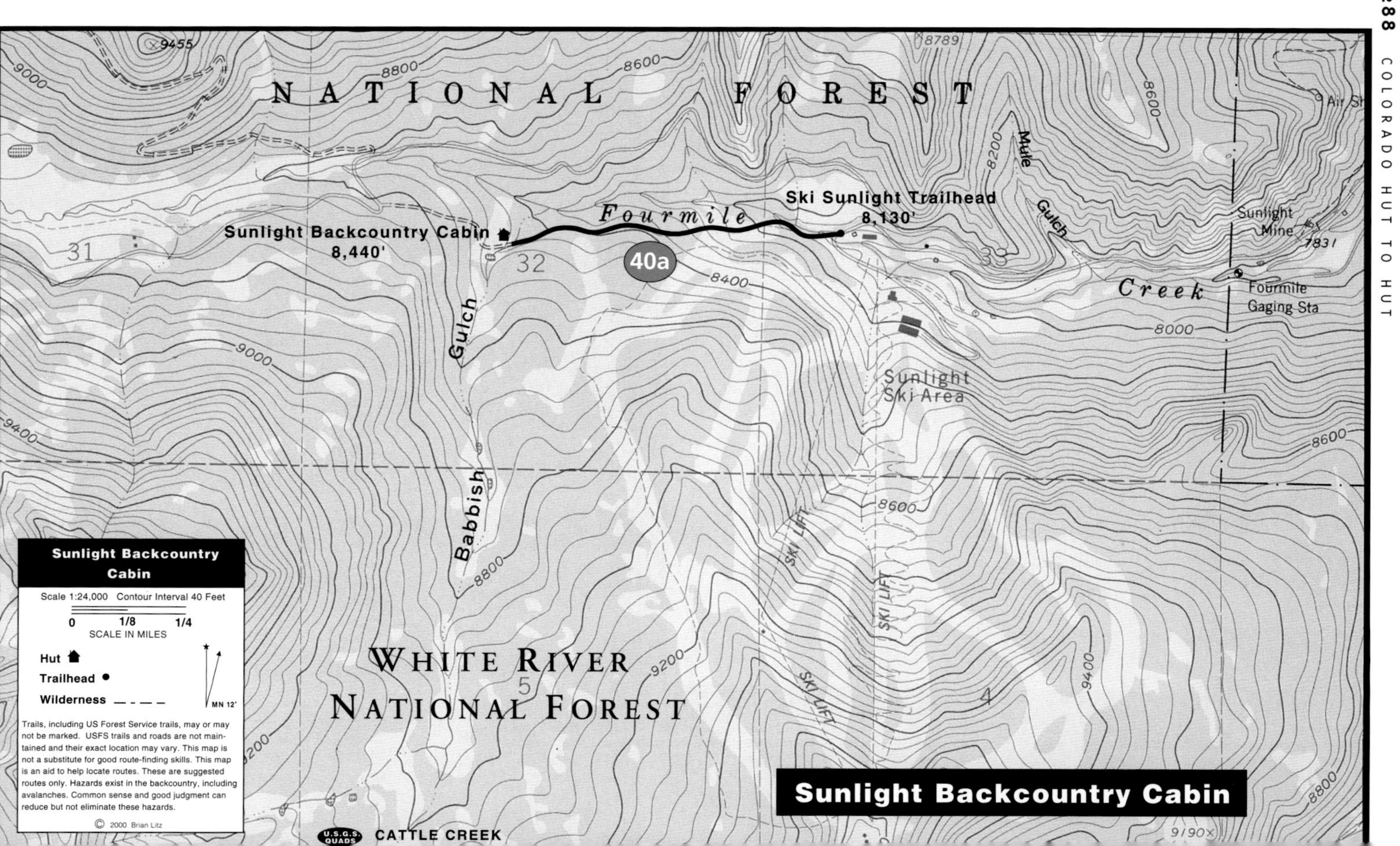
NATIONAL FOREST
Sunlight Backcountry Cabin 8,440'
Fourmile Creek
40a
Ski Sunlight Trailhead 8,130'
Mule Gulch
Sunlight Mine
Fourmile Gaging Sta
Gulch
Babbish
Sunlight Ski Area
SKI LIFT
SKI LIFT
SKI LIFT
WHITE RIVER NATIONAL FOREST
Sunlight Backcountry Cabin
U.S.G.S. QUADS CATTLE CREEK
Sunlight Backcountry Cabin
Scale 1:24,000 Contour Interval 40 Feet
0 1/8 1/4
SCALE IN MILES
Hut
Trailhead
Wilderness
MN 12°
Trails, including US Forest Service trails, may or may not be marked. USFS trails and roads are not maintained and their exact location may vary. This map is not a substitute for good route-finding skills. This map is an aid to help locate routes. These are suggested routes only. Hazards exist in the backcountry, including avalanches. Common sense and good judgment can reduce but not eliminate these hazards.
© 2000 Brian Litz

# APPENDIX A: Reservations and Information

**NORTHERN HUTS**

Never Summer Nordic Yurts and Nokhu Cabin (formerly Lake Agnes Cabin)
P.O. Box 1983
Fort Collins, CO 80522
970-482-9411
www.neversummernordic.com
E-mail: infor@neversummernordic.com

Brainard Lake Cabin and Guinn Mountain Hut
Colorado Mountain Club
825 South Broadway, Suite 40
Boulder, CO 80303
303-554-7688

Tennessee Mountain Cabin
Eldora Nordic Center
P.O. Box 430
Nederland, CO 80466
303-440-8700, x212

Squaw Mountain Fire Lookout
Reserve America (for reservations)
877-444-6777
Arapaho National Forest, Clear Creek Ranger District
P.O. Box 3307
Idaho Springs, CO 80452
303-567-3000

Second Creek Cabin (Gwen Andrews Hut) and First Creek Cabin
Arapaho National Forest, Sulphur Ranger District
P.O. Box 10
Granby, CO 80446
970-887-4100

High Lonesome Hut
P.O. Box 145
Fraser, CO 80442
970-726-4099
http://lonesome-hut.com
E-mail: lonesome-hut@lonesome-hut.com

**CENTRAL HUTS**

Summit Huts Association
P.O. Box 2830
Breckenridge, CO 80424
970-453-8583
E-mail: sumhuts@colorado.net
www.huts.org
For reservations, contact the 10th Mountain Division Hut Association.

**CENTRAL HUTS (continued)**

10th Mountain Division Hut Association
1280 Ute Avenue
Aspen, CO 81611
970-925-5775
www.huts.org

Double Diamond Bed and Breakfast (Provides overnight accommodations for 10th Mountain Division Hut visitors)
P.O. Box 2
Meredith, CO 81642
970-927-3404

Diamond J Ranch
Bill and Martha Simms
26604 Fryingpan Rd.
Meredith, CO 81642
970-927-3222

Alfred A. Braun Memorial Hut System*
P.O. Box 7937
Aspen, CO 81612
970-925-5775
www.huts.org
For reservations, contact 10th Mountain Division Hut Association.
*For information on gondola rides to the summit of Aspen Mountain, call 970-925-1220 or 800-525-6200.

Friends Hut
1280 Ute Avenue
Aspen, CO 81611
970-925-5775
www.huts.org
For reservations, contact 10th Mountain Division Hut Association.

Hidden Treasure Yurt
Hidden Treasure Adventures
P.O. Box 441
Edwards, CO 81632-0441
800-444-2813

Sunlight Backcountry Cabin
Sunlight Mountain Resort Nordic Center
10901 Road 117
Glenwood Springs, CO 81601
970-945-749; 800-445-7931
www.sunlightmtn.com

## APPENDIX B: Road and Weather Conditions

National Weather Service 303-494-4221
Colorado Road Conditions 303-639-1111

## APPENDIX C: County Sheriffs and National Forests

In case of immediate, life-threatening emergencies, always call 911. Dialing 911 will connect you with the nearest emergency-response network. Be prepared to provide as much information as possible concerning the type of emergency and your location (huts, roads, creek names, etc.). The sheriff department phone numbers listed below are non-emergency numbers that connect you with their dispatchers 24 hours a day. Use these numbers for problems such as stolen cars or to report lost skiers who have returned to safety on their own.

**Never Summer Nordic Yurts and Nokhu Cabin (formerly Lake Agnes Cabin)**
Jackson County Sheriff 970-723-4242
Colorado State Forest 970-723-8366

**Brainard Lake, Guinn Mountain, and Tennessee Mountain**
Boulder County Sheriff 303-441-4444
Arapaho and Roosevelt NF, Boulder Ranger District 303-444-6600

**Squaw Mountain Fire Lookout**
Sheriff 303-569-3232
303-569-3233
Arapaho and Roosevelt NF, Clear Creek Ranger District 303-567-2901

**First Creek Cabin, Second Creek Cabin (Gwen Andrews Hut), and High Lonesome Hut**
Grand County Sheriff 970-725-3343
Arapaho and Roosevelt NF, Sulphur Ranger District 970-887-4100

**Summit Huts Association**
Summit County Sheriff 970-668-8600
Arapaho and Roosevelt NF, Dillon Ranger District 970-468-5400

**10th Mountain Division Hut Association**
Eagle County Sheriff (Vail/Eagle area) 970-328-6611
Chaffee County Sheriff (Leadville area) 719-539-2596
Pitkin County Sheriff (Aspen area) 970-920-5310
Pike and San Isabel NF, Leadville Ranger District 719-486-0749
White River NF, Holy Cross Ranger District 970-945-2521
White River NF, Aspen Ranger District 970-925-3445

**Alfred A. Braun Memorial Hut Association**
Pitkin County Sheriff (Aspen) 970-920-5310
Gunnison County Sheriff (Crested Butte) 970-641-1113
White River NF, Aspen Ranger District 970-925-3445

**Friends Hut**
Gunnison County Sheriff (Crested Butte) 970-641-8000
Grand Mesa, Uncompahgre, and Gunnison NF, Taylor River Ranger District 970-874-7691

**Hidden Treasure Yurt**
Eagle County Sheriff (Vail/Eagle area) 970-328-6611
White River NF, Holy Cross Ranger District 970-945-2521

**Sunlight Backcountry Cabin**
Garfield County Sheriff 970-945-9151
White River NF, Sopris Ranger District 970-963-2266

**For general information about National Forests: 303-275-5350**
U.S. Forest Service
Rocky Mountain Regional Office
Box 25127
Lakewood, CO 80225

## APPENDIX D: Guide Services

For information on guide services, please call the reservation number for the particular hut system you are interested in visiting.

## APPENDIX E: Avalanche Training and Information

**American Avalanche Institute**
P.O. Box 308
Wilson, WY 83014
307-733-3315
E-mail: aai@wyoming.com

**American Association of Avalanche Professionals**
P.O. Box 1032
Bozeman, MT 59771
406-587-3830

**Silverton Avalanche School**
San Juan Search and Rescue
P.O. Box 178
Silverton, CO 81433
970-387-5531

**Avalanche Information Phone Numbers**
*Colorado Avalanche Information Center (CAIC):*
Denver/Boulder Area (statewide forecast) 303-499-9650
Fort Collins (statewide forecast) 970-482-0457
Colorado Springs (statewide forecast) 719-520-0020
Summit/Eagle County (regional forecast) 970-668-0600
Durango (regional forecast) 970-247-8187

**Avalanche Information Phone Numbers (continued)**
*United States Forest Service Backcountry Avalanche Information:*
Minturn (Vail/Eagle County regional forecast) 970-827-5687
Aspen (Aspen/Carbondale/Crested Butte regional forecast) 970-920-1664

*Utah Avalanche Information:*
Grand County, Utah 435-259-7669

Most ski and backcountry-equipment shops can provide skiers with information on groups and clubs offering avalanche training. In addition, many city and county recreation departments offer weekend and evening training courses.

Also, by becoming a "Friend of the Colorado Avalanche Information Center," you can receive daily e-mail updates on Colorado avalanche and weather conditions. At $25 (spring 2000), this is a steal for information critical to winter backcountry travelers. Call the CAIC office nearest you.

# APPENDIX F: Recommended Equipment Checklist

It is impossible to come up with a one-size-fits-all list of clothing and equipment that will satisfy the needs of the entire population of hut visitors. Just ask Joe Ryan of the San Juan Hut System, who travels sans gloves or mittens throughout the winter, year in, year out. Much of the time, he doesn't wear a shirt, even in brisk weather! Obviously, Joe's selection of garments (or lack thereof) wouldn't suit the majority of winter travelers. Whatever your preference, many sources of information are available on how to properly outfit yourself for mountain travel throughout the seasons, and the well-worn concept of layering still applies.

If you are new to backcountry life, take time to consult with an experienced friend, a professional ski or mountaineering retailer, or a ski/climbing guide or instructor before laying out your hard-earned cash on gear. The following are the most commonly carried items.

### Ski Clothing

*Base long underwear layer:* Moisture-transporting wool, synthetic, or blended layer worn under shell pants during warmer conditions, or under intermediate layers in extremely cold conditions and for the truly cold-blooded; examples are Capilene, polypropylene, and bi-component DriClime.

*Intermediate lower layers:* Traditional wool pants or fleece tights/pants that can be worn alone or under shell pants for average Colorado conditions; synthetics include 100-weight microfleeces or Polartec 100 stretch.

*Shell pants:* Laminated or coated waterproof/breatheable or highly wind/weather-resistant fabrics designed for the worst wet weather and deepest snow; scuff/edge guards and internal gaiters are helpful with lower-cut boots.

*Woven-fabric pants:* Four-way stretch-fabrics (Scholler-type fabric pants) are replacing traditional shell pants and wool pants for less-than-severe conditions; also good in summer.

*Intermediate upper layers:* Midweight or expedition-weight fleece, wool, or blended shirt or pullover worn over light, long underwear; fabrics similar to lower layer.

*Heavier insulating layers:* 200- to 300-weight fleeces, piles, or wool sweaters, or full-zip jackets; useful in very cold conditions or for lunch breaks and trips to the outhouse.

*Windbreaker or windshirt:* Super-light, simple windshirt for warmer days, and in colder temperatures during aerobic workouts; new and inexpensive windshells feature weather-resistant coatings and encapsulated fibers to enhance protection.

*Shell jacket:* One of the most important pieces of equipment; should have a generous cut that goes over all of your layers, and has superior venting capability, pockets large enough for gear (including skins), and a hood for blizzard conditions.

*Down or synthetic vest or coat:* Fluffy sweater or parka layered to fit over all of your clothes for emergency situations and lunch breaks; down works well in Colorado's relatively dry climate; new synthetic insulation includes, among others, MicroLoft, PrimaLoft, and PolarGuard HV and 3D.

*Lightweight gloves:* Synthetic or wool glove liners for warmer winter and spring conditions.

*Heavy gloves or mittens:* For general skiing, modular gloves that can be pulled apart to dry.

*Gaiters:* Useful for deep snow in winter and wet, slushy snow in spring.

*Wool or fleece stocking cap:* Available in a multitude of weights and styles.

*Balaclava or faceshield:* A lightweight shield that fits over or under your stocking cap for additional warmth and protection; neoprene-type facemasks also deflect wind.

*Sunglasses:* Should be made for high-altitude conditions and protect against UV radiation and visible light.

*Goggles:* Should have lenses suitable for flat light and storm conditions; an absolute necessity, winter or spring.

*Hat or cap:* A large-brimmed hat for additional sun protection for the face; a baseball cap will do.

*Sunscreen and lip balm:* An SPF factor of not less than 20–25 and, preferably, 30s to mid-40s for sunscreens.

*Neck gaiter or scarf:* Optional, additional protection for the neck.

*Hut slippers or booties:* Low-cut slippers for inside the hut, and taller booties or mukluks for outside; can be plastic ski boots with insulated liners and non-slip walking soles.

### Ski Equipment

*Performance free-heel or alpine touring setup:* Heavy-duty tele skis with shovel widths between 85 and 105 millimeters; they have shaped, single-camber designs optimized for downhill performance and for use with skins for touring and upward mobility; plastic or leather/plastic is best; used with modern cable bindings or alpine touring bindings.

*Wilderness touring setup:* Metal-edged, single or camber-and-a-half skis that can be used with wax or with skins; rooted in Nordic/cross-coúntry design; excel on trails, for touring (forward motion), and moderate telemark skiing with more moderate loads; ideal for beginner-to-advanced trails, especially roads and rolling terrain. Used with boots and "system" bindings such as NNNBC or SNSBC, or most traditional cable/three-pin bindings.

*Ski poles:* Most popularly, adjustable-length poles that convert into avalanche-probe poles; consider big powder baskets for mid-winter conditions; handy for touring.

*Backpack:* Capacity depends on length of trip and size of load; for most one- to three-night trips, a pack with a 2,800- to 4,000-cubic-inch volume will suffice; most compress in size for day trips and have side-straps for carrying skis. For extended trips (a week or more), consider a 5,000-cubic-inch pack or larger.

*Sleeping bag:* For basic sleeping purposes, a 20- to 40-degree sleeping bag; in case of emergency bivouacs—being forced to spend the night out—a zero- to –20-degree bag (+10 to –25 degree range). Yurts tend to cool off much more quickly (especially if the fire goes out), so yurt-to-yurters should carry a warmer bag, rated in the zero to +15 degree range.

*Climbing skins and/or wax kit:* Used for forward and upward movement; great for breaking speeds on long downhills; can buy trimmable skins to match your exact footprint or outline of the base of your skis (the wider and more shaped, or side-cut, your skis are, the more critical it is for skins to fit "wall-to-wall," but always leave metal edges exposed). Carry skin wax for wetter conditions.

*Snow shovel:* Made of metal or Lexan and light enough so you will always carry it.

*Avalanche transceiver:* Use only transceivers that transmit on the 457 kHz frequency and never old or questionable units; know how to use your unit before you go into the field; check the transceiver each morning.

*Spare batteries:* Lithium, for maximum performance in cold weather; carry extras for headlamps, GPS units, and transceivers.

*Avalanche probe:* Far outperforms a convertible ski pole for searching for buried victims in hardened avalanche debris.

*Headlamps:* Small, lightweight headlamps for short trips; for groups, several larger, professional-grade headlamps (and batteries). Though halogen bulbs provide better lighting, standard bulbs are adequate for normal use.

*"Hydration systems":* At least two quarts of fluids per day in anything from lightweight, insulated Camelbak-type systems to water bottles; during summer, carry a water filter/pump.

### Optional and Miscellaneous Equipment

**denotes possible group items*

*Ensolite pad:* To keep your bottom warm when sitting; for use during emergency bivouacs; and to splint broken or sprained limbs.

## APPENDIX F: Recommended Equipment Checklist (continued)

*Day pack or fanny pack:* Ultra lightweight, stuffable pack; some do double-duty as compression stuff-sacks for your sleeping bag.

*Mirror:* For signaling aircraft.

*Stove, pot, and fuel:* Essential for emergency camps and for treating hypothermic skiers trailside.

*Tarp*:* Lightweight tarp to construct emergency overnight shelter.

*Bivouac sack:* Used for simple overnight shelter; sometimes allows a lighter sleeping bag for the hut, as a bivy sack can add roughly 10 to 15 degrees to the sleeping bag's temperature rating.

*Maps and guidebooks:* Maps should be carried by every member of the group; guidebooks can be shared.

*First-aid kit*:* Build your own or purchase commercially; if using a group kit, bring a small, personal version for blisters, headaches, and the like.

*Snow kit for avalanche analysis*:* The popular Life Link or another kit, used to get a snapshot of what is going on underfoot in the snowpack.

*Altimeter*:* An essential navigation device for each group, if not every individual in a group; though wrist-watch models are the norm today, wind-gauge/thermometer weather instrument models also are available. Stand-alone Thommens model, serving skiers, guides, and mountaineers for decades, remains the professional choice.

### Ski Repair Kit/Emergency Kit

High-energy snacks and drinks
Space blanket
Duct tape
Stove parts
Long-burning candles
Webbing
Lighter and waterproof matches
Hot packs
Razor blades
Screws
Ski tips
Alpine cord
Steel wool
Glue sticks
Pocket knife or Leatherman
Sewing materials
Spare bindings, baskets, and cables
Wire
Notepad and pens
Safety pins
Flexible wire saw

### Bike/Hike Clothing

*See winter clothing list for more detailed descriptions of some of the following items.*

*Biking/hiking shorts:* Either road- or mountain-biking-type shorts.

*Insulating bike tights or long underwear:* Synthetic or wool.

*Medium-weight sweater or shirt:* Heavy long-underwear-weight or long-sleeved bike shirt.

*Heavy sweater, jacket, or vest:* Fleece, pile, wool, or synthetic insulators such as MicroLoft.

*Windpants and windshell:* Weather-resistant, yet highly breatheable, for high-aerobic activity.

*Rainshell:* Fully waterproof is recommended; waterproof breatheables work, too, but are not essential, especially if you carry weather-resistant wind-wear.

*Standard biking gloves*

*Shell gloves:* For colder temperatures or in rain and wind.

*Bathing suit/running shorts:* For saunas and creeks.

*Cap or hat:* Light, insulative stocking cap, baseball cap, or wide-brimmed hat.

*Biking/hiking socks and sock liners:* Wool, polypropylene, or Capilene.

*Walking shoes for day hikes*

**Bike Equipment**
Mountain bike
Water bottles (at least 2) or hydration system (like Camelbak)
Biking or hiking shoes
Sunscreen and lip balm
Helmet
Bike packs
Sunglasses
Day pack or fanny pack
First-aid kit
Flashlight or headlamp
High-energy snacks/energy bars

**Bike Repair Kit and Tools**
**Indicates group tools*
Phillips and flathead screwdrivers
Extra innertubes
Crescent wrench
Chain oil (small bottle)
Headset tools: 32mm, 36mm*
Tire patch kit
Hub wrenches: 13mm, 15mm*
Extra brake cables
Bottom bracket tools*
Spoke nipples
Extra tire*
Duct tape
Extra rear derailleur cable*
Tire pump
Chain lube*
Allen keys: 2.5, 4, 5, and 6mm
Large, adjustable, open-ended wrench*
Tire levers (2 to 3)
Box-ended wrench: 17mm*
Spoke wrench
Notepad and pens
Chain tool

# APPENDIX G: Bibliography and Recommended Reading List

The following listing is not necessarily a list of research materials. Rather, having had the opportunity to read, review, and use many books on backcountry living, I created a menu of resources that I think are most useful for anyone—novice and expert alike—who is interested in becoming a safer, more fit, more competent adventurer. These resources, organized by topic, are followed by the publisher's contact information and a brief description.

### Avalanche Safety Information

Daffern, Tony. *Avalanche Safety for Climbers and Skiers,* 2nd ed. Seattle: The Mountaineers, 1992. (206-223-6303, www.mountaineersbooks.org)
*This book is exhaustive and comes highly recommended—an excellent starting point.*

Fredston, Jill A., and Doug Fesler. *Snow Sense: A Guide to Evaluating Snow Avalanche Hazard,* 4th ed. Anchorage, AK: Alaska Mountain Safety Center, 1995. (907-345-3566)
*Field-totable with a unique perspective on route selection and decision-making, this book is concise and informative.*

LaChapelle, Edward R. *The ABCs of Avalanche Safety,* 2nd ed. Seattle: The Mountaineers, 1985. (206-223-6303, www.mountaineersbooks.org)
*Ed is the elder of the avalanche tribe and a true guru; all mountaineers should carry his book in their pack.*

Logan, Nick, and Dale Atkins. *The Snowy Torrents: Avalanche Accidents in the United States 1980–1986* (Special Publications 39). Denver: Colorado Geologic Survey, 1996. (303-866-2611, www.dnr.state.co.us/geosurvey)
*This detailed and analytical book from the CGS provides a fascinating look at recent avalanche accidents.*

## APPENDIX G: Bibliography and Recommended Reading List (continued)

McClung, David, and Peter Schaerer. *The Avalanche Handbook.* Seattle: The Mountaineers, 1993. (206-223-6303, www.mountaineersbooks.org)
*Based on older U.S. Forest Service publications, this is one of the most comprehensive books on the subject; extremely informative, if a bit dry.*

Moynier, John. *Avalanche Aware: Safe Travel in Avalanche Terrain.* Helena, MT: Falcon Publishing, 1998. (800-582-2665, www.falconguide.com)
*A Sierra climber, snowboarder, skier, and pro guide offers his angle on safety, culled from more than two decades of serious mountain living.*

**First Aid**

Steele, Peter. *Backcountry Medical Guide,* 2nd ed. Seattle: The Mountaineers, 1999. (206-223-6303, www.mountaineersbooks.org)
*Written by a physician, this super, general first-aid book fits easily into packs.*

Weiss, Eric. *Wilderness 911: A Step-by-Step Guide for Medical Emergencies and Improvised Care in the Backcountry.* Seattle: The Mountaineers, 1998. (206-223-6303, www.mountaineersbooks.org)
*From the editors of* Backpacker *magazine, this is an easy-to-understand first-aid resource.*

**Fitness**

Garfield, Doug. *SkiMuscle III: The Complete Musculoskeletal Tune-up for Skiers of All Ages and Abilities,* 2nd ed. Naperville, IL: Motioneering, 1998. (800-754-8353, e-mail: inmotion@mcs.com)
*Here are 100-plus pages of physics, physiology, and fitness woven into one of the most innovative, no-nonsense training programs available to skiers of all ages.*

Houston, Charles. *Going Higher: Oxygen, Man, and the Mountains,* 4th ed. Seattle: The Mountaineers, 1998. (206-223-6303, www.mountaineersbooks.org)
*Houston's master work is a captivating, enjoyable read for ski-mountaineers and armchair mountaineers alike.*

Ilg, Steve. *The Winter Athlete: Secrets of Wholistic Fitness for Outdoor Performance.* Boulder, CO: Johnson Books, 1999. (303-443-9766, e-mail: books@jppublishing.com)
*This volume is steeped in Ilg's unique spirituality/philosophy; no other book is so thorough or uniquely devoted to winter athletes and sports.*

Musnick, David, and Mark Pierce. *A.T.C. Conditioning for Outdoor Fitness.* Seattle: The Mountaineers, 1999. (206-223-6303, www.mountaineersbooks.org)
*This comprehensive fitness overview is appropriate for all abilities and fitness levels.*

Twight, Mark, and James Martin. *Extreme Alpinism: Climbing Light, Fast & High.* Seattle: The Mountaineers, 1999. (206-223-6303, www.mountaineersbooks.org)
*Though aimed at cutting-edge, high-altitude climbers, this take-no-prisoners book is chock-full of information, inspiration, hints, and tips useful for anyone heading for the high country.*

**History**

Dusenbery, Harris. *Ski the High Trail: World War II Ski Troopers in the High Colorado Rockies.* Portland, OR: Binford & Mort Publishing, 1991. (503-844-4960, www.binfordandmort.com)
*Based on the memoirs of a 10th Mountain Division soldier, this fun book provides a frame of reference for trips into the hut system of the same name.*

Ubbelohde, Carl, Maxine Benson, and Duane A. Smith. *A Colorado History,* 7th ed. Boulder, CO: Pruett Publishing, 1995. (303-449-4919, www.pruettpublishing.com)

**Navigation**

Burns, Bob, and Mike Burns. *Wilderness Navigation: Finding Your Way Using Map, Compass, Altimeter, and GPS.* Seattle: The Mountaineers, 1999. (206-223-6303, www.mountaineersbooks.org)
*This instructional book covers all the bases.*

Fleming, June. *Staying Found: The Complete Map & Compass Handbook,* 2nd ed. Seattle: The Mountaineers, 1999. (206-223-6303, www.mountaineersbooks.org)
*A good instructional book for beginners, this handbook focuses on the map and compass only.*

Letham, Lawrence. *GPS Made Easy: Using the Global Positioning System in the Outdoors,* 2nd ed. Seattle: The Mountaineers, 1999. (206-223-6303, www.mountaineersbooks.org)
*The Global Positioning System (GPS) is the basis for this in-depth look at the evolving area of navigation.*

**Skiing Information, Instruction, and Mountain Skills Training**

Brown, Nat. *The Complete Guide to Cross-Country Ski Preparation.* Seattle: The Mountaineers, 1999. (206-223-6303, www.mountaineersbooks.org)

Felkley, Dave, Ed., and Gene Prater. *Snowshoeing,* 4th ed. Seattle: The Mountaineers, 1997. (206-223-6303, www.mountaineersbooks.org)
*This is the best overview on contemporary snowshoeing (see also Mark Twight and James Marbin's* Extreme Alpinism, *under "Fitness").*

Gillette, Edward, and John Dostal. *Cross Country Skiing,* 3rd ed. Seattle: The Mountaineers, 1988. (206-223-6303, www.mountaineersbooks.org)
*Though a bit dated, this popular book provides an enjoyable read as well as a concise overview of all aspects of skiing, from cross-country to expedition skiing.*

Graydon, Don, ed. *Mountaineering: The Freedom of the Hills,* 6th ed. Seattle: The Mountaineers, 1997. (206-223-6303, www.mountaineersbooks.org)
*Always fresh, this is the definitive tome on general mountain travel skills.*

Masia, Seth. *Ski Maintenance and Repair.* Chicago: Contemporary Books, 1987. (847-679-5500, www.ntc-cb.com)
*This is an in-depth manual for the care of modern skis.*

O'Bannon, Allen, and Mike Clelland. *Allen & Mike's Really Cool Backcountry Ski Book: Traveling & Camping Skills for a Winter Environment.* Helena, MT: Falcon Publishing, 1996. (800-582-2665, www.falconguide.com)
*This informative book, illustrated with great cartoons, is a classic.*

O'Bannon, Allen, and Mike Clelland. *Allen & Mike's Really Cool Telemark Tips: 109 Amazing Tips to Improve Your Skiing.* Helena, MT: Falcon Publishing, 1998. (800-582-2665, www.falconguide.com)
*This neo-classic is not only informative but also is illustrated with uproariously funny cartoons.*

Parker, Paul. *Free-Heel Skiing: The Secrets of Telemark and Parallel Skiing in All Conditions,* 2nd ed. Seattle: The Mountaineers, 1995. (206-223-6303, www.mountaineersbooks.org)
*The instructional and equipment design guru of our generation has produced the undisputed classic free-heel overview covering parallel and telemark techniques, gear selection, maintenance, and fitness training.*

## APPENDIX G: Bibliography and Recommended Reading List (continued)

Randall, Glenn. *The Outward Bound Staying Warm in the Outdoors Handbook.* New York: Lyons Press, 2000. (800-836-0510, www.lyonspress.com)
*This is a good overview on layering and other strategies for maximizing comfort when living and exercising in colder climates.*

Vives, Jean. *Backcountry Skier: Your Complete Guide to Ski Touring.* Champaign, IL: Human Kinetics, 1998. (800-747-4457, e-mail: humank@hkusa.com)
*Written by a veteran skier who completed his doctoral research work on backcountry skiing, this book is a well-rounded resource for all types of modern off-piste skiing.*

Weiss, Hal. *Secrets of Warmth: For Comfort or Survival.* Seattle: The Mountaineers, 1988. (206-223-6303, www.mountaineersbooks.org)
*Although somewhat text-heavy, this book contains well-researched, detailed information on staying warm, comfortable, and safe in cold climates.*

Yule, Leigh Girvin, and Scott Toepfer. *The Hut Handbook: Planning and Enjoying a Backcountry Trip.* Englewood, CO: Westcliffe Publishers, 1996. (303-935-0900, www.westcliffepublishers.com)
*Though going out-of-print, this is the perfect primer for novice hut skiers.*

**Weather, Geology, and Ecology**

Chronic, Halka. *Roadside Geology of Colorado.* Missoula, MT: Mountain Press Publishing, 1988. (406-728-1900, www.mountainpresspublish.com)
*This is a best-selling guide to Colorado's "living geology museum" found along her highways and interstates.*

Chronic, John, and Halka Chronic. *Prairie, Peak & Plateau: A Guide to the Geology of Colorado* (Bulletin 32). Denver: Colorado Geological Survey, 1972. (303-866-2611, www.dnr.state.co.us/geosurvey)
*An excellent summary of Colorado's geologic history, this book is scheduled for revision and a new title by winter 2000–2001.*

Halfpenny, James C., and Roy Douglas Ozanne. *Winter: An Ecological Handbook.* Boulder, CO: Johnson Books, 1989. (303-443-9766, e-mail: books@jppublishing.com)
*This handbook provides an expert, in-depth study of winter mountain ecology.*

Halfpenny, James, and Todd Telander. *Scats and Tracks.* Helena, MT: Falcon Publishing, 1998. (800-582-2665, www.falconguide.com)
*For those who are curious about the animals living around the hut systems, this is an exhaustive study of the tracks they leave behind.*

Mutel, Cornelia Fleischer, and John Emerick. *Grassland to Glacier.* Boulder, CO: Johnson Books, 1984. (303-443-9766, e-mail: books@jppublishing.com)
*This is the best-selling guide to the ecology of Colorado.*

Nelson, Mike. *The Colorado Weather Book.* Englewood, CO: Westcliffe Publishers, 1999. (303-935-0900, www.westcliffepublishers.com)
*This best-selling book provides a basic overview of the science and history of Colorado's weather phenomena.*

Woodmencey, Jim. *Reading Weather: Where Will You Be When the Storm Hits?* Helena, MT: Falcon Publishing, 1998. (800-582-2665, www.falconguide.com)
*This small, packable book full of expert advice was written by a leading avalanche and weather forecaster.*

**Videos**

*Avalanche Awareness: A Question of Balance.* Alliance Communications (distributed exclusively by Pyramid Film & Video), 1989. (800-421-2304, www.pyramidmedia.com)
*This offers an easy-to-understand introduction to avalanche safety awareness.*

*Avalanche Rescue: Not a Second to Waste.* Lakewood, CO: Colorado Avalanche Information Center and National Ski Patrol, 1992. (303-988-1111, www.nsp.org)
*This is an in-depth, 30-minute avalanche rescue how-to video.*

*Beyond the Groomed: Freeheel Skiing Off-Piste.* Curlew, WA: Freeheels, 1995. (800-227-2054,www.freeheels.com)
*In this superb video, inspirational ski footage is interspersed with instructional segments that focus on the body mechanics of skiing, as well as skiing in different snow conditions.*

*Big Mountain, Little Skiers.* Curlew, WA: Freeheels, 2000. (800-227-2054, www.freeheels.com)
*The awesome skiing footage shot throughout Canada, the West Coast, and Alaska will get you pumped.*

*Freedom of the Heels.* Curlew, WA: Freeheels, 1997. (800-227-2054, www.freeheels.com)
*A nice introduction to backcountry skiing, this video covers topics such as skins, transceivers, route-finding, uphill travel, avalanche awareness, downhill skiing, and general backcountry awareness.*

*Winning the Avalanche Game.* Salt Lake City: Friends of the Utah Avalanche Center, 1993. (801-488-1003, or for Backcountry Access: 800-670-8735, www.bcaccess.com)
*This overview features spectacular avalanche footage and interviews with people who were caught in slides.*

## APPENDIX H: Map Sources

Colorado Atlas & Gazetteer
DeLorme Mapping
P.O. Box 298
Freeport, ME 04032
207-865-4171

Trails Illustrated
P.O. Box 3610
Evergreen, CO 80439
303-670-3457
800-962-1643

United States Geological Survey
Denver Federal Center
P.O. Box 25286
Lakewood, CO 80225
303-236-7477

USGS Topographical Maps
National Cartographic Center
507 National Center
Reston, VA 22092
703-648-6045

Most USGS topographic maps and Trails Illustrated maps can be purchased through outdoor, ski, and mountaineering shops. U.S. Forest Service maps can also be purchased through retail sporting goods stores as well as from their respective offices (see Appendix C for phone numbers).

## APPENDIX I: GPS Coordinates

This edition of *Colorado Hut to Hut* does not include the current crop of GPS coordinates. Within a year of press time, most hut systems that provide GPS coordinates are going to be in the process of re-gathering these data. Recent changes in U.S. Defense Department policy will allow for vastly more accurate readings to be taken. Though this process will take some time, these new, more reliable readings will be phased in.

In the meantime, please contact each hut system for the latest readings, and for further information refer to "On the Trail" in the introductory section of this book, pages 25 and 26. Also, please consult Appendix G for suggested reading on navigation.

## APPENDIX J: Difficulty Ratings for Tours

| NORTHERN HUTS | Difficulty Rating | Page |
|---|---|---|
| *Never Summer Nordic Yurts and Nokhu Cabin* | | |
| **1** Grass Creek Yurt | | 39 |
| **1a.** North Michigan Trailhead to Grass Creek Yurt | Novice | 40 |
| **1b.** Grass Creek Yurt to Montgomery Pass Yurts | Novice/Intermediate | 41 |
| **1c.** Grass Creek Yurt to Ruby Jewel Yurt | Novice/Intermediate | 42 |
| **2** Montgomery Pass Yurts | | 44 |
| **2a.** North Fork Michigan TH to Montgomery Pass Yurts | Novice/Intermediate | 45 |
| **2b.** Zimmerman Lake/Montgomery Pass Trailhead to Mountain Pass Yurts | Advanced/Expert | 46 |
| **2c.** Montgomery Pass Yurts to Ruby Jewel Yurt (Valley Route) | Novice/Intermediate | 48 |
| **2d.** Montgomery Pass Yurts to Ruby Jewel Yurt (High Traverse Route) | Intermediate | 49 |
| **3** Ruby Jewel Yurt | | 50 |
| **3a.** Jewel Lake Trailhead to Ruby Jewel Yurt | Novice | 51 |
| **3b.** Ruby Jewel Yurt to North Fork Canadian Yurt | Intermediate | 52 |
| **4** North Fork Canadian Yurt | | 53 |
| **4a.** N. Fork Canadian TH to N. Fork Canadian Yurt | Novice | 54 |
| **5** Dancing Moose Yurt | | 56 |
| **5a.** Dancing Moose Trailhead to Dancing Moose Yurt | Novice | 57 |
| **6** Nokhu Cabin | | 58 |
| **6a.** Lake Agnes Trailhead to Nokhu Cabin | Novice | 59 |
| *Colorado Mountain Club and Northern Independent Huts* | | 62 |
| **7** Brainard Lake Cabin | | 65 |
| **7a.** Red Rock Lake Trailhead to Brainard Lake Cabin | Novice | 67 |
| **7b.** North and South Trails to Brainard Lake Cabin | Intermediate | 68 |
| **8** Guinn Mountain Hut | | 70 |
| **8a.** Eldora Nordic Center TH to Guinn Mtn. Hut | Advanced | 71 |
| **9** Tennessee Mountain Cabin | | 75 |
| **9a.** Eldora Nordic Center TH to Tenn. Mtn. Cabin | Novice | 76 |
| **10** Squaw Mountain Fire Lookout | | 77 |
| **10a.** Squaw Pass Road to Fire Lookout | Novice | 79 |
| **11** First Creek Cabin | | 81 |
| **11a.** Berthoud Pass Road to First Creek Cabin | Novice/Intermediate | 83 |

| **NORTHERN HUTS** *(continued)* | **Difficulty Rating** | **Page** |
|---|---|---|
| **12** Second Creek Cabin (Gwen Andrews Hut) | | 84 |
| **12a.** Berthoud Pass Road to Second Creek Cabin | Intermediate | 85 |
| **13** High Lonesome Hut | | 87 |
| **13a.** Meadow Creek Road TH to High Lonesome Hut | Novice | 89 |
| **13b.** High Lonesome Hut to Arapaho Bay/Doe Cr. TH | Intermediate/Advanced | 91 |
| **CENTRAL HUTS** | | |
| *Summit Huts Association* | | 96 |
| **14** Section House and Ken's Cabin | | 99 |
| **14a.** Boreas Pass TH (Breckenridge) to Section House and Ken's Cabin | Novice/Intermediate | 100 |
| **14b.** Peabody TH (South Park) to Section House and Ken's Cabin | Novice/Intermediate | 101 |
| **14c.** Gold Dust TH to Section House and Ken's Cabin | Intermediate | 102 |
| **15** Francie's Cabin | | 106 |
| **15a.** Burro Trail Trailhead to Francie's Cabin | Intermediate | 107 |
| **15b.** Wheeler Flats Trailhead to Francie's Cabin | Advanced | 109 |
| **16** Janet's Cabin | | 111 |
| **16a.** Union Creek Trailhead to Janet's Cabin | Intermediate | 113 |
| **16b.** Vail Pass Trailhead to Janet's Cabin | Advanced | 115 |
| **16c.** Janet's Cabin to Fowler/Hilliard Hut | Advanced | 116 |
| **16d.** Janet's Cabin to Shrine Mountain Inn | Advanced | 117 |
| *10th Mountain Division Hut Association* | | 120 |
| **17** Eiseman Hut | | 126 |
| **17a.** Spraddle Creek Trailhead to Eiseman Hut | Advanced | 128 |
| **17b.** Red Sandstone Creek Trailhead to Eiseman Hut | Advanced | 132 |
| **18** Shrine Mountain Inn (Jay's, Chuck's, and Walter's Cabins) | | 133 |
| **18a.** Vail Pass Trailhead to Shrine Mountain Inn | Novice | 136 |
| **18b.** Red Cliff Trailhead to Shrine Mountain Inn | Intermediate/Advanced | 137 |
| **18c.** Shrine Mountain Inn to Fowler/Hilliard Hut | Advanced | 138 |
| **19** Fowler/Hilliard Hut | | 141 |
| **19a.** Red Cliff Trailhead to Fowler/Hilliard Hut | Advanced | 144 |
| **19b.** Pando Trailhead to Fowler/Hilliard Hut | Intermediate/Advanced | 146 |
| **19c.** Camp Hale Trailhead to Fowler/Hilliard Hut | Intermediate/Advanced | 147 |
| **19d.** Fowler/Hilliard Hut to Jackal Hut | Advanced | 149 |
| **19e.** Fowler/Hilliard Hut to Jackal Hut via High Traverse | Advanced | 150 |
| **20** Jackal Hut | | 154 |
| **20a.** Camp Hale TH to Jackal Hut via Pearl Creek | Intermediate/Advanced | 155 |
| **20b.** S. Camp Hale TH to Jackal Hut via Ranch Creek | Intermediate/Advanced | 156 |
| **20c.** S. Camp Hale TH to Jackal Hut via Cataract Creek | Intermediate/Advanced | 157 |
| **20d.** Jackal Hut to Vance's Cabin | Intermediate/Advanced | 159 |
| **21** Vance's Cabin | | 160 |
| **21a.** Tennessee Pass Trailhead to Vance's Cabin | Novice/Intermediate | 161 |
| **21b.** Vance's Cabin to 10th Mountain Division Hut | Intermediate | 163 |
| **22** Sangree M. Froelicher Hut | | 164 |
| **22a.** Buckeye Gulch TH to Sangree M. Froelicher Hut | Novice/Intermediate | 166 |
| **22b.** Sangree M. Froelicher Hut to Chalk Creek Traverse | Advanced/Expert | 167 |

## APPENDIX J: Difficulty Ratings for Tours (continued)

| CENTRAL HUTS *(continued)* | Difficulty Rating | Page |
|---|---|---|
| **23** 10th Mountain Division Hut | | 170 |
| **23a.** Tennessee Pass TH to 10th Mtn. Division Hut | Intermediate | 171 |
| **23b.** Crane Park Trailhead to 10th Mtn. Division Hut | Intermediate | 172 |
| **23c.** 10th Mountain Division Hut to Uncle Bud's Hut | Intermediate | 174 |
| **24** Uncle Bud's Hut | | 176 |
| **24a.** Turquoise Lake Trailhead to Uncle Bud's Hut | Intermediate | 177 |
| **24b.** Uncle Bud's Hut to Skinner Hut | Advanced | 178 |
| **25** Skinner Hut | | 182 |
| **25a.** Turquoise Lake Trailhead to Skinner Hut | Advanced | 183 |
| **25b.** Skinner Hut to Betty Bear Hut | Intermediate/Advanced | 184 |
| **26** Betty Bear Hut | | 188 |
| **26a.** Forest Road 505 Trailhead to Betty Bear Hut | Intermediate/Advanced | 190 |
| **27** Polar Star Inn and Carl's Cabin | | 194 |
| **27a.** West Lake Creek TH to Polar Star Inn/Carl's Cabin | Intermediate/Advanced | 196 |
| **27b.** Yeoman Park TH to Polar Star Inn and Carl's Cabin via Fulford Road | Intermediate | 198 |
| **27c.** Yeoman Park Trailhead to Polar Star Inn and Carl's Cabin via Newcomer Spring | Intermediate/Advanced | 199 |
| **27d.** Polar Star Inn to Peter Estin Hut | Advanced | 201 |
| **28** Peter Estin Hut | | 204 |
| **28a.** Yeoman Park Trailhead to Peter Estin Hut via Ironedge Trail | Intermediate/Advanced | 206 |
| **28b.** Yeoman Park Trailhead to Peter Estin Hut via Hat Creek Trail | Intermediate | 207 |
| **28c.** Sylvan Lake Trailhead to Peter Estin Hut via Crooked Creek Pass | Intermediate/Advanced | 208 |
| **28d.** Peter Estin Hut to Harry Gates Hut | Intermediate | 212 |
| **29** Harry Gates Hut | | 214 |
| **29a.** Sylvan Lake Trailhead to Harry Gates Hut | Intermediate/Advanced | 215 |
| **29b.** Spring Creek Trailhead to Harry Gates Hut | Intermediate | 216 |
| **29c.** Diamond J Trailhead/Montgomery Flats to Harry Gates Hut | Intermediate | 218 |
| **30** Margy's Hut | | 222 |
| **30a.** Norrie Trailhead to Margy's Hut | Intermediate | 223 |
| **30b.** Granite Lakes Trailhead to Margy's Hut | Intermediate | 224 |
| **30c.** Lenado Trailhead to Margy's Hut | Intermediate/Advanced | 226 |
| **30d.** Margy's Hut to McNamara Hut | Intermediate/Advanced | 227 |
| **31** McNamara Hut | | 230 |
| **31a.** Hunter Creek Trailhead to McNamara Hut | Intermediate | 231 |
| **32** Benedict Huts: Fritz's and Fabi's Cabins | | 233 |
| **32a.** Hunter Creek Trailhead to Benedict Huts | Intermediate/Advanced | 234 |
| **32b.** Benedict Huts to McNamara Hut via Thimble Rock | Advanced/Expert | 236 |
| **32c.** Benedict Huts to McNamara Hut via Van Horn Park | Intermediate/Advanced | 239 |

| CENTRAL HUTS *(continued)* | Difficulty Rating | Page |
|---|---|---|
| *Alfred A. Braun Memorial Hut System* | | |
| **33** Barnard Hut | | 245 |
| **33a.** Ashcroft Trailhead to Barnard Hut | Advanced | 246 |
| **33b.** Sundeck Trailhead to Barnard Hut | Intermediate/Advanced | 248 |
| **33c.** Barnard Hut to Goodwin-Greene Hut | Advanced | 250 |
| **34** Goodwin-Greene Hut | | 254 |
| **34a.** Ashcroft Trailhead to Goodwin-Greene Hut | Advanced | 255 |
| **35** Markley Hut | | 256 |
| **35a.** Ashcroft Trailhead to Markley Hut | Novice/Intermediate | 257 |
| **36** Lindley Hut | | 258 |
| **36a.** Ashcroft Trailhead to Lindley Hut | Novice/Intermediate | 259 |
| **37** Tagert and Green-Wilson Huts | | 262 |
| **37a.** Ashcroft TH to Tagert/Green-Wilson Huts | Intermediate/Advanced | 265 |
| **37b.** Tagert/Green-Wilson Huts to Friends Hut via Pearl Pass | Advanced/Expert | 267 |
| **38** Friends Hut | | 272 |
| **38a.** East River Trailhead to Friends Hut | Advanced | 273 |
| *Central Independent Huts* | | |
| **39** Hidden Treasure Yurt | | 280 |
| **39a.** West Lake Creek Trailhead to Hidden Treasure Yurt | Intermediate/Advanced | 281 |
| **39b.** Yeoman Park Trailhead to Hidden Treasure Yurt via Fulford Road | Intermediate | 282 |
| **40** Sunlight Backcountry Cabin | | 285 |
| **40a.** Sunlight Mountain Resort to Sunlight Backcountry Cabin | Novice | 287 |


## APPENDIX K: Hut Rental Rates

The hut fees listed here are for the 2000–2001 season. Although prices could increase in the future, this appendix enables a rough price comparison. These are base fees and do not reflect applicable taxes or hut association memberships if they apply. *Note:* Designations for days of the week are Su, M, T, W, Th, F, S; and PPPN = Per Person Per Night.

### Northern Huts

*Never Summer Nordic Yurts and Nokhu Cabin*

Grass Creek Yurt, Ruby Jewel Yurt, North Fork Canadian Yurt, Nokhu Cabin:
$99 flat fee/winter weekends (F, S, Su)

Dancing Moose Yurt, Montgomery Pass Yurts:
$79 flat fee/winter weekdays (M-Th)

Summer flat fee rates: weekends (F, S, Su), $59; weekdays (M-Th), $49

*Colorado Mountain Club and Northern Independent Huts*

Brainard Lake Cabin: $8 members; $15 non-members; $100 deposit required
Guinn Mountain Hut: donation requested
Tennessee Mountain Cabin: $75 weekends; $50 weekdays
Squaw Mountain Fire Lookout: $60 flat fee

## APPENDIX K: Hut Rental Rates (continued)

*Northern Independent Huts (continued)*

First and Second Creek Cabins (Gwen Andrews Hut): temporarily closed
High Lonesome Hut: $25 PPPN; $10 per child; $180 for entire hut

**Central Huts**

*Summit Huts Association*

Janet's and Francie's Cabins: $27 PPPN
Section House: $26 PPPN
Ken's Cabin: $69 flat fee

*10th Mountain Division Hut Association (Association-owned huts)*

Eiseman Hut, Fowler/Hilliard Hut, Jackal Hut, 10th Mountain Division Hut, Uncle Bud's Hut, Skinner Hut, Betty Bear Hut, Peter Estin Hut, Harry Gates Hut, Margy's Hut, McNamara Hut, Benedict Huts/Fritz's Cabin & Fabi's Cabin: $22 PPPN

*10th Mountain Division Hut Association (private huts)*

Shrine Mountain Inn—Jay's Cabin: $35 PPPN
Shrine Mountain Inn—Chuck's Cabin: upstairs, $200 flat fee; downstairs, $25 PPPN
Shrine Mountain Inn—Walter's Cabin: upstairs, $200 flat fee; downstairs, $200 flat fee
Vance's Cabin: $22 PPPN
Sangree M. Froelicher Hut: $28 PPPN
Polar Star Inn: $28 PPPN
Carl's Cabin at Polar Star Inn: $200 flat fee

*Alfred A. Braun Memorial Hut System*

Barnard Hut, Goodwin-Greene Hut, Markley Hut, Lindley Hut, Tagert Hut, Greene-Wilson Hut: $17.50 PPPN
Friends Hut: $15 PPPN, or $100 flat fee for entire hut

*Central Independent Huts*

Hidden Treasure Yurt: $25 PPPN
Sunlight Backcountry Cabin: $40 per night flat fee year-round

# Index

**NOTE:** Citations followed by the letter "p" denote photos; citations followed by the letter "m" denote maps.


Acute Mountain Sickness (AMS), 28
"Advanced/expert" route rating, 17–18
"Advanced" route rating, 17
Alfred A. Braun Memorial Hut System, 94–95, 242–277
Altitudes, high, 27
Arapaho Bay/Doe Creek Trailhead, High Lonesome Hut to, 88m, 91–92, 93m
Ashcroft Trailhead
- to Barnard Hut, 244m, 246–247, 252m–253m, 270m–271m
- to Goodwin-Greene Hut, 244m, 252m–253m, 255, 270m–271m
- to Lindley Hut, 244m, 252m–253m, 259–260, 270m–271m
- to Markley Hut, 244m, 252m–253m, 257, 270m–271m
- to Tagert and Green-Wilson Huts, 244m, 252m–253m, 265–266, 270m–271m

Avalanches
- assessing slide potential, 30
- carrying a shovel and probe, 31
- hazard rating system, 19–20
- surviving, 31
- types of, 29–30
- wearing a transceiver, 31

Barnard Hut, 244m, 245–251, 252m–253m, 270m–271m
- Ashcroft Trailhead to, 244m, 246–247, 252m–253m, 270m–271m
- to Goodwin-Greene Hut, 244m, 250–251, 252m–253m, 270m–271m
- Sundeck Trailhead to, 244m, 248, 250, 252m–253m

Benedict Huts: Fritz's and Fabi's Cabins, 124m–125m, 233–239, 235p, 236p, 239p, 240m–241m
- Hunter Creek Trailhead to, 124m–125m, 234–235, 240m–241m
- to McNamara Hut via Thimble Rock, 124m–125m, 236–238, 240m–241m
- to McNamara Hut via Van Horn Park, 124m–125m, 239, 240m–241m

Berthoud Pass Road
- to First Creek Cabin, 82m, 83, 86m
- to Second Creek Cabin (Gwen Andrews Hut), 82m, 85, 86m

Betty Bear Hut, 124m–125m, 186m–187m, 188–190, 188p, 189p, 192m–193m
- Forest Road 505 Trailhead to, 124m–125m, 186m–187m, 190, 192m–193m
- Skinner Hut to, 124m–125m, 184–185, 186m–187m, 192m–193m

Boreas Pass Trailhead (Breckenridge) to Section House and Ken's Cabin, 98m, 100, 104m–105m
Brainard Lake Cabin, 64m, 65–68, 69m
- North and South Trails to, 64m, 68, 69m
- Red Rock Lake Trailhead to, 64m, 67, 69m

Buckeye Gulch Trailhead to Sangree M. Froelicher Hut, 124m–125m, 166, 169m
Burro Trail Trailhead to Francie's Cabin, 98m, 107–108, 110m

Camp Hale Trailhead
- to Fowler/Hilliard Hut, 124m–125m, 142m–143m, 147–148, 152m–153m
- to Jackal Hut via Pearl Creek, 124m–125m, 152m–153m, 155

Carl's Cabin. *See* Polar Star Inn and Carl's Cabin
Cell phones, 33
Chalk Creek Traverse, Sangree M. Froelicher Hut to, 124m–125m, 167–168, 169m
Chuck's Cabin (Shrine Mountain Inn), 124m–125m, 133–140, 142m–143m
Colorado Mountain Club and northern independent huts, 35, 62–93
Crane Park Trailhead to 10th Mountain Division Hut, 124m–125m, 172–173, 180m–181m, 186m–187m

Dancing Moose Trailhead to Dancing Moose Yurt, 38m, 57, 60m–61m
Dancing Moose Yurt, 38m, 56–57, 60m–61m
Dancing Moose Yurt, Dancing Moose Trailhead to, 38m, 57, 60m–61m
Dehydration, 28

Diamond J Trailhead/Montgomery Flats to Harry Gates Hut, 124m–125m, 210m–211m, 218–219, 220m–221m
Difficulty ratings, 17–18
Distances, 18
Doe Creek Trailhead/Arapaho Bay, High Lonesome Hut to, 88m, 91–92, 93m

East River Trailhead to Friends Hut, 244m, 270m–271m, 273–274, 276m–277m
Eating, 28
Eiseman Hut, 124m–125m, 126–129, 126p, 130m–131m, 132
  Red Sandstone Creek Trailhead to, 124m–125m, 130m–131m, 132
  Spraddle Creek Trailhead to, 124m–125m, 128–129, 130m–131m
Eldora Nordic Center Trailhead
  to Guinn Mtn. Hut, 64m, 71–72, 73m
  to Tennessee Mtn. Cabin, 64m, 73m, 76
Elevations, 18
Equipment. *See* Gear

Fabi's Cabin (Benedict Huts), 124m–125m, 233–239, 239p, 240m–241m
First Creek Cabin, 81, 82m, 83, 86m
First Creek Cabin, Berthoud Pass Road to, 82m, 83, 86m
Food, 28
Forest Road 505 Trailhead to Betty Bear Hut, 124m–125m, 186m–187m, 190, 192m–193m
Fowler/Hilliard Hut, 24p, 32p, 124m–125m, 141, 142m–143m, 144–151, 152m–153m
  Camp Hale Trailhead to, 124m–125m, 142m–143m, 147–148, 152m–153m
  to Jackal Hut, 124m–125m, 142m–143m, 149–150, 152m–153m
  to Jackal Hut via High Traverse, 124m–125m, 142m–143m, 150–151, 152m–153m
  Janet's Cabin to, 98m, 116, 118m–119m, 124m–125m, 152m–153m
  Pando Trailhead to, 124m–125m, 142m–143m, 146–147, 152m–153m
  Red Cliff Trailhead to, 124m–125m, 142m–143m, 144–145, 152m–153m
  Shrine Mountain Inn (Jay's, Chuck's, and Walter's Cabins) to, 124m–125m, 138, 140, 142m–143m
Francie's Cabin, 98m, 106–109, 110m
  Burro Trail Trailhead to, 98m, 107–108, 110m
  Wheeler Flats Trailhead to, 98m, 109, 110m
Friends Hut, 244m, 270m–271m, 272–274, 274p, 276m–277m
  East River Trailhead to, 244m, 270m–271m, 273–274, 276m–277m
  Tagert and Green-Wilson Huts to via Pearl Pass, 244m, 267–269, 270m–271m
Fritz's Cabin (Benedict Huts), 124m–125m, 233–239, 235p, 236p, 240m–241m
Frostbite, 27

Gear
  caring for, 24
  skis, 23–24
  snowshoes, 22
  for summer travel, 22
Global Positioning System (GPS), 25–26
Gold Dust Trailhead to Section House and Ken's Cabin, 98m, 102, 104m–105m
Goodwin-Greene Hut, 244m, 247p, 252m–253m, 254–255, 254p, 270m–271m
  Ashcroft Trailhead to, 244m, 252m–253m, 255, 270m–271m
  Barnard Hut to, 244m, 250–251, 252m–253m, 270m–271m
GPS (Global Positioning System), 25–26
Granite Lakes Trailhead to Margy's Hut, 124m–125m, 192m–193m, 220m–221m, 224–225
Grass Creek Yurt, 38m, 39–43, 60m–61m
  to Montgomery Pass Yurts, 38m, 41, 60m–61m
  North Fork Michigan Trailhead to, 38m, 40, 60m–61m
  to Ruby Jewel Yurt, 38m, 42, 60m–61m
Greene Hut. *See* Goodwin-Greene Hut
Green-Wilson Hut. *See* Tagert and Green-Wilson Huts
Guinn Mtn. Hut, 64m, 70–72, 71p, 73m
Guinn Mountain Hut, Eldora Nordic Center Trailhead to, 64m, 71–72, 73m
Gwen Andrews Hut (Second Creek Cabin), 82m, 84–85, 86m
Gwen Andrews Hut (Second Creek Cabin), Berthoud Pass Road to, 82m, 85, 86m

Harry Gates Hut, 124m–125m, 210m–211m, 214–219, 217p, 220m–221m
Diamond J Trailhead/Montgomery Flats to, 124m–125m, 210m–211m, 218–219, 220m–221m
Peter Estin Hut to, 124m–125m, 202m–203m, 210m–211m, 212–213
Spring Creek Trailhead to, 124m–125m, 210m–211m, 216, 220m–221m
Sylvan Lake Trailhead to, 124m–125m, 210m–211m, 215–216, 220m–221m
Hidden Treasure Yurt, 279m, 280–283, 284m
West Lake Creek Trailhead to, 244m, 279m, 281–282, 284m
Yeoman Park Trailhead to via Fulford Road, 244m, 279m, 282–283, 284m
High-Altitude Pulmonary Edema (HAPE), 28
High altitudes, 27
High Lonesome Hut, 87, 88m, 89–92, 92p, 93m
to Arapaho Bay/Doe Creek Trailhead, 88m, 91–92, 93m
Meadow Creek Road Trailhead to, 88m, 89–90, 93m
Hilliard Hut. *See* Fowler/Hilliard Hut
Hunter Creek Trailhead
to Benedict Huts: Fritz's & Fabi's Cabins, 124m–125m, 234–235, 240m–241m
to McNamara Hut, 124m–125m, 231–232, 240m–241m
Hut-to-hut travel
avalanche safety, 19–20, 29–31
avoiding dehydration, 28
bringing maps and compasses, 25
carrying emergency equipment, 24
eating properly, 28
frostbite, 27
functioning at high altitudes, 27
hut amenities, 31–32
hut etiquette, 33
hypothermia, 26
navigation tips, 26
preparations checklist, 21–22
selecting gear, 22–24
staying together, 24
sun protection, 27
using cell phones, 33
using GPS coordinates, 25–26
weather considerations, 28–29
Hydration, 28
Hypothermia, 27

Icons, 18
"Intermediate" route rating, 17

Jackal Hut, 124m–125m, 152m–153m, 154–159, 155p, 158p
Camp Hale Trailhead to via Pearl Creek, 124m–125m, 152m–153m, 155
Fowler/Hilliard Hut to, 124m–125m, 142m–143m, 149–150, 152m–153m
Fowler/Hilliard Hut to via High Traverse, 124m–125m, 142m–143m, 150–151, 152m–153m
South Camp Hale Trailhead to via Cataract Creek, 124m–125m, 152m–153m, 157
South Camp Hale Trailhead to via Ranch Creek, 124m–125m, 152m–153m, 156
to Vance's Cabin, 124m–125m, 152m–153m, 159
Janet's Cabin, 98m, 111–117, 112p, 114p, 118m–119m, 124m–125m, 152m–153m
to Fowler/Hilliard Hut, 98m, 116, 118m–119m, 124m–125m, 152m–153m
to Shrine Mountain Inn (Jay's, Chuck's, and Walter's Cabins), 98m, 117, 118m–119m, 124m–125m, 152m–153m
Union Creek Trailhead to, 98m, 113–114, 118m–119m, 124m–125m, 152m–153m
Vail Pass Trailhead to, 98m, 115, 118m–119m, 124m–125m, 152m–153m
Jay's Cabin (Shrine Mountain Inn), 124m–125m, 133–140, 139p, 142m–143m
Jewel Lake Trailhead to Ruby Jewel Yurt, 38m, 51, 60m–61m

Ken's Cabin. *See* Section House and Ken's Cabin

Lake Agnes Trailhead to Nokhu Cabin, 38m, 59, 60m–61m
Lenado Trailhead to Margy's Hut, 124m–125m, 220m–221m, 226–227, 240m–241m
Lindley Hut, 244m, 252m–253m, 258–260,270m–271m
Lindley Hut, Ashcroft Trailhead to, 244m, 252m–253m, 259–260, 270m–271m

Maps, 20
Margy's Hut, 124m–125m, 210m–211m, 220m–221m, 222–228, 226p, 240m–241m
  Granite Lakes Trailhead to, 124m–125m, 192m–193m, 220m–221m, 224–225
  Lenado Trailhead to, 124m–125m, 220m–221m, 226–227, 240m–241m
  to McNamara Hut, 124m–125m, 220m–221m, 227–228, 240m–241m
  Norrie Trailhead to, 124m–125m, 210m–211m, 220m–221m, 223–224, 240m–241m
Markley Hut, 244m, 252m–253m, 256–257, 256p, 270m–271m
Markley Hut, Ashcroft Trailhead to, 244m, 252m–253m, 257, 270m–271m
McNamara Hut, 124m–125m, 230–232, 240m–241m
  Benedict Huts: Fritz's and Fabi's Cabins to via Thimble Rock, 124m–125m, 236–238, 240m–241m
  Benedict Huts: Fritz's and Fabi's Cabins to via Van Horn Park, 124m–125m, 239, 240m–241m
  Hunter Creek Trailhead to, 124m–125m, 231–232, 240m–241m
  Margy's Hut to, 124m–125m, 220m–221m, 227–228, 240m–241m
Meadow Creek Road Trailhead to High Lonesome Hut, 88m, 89–90, 93m
Montgomery Flats/Diamond J Trailhead to Harry Gates Hut, 124m–125m, 210m–211m, 218–219, 220m–221m
Montgomery Pass Trailhead/Zimmerman Lake to Montgomery Pass Yurts, 38m, 46–47, 60m–61m
Montgomery Pass Yurts, 38m, 44–49, 48p, 60m–61m
  Grass Creek Yurt to, 38m, 41, 60m–61m
  North Fork Michigan Trailhead to, 38m, 45–46, 60m–61m
  to Ruby Jewel Yurt (High Traverse Route), 38m, 49, 60m–61m
  to Ruby Jewel Yurt (Valley Route), 38m, 48, 60m–61m
  Zimmerman Lake/Montgomery Pass Trailhead to, 38m, 46–47, 60m–61m

Navigation
  tips for, 26
  using GPS coordinates, 25–26
Never Summer Nordic Yurts and Nokhu Cabin, 35, 36–61
Nokhu Cabin, 38m, 58–59, 60m–61m
  Nokhu Cabin, Lake Agnes Trailhead to, 38m, 59, 60m–61m
Nokhu Cabin and Never Summer Nordic Yurts, 35, 36–61
Norrie Trailhead to Margy's Hut, 124m–125m, 210m–211m, 220m–221m, 223–224, 240m–241m
North and South Trails to Brainard Lake Cabin, 64m, 68, 69m
North Fork Canadian Trailhead to North Fork Canadian Yurt, 38m, 54, 60m–61m
North Fork Canadian Yurt, 12p, 36p, 38m, 53–54, 60m–61m
  North Fork Canadian Trailhead to, 38m, 54, 60m–61m
  Ruby Jewel Yurt to, 38m, 52, 60m–61m
North Fork Michigan Trailhead
  to Grass Creek Yurt, 38m, 40, 60m–61m
  to Montgomery Pass Yurts, 38m, 45–46, 60m–61m
"Novice" route rating, 17
Nutrition, 28

Pando Trailhead to Fowler/Hilliard Hut, 124m–125m, 142m–143m, 146–147, 152m–153m
Peabody Trailhead (South Park) to Section House and Ken's Cabin, 98m, 101, 104m–105m
Peter Estin Hut, 124m–125m, 202m–203m, 204–209, 205p, 210m–211m
  to Harry Gates Hut, 124m–125m, 202m–203m, 210m–211m, 212–213
  Polar Star Inn to, 124m–125m, 201, 202m–203m
  Sylvan Lake Trailhead to via Crooked Creek Pass, 124m–125m, 202m–203m, 208, 210m–211m
  Yeoman Park Trailhead to via Hat Creek Trail, 124m–125m, 202m–203m, 207, 210m–211m
  Yeoman Park Trailhead to via Ironedge Trail, 124m–125m, 202m–203m, 206, 210m–211m

Polar Star Inn and Carl's Cabin, 124m–125m, 194–201, 195p, 196p, 202m–203m
to Peter Estin Hut, 124m–125m, 201, 202m–203m
West Lake Creek Trailhead to, 124m–125m, 196–197, 202m–203m
Yeoman Park Trailhead to via Fulford Road, 124m–125m, 198–199, 202m–203m
Yeoman Park Trailhead to via Newcomer Spring, 124m–125m, 199–200, 202m–203m

Red Cliff Trailhead
to Fowler/Hilliard Hut, 124m–125m, 142m–143m, 144–145, 152m–153m
to Shrine Mountain Inn (Jay's, Chuck's, and Walter's Cabins), 124m–125m, 137–138, 142m–143m
Red Rock Lake Trailhead to Brainard Lake Cabin, 64m, 67, 69m
Red Sandstone Creek Trailhead to Eiseman Hut, 124m–125m, 130m–131m, 132
Route difficulty ratings, 17–18
Ruby Jewel Yurt, 38m, 43p, 50–52, 60m–61m
Grass Creek Yurt to, 38m, 42, 60m–61m
Jewel Lake Trailhead to, 38m, 51, 60m–61m
Montgomery Pass Yurts to (High Traverse Route), 38m, 49, 60m–61m
Montgomery Pass Yurts to (Valley Route), 38m, 48, 60m–61m
to North Fork Canadian Yurt, 38m, 52, 60m–61m

Sangree M. Froelicher Hut, 124m–125m, 164–168, 169m
Buckeye Gulch Trailhead to, 124m–125m, 166, 169m
to Chalk Creek Traverse, 124m–125m, 167–168, 169m
Seasonal considerations, 28–29
Second Creek Cabin (Gwen Andrews Hut), 82m, 84–85, 86m
Second Creek Cabin (Gwen Andrews Hut), Berthoud Pass Road to, 82m, 85, 86m
Section House and Ken's Cabin, 98m, 99–102, 101p, 102p, 104m–105m
Boreas Pass Trailhead (Breckenridge) to, 98m, 100, 104m–105m
Gold Dust Trailhead to, 98m, 102, 104m–105m
Peabody Trailhead (South Park) to, 98m, 101, 104m–105m
Shrine Mountain Inn (Jay's, Chuck's, and Walter's Cabins), 124m–125m, 133–140, 135p, 139p, 142m–143m
to Fowler/Hilliard Hut, 124m–125m, 138, 140, 142m–143m
Janet's Cabin to, 98m, 117, 118m–119m, 124m–125m, 152m–153m
Red Cliff Trailhead to, 124m–125m, 137–138, 142m–143m
Vail Pass Trailhead to, 124m–125m, 136–137, 142m–143m
Skinner Hut, 124m–125m, 182–185, 185p, 186m–187m, 192m–193m
to Betty Bear Hut, 124m–125m, 184–185, 186m–187m, 192m–193m
Turquoise Lake Trailhead to, 124m–125m, 183–184, 186m–187m, 192m–193m
Uncle Bud's Hut to, 124m–125m, 178–179, 180m–181m, 186m–187m
Skis, 23–24
Snowshoes, 22
South and North Trails to Brainard Lake Cabin, 64m, 68, 69m
South Camp Hale Trailhead
to Jackal Hut via Cataract Creek, 124m–125m, 152m–153m, 157
to Jackal Hut via Ranch Creek, 124m–125m, 152m–153m, 156
Spraddle Creek Trailhead to Eiseman Hut, 124m–125m, 128–129, 130m–131m
Spring Creek Trailhead to Harry Gates Hut, 124m–125m, 210m–211m, 216, 220m–221m
Squaw Mountain Fire Lookout, 77, 78m, 79, 79p, 80m
Squaw Mountain Fire Lookout, Squaw Pass Road to, 78m, 79, 80m
Summit Huts Association, 94–95, 96–119
Sundeck Trailhead to Barnard Hut, 244m, 248, 250, 252m–253m
Sunlight Backcountry Cabin, 285, 286m, 287, 288m
Sunlight Backcountry Cabin, Sunlight Mountain Resort to, 286m, 287, 288m
Sunlight Mountain Resort to Sunlight Backcountry Cabin, 286m, 287, 288m
Sun protection, 27

Sylvan Lake Trailhead
- to Harry Gates Hut, 124m–125m, 210m–211m, 215–216, 220m–221m
- to Peter Estin Hut via Crooked Creek Pass, 124m–125m, 202m–203m, 208, 210m–211m

Tagert and Green-Wilson Huts, 244m, 252m–253m, 262–269, 263p, 268p, 270m–271m
- Ashcroft Trailhead to, 244m, 252m–253m, 265–266, 270m–271m
- to Friends Hut via Pearl Pass, 244m, 267–269, 270m–271m

Tennessee Mtn. Cabin, 64m, 73m, 75–76

Tennessee Mountain Cabin, Eldora Nordic Center Trailhead to, 64m, 73m, 76

Tennessee Pass Trailhead
- to 10th Mountain Division Hut, 124m–125m, 171–172, 180m–181m, 186m–187m
- to Vance's Cabin, 124m–125m, 152m–153m, 161

10th Mountain Division Hut, 124m–125m, 170–175, 173p, 180m–181m, 186m–187m
- Crane Park Trailhead to, 124m–125m, 172–173, 180m–181m, 186m–187m
- Tennessee Pass Trailhead to, 124m–125m, 171–172, 180m–181m, 186m–187m
- to Uncle Bud's Hut, 124m–125m, 174–175, 180m–181m, 186m–187m
- Vance's Cabin to, 124m–125m, 152m–153m, 163

10th Mountain Division Hut Association, 94–95, 120–241

Times, 18

Tour difficulty ratings, 17–18

Transceivers, 31

Travel times, 18

Turquoise Lake Trailhead
- to Skinner Hut, 124m–125m, 183–184, 186m–187m, 192m–193m
- to Uncle Bud's Hut, 124m–125m, 177, 180m–181m, 186m–187m

Uncle Bud's Hut, 124m–125m, 176–179, 179p, 180m–181m, 186m–187m
- to Skinner Hut, 124m–125m, 178–179, 180m–181m, 186m–187m
- 10th Mountain Division Hut to, 124m–125m, 174–175, 180m–181m, 186m–187m
- Turquoise Lake Trailhead to, 124m–125m, 177, 180m–181m, 186m–187m

Union Creek Trailhead to Janet's Cabin, 98m, 113–114, 118m–119m, 124m–125m, 152m–153m

Vail Pass Trailhead
- to Janet's Cabin, 98m, 115, 118m–119m, 124m–125m, 152m–153m
- to Shrine Mountain Inn (Jay's, Chuck's, and Walter's Cabins), 124m–125m, 136–137, 142m–143m

Vance's Cabin, 124m–125m, 152m–153m, 160–163
- Jackal Hut to, 124m–125m, 152m–153m, 159
- Tennessee Pass Trailhead to, 124m–125m, 152m–153m, 161
- to 10th Mountain Division Hut, 124m–125m, 152m–153m, 163

Walter's Cabin (Shrine Mountain Inn), 124m–125m, 133–140, 135p, 142m–143m

Weather considerations, 28–29

West Lake Creek Trailhead
- to Hidden Treasure Yurt, 279m, 281–282, 284m
- to Polar Star Inn and Carl's Cabin, 124m–125m, 196–197, 202m–203m

Wheeler Flats Trailhead to Francie's Cabin, 98m, 109, 110m

Wilson Hut. *See* Tagert and Green-Wilson Huts

Yeoman Park Trailhead
- to Hidden Treasure Yurt via Fulford Road, 279m, 282–283, 284m
- to Peter Estin Hut via Hat Creek Trail, 124m–125m, 202m–203m, 207, 210m–211m
- to Peter Estin Hut via Ironedge Trail, 124m–125m, 202m–203m, 206, 210m–211m
- to Polar Star Inn and Carl's Cabin via Fulford Road, 124m–125m, 198–199, 202m–203m
- to Polar Star Inn and Carl's Cabin via Newcomer Spring, 124m–125m, 199–200, 202m–203m

Zimmerman Lake/Montgomery Pass Trailhead
- to Montgomery Pass Yurts, 38m, 46–47, 60m–61m

Since his first hut trip to the Tagert and Markley Huts with the Denver Junior Group of the Colorado Mountain Club in 1977, **Brian Litz** has been a confirmed hut addict. His mountain travels began at an early age with family ski trips and climbing ventures with friends.

Litz is an avid downhill and cross-country skier, mountaineer, rock climber, and bicyclist whose insatiable appetite for exploration, adventure, and photography has led him through the western United States and Alaska, as well as Mexico, Canada, New Zealand, Australia, and western Europe.

A graduate of the University of Colorado, Litz is managing editor and founding partner of *Back Country Magazine.* He is also a member of the North American Snowsport Journalists Association and is coauthor of the book, *Skiing Colorado's Backcountry: Northern Mountain Trails & Tours,* with Kurt Lankford. His photos and articles have appeared in books, newspapers, and periodicals such as *Skiing, Ski, Powder, Outside Magazine, Outdoor Explorer, Outdoor Photographer, Summit,* and *Mercedes-Benz Momentum Magazine.* Litz's *Colorado Hut to Hut* calendar is also available through Westcliffe Publishers.

Litz serves as president of the Backcountry Skiers Alliance and as trainer/instructor for the Colorado Outward Bound School, where he has worked with mountaineering programs and the Professional Development Program. A Colorado resident for 35 of his 39 years, Litz lives in Boulder.

Brian Litz photo by Ruedi Beglinger